The Workplace Constitution from the New Deal to the New Right

Today, most Americans lack constitutional rights on the job. Instead of enjoying free speech or privacy, they can be fired for almost any reason, or for no reason at all. This history explains why. It takes readers back to the 1930s and 1940s when advocates across the political spectrum – labor leaders, civil rights advocates, and conservatives opposed to government regulation – set out to enshrine constitutional rights in the workplace. The book tells of their interlocking fights to win constitutional protections for American workers, recovers their surprising successes, explains their ultimate failure, and helps readers assess the outcome.

Sophia Z. Lee is Professor of Law and History at the University of Pennsylvania Law School. She earned her JD and her PhD in history from Yale.

Studies in Legal History

To my amazing postnuclear family, with love and gratitude

The Workplace Constitution from the New Deal to the New Right

SOPHIA Z. LEE

University of Pennsylvania Law School

CAMBRIDGE
UNIVERSITY PRESS

CAMBRIDGE
UNIVERSITY PRESS

32 Avenue of the Americas, New York, NY 10013-2473, USA

Cambridge University Press is part of the University of Cambridge.

It furthers the University's mission by disseminating knowledge in the pursuit of education, learning, and research at the highest international levels of excellence.

www.cambridge.org
Information on this title: www.cambridge.org/9781107613218

© Sophia Z. Lee 2014

First published 2014

Printed in the United States of America

A catalog record for this publication is available from the British Library.

Library of Congress Cataloging in Publication data
Lee, Sophia Z. (Sophia Zoila), 1970– author.
The workplace constitution from the New Deal to the New Right / Sophia Z. Lee.
   pages cm – (Studies in legal history)
Includes bibliographical references and index.
ISBN 978-1-107-03872-1 (hardback) – ISBN 978-1-107-61321-8 (paperback)
1. Industrial relations – United States – History. 2. Employee rights – United States – History. 3. Constitutional law – United States – History. 4. Labor laws and legislation – United States – History. 5. United States – Race relations. I. Title.
KF3369.L36 2014
344.7301'12–dc23   2014002496

ISBN 978-1-107-03872-1 Hardback
ISBN 978-1-107-61321-8 Paperback

Contents

Acknowledgments

Thanking all those who have made this book possible is a daunting, probably impossible, yet deeply rewarding task. Like many first books, this one was inspired by research I did for a professor, which grew into a seminar paper, from there into a dissertation, and then finally into this book. I made it through each of these steps owing to the support of an incredible community of teachers, mentors, classmates, colleagues, and friends. There is no way to rank their gifts, each of which has been invaluable.

One person to whom you as a reader, no less than I as a writer, owe tremendous thanks is Sarah (Sally) Barringer Gordon. Sally has been a mentor, colleague, editor par excellence, and dear friend. She has provided the best kind of tough love: she has balanced unfailing advice, boundless encouragement, unwavering faith, and a seemingly infinite willingness to read, discuss, and mark up the manuscript with hard questions about everything from word choice to framing concepts to the necessity of entire chapters. She and her coeditors of the Studies in Legal History series at Cambridge University Press have provided a level of engagement and support that is rare in academic publishing today and that greatly enriched this book.

I could not have conceived of this project without excellent teachers. My adviser and the chair of my dissertation committee, Glenda Gilmore, taught me the craft of history and has been an endless source of wise counsel. Reva Siegel steered me to this project and gave me the scholarly tools with which to proceed. Robert Gordon shaped my

understanding of legal history. Erudite and encyclopedic, his insight-
ful feedback was invaluable. Jennifer Klein gave me my bearings in
labor history and has been at the ready with careful reads and keen
advice.

This project was nourished by the many academic communities
to which I have belonged since its inception. Yale historians Jean
Christophe-Agnew, John Demos, and Beverly Gage helped me grow as
a historian and writer. At Yale Law School, Richard Brooks, William
Eskridge, Owen Fiss, Heather Gerkin, Daniel Markovitz, Jerry
Mashaw, Robert Post, Judith Resnik, and Vickie Schultz provided welcome support and intellectual inspiration. At New York University
School of Law, Cynthia Estlund, Barry Friedman, Daniel Hulsebosch,
and William Nelson provided lively feedback and welcome encouragement. Deborah Malamud deserves special mention: not only has
her work on race and labor critically informed my own, but she also
generously shared primary sources without which Chapter 1 would
not have been possible.

Since joining the faculty at the University of Pennsylvania Law
School, I have found among my colleagues a tremendously creative
and rigorous community. I am particularly indebted to Shyamkrishna
Balganesh, Cary Coglianese, Frank Goodman, Seth Kreimer, Howard
Lesnik, David Skeel, Thomas Sugrue, Michael Wachter, Tess Wilkinson-
Ryan, Tobias Wolff, and Christopher Yoo for their friendship, advice,
support, and comments. Serena Mayeri, in particular, generously read
the entire manuscript, saving me from errors and infelicities large
and small; my dean, Mike Fitts, deserves special thanks for the financial backing he secured for my research and the time he gave me for
focused writing. I have also been extremely lucky to have Writers
Bloc(k), our legal history writing group, the members of which have
provided incredible camaraderie and excellent feedback.

I have benefited immeasurably from the guidance and support of a
more diffuse community of scholars, as well. Special thanks are owed
to Nelson Lichtenstein and Theodore St. Antoine, both of whom provided that most precious gift in the book's final stages: they read the
full manuscript and provided valuable correction, guidance, and reassurance. Susanna Blumenthal, Tomiko Brown-Nagin, Mary Dudziak,
Daniel Ernst, Risa Goluboff, Kenneth Mack, Bill Novak, James Pope,
Reuel Schiller, and Barbara Welke have inspired and advised me; they

have also given generously of their time to read and comment on my work. I have had the good fortune of receiving perceptive responses to presentations of my work from Bruce Ackerman, Eric Arnesen, Brian Balogh, Christopher Capozzola, Anthony Chen, David Chappell, Drew Days III, William Forbath, John Harrison, Meg Jacobs, Laura Kalman, Randy Kozel, Robert Lieberman, Nancy MacLean, Wendell Pritchett, Gretchen Ritter, James Sparrow, Steven Teles, Christopher Tomlins, and Dorian Warren. Margot Canaday and Paul Frymer have enlightened, counseled, and encouraged me at key junctures.

As immensely grateful as I am to these scholars for all they have shared with me, I could not have written this book without the incredible friends and colleagues who have made the journey through graduate school and beyond with me. Adam Arenson, Kevin Arlyck, Christopher Beauchamp, Deborah Dinner, Nicholas Parillo, Gautham Rao, Christopher Schmidt, Jed Shugerman, Karen Tani, Laura Weinrib, and R. Owen Williams have challenged me in the most wonderful ways; kept me sane, well fed, and in good humor; and have shown me by their example what the best work of my generation of historians will be. Dara Orenstein's friendship, counsel, and encouragement have been particularly critical, right down to enlisting her talented friends Brett Snyder and Irene Cheng to help with the cover design.

The book would not have been possible without generous financial assistance. I am indebted to Yale University, including its John F. Enders Fund; Yale Law School, including its Legal History and Coker Teaching Fellowships as well as the Benjamin Scharps and Joseph Parker Prizes; the William Nelson Cromwell Foundation; New York University School of Law's Samuel I. Golieb Fellowship; the University of Pennsylvania Law School; the American Historical Association's Littleton-Griswold Research Fund; and the American Society for Legal History's J. Willard Hurst Summer Institute in Legal History and Kathryn T. Preyer Prize.

Portions of the book have appeared in *Law and History Review*, the *Virginia Law Review*, and *The Right and Labor in America: Politics, Ideology, and Imagination*, ed. Nelson Lichtenstein and Elizabeth Tandy Shermer (Philadelphia: University of Pennsylvania Press, 2012). I thank those publishers for allowing me to reprint the material here. I am also indebted to David Tanenhaus, Tamara Fishman, Lauren Willard, Kasey Levit, Nelson Lichtenstein, Elizabeth Tandy-Shermer, and the anonymous reviewers for *Law and History Review* for their expert editing and suggestions.

I was lucky to receive excellent assistance with my research from numerous archivists, librarians, and clerks of the court. In addition to enjoying the many conversations I had across the country about the future of archives in a digital age, I benefited greatly from the quick, professional, and illuminating help of archivists at the Archive of Labor and Urban Affairs, the George Meany Memorial Archives, the Harris County Courthouse in Texas, Harvard Law School Library, the Hoover Institution, the John F. Kennedy Presidential Library, the Library of Congress Manuscript Division, the Moorland-Spingarn Research Center at Howard University, Notre Dame University Archives, the Seeley G. Mudd Manuscript Library at Princeton University, the L. Tom Perry Special Collections at Brigham Young University, the Ronald Reagan Presidential Library and Museum, the Wisconsin Historical Society, and the Wisconsin Supreme Court. Staff at the National Archives locations across the country were of tremendous help locating and copying court records.

I am particularly indebted to several individuals. At the National Archives in College Park, Maryland, James Matthis moved mountains to expeditiously screen files for me. In addition, he and Tab Lewis located National Labor Relations Board and Department of Justice records without which I would not have been able to piece together the story told herein. Linda Whitaker at the Arizona Historical Society was not only extremely helpful during the time I spent in Phoenix researching the Barry M. Goldwater Papers but also continued to send me useful finds long after my visit. Professor Roberto Corrada of the Sturm College of Law at the University of Denver greatly enhanced my visit to the Penrose Library with his personal insights into the remarkable Howard Jenkins Jr. At Cornell's Kheel Center, Patrizia Sione diligently tracked down mislabeled material. The library staff at the University of Pennsylvania Law School's Biddle Law Library, especially Alvin Dong, have been a joy to meet and a pleasure to work with. I have also benefited from excellent research assistance by graduate students Anne Fleming, Smita Ghosh, Rebecca Serbin, and David Williams as well as professional researchers Debby Cooney, Carolyn Harbus, Rosemary Lewis, Andrew Skabelund, and Anita Sower. Chaz Lively and Collin Payne provided expertise I lacked, generating the book's study of workers' understanding of their constitutional rights and its figures, respectively.

Books would not make the leap from electronic file to tangible object without the support of a press and the collective efforts of many. I have been in particularly good hands at Cambridge, thanks not only to my series editors, but also to Lew Bateman, Eric Crahan, Shaun Vigil, copy editor extraordinaire Julie Hagen, and the crew at Newgen. The blind reader reports Cambridge solicited were also incredibly helpful in shaping and refining the book-in-process.

To my parents, sisters, sister-in-law, nephew, and the family to come, you've given and give me so much. My mother, Melissa Nelken, is owed special thanks for her tireless support and for her patient and lifelong efforts to teach me the craft of writing. Nicole, Julian, Lauren, Ellis, Shea, Mike, and Lorin, thank you for making your family my own, for drawing my head out of the books and into the present, and for the extreme joy of discovering the world together. My wife, Nicole, deserves more than thanks for holding our family together when the book has consumed me and for sacrificing so much to help Julian and me thrive. She is the most loyal and loving person I know. I would be lost without her.

Introduction

C. W. Rice did not know it, but he set the stage for a fifty-year struggle that has left Americans today with little or no constitutional protections in the workplace. Born in rural Tennessee at the close of the nineteenth century, Rice settled in Houston in the 1920s. There, he established the Texas Negro Business and Laboring Men's Association, a labor brokerage that placed black workers in industrial jobs. Like most African Americans in the early twentieth century, Rice was harshly critical of the American Federation of Labor (AFL). The AFL's member unions generally organized workers in a single craft, such as carpenters or machinists. These unions protected jobs and wages by limiting who could join their locals or work alongside their members. This restrictiveness built solidarity and shored up the members' economic power. It also hurt African Americans because most unions limited membership to "white candidate[s]." These rules and employers' long-standing hiring practices left African Americans "only those jobs ... [with] low wages, disagreeable dust, and ... tasks regarded as too heavy for native-born white Americans." Black leaders of Rice's generation favored thrift, hard work, and self-help to redress this economic hardship. Rice also favored black *independent unions* (those not affiliated with the AFL). He promoted them in his paper, the *Negro Labor News*, and organized workers at Houston's Hughes Tool Company. To many, Rice was a champion of black solidarity and economic advancement who was prolabor yet courageously critical of discriminatory unions.[1]

Rice's opponents, however, thought he helped employers exploit workers and served as a tool in their antiunion campaigns. Employers had resisted unionization since the nineteenth century. They preferred *open shops*, in which they could hire whomever they wanted and refuse to bargain with unions. They claimed that unions interfered with management, inflated wages, and were inconsistent with American ideals of individualism and free contract. When Rice built ties with white industrialists, promoted open shops, and encouraged African Americans to take jobs even when they would replace striking white workers, he seemed to side with employers and against organized labor. To his critics, Rice's all-black independent unions were just *company unions*: formed with the employer's blessing, they did not make tough demands and kept out unions that would. In the 1920s, the AFL criticized Rice while civil rights leaders and black Houstonians generally sided with him. But during the New Deal 1930s, a growing number of African Americans switched sides. The federal government promoted unionization, organized labor offered new interracial unions, and radicals argued that only a united working class could end racism. Rice's approach now seemed outdated: many African Americans believed that they should unite with white workers, not with employers.[2]

Rice is not this book's central character. But the puzzle of Rice – was he a prolabor champion of African Americans' rights, a proworker check on oppressive union power, or a tool in employers' antiunion campaigns? – *is* central. This puzzle attached equally to an idea Rice embraced: that workers had constitutional rights on the job and in the union, what I call the *workplace Constitution*. In the 1930s, Rice turned to the United States Constitution to defend independent black unions. He was one of the first to use the federal Constitution in an effort to redistribute power among and between workers, unions, and employers under the New Deal labor regime. Over the next fifty years, his African American and labor critics, as well as his open shop allies, followed in his path. Often their efforts were as politically confusing as Rice's had been. The perplexing quality of the workplace Constitution, and the uses to which it has been put, help explain why most people in the United States today do not have constitutional rights at work.[3]

Why Care about the Workplace Constitution?

Many of the workplace rights people expect under the U.S. Constitution are recognized in other industrial countries today: protection from arbitrary firings, due process before workers are terminated, and freedoms of speech, association, and privacy. In the mid-twentieth century, one-third of American workers had similar protections through union contracts. The rest worked under the "at-will doctrine," a judge-made rule that allowed employers to fire and discipline workers for any reason or for no reason at all. Advocates' subsequent efforts to use legislation or ordinary contract and tort law to win these protections for nonunion workers have had only limited success. Today, only about one in ten American workers is unionized. For the rest, it seems that constitutional rights offer an attractive alternative to the harshness of at-will employment. In fact, the idea of a workplace Constitution is so appealing that most American workers believe they *do* have these constitutional rights on the job.[4] The history that follows corrects this mistaken assumption. After examining the workplace Constitution's contradictory uses, however, readers of this book may well feel relieved, rather than wistful, about its fate.

From the vantage point of the mid-twentieth century, the workplace Constitution's future looked promising. In the 1930s and 1940s, two movements began trying to extend the Constitution to the workplace. They were opposed to each other politically but they shared this legal goal. One, the civil rights movement, would go on to capture the attention of the nation and dismantle Jim Crow. The other, the right-to-work movement, fought for open shops. Although its history is less well known, this second movement was supported by prominent politicians and opinion makers. Together, the two movements created a strange and contentious but potentially powerful combination. Their successes and failures change the historical understanding of constitutional law, labor politics, civil rights struggles, and conservative movements.

Moving Constitutional History Outside of the Courts
In recent years, historians have recovered civil rights advocates' focus on workplace discrimination from the 1930s to the 1980s by looking for law in arenas other than courts and in sources other than the Constitution.[5] Legal scholars have also demonstrated the role non-court actors played in shaping the Constitution's meaning.[6] This book

advances these trends by attending to the influence that institutions other than courts have had on the *constitutional* dimension of civil rights history. It focuses on an overlooked but omnipresent constitutional force in the modern American state: administrative agencies.[7] Agencies' explosive growth during the twentieth century created new venues for advocates' constitutional claims. At the same time, administrators grappled newly with their constitutional responsibilities.[8] Administrators at agencies such as the National Labor Relations Board and the Federal Communications Commission recognized a robust version of the workplace Constitution even though it was rejected by other federal actors, including the Supreme Court, Congress, and the president.

Reworking Civil Rights History

The meaning of civil rights under the Constitution was up for grabs during the 1930s and 1940s and was as likely to protect the mass of workers as the minority of African Americans. During this time, historians write, lawyers made constitutional claims that could protect African Americans economically and might safeguard all workers from exploitation. By the 1950s, they argue, the lawyers had moved on. Efforts to win protection against racial discrimination in the workplace focused on legislation instead. Eventually, monumental lobbying efforts by labor unions and civil rights groups, as well as considerable pressure from President Lyndon Johnson, produced a coalition of northern Democrats and Republicans in Congress that passed the Civil Rights Act of 1964. Title VII of that act barred employment discrimination on the basis of race, sex, national origin, and religion. Thereafter, Title VII dominated challenges to employment discrimination.[9]

This book enriches the preceding account of the fight for legal protections against workplace discrimination. As Part I argues, the 1930s and 1940s were just the beginning, not the end, of constitutional challenges to discrimination on the job and in the union. Part II demonstrates that the 1950s were not fallow years for such claims. Instead, throughout the decade civil rights and labor advocates pursued them with even more determination. Finally, Part III shows that the workplace Constitution did the most to protect African Americans in the 1960s and 1970s, Title VII's passage notwithstanding. During this time, administrators also extended the workplace Constitution to protect women and a range of other racial and ethnic groups.[10]

If constitutional challenges to workplace discrimination diminished in the late 1970s rather than the 1950s, then new explanations for their decline are needed. Histories that argue the civil rights movement stopped focusing on working-class African Americans in the 1950s rely heavily on the start of the Cold War to explain the shift. This explanation has little relevance to the 1970s, however. Instead, other legal, political, and institutional forces assume prominence, especially the rise of the New Right, an increasingly influential and broad-based conservative bloc within the Republican Party.

Race, Rights, and Post–New Deal Conservatism

Historians have produced a robust, complex history of conservatism in the past fifteen years, discovering how, during the 1940s and 1950s, suburban housewives helped it spread, religion fed its rise, business conservatives and free-market economists generated its intellectual infrastructure, and Barry Goldwater became its poster boy.[11] These historians wrote against an earlier literature that attributed conservatism to racial bigotry or paranoid anticommunism.[12] Many have instead downplayed race, arguing that, outside the South, racial backlash is an overly simplistic and often inaccurate explanation. At the same time, recent histories of the South's turn from solidly Democrat at midcentury to strictly Republican at its close put race at the center.[13] Those who examine why working-class whites, long the backbone of the Democratic Party's New Deal coalition, gradually shifted their allegiance to the New Right during the 1970s also emphasize race, particularly white workers' anger over affirmative action and school bussing policies.[14]

This history of the workplace Constitution offers a fresh take on the Right's rise. Historians have not focused much on how conservatives, especially anti–New Deal conservatives, used the law, and in particular how they sought to shape the Constitution.[15] The following chapters offer a novel legal history of conservatism. Beginning in the 1940s, conservatives who supported state right-to-work laws simultaneously claimed that workers had a constitutional right not to join or support a union. This book also provides a new twist on the role of race in post–New Deal conservatism. As early as the 1950s, some right-to-work advocates allied themselves *with* rather than against African Americans and their civil rights struggle, pioneering an approach

currently associated with late twentieth-century conservatives.[16] These
two insights show that the Right blunted its elite, ultraright image
before the mid-1970s and 1980s. They also demonstrate that it did
so with economic issues, not only with the better-known social issues
such as abortion, feminism, and gay rights.[17]

Loosening Coalitions and Consensus

Historians have eroded the assumption that a stable liberal consensus
reigned in the decades after the New Deal. They have shown that the
alliance the New Deal produced between labor and civil rights advocates fractured long before the affirmative action and bussing debates
of the late 1960s and 1970s.[18] They have also challenged the view
that American businesses reached a stable accord with labor by the
1950s.[19] The account in these pages brings together these two conflicts – that between labor and management, on the one hand, and
civil rights and labor, on the other – to reveal previously overlooked
strains.[20] This history also brings to conservatism some of the tempering scholars have given liberalism. Current work on conservatism
tends to depict the New Right as a juggernaut.[21] Just as the New Deal
order was far less stable than initial histories suggested, conservatism's
ascendency was also more fragile, fractured, and contingent than is
often recognized. This book emphasizes conservatives' failures as well
as their triumphs and, importantly, the losers as well as the winners
created by the New Right order.

Terminology

The story that follows involves numerous moving parts; technical legal
doctrines and complex regulatory statutes; an alphabet soup of agencies and organizations; and many previously obscure actors. To help
readers navigate and to highlight the book's key arguments, I use several terms entirely of my own creation. Their expository benefits outweigh their potential pitfalls, but they bear definition and explanation
up front.

In addition to the term the "workplace Constitution," which I have
defined, I distinguish between "liberal" and "conservative" workplace
Constitutions. These are not ideological or partisan labels; rather, they
refer to the political coalitions that particular claims were meant to

serve and in which they arose. Liberal refers broadly to claims made by those who accepted, even embraced, the New Deal labor regime. Conservative refers to claims by those who opposed the New Deal labor regime. Neither was perfectly identified with the Democratic or Republican Party, although there were often overlaps, nor were they always ideologically cohesive.

For the most part I use the actors' own language to tell this history, including Hollywood mogul Cecil B. DeMille's claim to a constitutional "right to work" in the 1940s and the simultaneous assertion by the National Association for the Advancement of Colored People (NAACP) that the "Fifth Amendment extends to ... union's activities." But at times I use my terms to distinguish historical actors' varied claims or to highlight important and often unintended interconnections among them. Civil rights and right-to-work advocates could help each other through the constitutional arguments they made, the strategies they honed, and the precedents or policies they won. My terms also help underscore divisions within each coalition over the wisdom of a workplace Constitution and help gauge the fit between a coalition and its claims as the coalition shifted, grew, and splintered over time.

Structure

The book is divided into four chronological parts. Each contains thematic chapters that are generally titled to indicate whether they involve courts versus agencies or liberals' versus conservatives' claims. Part I covers the 1930s and 1940s, explaining why liberals and conservatives turned to the workplace Constitution despite substantial hurdles. Together, its chapters demonstrate that these claims were barely formulated by the end of the 1940s, which marked merely the beginning of the quest for a workplace Constitution. Part II focuses on the 1950s, an extremely busy period for the workplace Constitution, when liberals and conservatives advanced coordinated litigation campaigns akin to the NAACP's better-known assault on public school segregation. Part III covers the liberal workplace Constitution's triumph during the 1960s and 1970s, when federal agencies implemented it broadly and to notable effect. Part IV describes how new and lingering doubts within both coalitions complicated the workplace Constitution's journey. You will have to read on to find out how it all ended.

PART I

CRAFTING THE WORKPLACE
CONSTITUTION IN THE NEW DEAL
1930S AND 1940S

I

Liberals Forge a Workplace Constitution in the Courts

"We were not antagonistic to collective bargaining."

Charles Hamilton Houston

On July 5, 1939, a solemn C. W. Rice took the floor before the House Committee on Labor. "Having organizations which do not allow persons of color to belong to them, representing the colored people, is not due process of law and is illegal," Rice insisted. Those gathered before him had just returned from celebrating the nation's Declaration of Independence. Rice's message resonated with a core precept of that document, as well as of the Constitution to which it led: that a government in which the people had no representation was tyrannical. Rice was not testifying about political government, however. Instead, he spoke of the labor unions newly empowered by the 1935 National Labor Relations Act (NLRA). Along with the similar 1934 Railway Labor Act, the NLRA had transformed the relationships among workers, unions, and employers, for the first time giving workers a right to unionize, and legally requiring an employer to bargain with the union its workers chose.[1]

Rice favored unionization but criticized the new labor laws. "Exclusive representation" was a cornerstone of both. Once a union demonstrated that it was supported by a majority of the workers it sought to represent, these laws gave the union the right to represent *all* of those workers, prohibiting the employer from contracting with its workers directly or with any other unions claiming their support.

Proponents contended that exclusive representation was needed to prevent employers from fomenting company unions to undercut the very right to organize that the laws were intended to secure. Rice countered that it gave unions the right to represent black workers whom they excluded from membership and to whom they had long been hostile. He urged Congress to amend the NLRA to prohibit racially discriminatory unions from serving as the exclusive representative for black workers.[2]

If anyone should have been expected to support Rice's position, it was the other African Americans testifying before the committee. The Declaration and the Constitution had long provided African Americans an aspirational if not an actual guarantee of equal citizenship. John P. Davis, the head of the National Negro Congress (NNC), granted that Rice had "the interests of the Negro workers deeply at heart" but he nonetheless took "very sharp exception" to Rice's position. An outspoken recent graduate of Harvard Law School, Davis had pressured New Deal agencies to end their racially discriminatory practices before helping to found and lead the NNC in 1936. The NNC promoted economic justice for working-class African Americans, and its leaders believed that justice could best be secured through allying with organized labor. Rice's proposed amendments, Davis cautioned, would "make it possible for employer groups to come in and destroy the rights of labor by simply claiming that ... a local union prohibited Negro membership" and was therefore ineligible to be a representative. Such tactics would not serve the interests of African American workers or the labor movement, Davis warned. They would instead return the country to those "dark days when greedy employers had a free hand to split and divide employees and to destroy their security and living standards." Tyranny of the employer, Davis implied, was far worse for black workers than tyranny of the union.[3]

Just a few years earlier, Rice could have expected African American leaders' support. But in 1939, it was Davis who spoke most authoritatively. Massive changes in black politics, federal law, and the labor movement had rapidly isolated Rice. They had also rendered it very unlikely that civil rights advocates who allied themselves with the labor movement would follow Rice and turn to the Constitution to protect African Americans from discrimination on the job and in the unions.

Race and Labor on the Rails

Rice's constitutional argument to the House Committee stemmed from a tense 1937 gathering in a Dallas hotel room. Rice and four aging black labor leaders – railway coach cleaners – were meeting with Robert Cole, an official with the National Mediation Board, one of the federal labor agencies created by the Railway Labor Act. Cole was planning an election to decide which union would represent the mostly black coach cleaners serving the Texas and Pacific Railway Company. The men meeting with Cole were leaders in the all-black National Federation of Railway Workers (the Federation), an independent union that represented most of the line's coach cleaners. The AFL's all-white Brotherhood of Railway Carmen (the Carmen) had recently petitioned Cole's Mediation Board to take over representing the line's cleaners, both the black majority and the Mexican American minority: hence the forthcoming election. The Federation would need a majority of the votes to remain the coach cleaners' representative; conversely, if the Carmen garnered more votes, under the Railway Labor Act, the Mediation Board would certify it as the coach cleaners' exclusive representative. At the Dallas meeting, Rice and the coach cleaners tried to forestall the election and sought assurances that, if the election did go forward, it would be free and fair.[4]

Racial tension coursed through the Dallas meeting. Given the history of race and labor on the rails, how could it have been otherwise? African Americans' fragile relationship with organized labor dated to the end of slavery. During the 1880s and 1890s, cross-racial (if not fully equal) unions had seemed possible. The AFL pledged to organize workers regardless of race and refused to allow railroad brotherhoods such as the Carmen to join unless they dropped their white-only membership rules. The AFL soon reversed course, however, and the color line in the unions persisted, even hardened, during the first decades of the twentieth century. Nowhere was this line more strictly drawn or more violently enforced than in the railroad brotherhoods. The South was unique in having skilled black workers on the rails, a relic of a time when slaves who assisted their white masters learned their masters' craft. In the twentieth century, white railroad workers brutally opposed efforts to integrate their unions and tried to eliminate skilled African Americans from their crews. During the Depression, white railroaders carried out deadly attacks, riddling black brakemen and firemen with bullets and crushing their skulls with lead pipes in a murderous wave of violence that wreaked havoc across the South. The 1937 Dallas meeting occurred just a few years after the last black railway worker turned up dead, his body found in a Baton Rouge roundhouse. Cole, the Mediation Board representative, was a Texan and a former member of the union behind the violence, the all-white Brotherhood of Locomotive Firemen and Enginemen (the Firemen's Brotherhood). The Federation leaders had every reason to distrust him.[5]

At the Dallas meeting, the Railway Labor Act, not Cole's union, was the threat that concerned the Federation's leaders. The Federation had been founded in 1928, rising out of the ashes of a post–World War I assault by employers on unions black and white. It represented black railroad workers throughout the South to "promot[e] a mutual understanding and cooperation" with the "officers of the Texas and Pacific Railroad Company." In most railroad jobs (what the Railway Labor Act referred to as the "class" or "craft" that a union represented) African Americans were a small minority. As a result, the white brotherhoods had easily won previous elections conducted under the act and thus the right to represent the African American minority. This had left the displaced all-black independent unions powerless to negotiate with employers. The brotherhoods had then used their exclusive status to win agreements that closed new mechanized jobs to black workers and allowed white workers to replace more senior African Americans. The Federation leaders knew of this pattern. Coach cleaning, like other service classes, was a rare exception in which African Americans were the majority. The Federation leaders feared that the Carmen intended to change that. They asked Cole whether the Carmen, if certified, would allow the Federation's members to keep their seniority, the basis on which jobs were given and taken away, or whether "young [white] Carmen would be placed over the old coach cleaners."[6]

The Federation leaders were so concerned because they knew African American cleaners would have no say in what the Carmen did, despite their large numbers. One Federation leader recalled trying to join the Carmen in 1925. "The [proffered dues] money was refunded," he recounted, and was accompanied by "the statement that there was no place in the organization for Negroes." Even if they could join, Rice observed, "in the South ... Negroes are not permitted to participate in joint board meetings and deliberations." Instead they were segregated into all-black *auxiliary locals* that were free to govern themselves but were excluded from voting on general union policy or leadership, including on who negotiated with the employers. Presaging the argument that Rice would later make in his House testimony, the Federation complained that African Americans had "no suffrage nor representation" within the Carmen. Without a voice in the union, the black coach cleaners' seniority would be at the mercy of their white brethren.[7]

Race, Labor, and Party Politics

Rice did not succeed in preventing the requested election, which the Mediation Board determined the Federation lost by seven votes. The Carmen now merited certification as the coach cleaners' exclusive representative. Rice challenged the election, contending that Cole had wrongfully excluded Rice from it and that the board's vote count was inaccurate. The Mediation Board refused to set the election aside and Rice went to court, driven by pride and reputation as well as justice for the coach cleaners. Righting the election, he contended, was necessary to clear his name among the Federation's members. Many of them thought their leaders had thrown the election at the Carmen's behest and that Rice was a "thief" like the others. But Rice's suit against the Carmen also played into a political battle he was waging on the national stage.[8]

The massive changes during the 1930s sent shockwaves through black America. Like the NNC's John Davis, a new generation of African American leaders and the majority of northern blacks said "farewell to the party of Lincoln," joining President Franklin Roosevelt's Democratic Party and backing his New Deal. Many also embraced organized labor, pressing for change within the AFL or joining cause with the Congress of Industrial Organizations (CIO), which splintered off from the AFL after the passage of the NLRA. Frustrated with the AFL's craft-based approach to unions, the CIO's leaders wanted to organize *un*skilled workers and whole industries. Whereas one AFL union organized machinists in an auto plant and another its electrical workers, for instance, the CIO's United Automobile Workers (UAW) sought to organize all of a plant's workers in a single union. Because the CIO targeted the jobs and industries in which African Americans were clustered, it also promised to unite black and white workers, thus winning the support of many African Americans.[9]

Rice opposed African Americans' shifting allegiances. In his *Negro Labor News*, he urged readers to stick to all-black independent unions. The CIO's talk of racial equality, Rice warned, was just that. In addition, Rice cautioned, the CIO was full of Communists, which was true. During the 1930s, the American Communist Party abandoned its policy of organizing its own unions and instead pursued change within the New Deal's "Popular Front" of liberals and leftists, including, most notably, the CIO. It was the Communists who often demonstrated the greatest commitment to organizing black workers and interracial unions. But Rice warned that they imperiled the CIO's future, especially in the South, where red-baiting and race-baiting went hand in hand. He also argued that even if CIO organizers wanted interracial unions, white workers did not, making these workers fickle allies that African Americans would be foolish to trust.[10]

Rice was similarly critical of African Americans' embrace of the Democratic Party. With white supremacists in firm control and blacks excluded from participating, the Democratic Party had little to offer southern blacks such as Rice. Their only opportunity for a political voice and leadership lay instead with the Republican Party. In some southern states (though not Rice's Texas), African Americans even controlled the Republican Party. Although they were shut out of office by Democrats' overwhelming majority, black Republicans benefited from patronage in their home states and on the national stage. Rice's affinity for the Republican Party, in other words, was akin to his support for black independent unions.[11]

Rice, like other Republican elder statesman, also argued that the New Deal was a bad deal for African Americans. In 1939, a black representative for the Republican National Committee attacked the "brutalitarian tactics of ... [the] alphabet agencies," which he argued had done more to entrench racial inequality than to counter it. Rice likewise declared, "Negroes, both in the North and in the South are disappointed with the New Deal." The NLRA, according to Rice, had empowered unions with a "color bar and discriminatory practices" to "caus[e] the wholesale replacement of Negroes on practically all jobs ... in all sections of the country." In Rice's opinion, the main thing the New Deal had accomplished "for Negro employment is the hiring of some few Negroes in strategic positions to travel over the country and picture Utopias to the working class of Negroes." Rice's lawsuit gave him a new venue in which to make his case against the New Deal labor laws.[12]

Rice turned to lawyers who were like him to pursue his claim, southern Republicans associated not with the new guard and John Davis's NNC but with the old order of black leadership: the venerated Washington, D.C., law firm of Cobb, Howard, and Hayes. The firm's partners were born in the first decades after Emancipation and came of age during the imposition of Jim Crow. Perry Wilborn Howard was the kind of Republican who drew criticism from Davis's crowd. During the 1930s, national Republican leaders attempted to build strength in the South by promoting a "lily-white" party. Black Republicans such as Howard, a leader in Mississippi's party, joined forces with white Democrats, who were determined to keep the Republican Party weak. An ally of Davis's quipped that Howard, who opposed a federal anti-lynching law, could be a "better 'lily-white' than a white Mississipian could be."[13]

Howard's partner James A. Cobb had a more complicated relationship with the new guard. Born in Louisiana, Cobb received his law degree in 1900 from Howard University. Cobb never married – his firm and his Howard law students were his family. African Americans' equal citizenship was his vocation. In the 1920s Cobb was the nation's foremost black civil rights litigator and one of the NAACP's leading attorneys. He worked on such seminal Supreme Court cases as *Nixon v. Herndon*, a successful challenge to a Texas law barring African Americans from voting in the state Democratic primary, and *Corrigan v. Buckley*, an unsuccessful test of a racially restrictive covenant on a Washington, D.C., property. Cobb was active in the Republican Party: he served as a delegate to the 1920 Republican convention and received judgeships on the Washington, D.C., municipal court from Presidents Coolidge and Hoover. But unlike Howard, Cobb engaged and at times collaborated with the up-and-coming generation. A leader of the black bar, in the 1930s he urged the relevance of law to the civil rights movement when younger advocates, such as Davis, insisted that mass politics was the only way to win change.[14]

Black Republicans and the Workplace Constitution

Despite Rice's invocation of due process in his 1939 House testimony, his suit challenging the Carmen's election on behalf of the Federation did not initially focus on the Constitution. Rice's lawyers instead relied on his claim that the Mediation Board's election was defective. According to affidavits Rice had collected, enough Federation members had voted for the Federation that it, not the Carmen, should have won. At trial, however, this tactic foundered. Federation members testified that Rice had coerced or deceived them into signing the affidavits. The ballots also showed that several of Rice's affiants had actually voted for the Carmen or failed to vote altogether, further undermining his case. This left Rice much more dependent on his claim that the Carmen could not represent workers to whom the union denied full membership. His constitutional claims, which had taken a backseat at trial, might have to carry his case on appeal.[15]

The Federation's constitutional claims faced a formidable legal hurdle: the state action doctrine. According to this rule, many constitutional guarantees (for instance, freedom of speech and equal protection) applied only to the state and its agents. The doctrine thus drew a strict line between public and private acts, constitutionally restricting the former but not the latter. The Supreme Court most famously articulated the state action doctrine in the 1883 *Civil Rights Cases*. That decision struck down part of a federal law prohibiting racial discrimination in public accommodations on the theory that such discrimination was a private action, placing it outside the Constitution's (and thus Congress's) reach. Where to draw the line between public and private was never obvious, however, and has been frequently contested. To many African Americans, the *Civil Rights Cases* "nullified the Fourteenth Amendment," an abdication lawyers such as Cobb set about undoing.[16]

Cobb based his state action arguments in Rice's suit on *Corrigan v. Buckley*, his 1920s challenge to racially restrictive covenants. *Corrigan* began when a neighbor sued Irene Corrigan to stop her from selling her house to an African American buyer, based on a covenant between Corrigan and her neighbors not to sell their property to "any person of the negro race or blood." In 1917, the U.S. Supreme Court had found unconstitutional a city ordinance that barred African Americans from occupying houses on majority-white city blocks. Cobb moved to dismiss the suit against Corrigan, arguing that the neighbors' covenant was as unconstitutional as that city ordinance had been. The court denied Cobb's motion. The Fifth and Fourteenth Amendments' "inhibition is upon the power of the state," the appellate court explained, "and not [on] action by individuals" such as Corrigan and her neighbors.[17]

When Cobb asked the Supreme Court to review *Corrigan*, he tried a new approach to state action, one he would reuse in Rice's case. The lower courts had provided the requisite state action, Cobb now argued, when they enforced the covenant. "It seems inconceivable that" a court could "give the sanction of the judicial department ... to an act which it was not within the competency of its legislative branch to authorize," Cobb reasoned. The Court had long held, Cobb noted, that "a State may act ... either by its legislative, its executive, or its judicial authorities; and the prohibitions of the [Fourteenth] amendment extend to all." But Cobb did not identify any decisions finding that judicial enforcement of a litigant's discrimination violated the Constitution. The Supreme Court deemed Cobb's argument "lacking in substance" and not properly raised. Cobb had great confidence in it, however, predicting that "when the matter ... is put squarely before the ... Court, ... it will be forced to hold that covenants made by private contract are against public policy and invalid."[18]

The Federation's case gave Cobb a chance to test his prediction – albeit with a version of his state action theory repurposed for the New Deal administrative state. The *Civil Rights Cases* seemed to establish that businesses and, by extension, unions were quintessentially private. The Federation thus faced the same doctrinal hurdle as Irene Corrigan: the Carmen's decision to exclude African Americans was seemingly made by private individuals. To succeed, Cobb would have to sufficiently connect the Carmen's actions to the state. Cobb argued that the Mediation Board's certification of the Carmen as exclusive representative was no different than the courts' enforcement of the restrictive covenant in *Corrigan*. Here, the board's action – as there the courts' action – "deprive[d] plaintiffs of their property right without due process of law, [and] denie[d] them the equal protection of the laws." Not only would the black coach cleaners lose "their right to contract for representation of their own choosing," but they would also be bound to an employment contract that they had no role in negotiating and to a union they had no role in governing.[19]

Cobb's confidence had been misplaced. The trial court dismissed the Federation's action, and the D.C. Circuit Court of Appeals affirmed. The record amply demonstrated that the Federation's challenges to the election lacked merit, the appellate court found. In response to the Federation's constitutional claims, the court held that the Carmen's Brotherhood was a "private association, acting on its own initiative." Thus, according to the state action doctrine, it could "limit the rights of its colored members, without thereby offending the guarantees of the Constitution." The Mediation Board was plainly a government actor, the court conceded, but the Carmen had gained representative status "because a majority of the coach cleaners voted for it, and not by reason of any governmental action." There was nothing constitutionally suspect about certifying a union chosen by the majority in an "honestly and fairly conducted" election. On petition to the Supreme Court, Cobb repeated the state action arguments he had made in *Corrigan* and urged that the Constitution limited the New Deal labor regime's majority-rule principle. If the courts allowed "white labor organizations ... [to] make contracts for Negroes who are not permitted to belong to them," and thus allowed them to "be forbidden to work at their own trade by a majority of the white vote," Cobb insisted, then "the [Civil] war amendments [that] were framed to defend the colored peoples ... become dead letters." The Supreme Court anticlimactically denied review.[20]

Rice's suit was a client-driven effort to vindicate the Federation and himself, not a test case by movement lawyers. The injustice would have appeared starker if African Americans had been a minority of the electorate rather than its vast majority. Still, the lawsuit marked a transition. Redemption-era civil rights litigation had focused on advancing the black middle class so it could uplift poor African Americans and project respectability to whites. Cobb, Rice, and the Federation's members, part of the Republican old guard and pillars of the black elite, had repurposed a pre–New Deal constitutional argument made on behalf of would-be homeowners and applied it to the emerging fulcrum of black politics: labor unions. They had done so for pragmatic and personal rather than ideological reasons; nonetheless, they had forged a *workplace* Constitution, opening a new path for civil rights lawyering. But how would it be received, given the shifting terrain of black politics?[21]

Liberals, Labor, and the Constitution

African Americans "are not antagonistic to collective bargaining, but we d[o] insist on being part of the collection as well as part of the bargain," Charles Hamilton Houston explained in 1940. Houston knew Cobb well; apart from belonging to the same small social circle of Washington's black elite, Houston was vice dean of the Howard Law School, where Cobb taught. But whereas Cobb believed in using law, qua law, to secure rights, the younger Houston believed such legal battles should be linked with mass politics. In the late 1930s, a number of black independent unions, Rice's Federation among them, joined together to better defend against the all-white brotherhoods' attack on their members' jobs. This time, they hired Houston, not Cobb, to represent them. There was good reason to expect Houston to forgo Cobb's fledgling workplace Constitution, just as Houston's ally John Davis had rejected Rice's proposed amendments to the NLRA.[22]

The 1930s transformed black lawyering. In the first decades of the twentieth century, black lawyers focused primarily on developing independent black institutions: founding black law firms to serve black businesses, for instance. Like Rice, leading legal thinkers saw the labor movement primarily as a threat to African American workers. Given that legislatures justified Jim Crow laws as protecting public health and welfare, black lawyers were painfully aware that government regulation could be oppressive. To defend against Jim Crow, they embraced the liberty-of-contract doctrine associated with business interests and used by the Supreme Court to strike down Progressive legislation, from wage and hour laws to child labor laws. One of liberty of contract's key components, the right to work, was a revered tenet of the black bar, wielded against discriminatory unions seeking to close African Americans out of jobs and restrictive licensing laws that excluded them from particular trades. Houston, the son of an attorney, was born into this tradition.[23]

Houston, like many others in his generation, ultimately forged a different path. He trained at Harvard Law School, where mentors such as Felix Frankfurter taught him that law shaped and was shaped by society more than by legal doctrine or logic. As Houston told the Howard law students taking his pioneering course on civil rights law in 1940, "The young lawyer [is a] social engineer or … craftsman." This approach heightened his focus on law's effects while sobering him to its potential. "Civil rights," he told his students, were "luxuries extended the minority by the majority in an expanding economy." Winning those rights would require "a long record of persecution." In order to succeed, advocates must connect them to "the general problem of civil rights for America and all the world," whether stemming from the repression of labor or religious minorities. African Americans would win civil rights, in Houston's view, not simply by litigating but through linking their fate to a majority willing to support their cause.[24]

For Houston, the labor movement promised to generate that majority. He immersed himself in the radicalism of the 1930s, collaborating with the Communist Party's legal outfit and with the Marxists filling the halls of Howard University. When he went to work for the NAACP in 1935, he pressed the organization to use litigation to "stimulate mass action." Houston was involved in Davis's NNC as well as the National Lawyers Guild, a left-leaning alternative to the American Bar Association. Like Davis, Houston concluded that African Americans' best hope lay in joining and advancing the labor movement.[25]

New-guard leaders disagreed, however, about whether racial equality had to be fought for from within labor or legally imposed upon it. Their disagreement was driven in part by larger debates labor supporters were having about the wisdom and proper scope of federal labor laws. Labor viewed the state as a dubious ally. For decades, its courts had enjoined unions as criminal conspiracies or tortious combinations, and its armed forces had suppressed labor's strikes. Even Congress and the Democratic Party had proved fickle. As a result, many labor supporters appreciated the state's guarantee of the right to organize but wanted to keep its role minimal. They worried, as Davis did in his House testimony, that any regulation of unions' practices would redound mainly to the benefit of the "capitalist class" that the state ultimately served.[26]

The principles guiding New Deal labor law reformers also made barring discriminatory unions a controversial policy. The idea of transforming the workplace from a tyranny of the employer into an "industrial democracy" had long animated the labor movement. By the 1930s, reformers had settled on collective bargaining as the best means to this end. Under what they called *industrial pluralism*, unions would give workers a representative in the workplace while the contracts they negotiated would determine its governance. All agreed that the state should facilitate this regime by ensuring that workers could form unions and that employers would bargain with them. But adherents disagreed over whether the state had an ancillary duty to police the unions it helped create, to ensure that tyranny did not merely migrate from the workplace to the union. Those pluralists who viewed groups such as unions, not individuals, as the basic organic building blocks of society disfavored state meddling in how unions ran themselves, including their racial practices. Those who worried that the state, in establishing a majority-rule system of exclusive representation, might be "ratify[ing] and empower[ing] imbalances of power and other inequities in the group" favored further state intervention into unions' inner workings.[27]

African Americans' differing views on how to address union discrimination reflected these debates. The NAACP and the National Urban League, as well as the radical-labor-aligned American Civil Liberties Union (ACLU), had fought unsuccessfully for the original NLRA to prohibit racial discrimination by unions. In 1935 and in 1939, John Davis opposed those efforts. He insisted that it was "the loyalty which the Negro people display toward" the labor movement, and not legislation, that would secure their place in the movement. Davis was not an outlier. In 1935, those who supported civil rights but favored the NLRA as drafted thought that "racial discrimination ... will only be eliminated after economic injustices are corrected." The position Davis took before the 1939 House Committee was formulated by the NNC's national labor committee, composed of leaders from the most racially progressive unions, and ratified at numerous NNC conventions attended by thousands of delegates from thirty-eight states. Although the NAACP ultimately backed amending the NLRA, the decision was its convention's most contentious. Houston sided with those who thought that unions had to be restrained legally from racial discrimination. During the 1930s, he fought to place employment discrimination at the center of civil rights lawyering and, while at the NAACP, sought funding to "safeguard the rights of Negro workers under the collective bargaining acts."[28]

But how to do it? As Houston taught his students, most of the Constitution's provisions limited only state actors, a point he illustrated with *Corrigan*. The New Deal had vastly expanded government's relationship with private industry. The federal government contracted more frequently with private companies, adopted novel union- and employer-designed codes for industry, and regulated with new breadth and depth. Angered when contractors excluded African Americans from precious public employment, or industry codes granted them lower wages, members of the black bar fought back. If private industry acted at the behest of or under authority given by the government, they argued, it acquired public duties, including the duty not to discriminate. But their advocacy was directed at government officials, not courts, and thus did not translate into usable legal precedent. Indeed, when Houston lectured about employment discrimination in 1938 he referenced only five cases, most of which applied the common law and involved boycotts or workplace injuries. The only constitutional decision he discussed involved an Atlanta ordinance restricting the business of black barbers, but that case did not present a state action problem.[29]

Even if Houston found a way to surmount the state action limit, the right-to-work tradition was in tension with Houston's new prolabor position. Labor was not categorically averse to the Constitution. Since the nineteenth century, labor had invoked the Thirteenth Amendment to decry "wage slavery," and labor radicals asserted a First Amendment "right to agitate." When Congress debated the NLRA, labor leaders proposed grounding it in the Thirteenth Amendment or a Fourteenth Amendment liberty to engage in collective action. But courts' persistent use of the Constitution to restrict strikes and boycotts or invalidate labor-friendly laws in the decades before the New Deal had made labor leery of the *judicially* enforced Constitution. If Houston wanted to protect African Americans under the New Deal collective-bargaining regime, he would have to forge a middle path between the antilegalism of labor and the antiunion liberty-of-contract tradition.[30]

Liberals' Strategic Need for the Constitution

There is an "axiom in America … crystallized out of bitter experience: that the Negro's work ends where the machine begins," Houston explained in 1940 to federal district court Judge Donelson Martin Sr. For black railroad firemen, that machine was the mechanical stoker. Firemen had long held the dirty and dangerous job of manually feeding coal-fired engines. Mechanical stokers turned firemen into machine operators. Hand-stoked engines were replaced by mechanical stokers at an alarming rate during the 1930s, and along with them, black firemen were replaced by junior white operators. But the legal challenge Houston brought on fireman Ed Teague's behalf had implications beyond the rails. As he told NAACP leaders, this "far reaching case ... aims to settle the rights of minorities under collective bargaining legislation" generally. If successful, Houston's lawsuit before Judge Martin would impose legal restraints similar to those Rice had proposed adding to the NLRA and Cobb had pursued in court. But Houston used quite different means to achieve that end.[31]

Houston's complaint in *Teague v. Brotherhood of Locomotive Firemen and Enginemen* made no mention of the Constitution and sought to include African Americans in the New Deal labor regime, rather than except them from it. He relied on common-law concepts and New Deal statutes only. After the Railway Labor Act passed in 1934, the Firemen's Brotherhood, the same union that had led the violent crusade against black railroad workers in the 1920s and 1930s, easily won representation of *all* firemen, including the African American minority. Houston did not challenge the brotherhood's right to represent his clients as Cobb had the Carmen's. Instead, he argued that, as their representative, the Firemen's Brotherhood had a duty to "conform to and regard the rules of law governing the relationship between principal and agent," including a duty to represent all workers "loyally and in good faith." The Firemen's Brotherhood, Houston contended, was legally required to give black workers notice of, and an opportunity to be heard and vote on, matters affecting them. His clients had property interests in their jobs and seniority, Houston asserted. When the brotherhood negotiated secret agreements that gave black workers' jobs to more junior white firemen, Houston argued, it had violated this duty. Unlike Cobb, Houston also sued the employer, arguing that the brotherhood had "unlawfully induce[d] and maliciously cause[d] the defendant railroad" to break its employment contracts with its African American employees and "violate their vested seniority preference rights."[32]

Houston's focus on common-law agency doctrines left him vulnerable, however. He brought suit in a Tennessee federal court because he thought his clients stood a better chance there than in the state courts. To be heard in federal court, however, either the plaintiff had to be from a different state than those he was suing or the suit had to raise a claim under a federal statute or the U.S. Constitution – that is, it had to raise a "federal question." The railroad contended that Houston lacked any such basis and moved to dismiss the suit. In 1940 Houston argued before a sympathetic Judge Martin that his clients were "in court ... strictly on the question of the interpretation of the R[ailwa]y Labor Act," a federal question. Picking up on a term used by the brotherhood's attorney, Houston began referring to the duty that the union owed his clients as arising from its "statutory agency." He distinguished this type of agency from that of a "private agent" such as the plaintiffs' lawyer. Houston's clients could fire him, he noted, but not the Firemen's Brotherhood, which was imposed on them by the Railway Labor Act. "The [federal] question here," he concluded, "was a direct question of statutory construction of the R[ailwa]y Labor Act."[33]

But for a fluke, Houston would have surmounted this jurisdictional hurdle. Judge Martin denied the railroad's motion to dismiss. President Roosevelt had recently elevated Martin to the Sixth Circuit Court of Appeals, however, which meant that Martin had to hand *Teague* off to his replacement, Judge Marion Speed Boyd. The Firemen's Brotherhood soon moved to dismiss the action on the same jurisdictional grounds as had the railroad. Judge Boyd came to the opposite conclusion as Judge Martin. "In this case there is no right or immunity ... that is created by the Railroad Labor Act," Judge Boyd found, nor does it "involve a dispute with respect to the [Act's] validity or ... construction."[34]

New Dealers' different views on the state's role in labor relations help explain how these two Roosevelt appointees could disagree on this critical issue. Judge Martin represented the contingent of pluralists worried about those caught in the maw of newly empowered unions. He responded sympathetically to Houston's account of railroad men victimized by large forces beyond their control – mechanization, collective violence, secret agreements, exclusive representation. Judge Boyd embodied the contrary pluralist perspective that the state, even as it helped level the playing field between capital and labor, should leave businesses and unions otherwise free to order their affairs. Adopting Houston's argument that the term "representative" in the Railway Labor Act entailed the duties outlined in his complaint, Judge Boyd contended, would be inconsistent with Congress's intent and "would mean that we [judges] would just be forever and eternally litigating internal differences of the Labor Unions."[35]

Confronted with the vulnerability of his Railway Labor Act claim, Houston repurposed anti–New Deal constitutional arguments in defense of the New Deal state. Before the district court, Houston had likened the duties of a statutory agent to the government's obligations to ensure equal protection and due process. But he asserted federal jurisdiction based only on the Railway Labor Act. On appeal to the Sixth Circuit, Houston for the first time argued that his case also involved constitutional violations. There was no direct precedent for this assertion, so Houston turned to anti–New Deal doctrine to make his case. Congress, Houston insisted, could not constitutionally pass a law that destroyed his client's seniority rights or his "right to follow his trade or calling." Nor could it do "indirectly what it cannot do directly," Houston reasoned, "by conferring on the majority of a craft or class, or [its] representative …, arbitrary power over the vested rights of the minority." In support, Houston turned to *Carter v. Carter Coal Co.* That case involved a New Deal statute that authorized a majority of coal producers and mine workers to fix wages and hours for the industry as a whole, including for "an unwilling minority." The provision, the Supreme Court found in 1936, improperly delegated a "governmental function" to private actors and was "so clearly arbitrary, so clearly a denial of [personal liberty and private property] rights safeguarded by the due process clause of the Fifth Amendment" that it had to be struck down. Employers had since used *Carter* to challenge the constitutionality of the New Deal labor laws. Now Houston invoked it to argue that the Sixth Circuit must interpret the Railway Labor Act to impose Houston's proffered duties or it had to strike down the act under *Carter*. Either way, a federal question was involved. Houston ended his oral argument confident that he had won over the court.[36]

Contrary to Houston's instincts, however, the Sixth Circuit quickly affirmed the trial court. The rights Houston asserted arose from and had "to be adjudicated upon the applicable common law of the state"; the Railway Labor Act neither protected them nor "permits their invasion," the court held. "Nor does plaintiff establish a basis for Federal jurisdiction by assertion of right under the Fifth Amendment," it

continued. Citing *Corrigan* and Rice's case, the court noted that the
Fifth Amendment applied only to governmental action. Congress's
enactment of the Railway Labor Act involved such action, the court
conceded, but did not violate the Fifth Amendment because "nothing
in the Act ... authorizes [the] representative to impair the personal or
property rights of the employees for whom" it acts. There was, in other
words, no federal question involved and thus no basis for bringing suit
in the friendlier federal courts.[37]

Forging a Liberal Workplace Constitution

The Sixth Circuit's opinion was a "very fair interpretation of the law,"
Houston's cocounsel thought. Henceforth, he wrote, "all of these cases
must be tried in the State Court unless you get in [to federal court]
by way of a diversity of citizenship." Houston disagreed. By now he
was pursuing numerous cases throughout the South on the black railroad workers' behalf. Four months after the Sixth Circuit's decision,
Houston once again filed a complaint in the federal district courts, this
time on behalf of a worker named Tom Tunstall. Houston brought
Tunstall's case specifically "to avoid the defects in pleading in the
Teague case and to state a case where an interpretation of the Railway
Labor Act could not be avoided."[38]

In *Tunstall*, Houston emphasized from the start that the duties he
attributed to the brotherhood were imposed by the Railway Labor
Act. A familiar trajectory followed: the defendants moved to dismiss
for want of a federal question, which the district court, citing *Teague*,
granted. Stymied in his efforts to establish jurisdiction on the basis of
the Railway Labor Act, on appeal Houston added a Fifth Amendment
argument based on *Carter*. This time the appellate court did not even
discuss Houston's constitutional theories. In 1944, it found simply that the Supreme Court's recent decisions instructed that federal courts should hew closely to Congress's instructions and avoid
"afford[ing] relief ... except where express provisions of the act so
indicate." Deference to Congress, not pre–New Deal policing of legislative overreach nor New Deal liberal concern for minorities, governed the appellate court.[39]

Houston sensed opportunity nonetheless and petitioned the
Supreme Court for review. With his firm belief that social, political, and

economic forces won cases as much as legal reasoning did, Houston must have counted more than his perfected pleadings in his favor. Notwithstanding the appellate court's decision, much had changed since Houston first filed Ed Teague's complaint in 1940. Now the country was engaged in a world war against totalitarianism, thanks to which it was experiencing the kind of expanding economy Houston believed favored civil rights claims. African American leaders used the fight against fascism abroad to push for equality at home. In response, President Roosevelt created a Fair Employment Practices Committee (FEPC) in 1941 to investigate racial discrimination by government contractors. The committee soon launched an inquiry into discrimination on the railroads. When Houston filed his 1944 petition in *Tunstall* and a companion case from the Alabama courts, *Steele v. Louisville & Nashville Railroad Co.*, he had recently joined Roosevelt's FEPC.[40]

Houston's claims would not have the antiunion tinge that plagued Rice and his lawsuit. With the CIO organizing interracial industrial unions, the railroad brotherhoods and their race policies looked increasingly outmoded. This created space for a Supreme Court friendly to the New Deal's majoritarian labor regime to nonetheless oppose the brotherhood's old-fashioned exclusivity. John Davis's anti-legislation position during his 1939 House testimony also no longer defined the labor-liberal position. In 1940, the CIO decided to support NLRA amendments that would deny exclusive representation to unions that practiced the kind of overt, systematic discrimination associated with the railroad brotherhoods. Houston's effort to win their equivalent through litigation now seemed in keeping with liberal laborites' stance.[41]

Recent Court decisions also augured well. In several instances, the Supreme Court had used the Constitution to protect disfavored minorities, even handing the NAACP a promising victory in its renewed challenge to the Texas Democratic Party's whites-only primary. Despite the Court's acceptance of the New Deal's constitutionality and the preponderance of New Deal proponents among the justices, the Court expressed increasing concern about the fairness of the resulting apparatus. The Court cautioned the National Labor Relations Board (NLRB, or the Board) to respect employers' freedom of speech and chastised agencies for failing to provide adequate procedures to those they regulated. These changes created an opening for Houston. No longer was the New Deal endangered by the courts, nor did it seem incompatible with rights claims. Houston crafted a constitutional challenge that threatened neither his nor the justices' liberal credentials by seeking to perfect, rather than attack, the New Deal labor regime.[42]

The case the Supreme Court heard on behalf of Tunstall was, as a result, notably different from anything that preceded it. Most prominently, the constitutional dimension of Houston's argument took center stage. Houston argued that the text and structure of the Railway Labor Act, as well as the principles of "industrial democracy" that it imposed, justified interpreting the act's term "representative" to include the "fiduciary and statutory" duties Houston had long urged. Houston, joined now by the NAACP as amicus, also insisted that if the act failed to impose these duties, it delegated unconstitutional authority to exclusive representatives much like in *Carter*. The Railway Labor Act's exclusive representation provision "fastened [the Firemen's Brotherhood] on the Negroes against their consent," Houston argued. "Unless [that] grant of power is to violate both the Fifth and Thirteenth Amendments and place the Negro firemen in economic serfdom to the Brotherhood," he reasoned, "the grant must be subject to constitutional restraints."[43]

Houston also experimented with the possibility that the New Deal labor laws transformed unions, at least in some respects, from private entities into state actors. Relying on the Court's white-primary cases, he argued that the brotherhood, when it was certified as exclusive representative, began to "speak with the voice of Congress" and to "exercise power delegated to it by Congress." The NAACP reassured the Court that it need not "decide to what extent this transforms the Brotherhood into a governmental agency." But, it argued, if unions acted as "repositories of official power," as the Texas Democratic Party had, then "the great restraints of the Constitution [likewise] set limits to their actions." Because the brotherhood's "restrictive agreements were made only by virtue of a grant of governmental authority under the Railway Labor Act," chimed in another amicus, the ACLU, they were "not more free from constitutional restraint on the denial of property without due process of law than were the restrictions at issue in" Texas's all-white primary.[44]

The railroad cases, as they were now known, also featured new theories about what the Constitution required. In *Teague* Houston had insisted his client was "not contend[ing] that the Act confers on him or the minority non-member Negro firemen the power to force his way into the ... Brotherhood against the will of the Brotherhood members." The union merely had to represent black workers impartially and give them a voice in union matters affecting them. Now Houston argued that the Fifth Amendment gave black workers a right to membership if that was needed to secure their participation in the union. The NAACP went further, arguing that "the Railway Labor Act violates the Fifth Amendment if it empowers a union composed solely of members of one race to act as statutory bargaining representative for ... members of another race whom it excludes from membership." Industrial democracy, like political democracy, must enfranchise black workers.[45]

Even as Houston and the amici made the most aggressive arguments yet for a workplace Constitution, they harmonized their claims with the New Deal. Houston had carefully drafted his complaint in *Teague* "to show that we were not antagonistic to collective bargaining." Houston and the NAACP similarly insisted to the Supreme Court that their position was prounion. They merely demanded "a democratic union" that gave the African American worker "a degree of control over the representative and plac[ed] the representative under a degree of responsibility to him." This could only be accomplished, they urged, by giving the worker "the protection of membership, the right to the floor in union meetings, [and] the right of appeal thru [*sic*] [union] channels." The Court need not even hold the Railway Labor Act unconstitutional, Houston and the amici reassured the Court; it could instead find black workers' rights to fair representation and full participation already embedded in this signature New Deal labor law.[46]

The Court's 1944 decisions in the railroad cases were a great victory. The Court held that the brotherhoods must represent the interests of black workers in their bargaining units, known as a union's "duty of fair representation." Together, *Steele* and *Tunstall* had "knock[ed] out" or "substantially knocked out" all the Firemen's Brotherhood's discriminatory agreements, Houston announced to his clients triumphantly. Additionally, "Judge Martin," who sided with Houston in *Teague*, "has now been vindicated," Houston celebrated. Contrary to the string of lower court dismissals, the Supreme Court in *Tunstall* established that this duty of fair representation arose from federal law, creating a basis for federal-question jurisdiction and securing black workers' access to federal courts.[47]

Houston nonetheless indulged in an advocate's creative reimagining when he crowed that the Court had adopted "every single proposition we have advocated for five years." The decisions were actually more limited than Houston had sought. The Court stated that it was *not* requiring exclusive bargaining representatives to let the workers they represented join their organizations. They simply had to represent the workers fairly. In addition, while the Court conceded that there might be exceptions, it emphasized that excluded nonmembers did not have a general right to a voice or vote in the union that represented them. Houston now insisted that he and his clients had "taken the position consistently that we were not directly concerned at this stage with union membership." He even cautioned that doing so would have been to "bite off too much at one time." Turning defeat into victory, he instead praised the decisions: "The ground work has now been laid so that in the near future we will be in position to" win the membership issue.[48]

Houston also simplified the Constitution's role in the Court's decisions. In *Steele*, the Court concluded that although "Congress has seen fit to clothe the bargaining representative with powers comparable to those possessed by a legislative body[,] ... it has also imposed on the representative a corresponding duty ... to exercise fairly the power conferred upon it in behalf of all those for whom it acts." By equating an exclusive bargaining representative with a legislature and suggesting that both were subject to "constitutional limitations," the Court implied that the Constitution imposed this fair representation duty. Notwithstanding his late and instrumental decision to rely on the Constitution, it was central to Houston's subsequent account of the cases. Thanks to the Constitution, Houston predicted, *Steele*'s duty of fair representation would be applicable not only to unions certified under the Railway Labor Act, but also to those certified under the NLRA, which was likewise "controlled by the Fifth Amendment," and which governed the vast majority of workers. The duty would even apply to state labor laws, which were "controlled by the Fourteenth Amendment," Houston thought. This was because "the principle is the same under each Amendment: that the bargaining representative must represent all members of the craft, class or unit without hostile discrimination." In subsequent briefs, Houston cited *Steele* along with the white-primary cases to support the proposition that "private persons and associations exercising governmental functions are subject to constitutional restraints."[49]

Steele's relationship to the Constitution was murkier than Houston allowed, however. Much of the Court's opinion, like Houston's briefs, focused on the text, history, and postenactment interpretation of the Railway Labor Act. Whether the Constitution created unions' duty, compelled the Court's interpretation of the act, or merely happened to coincide with it, was unclear. Justice Frank Murphy remarked on the opinion's ambiguity. Murphy agreed with the Court's opinion if its interpretation of the Railway Labor Act resulted from finding that the act would violate the Fifth Amendment if it "permit[ted] or allow[ed]" the bargaining representative any exercise of "its delegated powers which would in effect violate the constitutional rights of individuals." But, Murphy puzzled, "I am not sure that such is the basis."[50]

The railroad cases' ambiguous relationship to the Constitution was reflected in their subsequent reception. Houston's analysis received some support when, in 1946, the Kansas Supreme Court found in *Betts v. Easley* that a government-certified railroad brotherhood was a state actor because it was "created and function[ed] under provisions of Federal law." The brotherhood therefore had to provide African American workers an equal voice in the union, the Kansas court held, and in all "matters vitally affecting their economic welfare." William Hastie, who had helped write the NAACP's amicus brief, agreed with Houston that the railroad cases were a constitutional milestone. *Steele* added "labor unions ... to political parties in the new catalogue of social instrumentalities whose conduct must on occasion conform to the constitutional standards of governmental action," Hastie observed. But others disagreed. A leading (and sympathetic) labor-law scholar thought the Court had found it "unnecessary to decide the constitutional issue." And Houston quickly learned that many of the federal courts he had won access to understood *Steele* to impose on exclusive representatives narrowly circumscribed "statutory" or "fiduciary" duties, not broad constitutional constraints.[51]

Whether or not Houston's confident predictions came to pass, this legal lion of the now not-so-new guard had accomplished what only ten years earlier had seemed an unlikely and quite possibly ill-advised task: he had forged a *liberal* workplace Constitution. Houston's efforts to use the Constitution to strengthen and perfect the New Deal labor regime would shape civil rights lawyering for decades to come. Whether his railroad cases actually anchored that workplace Constitution in Supreme Court precedent, however, would continue to bedevil this book's protagonists for a long time hence.

2

Agencies Discover the Liberal Workplace Constitution

The NLRB: "… a little FEPC"?

Clarence Mitchell

In 1941, George Benjamin became the first African American vice president of the Tobacco Workers International Union, an American Federation of Labor affiliate. For decades the Tobacco Workers had mostly ignored black workers. In 1930, only 100 of its 3,000 members nationwide were black. By the early 1940s, however, the union was scrambling to improve those numbers. The National Labor Relations Board had initially let unions define the group of workers they wanted to represent. Recently, however, it had required that the "bargaining units" have an economic justification, not merely a racial one, ending the Tobacco Workers' practice of targeting a plant's white workers only. Meanwhile, rival Congress of Industrial Organizations unions had steadily organized black workers at tobacco processing plants around Richmond, Virginia, getting a head start on winning their allegiance. Benjamin was a skilled and tested organizer, adept at operating within the constraints of Jim Crow. The Tobacco Workers' new president wanted Benjamin to help the union organize "at least 90% of the colored workers" in Richmond. Unfortunately, it was "still in the minds of some of the people that our international don't want the Negro," Benjamin warned. Richmond's Larus & Brother tobacco plant became the testing ground for the Tobacco Workers' new strategy.[1]

Instead of the racial exclusion so common among the railway brotherhoods, the Tobacco Workers organized African Americans into segregated locals. "I am not telling you that [Tobacco Workers] Local 219 will not bargain for you," Benjamin informed Larus & Brother's African American workers. "But ... my experience in the labor movement [is] that it would be better ... to be in a local union to [your] selves." With the CIO promising them an interracial union, Larus & Brother's black workers had to weigh the merits of segregated versus interracial membership.[2]

The ensuing dispute between the two unions forced the NLRB to decide whether, having prohibited race-based bargaining units, it would also forbid those unions representing interracial units from excluding African Americans or from segregating them into a separate local. What began as a question of policy evolved into arguments over the meaning of the Constitution and federal agencies' role in its implementation. If the liberal workplace Constitution took a different course before the NLRB than it had in the Supreme Court's railroad cases, the Board might become an attractive alternative to the Fair Employment Practices Committee (FEPC).

Race and Industrial Labor in Richmond and Beyond

Larus & Brother was a shrewd country squire among Richmond tobacco companies. Not as big or popular as the industry giants like American Tobacco, Larus & Brother was nonetheless elite among Richmond's smaller tobacco firms. The company was most famous for its pipe tobacco. Larus & Brother was also beloved for its local state-of-the-art radio station, which served listeners folksy fare such as the popular Corn Cob Pipe Club alongside the modern country music group Sunshine Sue and the Rangers. During World War II, Larus & Brother's business boomed. The federal government requisitioned the entire plant to sate American soldiers' taste for tobacco. The labor showdown brewing at Larus & Brother, like its business, blended local and national interests as well as traditional and pioneering practices. The dispute at Larus & Brother reflected broad changes in the dynamics of race, work, and unionization, albeit with a southern twist.[3]

When black workers arrived at Larus & Brother's manufacturing plant, they headed for the third floor. Unlike the textile mills dotting the upper South, where white workers predominated, the tobacco industry traditionally employed black and white workers in nearly equal numbers. Tobacco companies also hired black women, providing one of their few alternatives to domestic labor. But Larus & Brother, like other tobacco processing plants, intricately segregated its workforce by race and gender. Nearly all those sorting tobacco leaves in the dirty, at times suffocatingly hot stemmery were African American, and most were women. Less than half the workers in the manufacturing plant were black, and they were given the least skilled, most labor intensive jobs. There was nothing particularly southern about this kind of occupational segregation. But southern firms particularly emphasized spatial segregation, shunting black workers into separate spaces like Larus & Brother's third floor.[4]

Richmond's tobacco unions were as racially segregated as its manufacturing plants. After the CIO was founded in 1937, its unions organized black workers, from the steel mills of Birmingham to the auto plants of Detroit, influenced by a Communist Party ideology that emphasized cross-racial class solidarity, the opportunity to organize the workers the AFL ignored, and the pragmatics of winning elections in industrial units with a significant African American presence. These CIO unions began to transcend, however imperfectly, the AFL unions' trade, ethnic, and racial schisms. Nonetheless, in places like Richmond, CIO unions initially worked within segregation's confines, targeting only the black workers long shunned by the Tobacco Workers. During the 1930s, Communists organized Richmond's black tobacco workers, staging a dramatic sit-down strike and winning an unprecedented contract in 1937. The resulting Tobacco Stemmers and Laborers Union joined the CIO and in 1942 merged into the United Cannery, Agricultural, Packing and Allied Workers of America (Cannery Workers), organizing Larus & Brother's stemmery and third-floor manufacturing workers along the way.[5]

The Cannery Workers union stood out within the CIO for its radicalism. The president was a former economics professor who began organizing rural workers for the Communist Party in 1933. He founded the Cannery Workers in 1937 and affiliated with the CIO. Like its president, many who worked for the Cannery Workers were Communist Party members or sympathizers. The Cannery Workers targeted those the labor movement had long written off: women, seasonal workers, illiterate farmers, and migrants. Its members came from around the globe, and included Mexican, Filipino, Chinese, and Japanese workers employed in fields and canneries across the United States.[6]

The CIO's presence in Richmond caused the Tobacco Workers to shift from excluding black workers to segregating them. The international president of the Tobacco Workers relished competition from the Cannery Workers because he thought that Richmond's employers would embrace his union as a less radical and thus less threatening alternative. Local Tobacco Workers officials saw the situation differently. They beseeched their parent union to help them organize in the black community. The Tobacco Workers risked getting blamed by employers for letting the radical CIO gain a foothold in their plants, one pleaded. "It is the wrong psychological time," he acknowledged, "but it should be done ... to prevent anyone from saying we have not tried to organize them." In 1943, the Cannery Workers and Tobacco Workers agreed to merge their separate, racially defined bargaining units at Larus & Brother's manufacturing plant, and then to fight to represent the new merged unit. With an NLRB election between the two unions looming, the Cannery Workers promised an interracial union. The Tobacco Workers courted white workers' support (and the employer's favor) by pledging to establish segregated locals, as it had at a number of the South's major tobacco processers.[7]

Battles over the racial order, union power, and the South's place in the nation raged during the run-up to the Larus & Brother election. Economic and political opportunities opened for African Americans in the 1940s. America's factories were already pulling the country out of the Depression by arming its allies. Once the United States joined the war in 1941, job opportunities increased for those who remained at home while others entered the fight for democracy overseas. African American leaders used the fight against fascism abroad to push for equality at home. A. Philip Randolph, the leader of the AFL's mostly black Brotherhood of Sleeping Car Porters (the Sleeping Car Porters), called for African Americans to join the March on Washington. Meanwhile, NAACP branches observed a "National Defense Day" with protest meetings in about two dozen cities. Their "Double V" campaign – for victory overseas and at home – worked: in 1941 President Roosevelt created his controversial and unprecedented

FEPC and charged it with investigating racial discrimination by government contractors.[8]

The war created conflict as well as opportunities. African Americans' search for jobs off the farm and out of the South accelerated. At the same time, black servicemen found themselves posted to southern towns where they faced the strictures of Jim Crow and the hostility of local whites. The scope and speed of these changes sparked conflict and violence. In 1943, black and white mobs clashed in wartime production centers such as Detroit, Mobile, and Los Angeles. In San Francisco, more than a thousand gathered to protest Jim Crow unions, and white workers struck in Houston after their CIO union tried to integrate its membership. Racial violence roiled military bases and nearby towns in the South as well. These mass confrontations magnified the low-level, intimate, and daily racial clashes occurring in workplaces and communities across the country.[9]

Richmond was not immune to the conflicts. In April 1942, an interracial group of church leaders met in Richmond to discuss "the greatly accentuated racial tensions of the present war emergency." They did not have to look further than Larus & Brother to witness the problem they sought to address. In 1941, Larus & Brother's all-white Tobacco Workers local went on strike. Initially, members of the Cannery Workers respected the picket line. Without a strike fund to sustain them, however, and with Larus & Brother accusing them of striking illegally, they gradually returned to work, exacerbating conflict between the plant's black and white workers. Meanwhile, the black women working in Larus & Brother's stemmery complained to the FEPC that white women working in the manufacturing plant made nearly double their wages. Pay rates were not the only concern of Larus & Brother's black workers. The tobacco industry was rapidly mechanizing, and machine work was generally given to whites only. African Americans would soon lose their jobs to whites, unless they were allowed to operate the gleaming cigarette rollers and packing machines crowding plants like Larus & Brother.[10]

Larus & Brother's black workers faced internal pressures as well. Unionization skyrocketed during the war, with AFL and CIO unions adding millions of members. Due to wartime job opportunities, many new workers were African American. They had to decide how to unionize so as to protect their jobs and better their wages. Chapter 1 described how black railroad workers debated whether to fight for independent unions or join the brotherhoods. When segregated AFL unions competed with interracial CIO unions, as was the case at Larus & Brother, black workers faced a different choice. Segregated locals provided some benefits. As George Benjamin advised, a segregated local created leadership opportunities. Even an auxiliary local that had no voice in the white local's dealings with the employer, like the one the Tobacco Workers offered, at least gave black workers a chance at self-government. They might even have more power than in the Cannery Workers' interracial union, given that they constituted only a minority of that unit. Where unions operated a *closed shop*, one in which the employer could hire only union members, a segregated local could still provide access to jobs.[11]

African Americans at Larus & Brother initially stood together. In March 1944, the two unions faced off to represent the new, integrated unit. When workers lined up to vote that month, they took a stand in the racially tinged labor politics roiling the nation, choosing between a radical and a conservative union, an industrial and a craft union, an interracial and a Jim Crow union. In the end, most workers voted for *their* union, and the white majority handed the Tobacco Workers an easy victory.[12]

Larus & Brother's black workers ultimately proved divisible, however. The NLRB soon certified the white Tobacco Workers local as the exclusive representative. Now the erstwhile members of the Cannery Workers had to decide whether to join the Tobacco Workers on a segregated basis or fight against its victory. Some joined an all-black Tobacco Workers local, contending that "all we want is to be in the A.F. of L., where we can all bargain together." Many more did not; they declared that the Tobacco Workers, by establishing segregated locals, "had sold us out." Acting at their behest, the Cannery Workers requested that the NLRB rescind its certification of the Tobacco Workers, contending that the union discriminated against the members of its all-black local. Thus far, proposals to amend the NLRA to deny certification to discriminatory unions had gone nowhere. Now the NLRB would have to decide whether to find this prohibition in fact already existed in the statute as originally enacted.[13]

Race and Labor at the NLRB

During a Senate appropriations hearing in the summer of 1944, Georgia Democrat Richard Russell grilled an NLRB member about the Board's rumored plan to revoke the certifications of southern unions that did not merge their segregated locals. The chairman of the FEPC also took notice, informing the NLRB that his committee was "very much interested" in the Cannery Workers' petition and whether the Board would decertify unions "which refused to represent equitably Negro members." The Cannery Workers' request had brought Larus & Brother to the nation's attention and shone a spotlight on the NLRB's race policies.[14]

The war had displaced debates about amending the NLRA to bar union discrimination, but the NLRB had nonetheless waded gradually into the deeply controversial waters of federal fair employment policy. In the late 1930s, it had prohibited bargaining units defined by race alone. During the war, the NLRB courted opportunities to address racial discrimination in other ways. The Board directed its trial examiners, the administrative equivalent of a trial judge, to consider evidence of racial discrimination, including regarding a union's membership practices. In the past, the examiners had excluded such evidence as irrelevant. Now they, and eventually the NLRB, would consider whether racial discrimination affected a union's ability to represent workers adequately.[15]

Taking on the contentious issue of racial discrimination was an odd choice for a politically beleaguered agency. Immediately after the NLRA was enacted, business groups such as the National Association of Manufacturers sought to have the Supreme Court declare the law unconstitutional. After the Court upheld the NLRA in 1937, a coalition of conservative Republicans and southern Democrats in Congress sought to repeal it or severely curtail the NLRB's authority. In 1941, the House passed a raft of amendments by large margins, although they died in the Senate. In 1939 and 1940, a House committee also investigated the NLRB staff for everything from incompetence to communism. Accused leftists resigned and President Roosevelt overhauled the Board, appointing its first conservative member as well as a more moderate chairman. Even some civil rights supporters thought it a bad

idea for the Board to police union discrimination, given that it "has
been and continues to be the target of so much criticism, both in and
out of Congress."[16]

Perhaps due to its politically precarious position, the NLRB's first
decisions addressing union discrimination were bold in word but cautious in effect, intruding minimally on unions' membership practices.
In 1943, a year before the Supreme Court decided the railroad cases,
the Board said that it "entertain[ed] grave doubt whether" a *closed
union* (one that excluded African Americans) could represent "an
appropriate unit composed in part of members of the excluded race."
This "might have consequences at variance with the purposes of the
Act." After all, the Board mused, if a closed union were to negotiate a
closed-shop contract, those excluded from membership would lose their
jobs. Even absent a closed shop, the excluded workers might be denied
"their full freedom of association, self-organization, and choice of representatives, which the Act was designed to protect." When the NLRB
later required certified unions to "provide equal representation to all
employees in the unit ..., irrespective of race," however, it did not spec-
ify whether membership was an essential component of this equal representation. The Board's stance on racially exclusive unions may have
been murky, but its position on segregated locals was not: like the
FEPC, the Board tolerated them.[17]

The field examiner who investigated the Cannery Workers' charges
did not see discrimination in what he found. Because both locals participated in contract negotiations and voted at the union's national
convention, he found no basis for concern. The Tobacco Workers' segregated locals were simply part of the AFL's "historic policy in the
tobacco plants." This is precisely what made the *Larus & Brother Co.*
case such a potentially important one: the NLRB might be the first
government body to bar segregated locals.[18]

Bypassing the Workplace Constitution

The Cannery Workers' organizer thought *Larus* could strike "a blow
against the Jim Crow policies of the AFL" and the discrimination
"practiced against ... minority groups throughout ... the country."
At the least, it might remove "segregation from the Unions of the
South." The ACLU "expected [*Larus*] to set a far-reaching precedent"

on the novel question of segregated unions. An AFL official pressured the NLRB to defuse "the tremendous explosive nature of this case." Attorneys were busy arguing in the railroad cases that union discrimination was unconstitutional. When the trial examiner scheduled a hearing in the *Larus & Brother* dispute for early 1945, however, no one challenged the Tobacco Workers' segregated locals on constitutional grounds.[19]

Neither the ACLU nor the NAACP relied on the Constitution when they argued that racially segregated unions were illegal. The ACLU made state action–like arguments, urging that "the machinery of the Government should not be utilized to assist those who would create ... inferior classes in this country" and arguing that a "union is not a social club. It is an institution powerful in its organization and effect, in many instances controlling the conditions and terms of employment." The ACLU did not link these arguments to a constitutional claim, however. Instead, it argued that segregated locals violated the NLRA, Roosevelt's executive order creating the FEPC, and the public's interest in "a system of discrimination on the basis of color be[ing] uprooted." Even the NAACP, the premier advocate for African Americans' constitutional rights, saw courts as the exclusive site for constitutional advocacy. In a 1943 NLRB dispute, the NAACP made statutory and policy arguments against certifying unions that segregated African Americans into auxiliary locals, or otherwise denied them a "full voice or vote in union affairs." In 1944, the NAACP sought unsuccessfully to resubmit this earlier brief in *Larus*. Nowhere in its submissions to the Board did the NAACP mention the Constitution.[20]

The Cannery Workers similarly walked right past a constitutional argument. At the *Larus* hearing, the union's lawyer mentioned that the Tobacco Workers' segregated locals might violate the Constitution. But the union's primary claim was that the segregated locals violated the NLRA's purpose of "insur[ing] to workers the achievement of collective bargaining." In support, the Cannery Workers quoted at length from the Supreme Court's recent decision in the railroad cases, which held that exclusive representatives had a duty to fairly represent all the unit's members, irrespective of race. The Cannery Workers included the portions of the majority opinion and of Justice Murphy's concurrence suggesting that this duty was constitutionally required. The Cannery Workers nonetheless argued only that these quotes established that the Tobacco Workers' segregated locals "constitute perversions and violations of" the federal labor laws.[21]

The Tobacco Workers argued constitutional doctrine, but to defend rather than challenge segregated locals. The Cannery Workers' claims were unreliable because they were made by an organizer who had "communistic leanings or [was] a full-fledged fellow traveler," the Tobacco Workers warned. Anticommunism was a common refrain in southern opposition to the CIO, with southern Democrats promising on the Senate floor to resist any CIO "second 'carpetbag expedition' in the Southland, under the red banner of Soviet Russia." But the Tobacco Workers probably also hoped to chasten an NLRB still recovering from a Congressional investigation into its communist sympathies. The Tobacco Workers offered the Board a politically cautious and legally sound alternative. Under the Constitution, the Tobacco Workers insisted, segregation did not "per se create economic discrimination." The Supreme Court's decision in *Plessy v. Ferguson*, the union admonished, had long since established that segregation, "part of the warp and woof of society as we know it," was not discrimination. At worst, it was a "social problem" for society, not a regulatory agency like the NLRB, to address.[22]

Introducing an Administered Workplace Constitution

Frank Bloom was an unlikely civil rights crusader and constitutional pathbreaker: he had built his career by keeping the boat steady, not rocking it. A graduate of the University of Chicago and its law school, Bloom started his career at a local law firm. His colleagues included labor liberal Frank McCulloch, a settlement-house worker and League for Industrial Democracy officer who would eventually chair the NLRB in the 1960s. But Bloom's work was hardly radical: he represented banks and corporations in real estate litigation. In 1937, Bloom joined the NLRB as a trial examiner. He distinguished himself and was promoted a year later to assistant chief trial examiner. During the House's investigation of the NLRB, Bloom was briefly painted with a red brush by a former colleague. Bloom's level-headed and technocratic testimony to the House committee made the colleague's accusations of hot-headed cruelty as unbelievable as those of radical tendency. After the NLRB's shakeup, Bloom was promoted to chief trial examiner.[23]

In his February 1945 report and recommendations, Bloom none-theless delivered the blow against Jim Crow unions that the Cannery Workers sought. Bloom's legal reasoning was even more surprising than his conclusion that Larus & Brother's segregated locals were impermissible. In Bloom's opinion the locals defied the authorities the Cannery Workers and civil rights advocates had identified, including the NLRB's certification order, the NLRA's central mission of foster-ing workplace democracy, and President Roosevelt's fair employment executive order. The fact that the Tobacco Workers had "violated our constitutional policy against discrimination on account of race," how-ever, was "of even greater vital importance" to Bloom.[24]

The Constitution required both the Tobacco Workers and the NLRB to reject segregated locals, Bloom concluded, a possibility no one had suggested. "The Board, acting by virtue of an Act which itself must be construed in the broader terms of the Constitution," Bloom reasoned, "may not countenance infractions of constitutional rights or lightly ignore the practice of racial discrimination by a labor orga-nization which has sought and been accorded certification under the Act." Aspects of Bloom's analysis remained murky (for example, why the Tobacco Workers were state actors capable of violating the Fifth Amendment). His decision was nonetheless remarkable.[25]

Commentators, whether outraged or awestruck, grasped the signif-icance of Bloom's report but missed its most extraordinary aspect: his constitutional reasoning. "Sometimes quiet battles are waged on our behalf by men who have little or no direct contact with Negro leader-ship," a columnist for the *Pittsburgh Courier* said of Bloom. According to the black press, Bloom's report had far-reaching consequences, including "perhaps changing the AFL's policy throughout the South of maintaining separate locals for whites and Negroes." An irate AFL official accused Bloom of using his "misguided acrobatic bureaucratic totalitarian dictatorial authority in the best Robert Ley Nazi labor front manner" and of being a CIO stooge.[26]

Bloom's constitutional argument was pioneering even though it was largely ignored. Bloom gave new bite to agencies' obligation to the Constitution. Administrators had long interpreted and implemented the Constitution, typically with deferential supervision by the courts. During the New Deal, as the Supreme Court allowed agencies to wield broader powers, it also began scrutinizing more closely agency protection of regulated parties' constitutional rights, particularly their First Amendment free speech and Fifth Amendment due process rights. The Court had recently instructed the NLRB to define more broadly when its punishment of employers' antiunion statements violated free speech, for example. Despite the Court's direction, the Board seemed disinclined to stay its hand in the Constitution's name, however. Repeatedly it dismissed employers' claims that the First or Fifth Amendment limited its statutorily granted powers. Bloom, in contrast, recognized constitutional limits on the Board's exercise of its authority, determining that the Constitution denied the NLRB the power to certify the white Tobacco Workers local. This limit was also self-imposed; Bloom adopted it without prompting by the Court or the parties.[27]

More startling still, Bloom interpreted these constitutional restraints differently than the Supreme Court. In finding that he must construe the NLRA "in the broader terms of the Constitution," Bloom adopted an administrative analogue to the Court's approach in the railroad cases. The Court avoided constitutional problems in *Steele* by interpreting the Railway Labor Act to impose a duty of fair representation on exclusive representatives. The Court stated that the act did not "deny to such a ... labor organization the right to determine eligibility to its membership." Race-based membership practices, apparently, were not among the constitutional problems that must be avoided. Further, as the Tobacco Workers had noted, the Court's separate-but-equal doctrine was still intact. Bloom, in contrast, found that the Constitution reached unions' membership practices and declared that the Tobacco Workers' Jim Crow locals violated the Fifth Amendment.[28]

Bloom also departed from the Court and civil rights advocates by remaking, rather than trying to fit within, pre–New Deal understandings of the Constitution. In the railroad cases the NAACP and ACLU used well-established, if increasingly fragile, legal doctrines to justify a liberal workplace Constitution, including constitutional rules that limited the powers that Congress could delegate to others. These were the constitutional problems the Court sought to avoid in *Steele*. The white primary case *Smith v. Allwright*, also decided in 1944, evinced a similar dynamic. In *Allwright*, the NAACP argued and the Court held that the Texas Democratic Party was a state actor because of the public duties delegated to it by state statutes.[29]

Bloom's state action theory was more novel. Chapter 1 demonstrated that James Cobb could not convince a court that its *active enforcement* of discriminatory agreements was unconstitutional. Yet Bloom reasoned that government's mere tolerance of discrimination constituted impermissible state action (referred to here as a *sanctioning theory* of state action). Bloom's approach was not entirely unprecedented. At the time, Department of Justice lawyers were making a similar argument to reach mob violence under a federal civil rights statute. They noted that when Congress had debated the Reconstruction-era statute, a senator argued that the "State denies equal protection whenever it fails to give it. Denying includes inaction as well as action." In the 1870s and 1880s, the Supreme Court suggested it would recognize some versions of this inaction theory, although it never did. In the 1940s, Justice Department attorneys revived these inaction arguments to target official complicity in mob violence. Civil libertarians such as Bloom would have been familiar with these efforts. But it was hardly well established as a matter of law. In 1942, a Justice Department official conceded that the inaction theory was "still conjectural." It also went far beyond the rule the Court would later adopt in *Shelley v. Kraemer*, three years after Bloom's report: as Cobb had long urged, *Shelley* barred courts from *enforcing* private discrimination. Bloom instead prohibited merely "countenanc[ing]" or "ignor[ing]" discrimination.[30]

Bloom's broad theory of state action, coupled with his willingness to use the Constitution to restrain the NLRB's authority, opened up a new arena for advocating the liberal workplace Constitution: administrative agencies. Employers had brought constitutional claims before the Board for several years, but civil rights groups challenging workplace discrimination had yet to do so. Even the ACLU, which had filed briefs with the Board regarding employers' First Amendment rights, and with the courts challenging the constitutionality of unions' racial discrimination, did not rely on the Constitution in *Larus*. If the NLRB, like Bloom, began imposing constitutional limits on its authority and recognizing a liberal workplace Constitution, civil rights groups had much to gain from following Bloom's lead.

The Board Decides the Issue

"If two locals petition the Board for an election jointly and are certified by the Board, what is wrong with that?" John Houston asked an ACLU attorney at the NLRB's June 1945 hearing. President Roosevelt had recently appointed Houston to the Board to settle a political debt.

Houston knew little about labor relations, but as a Kansan, he knew plenty about segregation. "In the absence of any other special features I don't see anything wrong with that," the ACLU lawyer responded. "Suppose one is white and the other is colored," prodded Harry Millis, a quintessential industrial pluralist. Roosevelt had appointed the moderate Millis chairman of the NLRB in 1940 to mollify the Board's conservative critics. The ACLU lawyer responded with a clarity few others would provide during the Board's hearing: "Then I believe there is discrimination by segregation ... which we do not consider constitutional." "Even if voluntary?" Houston queried. "Yes, sir," the ACLU attorney responded. The Board's third and final member, Gerard Reilly, an established New Dealer, asked somewhat incredulously, "Do you use the words 'segregation' and 'discrimination' interchangeably?" The ACLU lawyer hedged, stating that the one amounted to the other "in this particular case." An AFL official countered that "there isn't anything under the Constitution, ... the Federal Acts of Congress, or any of the decisions of the Supreme Court that says segregation is a violation of the Constitution." The Tobacco Workers had a point. The parties were pushing the Board to decide pioneering constitutional questions.[31]

State action was a necessary predicate to debates about the constitutionality of segregation, and the parties pressed the Board on this issue as well. The Cannery Workers' lawyers picked up on the constitutional arguments they had bypassed before Bloom, relying on the railroad cases rather than Bloom's sanctioning theory to apply the Constitution to Larus & Brother's segregated locals. William Hastie, a Howard Law School professor and chairman of the NAACP's National Legal Committee, appeared on behalf of the National Lawyers Guild. Like the Cannery Workers, Hastie argued that the duty of fair representation "was based on this constitutional premise, that the union deriving its authority and power of representation from a statute of the United States, must treat workers in the same way that the government itself would have to treat workers." When Millis pressed Hastie about the consequences of his argument for "private organizations and labor organizations and private companies and religious and educational and other institutions," Hastie reassured Millis. Only because the union "claim[ed] certain rights under a Federal statute" could it "no longer enjoy the same privilege to discriminate that a private organization enjoys." The Tobacco Workers union was adamant that the railroad cases had not found certified unions to be state actors. The duty of fair representation, it insisted, "comes from the statute ... and not from the Constitution. The Federal Constitution has nothing to do with this case."[32]

The NLRB must have wondered whether Bloom had opened a Pandora's box as parties in other actions newly pressed constitutional arguments. A CIO union battling AFL unions at General Motors' St. Louis plant contended that, according to Bloom's report, the AFL's racially exclusive unions could not represent GM's interracial workforce. The NLRB, the CIO union urged, should adopt Bloom's approach and "affirm the legal right of American citizens to equal protection under the National Labor Relations Act regardless of race, creed or national origin." Bloom's report also proved useful to employers opposing unionization. The resolutely antiunion Atlanta Oak Flooring Company contended that it could not recognize, and the Board could not certify, an AFL union petitioning on behalf of racially segregated locals. According to the employer, the petition was "predicated upon ... an illegal and unconstitutional, discriminatory segregation of races." Echoing Bloom's state action reasoning, the company urged the Board that it would be "approving, or at least countenancing, the segregation" if it entertained the union's petition. The NLRB could expect many more such arguments if it adopted Bloom's sanctioning theory or the *Larus* parties' claim that certified unions were state actors.[33]

What was happening in Congress gave the NLRB pause. President Roosevelt's death in April 1945 raised doubt that the executive branch would maintain its commitment to fair employment. While *Larus* was pending, Congress debated the issue. At the *Larus* hearing, Millis asked whether it was "the function of this Board to make a law when other people are questioning what the law should be?" A week after the *Larus* hearing, southern Democrats blocked a proposed fair employment law. The next month, they dramatically defunded Roosevelt's FEPC, after failing to eliminate it altogether. Apparently Congress felt no constitutional obligation to prohibit unions' discriminatory membership practices. The ever-cautious Board had good reason to think twice before creating unprecedented fair employment policy.[34]

The NLRB decided to sharply delimit its role in policing unions'
racial practices. In the petition involving the St. Louis GM plant, the
Board authorized all-white unions to represent interracial units so long
as the union promised to "represent all employees of the unit." The
Board cautioned that if an AFL union was later shown to have "denied
adequate representation to any employee because of his race," the NLRB
would "consider such discriminatory practice as grounds for rescinding
the certification." In *Atlanta Oak Flooring*, the Board unequivocally
affirmed the *Plessy* principle that "segregation into separate locals is
[not], per se, a form of racial discrimination in violation of the National
policy and of the Fifth Amendment." If the segregated locals had equal
rights of affiliation and representation, the Board concluded, then there
was "no question of racial discrimination before us."[35]

The Board's decision two days later to allow Larus & Brother's
segregated locals was predictable in light of these earlier decisions.
The NLRB found that its statutory restraints shaped its constitutional
duties. The Board began from the premise that it was "solely a crea-
ture of Congress," constrained to dutifully apply the laws Congress
made. The NLRB had been "vigilant within the limited powers given
it by Congress to see to it that [its] certifications ... should not be
made the vehicle of discriminatory racial practices by labor organizations." These powers did not extend to demanding that unions provide
African Americans an equal voice in the union, however. Affirming the
industrial pluralist principles animating the NLRA, the Board insisted
that it lacked authority to police unions' internal policies. As evidence, it noted that the NLRA prohibited some employer conduct and
empowered the Board to issue "unfair labor practice orders" against
wayward employers but had no parallel provisions for unions. The
NLRB also observed that *Steele* stated that an exclusive representative retained the "right to determine eligibility to its membership." The
Tobacco Workers was required only to represent equally its all-black
local. The white Tobacco Workers local should not have required the
black local's members to pay dues, however, because the Board had certified only the white local as representative. Henceforward, the Board
would certify unions so long as segregated locals jointly petitioned the
NLRB to be the exclusive bargaining representative or racially exclusive unions represented black nonmembers and abstained from charging them dues.[36]

The Supreme Court dicta in *Steele*, Board members' industrial-pluralist leanings, the prospect of providing fodder for their congressional enemies, and their concerns about adding racial discrimination to the already thorny set of issues they oversaw all recommended caution. The NLRB's trilogy of decisions in *General Motors*, *Atlanta Oak Flooring*, and *Larus* unequivocally rejected Bloom's view that black workers had a constitutional right to integrated (or any) membership and an equal voice in unions seeking NLRB certification.

The Board Stands Firm

"The exponents of racism won a major victory in the flank attack they have executed with the supine acquiescence of the NLRB," the black press charged. If the Board had assumed a posture of "supine acquiescence" to racism in its trilogy of race decisions, however, an active and diverse network of civil rights supporters did not. During the fall of 1945, protest letters poured into the NLRB from across the country.[37]

Letter writers argued that segregated locals and racially exclusive unions undermined the NLRA. Irene Osborn of Columbia, Missouri, admonished that "to permit segregation, or exclusion of any group" thwarted harmonious labor relations by "split[ting] the ranks of labor." Mrs. R. P. Milburn, on behalf of a New Jersey Interracial Council, argued that exclusion from membership in the all-white local *was* discrimination and thus inconsistent with the NLRA's purposes and the NLRB's promise to revoke the certification of discriminatory unions.[38]

Others urged the Board to consider policy concerns beyond the NLRA. Julia Cooley Altrocchi, a member of the Berkeley, California, Interracial Committee queried, "What did we fight the war for – for the principles of Fascism, prejudice, superiority of pallor to sun-burn?" She exhorted the Board to "act according to the precepts of our Founding Fathers and the principles of American justice, which is justice, not to majorities, but to all!" Mrs. Milburn hoped that the NLRB would decertify racially exclusive unions, making its policy "truly representative of democracy." C. L. Dellums, a leader of A. Philip Randolph's union and president of the Alameda County, California, branch of the NAACP, succinctly implored, "We just must not come out of this war with less not more democracy."[39]

The Board was unpersuaded. In October 1945, the NLRB summarily dismissed the Cannery Workers' petition to reconsider its *Larus* decision. From Seattle, Washington, to Columbus, Missouri, disappointed letter writers opened their mailboxes to find a boilerplate response from Oscar M. Smith, director of the NLRB's Field Division. Congress sets labor policy, Smith wrote to those who had protested the Board's trio of race decisions. The NLRB was "limited to interpreting and applying this policy to cases as they arise in light of high Court decision." Congress had not granted the Board the power "to remedy undemocratic practices within the structure of union organizations," Smith insisted. If the precepts of the Founding Fathers were to the contrary, it was not the place of the Board to decide.[40]

Taft-Hartley's Effect on the Board

"Some persons are under the impression" that Section 8 of the Taft-Hartley Act "is a little FEPC," the NAACP's skeptical labor secretary, Clarence Mitchell, observed in 1947. World War II officially ended in September 1945 and the nation soon plunged into domestic turmoil. Returning soldiers and a demobilizing economy raised the specter of the Depression, while unions struck at record rates in an attempt to preserve their wartime gains. The public grew critical of labor, and Republicans swept Congress in 1946. Those Republicans and southern Democrats in Congress who had been "'hammering' at the NLRA since 1937" finally got satisfaction. Their amendments, which had died in committee in 1940, now passed over President Truman's veto. The resulting Taft-Hartley Act included new protections for employer speech, a requirement that union leaders file noncommunist affidavits, restrictions on strikes and boycotts, and a ban on closed shops. An enlarged Section 8 also gave the NLRB the power, for the first time, to issue unfair labor practice orders against unions, not just employers. The NAACP had opposed Taft-Hartley. Mitchell defended the closed shop and warned Congress that the proposed law would "return this country to involuntary servitude of the working man." Nonetheless, once Taft-Hartley became law in 1947, the NAACP and labor lawyers combined its provisions with the Constitution to argue that the NLRB now had the power to bar unions' racially discriminatory membership practices.[41]

The text and history of Section 8 left some doubt whether it could really function as a little FEPC. By empowering the Board to issue unfair labor practice orders against unions, Taft-Hartley seemingly undermined the NLRB's oft-stated claim that it lacked the power to inquire into unions' internal policies. One new provision barred unions from discriminating against workers on the basis of union membership, possibly providing a new remedy for racial discrimination. Yet it explicitly stated that it was not intended to "impair the right of a labor organization to prescribe its own rules with respect to the acquisition or retention of membership therein." Inauspiciously, one of the act's sponsors, Senator Robert Taft, reassured southern Democrats during floor debate that, under the new law, "unions which prohibit the admission of Negroes to membership ... may continue to do so." The Conference Report also specified that the amendments would not "disturb arrangements in the nature of those approved by the Board in *Larus.*" Opponents of workplace discrimination nonetheless hoped that the new provisions might create a legal wedge for their campaign.[42]

The NAACP and union lawyers renewed their challenges before the Board, now emphasizing the Constitution and adopting Bloom's state action theory. In 1948, NAACP lawyers still argued, as Hastie had to the Board in *Larus*, that under *Steele*, "the Fifth Amendment extends to the union's activities," barring discrimination by any union "acting pursuant to authorization by a Federal agency under a Federal statute." The NAACP also contended, echoing Bloom, that the "Board cannot lawfully lend its aid to any union seeking to discriminate." Accordingly, the NAACP "called upon [the Board] to ... refus[e] to certify a union in whose activities Negroes will not be entitled to participate fully nor benefit equally." Even AFL unions, typically the most averse to government regulation of unions' affairs, used charges of discrimination and the Constitution to challenge competitor unions. In 1947 a Teamsters local intervened before the NLRB to stop a rival racially exclusive union from representing workers at a southern trucking company. The Teamsters, not known for its racially progressive policies, may have been more interested in retaining its representation of the company's mechanics than in advancing the cause of racial justice. The local nonetheless argued that unions failed to "fulfill their statutory and constitutional duties" if they barred African Americans from membership.[43]

The Board did not view Taft-Hartley as a "little FEPC," however. Since the NLRB's first trilogy of race decisions, Congress had rebuked the Board by passing Taft-Hartley; the Board had also gained a new chairman who, even more than his predecessor, moved Board policy to the right. The NLRB repeatedly stated that it would not tolerate racially discriminatory unions, even as its decisions clarified that it did not see the recent Taft-Hartley amendments as a mandate for more aggressive action. Citing its earlier decisions, the Board merely reiterated that it would "not pass on the internal organization of petitioning unions in the absence of proof that they will not fairly represent all employees regardless of race, color, or creed."[44]

In 1949, Clarence Mitchell, the NAACP's labor secretary, called Taft-Hartley's membership nondiscrimination provision a "pure unadulterated fake" and accused Congress of pinning a "donkey's tail of second class citizenship on all of the colored people in the trade union movement." He also sardonically described the Board's interpretation of the labor laws: "Unions may exclude colored people from membership, they may segregate them into separate locals and they may refuse to let them share in the full benefits of the union, but no union may discriminate against them because of race."[45]

The NLRB's 1946 annual report reduced its pre–Taft-Hartley discrimination decisions to a simple rule: "Neither exclusion from membership nor segregated membership *per se* represents evasion on the part of a labor organization of its statutory duty to afford 'equal representation,'" the Board explained. An exclusive representative, however, "must not exclude employees upon a discriminatory basis if it holds a contract with the employer containing closed-shop features." By 1946, the "grave doubt" about closed unions that the Board expressed in 1943 had crystallized into a firm policy against allowing closed unions to organize closed shops. According to the NLRB, this policy resulted from interpreting the NLRA's term "representative" in light of that act's purposes, as well as "the national policy against discrimination," as "expressed in the Fifth Amendment to the Constitution and in the President's Executive Orders."[46]

The NLRB's report was remarkable for both the policy it established and the justification it provided. Barring closed unions from organizing closed shops was one of the NAACP's top litigation goals during the early 1940s. As of 1946, only the California courts had adopted the rule. Hidden in a relatively obscure annual report, the NLRB extended this principle to the majority of American workplaces. Taft-Hartley's ban on closed shops the following year rendered the Board's new policy of short-lived utility. But in a promising sign for civil rights advocates, the Board based its policy on the Fifth Amendment. Perhaps the space between the Board and Bloom did not result from different views of *whether* the Constitution constrained or authorized NLRB action, but of *what* the Fifth Amendment required of the Board. The report suggested that if the Board revised its understanding of discrimination under the Fifth Amendment, its racial discrimination policy might change as well.[47]

Bloom's report had transformed the liberal workplace Constitution. Agencies were now a site for civil rights advocates' constitutional claims, and Bloom had placed a new, potentially far-reaching theory of state action in their arsenal. With the NLRB in agreement that the Fifth Amendment governed its policy, it might yet become the little FEPC that the NAACP hoped for.

3

Conservatives Create a Workplace Constitution in the Courts

"The spirit at that particular time"

Neil McCarthy

"This is a rather startling document for an American citizen to receive," the renowned film director and beloved radio broadcaster Cecil B. DeMille wrote to his longtime attorney, business partner, and friend Neil McCarthy. It was August 1944 and DeMille was outraged. He had just received a letter from his union, the American Federation of Radio Artists (AFRA), telling him that all union members had to pay one dollar or face suspension. The dollar assessment was levied to fund AFRA's campaign against Proposition 12, a measure on the California ballot that would amend the state constitution to ban closed shops. AFRA had a number of closed-shop contracts, including one covering DeMille's popular *Lux Radio Theater* program. As a member of Hollywood's right wing and a conservative Republican, DeMille opposed the closed shop and supported Proposition 12. "I am not in favor," he wrote, "of any free man being forced to join a union in order to work." He did not want to pay even a dollar of his considerable fortune to support the closed shop. Yet if DeMille refused to pay the dollar and AFRA suspended him, he would lose his radio program. By threatening to deny him "the right of earning my livelihood" if he failed to pay the fee, DeMille fulminated, the union "is in direct violation of my Constitutional rights."[1]

Known among his employees for his temper and outsize ego, DeMille was used to getting his way. But the U.S. Constitution was not like one of the assistants whom he could bully into taking the position he desired. To win recognition of a conservative workplace Constitution, DeMille had to explain *why* AFRA's threat violated his constitutional rights. In the process, he created legal, rhetorical, and tactical links between his cause and that of African American workers. Like them, DeMille faced arduous doctrinal hurdles. Also like them, he turned initially to the pre–New Deal past, then gradually added more modern minority-rights claims to his repertoire. In another similarity, DeMille turned to forums other than courts to make his case. Unlike those fighting for a liberal workplace Constitution, however, DeMille was a multimillionaire with political connections, access to the ears and wallets of the wealthiest Americans, and national platforms at his disposal. For DeMille, low-stakes constitutional litigation served high-stakes constitutional politics.

Anti–New Deal Conservatives Make a Right-to-Work Movement

In November 1944 California's Proposition 12 was soundly defeated and the Los Angeles Superior Court declared legal a similar fee assessment by a different union; neither development ended AFRA's efforts to collect DeMille's dollar, nor his refusal to pay it. The union set a final deadline for early December, which came and went without the payment of DeMille's politically and legally freighted dollar. *Billboard Magazine* predicted that "the matter will come to a showdown ... [because] it appears that neither party is willing to back down." As predicted, AFRA suspended DeMille. An indignant DeMille insisted that "under the Constitution of the United States no organization should have th[e] right" to make an American voter "support or oppose any proposition on the ballot." DeMille had built a fortune catering to the masses. As he sought public support for his cause, he took pains to bridge the gap between himself and his audience.[2]

DeMille was immersed in an open-shop movement that was itself embedded in surging conservative opposition to the New Deal. Union gains during the New Deal and World War II gave conservative opposition to closed shops new urgency. Since at least the early twentieth century, employers had banded together to fight for open shops. Before the 1930s, employers mostly had the upper hand in disputes between capital and labor. But this control was tested during the Depression. Thanks to aggressive organizing campaigns and New Deal legislation like the National Labor Relations Act, union membership exploded. Closed shops, long favored by traditional AFL craft unions as a means to monopolize the market for their skill and bind workers to the union, proliferated. So did the *union shop* agreements championed by the CIO's industrial unions. These required new employees to join the union to keep their jobs, allowing the union to shift resources from recruiting and retaining members to administering contracts. They also gave the union an indicium of employer acceptance. Unions got a further boost as the economy revived in the early 1940s. Europe was at war and America supplied military goods to the world. Government agencies overseeing the industrial mobilization allowed, and at times even required, closed and union shops. By 1941, the Department of Labor reported that four million wage earners, nearly two-thirds of union members, worked in a closed or union shop.[3]

As unions' strength grew, their opponents' influence withered. Opposition to unions and to closed shops persisted during the 1930s among what one historian has termed the "belligerents" of large industrialists, men like the intensely antiunion du Pont brothers, Pierre, Lammot, and Irénée. In the mid-1930s, employer groups like the National Association of Manufacturers (NAM) opposed passage of the NLRA and then fought for its repeal or invalidation by the courts. The more euphemistically named but no less industrialist-driven American Liberty League tried to convince voters to abandon President Roosevelt. These activists' efforts came up short. NAM's opposition to New Deal legislation earned it, according to one historian, "a reputation as an ineffective, churlish lobby," and the Liberty League was seen as elitist and inconsequential.[4]

In the late 1930s, anti–New Deal conservatives gained new political muscle. Despite Roosevelt's decisive reelection in 1936, some of his supporters soon defected. Popular columnist Westbrook Pegler attributed his own turn against the New Deal to his encounter with rising fascism in Europe during a 1935 trip abroad and to what was, in his view, Roosevelt's eerily similar court-packing plan at home. Pegler then turned against labor after his union threatened to oust him if he refused to join its strike. In the late 1930s, Pegler led a crusade against the New Deal labor laws and the union bosses on behalf of "members against their will." The already ailing economy slumped further in 1937 and 1938, and the nation was rocked by headline-grabbing sit-down strikes. In the 1938 mid-term elections, Republicans gained seventy-one seats in the House. Conservatives of both parties now held a majority in the House and significant sway in the Senate. New Dealers were also hit at the state level, losing governorships in such labor strongholds as Wisconsin, Michigan, and Pennsylvania.[5]

Conservatives used their new power to challenge the rapidly growing labor movement. In the late 1930s, NAM undertook a major public relations campaign, producing films, radio programs, advertisements, and displays for schools and factories. Its leaders attacked the National Labor Relations Board and the NLRA, calling for a ban on closed shops. Virginia Democrat Howard W. Smith convened a special House Committee to investigate NLRB staff for everything from Communist sympathies to pro-CIO bias. On the House floor, Georgia Democrat Edward Cox called the NLRB's attorneys "an army of wild young men" and criticized the NLRB for moving "steadily toward compulsory unionization," a derogatory term for the closed and union shop. In 1940, Pegler published a Pulitzer Prize–winning exposé of mob corruption in two prominent unions.[6]

Thanks to World War II, anti–New Deal conservatives produced few policy results, however. Led by Howard Smith, in 1941 House conservatives passed restrictive amendments to the NLRA, after promising from the floor to liberate American workers from labor dictators and racketeers. But these amendments stalled in the Senate, as the nation's attention pivoted to the surprise bombing of Pearl Harbor. In a nation now at war, the federal government involved itself further in setting labor policy, regulating prices and trading a variety of dues- and membership-enhancing policies with labor for a pledge not to strike. Business organizations like NAM and the Chamber of Commerce were effectively sidelined.[7]

Regrouping, deep-pocketed executives like the du Ponts, anti–New Deal activist groups like NAM, and populist mobilizers like Pegler formed a loose and hazily defined movement in the early 1940s. "Right to work" was its emerging slogan. Those associated with the movement targeted a range of issues, from the union security agreements Representative Cox and NAM fought against, to the political assessments DeMille opposed, to the union corruption that Pegler deplored.

The meaning of "right to work" was not yet fixed or exclusive. The right to pursue a calling had deep roots in Anglo-American common law. In the late nineteenth century it migrated into constitutional law, where it was best known for limiting government's power to regulate the workplace. Its application to union power dated back at least to the early twentieth century, but open shop advocates had no monopoly on it. In 1930, it was as likely to be invoked by African Americans asserting a right to decent jobs as by closed-shop opponents. In the early 1940s, the black press still decried African American women "being denied the right to work in war plants," while other Americans complained that "workmen have lost their constitutional right to work [because they] now have to pay tribute to labor racketeers." Beginning in 1941, however, opponents of big labor sought to make the "right to work" term their own, and to make abolishing closed and union shops their most prominent issue.[8]

Right-to-work activists had considerable impact on state laws. As early as 1939, states in the Northeast through the upper Midwest and on out to Oregon enacted laws that restrained union activities. On Labor Day 1941, conservative newsman William Ruggles used the editorial page of the *Dallas Morning News* to offer what he termed the "Right to Work Magna Carta." Ruggles proposed a Twenty-Second Amendment to the United States Constitution that ensured no worker had to join or support a union. The Christian American Association, a Texas group funded by the du Ponts and associated with the far right of anti–New Deal politics, took up Ruggles's "right to work" banner, using it to promote similar state legislation throughout the South. The association did not have to wait long. The year 1943 proved "prolific of ... labor legislation which is predominantly anti-union in character," one legal scholar observed. The next year, right-to-work supporters launched their first legislative campaign to put Ruggles's proposed ban into state law. California was a prominent battlefield, and Hollywood, which was embroiled in sometimes violent jurisdictional battles among its craft unions, was arguably the campaign's ground zero.[9]

Cecil B. DeMille was active in the Republican Party. Described as "conservative, if not reactionary," DeMille served as a delegate to the Republican Party's national convention when the Liberty League mobilized to defeat Roosevelt in 1936. Sensing DeMille's ability to popularize the anti–New Deal cause, state Republicans tried unsuccessfully to convince DeMille to run for Senate in 1938. More locally, Hollywood was a hotbed for leftist Popular Front politics, from the recent Walt Disney cartoonists' strike to Orson Welles's allegorical films. DeMille was an ardent opponent of Hollywood's left turn. During the war, he informed for the FBI, reporting suspected Communists and investigating putative fascists in the Hollywood studios. In 1944, Hollywood's anticommunists and conservatives banded together as the Motion Picture Alliance for the Preservation of American Ideals. The alliance's short-term goal was to help the Republican Party win back the White House; its long-term goal was to purge Hollywood of leftists. DeMille was one of the alliance's founding members.[10]

DeMille had a particular interest in the right to work. He was convinced that the unions were run by Communists. In his view, union security agreements fed the leftists' power and subjected noncommunists unwillingly to their rule. As a film producer and director, DeMille was also an employer of many who had to deal with multiple unions about issues far more expensive than AFRA's one-dollar assessment.

Publicly, DeMille distanced himself from the elites with whom anti–New Deal politics was still associated. He insisted that when he received AFRA's notice of the fee, "I did not then know what Proposition 12 was." He also told a misleading but homey story about his decision to withhold his dollar when faced with AFRA's ultimatum. It was a December eve, getting on toward Christmas. As DeMille told it, he turned to his wife and asked her what to do. "She told me," he would later say, "that if I paid the dollar I would be telling the world I placed money above principle. Besides, she said she was a partner in the firm and would not pay her half of the dollar."[11]

In truth, DeMille's battle was far less personal and much more political than he let on. Contrary to his public statements, when DeMille first learned of AFRA's assessment, he wrote his lawyer, McCarthy, that his support for Proposition 12 was among the reasons he found the fee "startling." After receiving AFRA's letter, DeMille consulted not only his wife but also fellow conservative activists. One, Georgia native Y. Frank Freeman, was a vice president at Paramount who had recently tangled with the left-leaning Office of War Information over its regulation of Hollywood. The NAACP's Walter White referred to

Freeman as "a thoroughly unreconstructed Southerner." DeMille had recently turned out a number of blockbuster movies for Paramount and counted Freeman among his close associates. Another was William M. Jeffers, whose interest in DeMille's dollar dispute highlighted its national implications. Jeffers had worked his way up on the railroads. Due to a mixture of brawn and cunning, he now stood at the helm of the Union Pacific Railroad. Jeffers's industry combined strong unions with open shops and racial exclusivity. After receiving AFRA's letter, DeMille consulted Jeffers and Freeman about whether to pay or to challenge AFRA. Their advice to take a stand against the unions, as much as Mrs. DeMille's refusal to pay her fifty cents, fueled DeMille's fight. DeMille explained his decision to risk losing his lucrative radio show as an apolitical and private act of conscience undertaken by Mr. and Mrs. DeMille, but it was also a strategic move chosen by a cadre of conservative activists.[12]

Forging a Conservative Workplace Constitution

DeMille vowed to fight his ouster from AFRA in the courts. His belief that something was constitutionally amiss was understandable. Union opponents had long viewed courts and the Constitution as their best allies and legislatures as their worst enemy. While Progressives passed proworker laws barring antiunion contracts and ensuring a minimum wage, state and federal courts issued injunctions against threatened strikes and struck down workplace legislation. Unions were as leery of courts as their opponents were fond of them.

DeMille's attorney, McCarthy, predicted that it would be hard to secure a legal victory, however. McCarthy had been DeMille's lawyer and business partner for more than twenty years. When they first met, McCarthy was a smart, witty, and energetic upstart – a bit like the young DeMille. The two built their careers together. By the 1940s, McCarthy was a lawyer to the rich and powerful, from politicians like Herbert Hoover to the great industrialist Howard Hughes. "An Irish rogue," according to DeMille's granddaughter, McCarthy spent his career litigating commercial transactions in the California courts. Although not an expert, McCarthy agreed with DeMille "that compelling him to use his money in an election to oppose a proposed amendment ..., where he wanted to use that money to ... support that amendment, was ... a violation of his Constitutional rights." But "constitutional law was not an exact science," McCarthy warned. Instead, "The decisions of the courts in Constitutional questions w[ere] a matter of psychology and social viewpoint of the individuals composing the courts." In McCarthy's view, this did not bode well for DeMille. "The spirit at that particular time," McCarthy warned, "was so pro-labor that we would probably not find a court with sufficient courage to uphold our position."[13]

The spirit of the times was one barrier. The law of the times was another. When AFRA suspended DeMille in December 1944, McCarthy was ready. He immediately filed suit against the union and secured a temporary restraining order from the Superior Court. This saved DeMille from losing his *Lux Radio Theater* program, but AFRA quickly moved to dismiss DeMille's suit. McCarthy had to convince the court that there was a legal basis for invalidating AFRA's fee. McCarthy argued, among other things, that AFRA's assessment violated DeMille's constitutional rights and that it, and any contract authorizing it, was void as against public policy under the Fifth, Thirteenth, Fourteenth, and Fifteenth Amendments. McCarthy particularly insisted that the assessment unconstitutionally forced DeMille to sacrifice his "right of suffrage" if he paid the fee or his right to work if he did not.[14]

Like the lawyers representing black workers in the railroad cases, McCarthy turned to pre–New Deal precedent to make his case. When the right to work entered constitutional law in the late nineteenth century, it was variably derived from the Fifth and Fourteenth Amendment's due process clauses, the Fourteenth Amendment's privileges and immunities clause, or even the Declaration of Independence. However derived, it was among the freedoms of contract that state and federal courts relied on to strike down Progressive legislation. Unremarked yet remarkable is that state courts also justified injunctions against union activity based on a constitutional right to work. Some courts straightforwardly found the "right to earn a livelihood" sufficient to uphold a labor injunction. The right to work never shed its connection to the common law, however, and some courts fused the two, finding, for instance, that a union violated the public interest when it "deprive[d] a nonmember of his constitutional right of liberty and property." These were the cases to which McCarthy turned to support his claim that DeMille's assessment was "against public policy" and "an attempt to deprive plaintiff of his liberty and his property without due process of law."[15]

McCarthy had reason to think that his claims might succeed. Freedom of contract had fallen out of favor among intellectuals even before the Depression. During the 1930s, the Supreme Court stopped making it a check on economic regulation, throwing the doctrine in further doubt. But during the early 1940s, the constitutional right to work's future was far from resolved. The doctrine remained popular among conservatives who viewed freedom of contract as a bulwark against creeping statism. Rallying the troops in 1941, NAM's president gave a speech entitled "The Bill of Rights Today" that lionized a "vital natural right, namely the right to work at a lawful vocation of one's own choosing." True, the Supreme Court increasingly protected disfavored minorities, including religious minorities who resisted mandatory flag salutes in public schools and labor organizers faced with local laws restricting their activities. But as Risa Goluboff argues, "The judicial rejection of *Lochner*'s right to work was neither clean nor complete."[16]

Even liberals committed to the Court's new minority-rights jurisprudence saw promise in a constitutional right to work. A civil libertarian argued that the cases McCarthy cited demonstrated that, in assessing unions' growing power, "we can hardly avoid giving consideration to the standards set up by the Bill of Rights." In 1944, the NAACP brought right-to-work claims in state and federal courts on behalf of African Americans excluded from union membership. The NAACP cited the same precedent as McCarthy and similarly interwove constitutional and common law. An exhaustive article, "The Right to Equal Employment Opportunity," described the cases McCarthy cited as "pioneering."[17]

McCarthy's turn to pre–New Deal precedent affected how he addressed state action. The state action limit, crystallized by the Supreme Court's 1883 decision in the *Civil Rights Cases*, is generally thought to have remained stable into the 1940s. The historical record is more complicated, however. In the well-known freedom-of-contract cases, plaintiffs challenged statutes and ordinances, so state action was clear. As McCarthy's brief demonstrated, plaintiffs also sought injunctions against unions based on a constitutional right to work throughout the freedom-of-contract era. When the actions of a union rather than a legislature were challenged, state action appeared to be lacking. Abundant federal cases dismissed right-to-work claims against medical boards, bar associations, and, as black railroad workers found, unions, for precisely this reason. Indeed, a federal court had recently dismissed one of the NAACP's 1944 membership cases for lack of state action. State courts were different, however. Perhaps because they mixed constitutional and common law reasoning, state courts that enjoined unions to protect a constitutional right to work never mentioned this problem. McCarthy relied on this jurisprudence. His brief did not mention state action or concede any problem asserting Fifth, Fourteenth, or Fifteenth Amendment rights against AFRA.[18]

The legal regime on which McCarthy relied appeared to retain some purchase. Responding to DeMille's lawsuit, AFRA granted that he held a right to work, but contended that it, "like most other rights, is a qualified right and is subject to plaintiff's willingness to comply with working conditions decided upon by a majority of his fellow workers in the radio acting field." Perhaps primed by the rhetoric of industrial democracy, the union also seemed perfectly happy to equate itself with a state body. Denying a union the right to require contributions would be like telling a city it could only collect voluntary taxes, AFRA argued. "It is a part of the democratic process that the will of the individual should give way to the will of the majority." AFRA similarly conceded its *ability* to infringe DeMille's right of suffrage, instead claiming that, in this instance, its assessment left his right intact because he remained free to vote for Proposition 12.[19]

Judge Emmet Wilson of the Los Angeles Superior Court also objected to neither DeMille's asserted right to work nor the absence of state action. He found DeMille free to vote his conscience regarding Proposition 12, AFRA's assessment notwithstanding. "The dissemination of the principles of a union and opposition to their impairment differ widely from an attempt to elect or defeat a candidate for political office," Wilson held. The latter, Wilson reasoned, was a "political activit[y]," while the former, "oppos[ing] legislation it deems to be destructive to its principles," was not. That Wilson ignored the obvious state action ground for dismissal and instead grappled with the merits of DeMille's claim suggests he did not see state action as necessary. Bolstering this interpretation, Wilson implied that, had AFRA's assessment supported *political* activity, it would have violated DeMille's right of suffrage. On January 24, 1945, Wilson dismissed DeMille's complaint. AFRA was free to take DeMille off the air.[20]

DeMille vowed that he would press his case "to our highest courts before we accept the principle of tyranny as part of our American citizenship." Going forward, should DeMille conform to the increasingly pro-minority-rights spirit of the times or should he try to change that spirit to be more amenable to anti–New Deal conservatives' constitutional claims? DeMille hedged his bets. He appealed his case and simultaneously launched a campaign to sway the American public to his view of the Constitution. Before both audiences he bent to the spirit of the times and sought to mold it.[21]

Changing the Spirit of the Times

On March 17, 1945, DeMille stood on a stage in Omaha, Nebraska, looking out on the assembled members of the all-white railroad brotherhoods. The wires leading from his microphone also broadcast his speech to radios across the country. The occasion was the annual St. Patrick's Day luncheon hosted by William Jeffers, DeMille's conservative ally, and Jeffers had purchased DeMille a full hour on national radio to tell the story of his battle with AFRA. When DeMille demanded that "we must find a voice for the great mass of Americans who want to cry out against the rape of American Freedom," he spoke not only to the union men and railroad officials gathered before him eating their heartland meal, but also to millions of Americans across the nation. DeMille already had a voice in mind to speak on behalf of these silent millions: his own.[22]

DeMille was an organization man, whether it was the Republican Party or the anticommunist Motion Picture Alliance. He knew that you needed institutions, not only a lawsuit, to change the spirit and thus the law of the times. DeMille, McCarthy, Jeffers, and Paramount executive Frank Freeman quickly mobilized in the wake of DeMille's trial court loss to create a more favorable environment for his appeal. Business opposition to unions had spread in 1944 and 1945 as labor organized new firms and sectors. "Bitterly anti–New Deal" businessmen took over NAM and used their positions on the War Labor Board to oppose union security agreements, like those for closed or union shops. DeMille, Jeffers, and Freeman recruited a number of these businessmen, most prominently the resolutely antiunion president of Allis-Chalmers, along with several wealthy conservative activists, to establish the DeMille Foundation for Political Freedom. Their humble goal, in the words of Jeffers, was to jumpstart the "greatest movement in this country in the past century."[23]

In the growing pantheon of conservative organizations, the DeMille Foundation added a populist approach. In 1945, there was a plethora of conservative organizations but no good models for DeMille to emulate. NAM and the national Chamber of Commerce had retooled their tactics and by 1945 found themselves in a position to influence national labor policy. But they represented employers, not the masses. There was an increasing array of less explicitly employer-driven groups, but none of these was quite right either. The ultraright Christian American Association was too exclusive, associated as it was with the anti-Semitism and anti-Catholicism of organizations like the Ku Klux Klan. Those that sought to mint the ideas that would guide the nation off its statist course, like the recently founded American Enterprise Association (later Institute), were too elitist. A "seasoned anti–New Deal campaigner," the Committee for Constitutional Government had the kind of innocuous yet appealing name DeMille and his associates were looking for, but their foundation shifted the focus from the institution to the individual. Who, they must have reasoned, did not seek "political freedom"?[24]

DeMille and his comrades organized in defense of the Constitution, but they had a crassly political notion of how to achieve their goal. Unlike groups that focused on free enterprise and managerial prerogative, the DeMille Foundation, in Jeffers's words, was "seeking to ... hand down to posterity the Constitution of this country." Simply touting the Constitution, however, would not suffice. "The Bill of Rights ... has been there for a long time," DeMille noted, "and the Supreme Court doesn't seem to be paying much attention to it." His foundation would have to "change the minds of the city Councils, the legislatures, the governors, and the Congress" in order to ultimately "change the mind of the Supreme Court." And to transform American politics, DeMille's foundation needed to attack what its creators deemed the Constitution's greatest enemy, the CIO. The reason most conservative organizations had failed thus far, DeMille diagnosed, "is that they have started out to conquer the world like Don Quijote [*sic*] and Sancho Panzo [*sic*]." The DeMille Foundation, in contrast, would follow "the modern science of war" and "attack the enemy's supply." The "one thing that gives ... [the CIO] its power," DeMille reasoned, was the "political assessment." Mandatory contributions allowed the CIO to "terrorize the courts, the city Councils, the legislatures, the governors[,] the Congress and the very highest offices of government," DeMille insisted. By attacking the left's supply route and building "an organization with a voting power surpassing that of the unions," his foundation would transform the constitutional spirit of the times.[25]

Long before the DeMille Foundation could do battle with the CIO, however, it faced a number of more proximate hurdles. The founders first had to decide how to achieve their spirit-changing goal. Should the organization focus on education or political action? An obvious advantage of education was that it might result in a tax-exempt status much coveted among small conservative organizations. But as Freeman commented, they should not sacrifice principles to increase donations. Was Frank Doherty, prominent attorney and former president of the Los Angeles Chamber of Commerce, right that if they used education to "fix the principles of political freedom, laws will automatically follow"? Or were McCarthy and Freeman correct that an educational campaign was too limited in its scope and appeal? Jeffers, DeMille, and Doherty won the day: as Jeffers barked, the DeMille Foundation would "stick to the one issue of political freedom. Stick to educational activity. Take the message to the people against political coercion." DeMille's "first job," Jeffers insisted, "is to try to educate the American people – [by] telling them how to think."[26]

The founders also had to choose the best vehicle with which to pursue their strategy. One of their donors, E. F. Hutton, a wealthy financier and former Liberty League backer, liked the DeMille Foundation's emphasis on political freedom, but thought the right to work was too narrow and controversial an issue on which to focus. "Your appeal," he warned DeMille, "seems to be only to union labor, and all told that represents not more than ten or twelve million people." Nonunion folks are already "somewhat hostile to labor and would shed no tears or cough up money on behalf of freeing labor from the political domination of its unions." DeMille stood his ground, insisting on right to work's broad appeal. "Where one educated man will appreciate an appeal based upon the constitutional guarantee of liberty," DeMille predicted, "a hundred thousand will understand what it means to lose a job if you don't 'kick in' to a political campaign fund."[27]

Decisions about funding and membership also had to be treated with care. One group of wealthy donors offered enough cash that the DeMille Foundation could "depend upon a comparatively few rich men and corporations" rather than a large membership made up of donors big and small. But then it "would be an instrument for big business" instead of "enlisting big business support on behalf of our single aim," the foundation's secretary warned. The funders would set the agenda, and they wanted an uncontroversial program, the secretary cautioned; no more "talking about political assessments." DeMille was happy to have wealthy donors, but not if it meant forsaking a mass-movement attack on the enemy's supply chain. He also insisted that membership "be open to every American, without cost" so as "to enlist as great a number as possible and to highlight the difference between this movement and the opposition movements [namely, unions] which exist by forced assessments."[28]

A degree of discretion was required to maintain the DeMille Foundation's populist appeal. The "main task," its secretary advised "is to convince genuine middle-of-the-road leaders that we ... are not anti-labor, not anti-union, that we have one and only one aim, political freedom, and not undercover objectives beyond that." This is precisely how DeMille sold his foundation to potential funders. He told a gathering of the Los Angeles Realty Board in February 1946, "The DeMille Foundation is non-profit – non-partisan – and non-political. It is not anti-labor or anti-union. It is anti-political coercion." DeMille's foundation would talk publicly about the Communist threat and labor tyranny, but discussion of the CIO and its muscular Political Action Committee remained behind closed doors.[29]

The DeMille Foundation quickly settled on a strategy, but it was still unsure of its tactics. In the years following its charter, the foundation considered supporting individual right-to-work lawsuits, contemplated creating state-level DeMille Foundation committees to support local right-to-work campaigns, and pushed for a federal right-to-work law. One activity remained constant, however: DeMille used the many prominent platforms available to him to attempt to alter constitutional politics.

Popularizing and Modernizing the Conservative Workplace Constitution

February 14, 1947, was an especially sweet Valentine's Day for Cecil B. DeMille. He faced adoring Republican members of the Senate Committee on Labor and Public Welfare. The war had ended a little over a year before, just months after President Roosevelt died, leaving the nation in the hands of his untested successor, Harry Truman. Unions' record-breaking strike wave backfired as soldiers returned en masse just when industries, once buoyed by war, contracted, kindling fears of a renewed Depression. Republicans took control of both houses of Congress in the midterm elections after campaigning on charges of union abuses. After years in the political wilderness, they could finally enact the labor law reforms they had been promoting for nearly a decade. DeMille was ready. He had recently lost the appeal in his suit against AFRA. The California Court of Appeals easily found that AFRA could not have violated DeMille's rights of suffrage, free speech, and assembly – but not for lack of state action. Instead, the court found that no one attributed AFRA's position on Proposition 12 to DeMille and he remained "entirely free to work in support of the proposition, regardless of the union's opposition," the court reasoned.[30]

DeMille was always skeptical that a court would recognize his constitutional rights without a massive transformation in American politics. Now that transformation seemed to be occurring, and not two years had passed since his foundation set this as its goal. In the meantime, in dozens of speeches across the country DeMille had challenged the prolabor spirit that McCarthy identified as DeMille's chief barrier. In the process, DeMille fashioned a new constitutionalism for anti–New Deal conservatives, one that deemphasized *Lochner*-era freedom of contract in favor of newer minority-rights claims. He called his statement to the Senate Committee his "brief" against the closed shop for a reason.

Whether measured by turnout, speaking engagements, public response, or press attention, DeMille struck a chord with his public. As predicted, David and Goliath stories of individual workers pitted against powerful union leaders were compelling, their appeal only heightened by America's fight against totalitarianism abroad. That the "worker" who was speaking happened to be one of Hollywood's most successful filmmakers did not seem to matter. In May 1945, DeMille appeared at an intimate gathering of the Southern California Republican Women at the tony Los Angeles Biltmore Hotel. By September 1945, more than three thousand New Yorkers gathered in the streets of Manhattan to hear DeMille speak at the conservative American Legion's ceremony commemorating the Bill of Rights. Hundreds of sympathetic editorials in small papers across the country spread the word of DeMille's stand, and letters from listeners and readers poured in to his Hollywood studio. Although the DeMille Foundation received a twenty-thousand dollar donation from the president of General Motors and courted the financial support of "leading eastern industrialists, bankers and mercantilists," Junior Chamber of Commerce members, and Hollywood conservatives, thousands of ordinary members also made modest contributions. Whereas the Liberty League could never shake its reputation as an organization fighting for "the rights of the rich," DeMille and his foundation successfully framed DeMille's struggle against AFRA "as the case of every American workman."[31]

As DeMille campaigned in the court of public opinion, aspects of his constitutional case evolved while others remained constant. His line on union power hardened considerably. When his dispute with AFRA began, DeMille privately opposed "any free man being forced to join a union in order to work." Publicly, however, he initially insisted that he was neither "for [n]or against a closed shop." Because a closed shop "constitutes a monopoly of labor," like any other monopoly, DeMille argued, "it should be controlled and regulated for the welfare of the community." The right-to-work movement was gathering strength in the states, giving DeMille cover to make his private views public. His 1947 "brief" to the Senate Committee contended that the "closed shop, by its very nature, leads to the invasion of rights guaranteed by the Constitution." Closed shops, not political assessments, were now the central problem.[32]

DeMille remained focused on a constitutional right to work, but he refined the basis for that right. Whether speaking to conservatives in southern California, state officials in Sacramento, or the general public in Wichita, Kansas, DeMille championed a right to work that he variously described as "endowed by God," recognized in the Declaration of Independence, or protected by the Bill of Rights. By 1947, he had linked these three sources of law. DeMille still contended that the right to work was a predicate of the right to life guaranteed by the due process clauses of the Fifth and Fourteenth Amendments. He nonetheless sought alternative bases for the right to work, advancing a traditionalist account of natural rights and newly emphasizing the Ninth Amendment. The Constitution, according to DeMille, did not create rights, it just protected them. The rights thus protected were not limited to those enumerated in the Bill of Rights, or even those described in the Declaration of Independence. The Ninth Amendment stated that the rights described in the Constitution "shall not be construed to deny or disparage others retained by the people," implying that there was an open-ended spectrum of additional rights the Constitution protected. The right to work was among those unenumerated yet protected rights, DeMille insisted. The Declaration stated that the rights to life, liberty, and the pursuit of happiness were merely *among* those men held, DeMille pointed out, meaning its list was partial rather than complete. Because the Declaration described men as "endowed by their *Creator* with certain inalienable rights," natural law, which included a right to work, was the place to look for those additional rights.[33]

DeMille looked to the present as well as the past, aligning his claims with the Supreme Court's new solicitousness for political, religious, and racial minorities by describing his movement as one of the minorities the Constitution was designed to protect. In his 1945 St. Patrick's Day speech, DeMille had positioned himself and his sympathetic audience as among the "80 or 90 million citizens of the United States who still believe in Constitutional Government and the freedom of the individual." This mass of like-minded citizens, DeMille urged, must "unite to prevent our government, our Congress, our legislatures, and our courts from being high-pressured into submission by any minority groups of individuals operating for private purpose and gain." Soon, however, DeMille repositioned himself and his sympathizers as a minority of dissenting workers seeking protection from a domineering union majority. "All Americans believe in the concept of majority rule," but this "is only half the picture," he cautioned. "As long as the Constitution and the Bill of Rights remain in force," there was "a threshold at which the power of government itself must halt," as well as "the battering ram of any majority." Indeed, DeMille insisted, "the only reason ... Democracy has worked in this country is that majority rule has gone hand in hand with minority rights."[34]

DeMille translated his minority-rights rhetoric into new, more modern claims to a conservative workplace Constitution. Although far-fetched from a legal standpoint, he fashioned them out of the constitutional provisions most popular with civil libertarians. DeMille argued that the closed shop violated religious freedom. As an example, he offered the story of several workers who lost their jobs because it was against their religion to join the union. He also argued that the closed shop violated workers' freedom of speech because "no member dares to speak out or to combine with his fellow-members against the entrenched power of the union boss or so-called union majority." Pointing to the fate of five Hollywood clerical workers who lost their jobs over their involvement in a lawsuit against their union, DeMille argued that closed shops violated due process by making it practically impossible "for any union member to appeal to the courts." When McCarthy appealed DeMille's case to the California Supreme Court, he likewise described DeMille as a dissenting minority within the union. In 1944, the U.S. Supreme Court created a free speech exemption from public school's mandatory flag salutes for Jehovah's Witnesses. McCarthy likened paying AFRA's assessment to the "positive action ... required to make the flag salute."[35]

DeMille particularly plumbed the similarities between the right to work and the African American freedom struggle, drawing analogies between the closed shop and American slavery. In 1946 DeMille spoke to the powerful Western Growers Association, an organization active in right-to-work politics. DeMille recounted how he and William Jeffers perceived in 1944 a "new and desperately grave threat to freedom" posed by unions' "power to tell a worker that he could not earn his living unless he subscribed to the political designs of a group that controlled his right to work." They sensed this threat, DeMille intoned, "as other Americans had sensed the threat to freedom in an insignificant tax on tea or the fate of a runaway slave named Dred Scott." DeMille told the Senate Committee, "We need a Second Emancipation Proclamation to free those [workers] who have been forced to sign away their individual liberty." Elsewhere, he even argued that allowing closed-shop unions to compel contributions would bring slavery back to the United States.[36]

DeMille likened the right to work to African Americans' contem-
porary struggle as well. Conservative southern Democrats had already
drawn connections between right to work and racial discrimination.
In 1946 they opposed a fair employment bill before Congress in part
because it did not prohibit discrimination against nonunion workers in
closed or union shops. Georgia Democrat Richard Russell inveighed,
"It is almost a fraud on its face to give us a bill which seeks to regulate discrimination in employment ..., when it does not even deal with
... the discrimination which has been practiced against hundreds of
thousands of American citizens because they have not been members
of a certain labor union." In 1948, when Congress considered a federal
right-to-work law, one of DeMille's cotestifiers warned liberals that
advocating for African American civil rights but not the right to work
had "the quality of a deep hypocrisy." This was especially true because,
in his view, union discrimination against nonmembers was "a far more
serious discrimination than the incidental discriminations that may
occur or may not occur in regard to race, color, or ancestry."[37]

Like other conservatives, DeMille used the analogy between right
to work and African Americans' civil rights to bolster his own movement, not to support theirs. In 1947, DeMille first referred to his foundation's work as civil rights advocacy. The next year, a member of
the foundation's staff proposed to its congressional allies that they
add a right-to-work amendment to any proposed civil rights bills.
But DeMille was not trying to advance African American civil rights.
Pleased when *Readers Digest* ran a favorable piece on right to work
titled "Speaking of Civil Rights," DeMille wrote the author that "I like
the title particularly.... There is so much speaking of civil rights, with
dead silence about the Right to Work. You are helping much to correct
that."[38]

If DeMille had broadened and updated his constitutional claims in
many respects, one feature remained steadfast: he still had no notion
that state action might be a significant hurdle for his cause. Grounding
the right to work in natural law evaded the problem. DeMille argued
that the divine rights to property, liberty, and happiness recognized
in the Declaration were "rights which no power on earth can touch."
In DeMille's view, the First and Fifth Amendment rights about which
he testified to the Senate were equally inalienable. As DeMille asked
his audiences incredulously, "Do the constitution and by-laws of a

union ... take precedence over the Constitution of the United States?" McCarthy's brief to the California Supreme Court similarly argued that "the fundamental or constitutional rights of the individual may not be invaded by private associations or corporations any more than by the State or a public body." Although DeMille continued to describe unions as monopolies, term them a "government within a government," and even argue that they were "in a sense more powerful than government itself," he never used these attributions to argue that they were state actors.[39]

The Times' Stubborn Spirit

In the summer of 1947 Congress passed the Taft-Hartley Act over President Truman's veto. Among other things, the act prohibited closed shops, allowed states to mandate open shops, and outlawed penalizing nonmembers in union shops for any reason other than their nonpayment of regular dues and fees. A raft of states passed right-to-work laws later that year, bringing to fourteen the number that banned closed and union shops. Taft-Hartley's sponsors, conservative stalwarts in their respective chambers of Congress, flattered DeMille when they credited his foundation with the act's passage. Nonetheless, DeMille had put a familiar, grandfatherly face on the right-to-work cause and had gone a long way toward building the mass movement he and his fellow activists dreamed of.[40]

His favorable reception in Congress took some of the sting off his loss before the California Supreme Court in December 1947. Then again, the many draft statements he prepared in anticipation of the court's decision suggested that he considered it of great moment. As had the lower courts, the California Supreme Court dismissed DeMille's constitutional claims by finding no violation of his rights on the merits. There was no whiff of minority protection here: the court reasoned that majority rule foreclosed DeMille's claims. He also did not qualify for the free speech exception given to the compulsory flag salute because the assessment did not result in compelled *personal* expression. Nor did it force DeMille to oppose a proposition that he supported. DeMille's arguments, in the court's view, overlooked the fact that "the member and the association are distinct." The money spent and the message sent were AFRA's, not DeMille's.[41]

The merits might turn out to be the least of DeMille's concerns, however. DeMille had dodged the state action hurdle thus far because he was in state court, and particularly because he was in California. In the mid-1940s, the California Supreme Court interpreted the state's public policy in light of a constitutional right to work and declared a number of actions by closed-shop unions illegal. In the course of this hybrid common and constitutional law reasoning, the California Supreme Court stated that the "right to work ... [is] protected in some degree against arbitrary action by private organizations, including employers and labor unions." Unsurprisingly, the California courts had not tossed DeMille's action out for lack of state action. Having promised to "lay this vital constitutional question before the nation's highest tribunal," however, DeMille had to face the overwhelming federal precedent that imposed a state action requirement on the amendments he invoked.[42]

DeMille's fancy Washington lawyers wrangled the arguments below, with their tangled mix of common and constitutional law, into a form cognizable to the federal courts. Although they spent a fair amount of time arguing the merits of DeMille's forced speech and right-to-work claims, they also gave the state action requirement unprecedented attention and a novel twist. By 1948, when they wrote their brief, lawyers, scholars, administrators, and courts had developed state action theories that reached unions. Charles Houston and NAACP lawyers had evolved from using nondelegation-like arguments to asserting that unions were state actors because they were empowered by the state. In 1947, legal scholar Clyde Summers adopted this rationale and applied it to the broad question of workers' "right to join a union."[43]

DeMille's lawyers instead took an approach akin to that of the NLRB's Frank Bloom and the coach cleaners' attorney James Cobb. Echoing the civil rights attorneys' arguments in the racial covenant cases pending before the Supreme Court, they argued that the requisite state action existed in the California courts' failure to protect DeMille. "Action is no less governmental because it is taken by the judicial rather than the legislative or executive branch," they reasoned. Even when enforcing private common-law rights, his lawyers asserted, courts remained government actors. In the racial covenant cases, the state court had clearly engaged in such action by enforcing a private agreement prohibiting the sale of property to African Americans. But the California courts had not enforced anything. DeMille's attorneys thus had to take their argument a step further. "No distinction can properly be made as to whether the judicial action challenged on constitutional grounds is affirmative or negative," they argued. By failing to redress AFRA's actions against DeMille, the California courts were as responsible for those acts as if they had enforced AFRA's assessment or suspension directly.[44]

AFRA's lawyers raised alarms about DeMille's state action theory. This approach was not supported in precedent, they protested; previously, the Court had found constitutional violations only if the judiciary had wielded its "coercive power ... [the] enforcement of which violates the Fourteenth Amendment." DeMille's approach was also ill-advised, AFRA warned. If adopted, "everyone who claims a private person has violated his rights and thus has no constitutional claim, could convert it to a constitutional claim by losing his case in court and then claiming that Court, by denying relief, [committed] unconstitutional state action." Relaxing the state action requirement in this way "would be to abolish it entirely." The U.S. Supreme Court declined to hear DeMille's appeal, but its decision later that year in *Shelley v. Kraemer* held only that state court *enforcement* of racially restrictive covenants violated the Fourteenth Amendment.[45]

DeMille conceded that AFRA may have won in the courts, but crowed that "his position had been vindicated by Congress in the Taft-Hartley Act." AFRA probably thought DeMille's boast was unjustifiable. Labor assumed that its allies would regain Congress in the upcoming election and promptly repeal Taft-Hartley. But DeMille was adamant. He talked less about winning a constitutional right to work in the courts and more about pursuing this goal exclusively through politics. The DeMille Foundation also shelved plans to support right-to-work plaintiffs in favor of educating the public and supporting state right-to-work campaigns.[46]

If DeMille backed away from the courts, he did not back away from the Constitution. He began work on a never-completed book titled "Right to Work." The idea was to interweave his own personal story with economic and legal arguments in support of the right to work, arguments like his now-familiar claim that "the Declaration of

Independence gives you certain God-given rights that even you cannot dispose of, and the Constitution protects those God-given rights." By the end of the 1940s, conservatives had their own civil rights movement, one that shared more than a name with the liberal civil rights movement. Albeit to different ends, both fought for a workplace Constitution and looked to secure it beyond the courts.[47]

PART II

ADVANCING THE WORKPLACE CONSTITUTION IN THE COLD WAR 1950S

4

Liberals Test the Workplace Constitution
in the Courts

"If the Fifth Amendment precludes segregation ... in public education, it necessarily precludes segregation ... of Negro firemen."

Joseph Rauh

"To the Colored Firemen ... Employed on the Central of Georgia Railway," read the notice the Firemen's Brotherhood posted in the spring of 1953. In 1951, Congress had amended the Railway Labor Act to allow union shops. After overcoming two years of resistance from the railroads, the Firemen's Brotherhood was about to enforce its new union shop agreement. All eligible firemen would have to join the union or face dismissal. Given the brotherhood's history of running African Americans off the rails, whether through workplace lynchings or discriminatory agreements, the railway's black firemen had reason to worry. Many of them had recently asked to join the brotherhood but, as the notice reminded them, the "constitutional requirements of the Brotherhood does [sic] not permit you to become members thereof." The union shop agreement, the notice nonetheless reassured them, provided that "no employee refused membership in the Brotherhood shall be dismissed."[1]

Even if the Firemen's Brotherhood could be trusted, its reassurance no longer sufficed. When the Supreme Court decided the *Steele* and *Tunstall* railroad cases in 1944, Charles Houston described the decisions as laying the "ground work" for a future challenge to "the right of the railroad unions to ... [exclude] Negroes from membership."

Houston was felled in 1950 by a heart attack before achieving his ultimate goal. His clients, for their part, remained ambivalent about membership in the brotherhood, reasoning that they would be better off in their independent all-black unions than as a minority in the historically hostile, all-white Firemen's Brotherhood. A. Philip Randolph did not share their ambivalence, however. Randolph had been committed to fighting for equality from within organized labor since affiliating his Brotherhood of Sleeping Car Porters with the AFL in 1928. During the 1950s, he devoted himself to ending the color bar to union membership.[2]

Randolph's cases joined persistent challenges to the state action doctrine. One of the Supreme Court decisions legal scholars have found most difficult to justify was an easy case for the justices. Decided in 1948, *Shelley v. Kraemer* found that a court could not constitutionally enforce an otherwise valid racially restrictive covenant. Chief Justice Vinson thought the case involved the "letter of [the] 14th Amend[ment] as interpreted" and his brethren agreed. It would be the Court's last easy state action decision. Throughout the 1950s litigants argued that everything from *Shelley*-like enforcement to mere government permission or failure to intervene was sufficient to convert traditionally private action into state action.[3]

After the Supreme Court declared segregated public schools unconstitutional in 1954, the stage was set for Randolph to provoke a collision between its state action and antisegregation decisions. If the Court extended state action to unions, their racially exclusive or segregating membership practices seemed doomed. But would this eventuality prompt the Court to broaden or restrict state action? Its decision would determine whether Randolph would win a *Brown v. Board of Education* for the workplace.[4]

Looking to Congress

In 1950, Theodore Brown, an officer in Randolph's union, testified on Randolph's behalf before a House committee considering the Railway Labor Act's union-shop amendments. Brown decried "the vicious Hitlerite racial practices" of unions like the Firemen's Brotherhood, terming them "a very serious social, economic, undemocratic illness in our American industrial pattern." The all-white brotherhoods had "scoffed at the United States Supreme Court" by refusing to comply with its *Tunstall* decision, he informed Congress. As a result, black railroad workers were forced to sue for compliance worker by worker. This litigation was "expensive and cumbersome." Charles Houston's law partner, Joseph Waddy, testified to the same effect, calling the litigation *Steele* spurred "inadequate." He and Brown represented a labor-liberal alliance that had strengthened and broadened since Houston first brought his railroad cases. Brown spoke for them all when he insisted that, owing to litigation's failings, "*Congress* has to correct these racial-discrimination practices."[5]

By 1950, the labor-liberal alliance fused opposition to communism and discrimination with support for organized labor. Conservatism and anticommunism as much as civil rights fervor brought these activists together. The distance between the AFL and CIO now looked less dramatic than that between the labor organizations and their right-to-work foes. Because those foes opposed fair employment legislation and had ties to white supremacists, the AFL's interests converged with those of civil rights advocates. AFL officials served on President Truman's Committee on Civil Rights, sat on Randolph's National Council for a Permanent FEPC, and opened their unions to NAACP membership drives. Opposition to leftists also brought the labor and civil rights movements together. After the war, anticommunism dominated domestic and international politics. President Truman divided the world into Communist enemies and non-Communist allies, while the Taft-Hartley Act required all union leaders to disavow Communist Party involvement. The CIO ousted its most left-leaning (and racially progressive) unions, bringing itself in line with the AFL's doctrinaire anticommunism. Labor leaders then used their support of civil rights to neutralize Communist charges of racism. The civil rights and labor movements grew, to use the NAACP's term, more "indissolubly intertwined."[6]

These allies prioritized winning a federal fair employment law enforced by an administrative agency, or as a second best, adding anti-discrimination provisions to existing labor laws. Civil rights leaders expected political favors from Democrats in exchange for northern blacks' critical votes in the tight 1948 presidential election. In 1949, Randolph called on Congress to show the world that "the Constitution and the Bill of Rights are not Globaloney" by "remov[ing] the shackles

of second class citizenship" and ensuring African Americans' "right
to work." A coalition of conservative Republicans and southern
Democrats repeatedly dashed the alliance's legislative hopes, however.
Between 1945 and 1950, no less than forty-seven fair employment laws
were introduced only to die, most in committee. Antidiscrimination
amendments to Taft-Hartley met the same fate. During consideration
of the Railway Labor Act's union shop amendments, Brown and his
allies vainly urged Congress to deny this protection to any union
with racially discriminatory membership practices. By 1953, with
Republicans in control of the White House and Congress, alliance
members finally acknowledged that fair employment legislation might
not be forthcoming. For Randolph and his allies, these fading legislative hopes increased litigation's appeal.[7]

Turning to the Courts

"I am looking forward with great interest to our color bar membership case," Randolph wrote in 1955. Randolph was born in turn-of-
the-century Jacksonville, Florida, a town in which "locomotive firemen
represented the ... epitome of success for Negro workers." Randolph
never went to work on the rails, lured instead to Harlem and a life as a
Socialist orator and propagandist. When Pullman porters organized a
union in 1925, they recruited this outspoken critic of the AFL's racism
and champion of interracial working-class solidarity. Facing a hostile employer, Randolph's Brotherhood of Sleeping Car Porters might
well have folded were it not for the 1934 enactment of the Railway
Labor Act and the easily won union election it guaranteed. With the
porters' position strengthened, Randolph dedicated himself to fighting
more aggressively against racism within the labor movement, repeatedly urging the AFL to ban discrimination and promote interracial-
ism in its constituent unions. Randolph even fought his way into the
movement's lily-white inner sanctum: the committee through which
the leaders of the railroad brotherhoods strategized. He was eager to
do the same for the brotherhoods themselves.[8]

Randolph's Provisional Committee to Organize Colored
Locomotive Firemen provided the vehicle for his attack on unions'
color bar. The Provisional Committee did not seek to represent black
firemen. Randolph insisted that black workers "face and fight these

problems" and not "try to solve them by running away" into separate unions. The Provisional Committee thus helped its members challenge the brotherhoods in the courts and through the union. During the 1940s, it brought numerous suits to enforce *Steele* and *Tunstall*. In the 1950s, the committee concluded that the next front in fighting the brotherhoods' racism on their own turf would be "secur[ing] bonafide membership," what Congress had failed to provide in its union shop amendments to the Railway Labor Act.[9]

The Supreme Court's 1954 decision in *Brown* transformed the Provisional Committee's attack on closed unions. As Theodore Brown had complained to Congress, the committee found litigation expensive and ineffective. Despite dimmed hopes for a federal fair employment law, it initially reserved this tool for lingering *Steele* and *Tunstall* enforcement issues. Then the Court handed down its school desegregation decisions. Many court watchers surmised the Court was doing no more than ending segregation in the specific institutional context of public schools. Days later the justices instructed a lower court to reconsider an NAACP challenge to a racially segregated public park in light of *Brown*, suggesting that they might be prepared to address racial segregation more broadly. The decisions raised expectations enough to send the Provisional Committee into court, where Randolph hoped to close "the final chapter in vindicating the rights of" black railroad workers.[10]

Randolph turned to Joseph Rauh to litigate his membership cases. Rauh was a passionate New Dealer who spent his early legal career in government service, interpreting the federal wage and hour law and drafting Roosevelt's fair employment executive order. After leaving government, Rauh became a leader among anticommunist, prolabor liberals. He entered private practice, taking on like-minded labor leaders and their unions as his clients, including Walter Reuther's United Auto Workers. Rauh's home served as the war room for Americans for Democratic Action, a collection of "exiled New Deal liberals" who liked neither Communists nor insufficiently liberal Democrats. As the story goes, Rauh's performance during a 1940s mock trial of the army's discriminatory policies won him Randolph's business. By hiring Rauh, a rangy and imposing midwestern Jew, Randolph bucked the trend among African American workers of turning to black attorneys with civil-rights credentials rather than labor lawyers. It was a fitting choice for a stalwart union man.[11]

Rauh filed a challenge to the Firemen's Brotherhood's member-ship policies just six months after *Brown* was decided. Underscoring *Brown*'s catalytic effect, Rauh had begun planning his case only weeks before. Lee Oliphant, a fireman on the Central of Georgia Railroad, became the lead plaintiff in the class action Rauh filed in the Cleveland, Ohio, district court. In keeping with *Brown*'s rule that separate could never be equal, Rauh contended that the broth-erhood's racial exclusiveness alone rendered it "unable to represent plaintiffs and other Negro firemen fairly and equitably as required by the Railway Labor Act and the Fifth Amendment." Reflecting the ambient uncertainty about *Brown*'s reach, however, Rauh also alleged that the union had failed to provide equal representation in practice, adopting policies that hurt black workers and failing to grieve (advo-cate with management about) their complaints. This also, he asserted, violated the class members' "rights under the Railway Labor Act and the Fifth Amendment." [12]

Nearly three years passed before the case went to trial, afford-ing Randolph new opportunities to pursue his cause through union rather than court law. In 1955, the AFL and the CIO merged into a single federation that required all member unions to operate without racial discrimination. When the Firemen's Brotherhood affiliated with the AFL-CIO the next year, it promised to remove its color bar at its next convention, in 1959. Randolph might have let union law take its course. This would have been the AFL-CIO's preference. Its pres-ident, George Meany, insisted that labor "stood four-square on the Constitution of the United States and all its guarantees of equality" but favored "using the methods of persuasion, logic and hard solid facts," not litigation. The AFL-CIO's Civil Rights Department likewise preferred to handle union discrimination "without the intervention of lawyers." Randolph's ability to win change through the AFL-CIO was also at its apex. In 1955 he was elected to its top governing body, empowering him, as he promised, to "be of service to the labor move-ment in general and minorities in particular." Theodore Brown, who had testified for Randolph in 1950, now staffed the AFL-CIO's Civil Rights Department, giving Randolph influence there as well. When the Firemen's Brotherhood sought to settle the case based on its promise to remove its color bar at the 1959 convention, however, Randolph refused. "The time has come for a federal court decision," a leader in

Randolph's union insisted. "Such a decision," he predicted, "would be historic and would bring the breath of democracy to the entire trade union movement."[13]

Rauh offered the court three ways to rest this "historic" decision on the Constitution. He insisted that, after the school segregation decisions, "the Fifth Amendment precludes the exclusion of Negroes from membership in unions exercising exclusive statutory bargaining powers." To the extent that the Railway Labor Act permitted them to do so, it was unconstitutional. But, Randolph's lawyers urged the court, they much preferred that it "read into the Act a stricture against *exclusion* ... to save it from the same constitutional defect." They reassured the court that this was the approach taken in *Steele*, which had technically avoided the constitutional issue but nonetheless imposed the Fifth Amendment's "equal protection requirement." Now that separate could no longer be equal under the Fifth Amendment, it followed that exclusive representatives had to open their unions to black workers. Most narrowly, the court could avoid a sweeping precedent altogether by resting on the Supreme Court's pre-*Brown* cases finding segregation unconstitutional when it resulted in *actual* inequality. The court "need only find," Rauh reassured, "that admission is required in this particular case to secure" the "equal rights, guaranteed by *Steele*," to nonmembers.[14]

The trial court, however, focused on an issue the plaintiffs had assumed rather than argued: state action. The court did not find the union's bargained-for policies discriminatory. But this had "no bearing upon the single question to be resolved": whether the plaintiffs had an unconditional right to join the union. The court found it "impossible to interpret the Act" to grant this right, given that Congress rejected such a proposal when it amended the Railway Labor Act. The plaintiffs' only hope lay with establishing that "certification clothes the Brotherhood with some or all of the attributes of a Federal agency," thereby bringing the Fifth Amendment into play. But, the court held, certification was "not sufficient to change the character of the [labor] organization from that of a private association to that of a governmental agency." The situation might be unjust, but "the remedy does not lie with the courts."[15]

State action moved to the fore of Rauh's case. The Supreme Court had before it a similar lawsuit, *Conley v. Gibson*, challenging a railroad brotherhood's practice of segregating black workers into separate locals. Rauh took the unusual step of petitioning the Supreme Court to review the district court's decision alongside *Conley*. Rauh urged the justices that the trial court's state action holding was "clearly contrary" to the Supreme Court's fair representation decisions, which had found the Firemen's Brotherhood "sufficiently 'governmental' to warrant relief against its discrimination." Nor could *Steele*'s dicta respecting an exclusive representative's right to determine its membership qualifications govern, given its constitutional basis: "Such approval, had it been intended, [could not] have survived" *Brown*. The Firemen's Brotherhood, Rauh insisted, was a "federally-certified labor union exercising federally-created bargaining power" to implement "federally-sanctioned second-class citizenship" reminiscent of that found in segregated public schools. The Court should allow these "important and related constitutional questions of first instance ... [to] be heard and determined ... at one time."[16]

The Supreme Court and the State Action Doctrine

"The Supreme Court so far has not spelled out in detail at what point private acts become state-supported discrimination," Anthony Lewis wrote in 1957. His *New York Times* article was about not the workplace Constitution but the latest case to test the limits of *Shelley v. Kraemer*, the Court's easy racial covenant case. *Shelley* found it unconstitutional for a court to enforce a racial covenant by enjoining a sale. In 1953, the justices held additionally that a court could not award damages for such a sale. The question in the 1957 case was whether *Shelley* barred a court from replacing public trustees with private ones so that the school they oversaw could continue to admit only "white male orphans" without running afoul of *Brown*.[17]

The 1957 case raised concerns for white racial liberals. Since *Brown*, the Court had indicated that its antisegregation principle applied to a wide array of state actors other than public schools. The principle's breadth gave Lewis pause about further widening the sweep of state action. The Court had thus far expanded the state action doctrine with relative nonchalance. Lewis urged temperance. "Not every private discrimination backed by state enforcement can constitute 'state action,'" he cautioned. "If this were so, the private homeowner who called in the police to eject an unwelcome guest might be subject to the Fourteenth Amendment." Liberal legal scholars also supported preserving a zone in which racial exclusion would remain legal, and were concerned about the Court's colliding broad state action and antisegregation decisions. After *Brown*, one legal scholar opined, the Court must vigorously police the public-private distinction to protect "discrimination in the choice of friends and private associates." Another worried that "if *Shelley v. Kraemer* means that judicial action is state action in every context, it would become a mere procedural matter to make ejectment of an undesired guest from a tea party actionable discrimination." The union membership issue would force the justices to grapple with how their state action doctrine should limit or extend the reach of *Brown*'s antisegregation principle.[18]

After World War II, courts at all levels faced persistent and varied state action challenges. The Supreme Court's civil rights and civil liberties decisions recognizing new speech, association, and equal-protection rights only fueled the assault by providing new reasons to test the state action doctrine's limits. Litigants tried to bring institutions founded, funded, and run by a mix of public and private actors – whether libraries, housing developments, or parks – within the Constitution's reach. They targeted state-regulated streetcars and buses. And they met with considerable success. After *Shelley*, lower courts steadily expanded the ways public participation could open an ostensibly private entity to the Constitution's demands.[19]

In the midst of these state action challenges, the Court treated government-certified unions as state actors. In a case involving union discrimination, *Brotherhood of R.R. Trainmen v. Howard*, the Court explicitly likened the actions of exclusive representatives to state action. Decided in 1952, *Howard* explained that certified unions were prohibited from discriminating for reasons analogous to those that barred courts from enforcing racial covenants in *Shelley*. *Howard* also described the certified unions' efforts to eliminate black workers' jobs in state action terms, calling it "an unlawful use of power granted by a federal act." *American Communications Association v. Douds* was also suggestive. In this free speech case the Court stated that because union leaders' "authority derives in part from Government's thumb on the scales, the exercise of that power ... becomes closely akin, in some respects, to its exercise by Government itself." The Court retained some of *Steele*'s ambiguity. *Howard* referred to the duty of fair representation as one imposed by the "language of the [Railway Labor] Act" even as it alluded to the duty's constitutional roots. And in *Douds*, the Court insisted it was not "suggest[ing] that labor unions which utilize the facilities of the [federal labor boards] become Government agencies or may be regulated as such." But the justices nonetheless tethered exclusive representatives more firmly to state action and the duty of fair representation to the Constitution.[20]

The Court also decided cases involving union discrimination in ways that implied that unions were state actors. During the 1950s, the Supreme Court steadily expanded unions' fair-representation duty. *Steele* had involved a union's duty toward the *non*members that it represented under the Railway Labor Act. In 1956 the Supreme Court clarified that the duty of fair representation applied to unions organized under the NLRA and was owed to members as well as nonmembers. The *Howard* plaintiffs were not represented by the union *at all*. Nonetheless, the Court asserted that the union's discriminatory actions fell squarely within *Steele*'s scope. In these decisions, the duty the Court imposed on government-regulated unions grew so much broader than any statutory or fiduciary duties the unions may have had, that it seemed like it must derive from the Constitution.[21]

The Court's other state action decisions also came tantalizingly close to extending the Constitution to unionized workplaces. *Public Utilities Commission v. Pollak*, decided in 1952, involved a challenge to broadcasts of music in Washington, D.C., streetcars. The Court reasoned that the Public Utilities Commission's general regulation of the streetcar company and its specific dismissal of its investigation into the musical broadcasts created "a sufficiently close relation between the Federal Government and the radio service to make it necessary for" the Court to consider whether the broadcasts violated the First or Fifth Amendment. If state action inhered anytime a government agency regulated an otherwise private entity or the agency tacitly approved that entity's challenged actions, the Constitution could arguably reach discrimination by certified unions. The Court invited this conclusion in another decision by likening *Steele* and *Howard* to the state action ruling in *Pollak* and the white-primary case, *Smith v. Allwright*.[22]

Then the membership issue landed on the Court's docket. The *Conley* plaintiffs claimed that their required membership in a railroad brotherhood's segregated local and the union's unequal application of the collective bargaining agreement to their local violated the Fifth Amendment and the Railway Labor Act. The lower courts ignored the constitutional charges, dismissing on the grounds that the duty of fair representation gave federal courts jurisdiction over the *making* and *terms* of a collective bargaining agreement, not over how the union *conducted itself under* the agreement. In their private conference, all the justices agreed that the lower courts had it wrong. Where a "lack of equal protection favors white members," Chief Justice Earl Warren insisted, "there is jurisdiction." But the justices were divided on the membership issue. Justice Frankfurter agreed that the claim of unequal representation "comes down to *Steele*" but not "the complain[t] of segregation." Justice Harlan would not "go for abolition of the segregated union" and did not want the Court to "make any suggestion about [the permissibility of] segregated unions." Yet, if the duty of fair representation derived from the Fifth Amendment (as the chief justice assumed) *and* that amendment forbade segregation (as *Brown* and its progeny implied), then it would be impossible to satisfy Justices Harlan and Frankfurter, or any others who shared their concern.[23]

The membership issue impelled the Court to erase state action and the Constitution from the duty of fair representation. Justice Black wrote for a unanimous Court in *Conley v. Gibson*. Black did not mention the Constitution, cite *Shelley*, or use any state action–like reasoning. Instead, Black described the duty of fair representation as "statutory" and provided a Constitution-free gloss to the last thirteen years of case law: the Court had "squarely held in *Steele* and subsequent cases that discrimination in representation because of race is prohibited by the Railway Labor Act." Black's occlusion was intentional. Black's personal view was that unions were state actors. He had recently joined a Douglas dissent arguing that when a union "operates with the sanction of the State or the Federal Government behind it" the union becomes the "agency by which governmental policy is expressed." Black initially included state action reasoning in *Conley*, stating (as he had in *Howard*) that unions had a duty toward African American workers because "bargaining agents derive their power from a Federal statute." There is no certain proof that the Court severed the duty of fair representation from the Fifth Amendment to avoid imposing *Brown*'s antisegregation principle to unions' membership practices. But in another telling elision, although the Court took the optional step of addressing the merits in *Conley*, it chose to defend the merits of plaintiffs' contract performance claims but not their complaint of segregated membership. It was the first fair representation claim since *Steele* that the Court had failed to endorse.[24]

The Court's discomfort with the membership issue was not apparent to an outsider, however. To Rauh, the timing of his *Oliphant* petition must have seemed auspicious, given the trend in the Court's decisions and the fact that it had already accepted *Conley* for review. But the justices did not turn to it until after *Conley* was handed down. Having said nothing about membership in *Conley*, the justices easily refused to hear Rauh's case, sending it back for the usual next step of appellate court review. "We have no choice but to continue," Randolph's officer informed Rauh. The Sixth Circuit Court of Appeals affirmed the trial court, however, holding that there was no statutory bar on exclusion and insufficient state action to reach or avoid the black firemen's constitutional claims. The Court had not seen the last of the membership issue.[25]

Antisegregation Collides with State Action

"Federal laws have reshaped entire areas of personal activity and economic reality," including "in the labor field," Rauh reminded the justices in his second petition for review. Rauh favored the New Deal's proliferation of statutes. But "if ... basic constitutional prohibitions do not accompany statutory powers vested in private persons," Rauh urged the justices, "then Congress may do by indirection ... what it could not do directly," namely, segregate white and black workers. "The racial exclusion still practiced by some of the nation's largest labor unions," Rauh warned, "renders a substantial number of Negroes second class citizens ... under federal law." Rauh invoked a vein of liberalism tapped by Charles Houston before him, one concerned with protecting individuals and minorities in the face of a newly pervasive state. He must have hoped this concern would weigh more heavily on the justices than white liberals' countervailing worry that the expanding state action doctrine would swallow civil society whole, tea parties and all.[26]

Many liberals worried during the 1950s about individual liberty in an era of big government, big business, and big unions. American Telephone & Telegraph, one concerned scholar pointed out in 1957, "based on combined population and wealth would be somewhere around the thirteenth state of the union in terms of budget." Legal scholars and political theorists had argued since the early twentieth century that corporations had grown to exert as much coercive power as the state, if not more. Now unions were also thought to threaten democracy. That they were among the "private individuals and organizations" that exercised power derived from "a state or the federal government" only enhanced the problem. The liberal think tank Fund for the Republic commissioned studies titled not only "The Individual and the Corporation" but also "The Individual and the Trade Union." Liberal labor scholars debated how to ensure democratic unions, and a Democratic Congress added a bill of rights for union members to the labor laws. At the same time, "More and more of our activities are governmentally controlled," liberals worried, as regulation, military contracts, and federal investment in transportation and infrastructure burgeoned. According to court watchers, cases like *Oliphant*, in which "individuals [were] at the mercy of a 'private' organization," favored constitutionally limiting big labor and big business. Rauh hoped that the justices would agree.[27]

Rauh thought state action would be his greatest hurdle. From the white-primary cases to *Shelley* to *Pollak*, Rauh argued, "The consistent trend of th[e] Court's decisions [wa]s towards holding those exercising governmental or governmentally-derived power to a standard of non-discriminatory conduct." *Steele*, *Douds*, and, more sweepingly, *Howard* found that certified unions specifically, because of their "federally-created exclusive bargaining power," had acquired at least some constitutional obligations. Among them was ensuring that workers were not "denied voice, vote and information in the determination of their working conditions" because of their race. The intersection of the Court's state action and antisegregation decisions meant "that the Fifth Amendment forbids the exercise of exclusive statutory bargaining power for Negroes by a union open only to whites," Rauh insisted. "If the Fifth Amendment precludes segregation and exclusion of Negroes in public education," Rauh reasoned "it necessarily precludes segregation and exclusion of Negro firemen."[28]

Four justices had to vote in favor for the Court to grant review, yet only Justice Douglas, the recently appointed Justice William J. Brennan, and Chief Justice Warren favored granting Rauh's petition. Black's vote against review was decisive. The newest justice, Potter Stewart, did not participate, having sat on the panel that heard *Oliphant*'s appeal. The aversion of Justices Frankfurter and Harlan to opening membership was known. Frankfurter might count on winning Justices Clark and Whittaker to his view, but not any of the remaining justices, leaving him shy of a majority on the merits. Neither he nor his allies would vote to hear the case.[29]

To a court watcher, Justice Black's vote against review would have been surprising. He had written two of the Court's post-*Steele* union discrimination decisions and repeatedly sided with those finding unions to be state actors. There were also personal reasons to antici-pate Black's support. His son, a labor lawyer in Black's hometown of Birmingham, Alabama, often worked with Rauh on Randolph's cases, touting their merits to his father. Black confided to his son that he found these workers' claims "on the right side from the standpoint of justice and right." Behind the scenes, whether successful or not, Justice Black consistently voted to review black workers' claims.[30]

Counter to Rauh's prediction, the reach of the antisegregation prin-ciple, not state action, most likely drove the outcome. Black may not have wanted to hold that union segregation was constitutional, but he, like Frankfurter and his allies, was probably also unwilling to force unions to open their membership to African Americans. As Reva Siegel has noted, many perceived the Court to be deciding on a "case-by-case basis whether racial[ly]" exclusive government policies were unconsti-tutional. The Court had recently indicated a particular unwillingness to require what was called "social equality" when it avoided review of a Virginia law prohibiting marriage between whites and nonwhites. The brotherhoods served as fraternal societies and social clubs as well as collective bargaining representatives. Indeed, in the lower courts the Firemen's Brotherhood had defended its closed membership on the grounds that it held social functions with its ladies' auxiliary, invok-ing the specter of racially threatened white womanhood that was so often deployed in segregation's defense. The Firemen's Brotherhood tapped this fear again before the Supreme Court, urging it to rein in state action to preserve segregation. Like the liberals worrying about unwanted guests, the brotherhood warned the Court that Rauh's state action theories would require "every business man, farmer, and veteran who receives help from the government ... to operate his business, farm, and home without racial discrimination."[31]

The justices' denial of review suggested that concerns about social equality rather than state action drove their decision. On the same day that they denied review in *Oliphant*, they refused to hear an issue in which state action was clear but interracial intimacy could follow: segregated public bathrooms. The Court also took "the almost unheard-of action" of stating why "it had refused review" in *Oliphant*. After much quibbling, it ultimately fell to Justice Harlan to draft an acceptable statement. "In view of the abstract context in which the questions sought to be raised are presented by this record, the petition ... is denied," the Court's cryptic order read. An unwillingness to find an unconditional right to union membership apparently dictated the vote against review. As Rauh pointed out in a motion for rehearing, the Court seemed to assume that the lower courts had, as the appeals court put it, "subtracted" out the issue of actual inequality by finding the unions' policies nondiscriminatory, thus leaving only the "abstract" question of inherent inequality. Rauh disagreed that this was so, but even if it were, he contended, *Oliphant's* presentation of inherent inequality was "no more abstract than" in *Brown*, where the lower courts had also found no actual inequality. Unfortunately, this was precisely what five of the justices seemed to fear.[32]

"This is the last round for petitioners and their class," Rauh beseeched the Court. Only by agreeing to hear the case, he urged, "can [the Court] write a just and final chapter to one of the most unjust discriminations of our time." Legal rules prevented the firemen from raising the same challenge again, and their advanced age made them unlikely to benefit should some future litigants win where they had failed. The Court nonetheless refused to rehear their petition. "The door to first class citizenship," Rauh lamented, "is closed forever to these men."[33]

For other workers, the *New York Times* noted, the Court's statement "le[ft] the way open for possible later consideration ... whether a union has a right to restrict membership because of race." The justices' behind-closed-doors fissures, however, made it unlikely the Court would review the membership issue anytime soon, let alone decide it in black workers' favor. Notably missing from accounts of midcentury constitutional challenges to racial segregation is the line the Court drew at union membership. From today's perspective, scholars would most likely assume that the Court drew this line because it was unwilling to expand the state action doctrine to reach unions. The record suggests that concerns about extending the antisegregation principle were at least as important. It seems more plausible that the Court stopped treating unions as state actors because of its uneasiness about the membership issue than that it avoided the membership issue because of its implications for state action.[34]

As for the firemen, *Oliphant* proved to have been their last hope. The Firemen's Brotherhood was supposed to remove its color bar at its 1959 convention but the AFL-CIO's Civil Rights Department did not press the issue. The department's director may have been hoping that the Supreme Court would save him and AFL-CIO president George Meany from taking on the powerful brotherhood. After the Court closed the door on *Oliphant* in the spring of 1959, Theodore Brown, Randolph's officer turned Civil Rights Department staffer, reminded his boss that the time was nigh for the brotherhood to make good on its promise. But when the Firemen's Brotherhood convened in July, its delegates rejected the proposed change. The Sleeping Car Porters gathered the next month and Randolph rallied his troops: the "labor movement," he boomed, "can no more countenance [the existence of Jim Crow unions] than a democratic society can maintain jim crow [*sic*] public schools." But when Randolph called on the AFL-CIO in October to expel the Firemen's Brotherhood and all other unions with discriminatory membership practices, all he received was a rebuke. "Who the hell appointed you as the guardian of all Negroes in America?" President Meany roared. With the next Firemen's Brotherhood convention not to be held until 1963, union law had failed Oliphant and his fellow plaintiffs as well.[35]

As the NAACP and black industrial workers learned in Chapter 2, the growing administrative state provided new sites in which to pursue a liberal workplace Constitution. The administrative alternative was futile for black railroad workers like Oliphant, however. Since the railroads and the brotherhoods selected the officials who implemented the Railway Labor Act, those officials were predictably unsympathetic to black workers' claims. But off the rails at the NLRB, whose independent administrators were nominated by the president and confirmed by the Senate, the administrative option beckoned.

5

Agencies Consider the Liberal Workplace Constitution

"Persons are entitled to fair and equitable treatment."
Executive Order 10479

During the 1950s, the Esso Standard Oil refinery's gangly smokestacks and labyrinthine pipes brought the Gulf Coast's oil boom home to Baton Rouge, Louisiana. The physical difference between the gritty metallic refining plant and Esso's gleaming cube-shaped office building marked the distance between its white- and blue-collar workers. Esso separated its black and white workers less obviously, but no less completely. The office building, like others on the Gulf Coast, housed whites only. Within the refinery, work was also highly segregated. As in many industrial plants, African Americans were hired into an unskilled labor pool at the refinery, where they remained throughout their tenure. In contrast, white workers were hired into and progressed up lines of increasingly skilled and better-paying jobs.[1]

Job segregation like that practiced at Esso left African Americans vulnerable. The American economy boomed after World War II, buoyed by pent-up consumer demand and ambitious government spending on infrastructure and defense. But the war's end flooded the labor market with demobilized soldiers, many of whom had greater seniority than recently hired black workers. Mechanization continued apace, turning the United States into a majority white-collar workforce and eliminating the low-skilled jobs into which African Americans were shunted. Even the most secure among African American workers, those with skills and unions, were knocked from their elite perch as federally funded highways facilitated deindustrialization of the northern urban centers in which they clustered and corporations sought cheaper labor and weaker unions down South.[2]

In the early 1950s, black workers at Esso began to agitate for change. "We began to see," Thomas Davis remembered, "where we would be out of jobs," owing to mechanization. Like the refinery, the union that represented Esso's workers was segregated. Davis and his fellow union members urged Esso management to open more jobs to black workers. "We asked to ... raise our standards and put our ability to the best use," James Wilson reported, but "we couldn't get anywhere by doing this." During 1952 and 1953, shop-floor conversations "about the colored labor situation in the South," union hall meetings about their "dissatisf[action] with the labor conditions at the plant," and Masonic Lodge gatherings about where to turn for help prompted these Esso workers to seek the NAACP's assistance.[3]

From Louisiana to Texas and up through Arkansas, other black oil workers held conversations similar to the Esso workers'. Some hired lawyers and went to court. But those, like the Esso workers, who connected with the NAACP found themselves not before a judge but before a federal agency. Together, the NAACP and these frustrated black workers fueled the most concerted administrative challenge yet to the constitutionality of workplace discrimination, one that rivaled the railroad workers' efforts described in Chapter 4 and resembled the NAACP's more famous contemporaneous legal campaign against public school segregation.

African American Workers Challenge Workplace Discrimination

Roberson King was a Texas native, a doctor's son who grew up in Wichita Falls. King left home after high school to attend the all-black Lincoln University in Missouri and the University of Chicago Law School, punctuated by a two-year stint in the army. He founded a law practice in Houston, became active in its black bar association, and joined the faculty at the all-black Texas Southern University's law school. During the 1950s, King brought constitutional claims on behalf of black trade unionists in the steel, oil, and railroad industries, including the *Conley* case discussed in Chapter 4. King got the case that would lead to the Esso workers' administrative assault through happenstance, however. In 1953, workers at Houston's Shell Oil plant, unhappy with a union contract they believed limited their job prospects, visited Texas Southern's law library in search of a lawyer. They found King, who doubled as the law school's librarian but knew nothing about labor law. That soon changed.[4]

In January 1954, King filed a case in the Texas courts against the CIO-affiliated Oil Workers International and the integrated local representing Shell Oil's Houston plants. That May, he filed a second suit in federal court on behalf of black workers at the Gulf Oil plant in Port Arthur, Texas. Prior advocates of a liberal workplace Constitution had focused on union membership, but the Texas oil workers demonstrated that integrating unions did not liberate African Americans from the worst-paying, lowest-skilled jobs. The interracial unions at Shell and Gulf Oil still negotiated for segregated jobs, segregated lines of promotion, and segregated seniority rosters. In King's complaints, he argued that the unions and employers who agreed to these terms violated his clients' constitutional "rights without due process of law as condemned by the Fifth Amendment of the United States Constitution."[5]

The Shell workers spurred national action by the NAACP and its labor allies. George Weaver was an urban Rust Belt native. Between 1937 and 1942, he attended Chicago's interracial YMCA College and then Howard Law School, supporting himself as a redcap (a railway station porter) and then as an official in the predominantly African American redcap union. Weaver next joined the CIO's national office as its highest-ranking African American, directing the CIO's Civil Rights Committee and assisting its secretary treasurer. In March 1954, Weaver sent a copy of King's complaint to Robert L. Carter, Thurgood Marshall's second-in-command at the NAACP's Legal Defense Fund (LDF). Carter, a Howard Law School classmate of Weaver's, understood the African American workers' plight. Raised in Newark, New Jersey, by a single mother who supported the family as a maid, Carter attended Pennsylvania's all-black Lincoln University on scholarship and then earned degrees from Howard and Columbia Law Schools. After serving in World War II, he joined the LDF in 1945. "It would seem to me that [King's complaint] is an unexplored route and could be used with effect in eliminating discrimination," Weaver wrote Carter. King's suit targeted a CIO union. Weaver argued that similar action should be taken against other oil-worker unions. This strategy would prevent "the possibility of a group of [white] workers in Shell Oil from agitating to go independent or into the AFL" as a result of King's lawsuit.[6]

With litigation bubbling up at the local level, the NAACP's national office scrambled to initiate an industrywide attack. In June 1954, Carter held a special meeting about the oil cases with Weaver and LDF staff. The NAACP's labor secretary, Herbert Hill, a former CIO organizer, a socialist, and a strident anticommunist, urged NAACP officials throughout the Gulf Coast to secure plaintiffs who were members of AFL and independent unions. Esso's black workers, however, were already looking for Hill. During 1954 and 1955, Carter, Hill, and LDF staff met with the Esso workers, discussing their legal rights and building their case. At the Carbide and Chemicals Company plant in Texas City, Texas, members of a segregated AFL local were also interested in "get[ting] better jobs ... and ... mak[ing] a decent livin[g]." As Carbide worker Benjamin Hunter remembered, they sought out LDF after hearing of "a number of cases in the South where the NAACP had been of assistance in getting the [N]egro race better pay and better living conditions." In the fall of 1954, Hill met with more than fifty of Carbide's African American employees. Nearly one hundred showed up to hear him speak at a local church a few months later.[7]

By 1955, the NAACP was nearly ready to file its claims. Thanks to the initiative of the Esso and Carbide workers, Carter had secured plaintiffs from AFL and independent oil-worker locals. But one major oil-refining region on the Gulf remained to be canvassed: Arkansas. In February, Hill visited El Dorado, Arkansas, where he found a familiar pattern of discriminatory contracts and racially integrated but white-dominated unions. At the Lion Oil Company, Hill reported, even the "*time clocks* are segregated." Seven Lion Oil workers signed on to the NAACP's suit. The legal team was now ready to commence the coordinated actions that Hill believed would "creat[e] a new body of labor law to protect the rights of Negro workers."[8]

The NAACP's Administrative Approach

For legal, tactical, and political reasons, Carter brought his charges before administrative agencies rather than to court. In April 1955, Carter filed a complaint with President Eisenhower's Committee on

Government Contracts (PCGC), established in 1953. All government contracts had provisions prohibiting contractors from discriminating in their employment practices. Eisenhower's PCGC oversaw contracting agencies' enforcement of those provisions. After making "extensive study ... of the numerous problems of discrimination in employment," Carter urged attendees of a 1954 workshop on the subject to use the PCGC. Although "the President's Committee has not direct power of enforcement," Carter instructed, "the threat of a recommendation that the government withdraw its business from the concern involved ... [would be] enough of a hammer to secure compliance." A PCGC complaint, Carter predicted, "would obtain results far greater than those obtained in filing a law suit."[9]

Carter thought it was wise to bring challenges to the National Labor Relations Board as well. Sensitive to its labor allies' complaint that employers rather than unions controlled hiring, the NAACP sought ways to attack discrimination by employers, especially non-governmental employers against whom the state action doctrine made constitutional challenges tricky. In the 1940s, the NAACP and CIO challenged the NLRB's authority to certify a union with discriminatory membership practices as the exclusive representative for black workers. The NAACP now advised *against* seeking decertification, which "has the obvious disadvantage that, if ... de-certification actually takes place, the result is that there is no union, no collective bargaining relationship, and, therefore, no protection whatsoever against discrimination by the employer." Instead, NAACP attorneys preferred seeking an unfair labor practice order, which left a union's representative status intact but required it to change its practices.[10]

If Carter wanted to establish that the NLRB could issue unfair labor practice orders against discriminatory unions and employers, however, he could not head immediately to court. Generally, judges required litigants to exhaust any administrative remedies available to them before turning to the courts. As discussed in Chapter 1, Charles Houston argued that it was appropriate to bring his claims in court because federal agencies had no power under the Railway Labor Act to resolve his clients' complaints. But Carter wanted to argue that the NLRB *had* the power to issue unfair labor practice orders against discriminatory unions and employers. He could not credibly argue that his clients had no administrative options to justify bringing their claim in federal court, then, once there, argue that the Board *could* issue orders against discriminatory unions and employers. NAACP attorneys conceded that courts moved faster than the backlogged NLRB and gave litigants some ability to seek out friendly judges. But the NLRB's "cases and its personnel indicate that its reaction may be sympathetic," NAACP lawyers predicted. Carter thus followed his colleagues' advice that the "initial approach should be via the Labor Board" and filed NLRB complaints in the oil worker cases that mirrored his PCGC actions.[11]

Carter's claims invoked a workplace Constitution. In his PCGC complaint, Carter claimed that Esso, Carbide, Lion Oil, and the Lake Charles, Louisiana, Cities Service Refining Company, as well as their unions, had violated the terms of their collective bargaining and government contracts. Assuming that these employers and unions were state actors, perhaps based on their work for the government, Carter also claimed that they "deprived complainants and all other Negroes employed of rights and privileges guaranteed to them by the Constitution and laws of the United States."[12]

Carter was prepared to make constitutional arguments to the NLRB as well, if it decided to pursue his complaint. In the 1930s and 1940s, lawyers relied on nondelegation, inaction, and sanctioning theories of state action. The NAACP promoted instead what might be called a "sufficiency of contacts" theory: discriminatory employer-union agreements were the product of state action because the National Labor Relations Act altered extensively the bargaining process as well as the relationships between employers and unions, employers and workers, and unions and workers. The NLRA required employers to bargain with unions over certain subjects, for instance, and exclusive representation foreclosed individual workers from negotiating with their employer. The NLRA also made it an unfair labor practice for unions and employers to "restrain or coerce" certain employee rights. NAACP attorneys reasoned that fair representation was one of those basic rights. Using the arguments surveyed in Chapter 4, they contended, in turn, that the right to fair representation was derived from the Constitution.[13]

The NLRB and Discrimination after *Brown*

Luckily for the NAACP, the NLRB was already reviewing whether recent Supreme Court decisions required it to broaden its "policies respecting discriminatory racial practices of unions." The composition of the committee to which the Board delegated the review boded well for the NAACP's complaint. Arthur Christopher Jr. was a native of Jacksonville, Florida, who began his Washington, D.C., career in 1934 as a skilled laborer for the federal government. During the next twelve years, Christopher steadily moved up the civil service ladder while putting himself through college and law school at Howard University. A member of various civil rights and civil liberties organizations, in 1946 he joined the NLRB's staff and soon became a legal assistant to the Board chairman, akin to a judge's clerk, making him the highest-ranked African American at the agency. The other committee members also supported civil rights: the wonkish head of the Board's Industrial Analysis Branch was "forthright and strong in his denunciation of racial bias," and the Board's associate solicitor was sympathetic to the desire for "stronger action on the part of the NLRB" against union discrimination.[14]

Broad theories of state action still held purchase at the NLRB. By convening Christopher's committee to consider the Court's constitutional race cases the Board indicated it still thought the Fifth Amendment guided its certification policy. In his 1955 draft report, Christopher pushed his committee to conclude that the Constitution required the NLRB "to refuse to lend its processes to a union engaging in such [discriminatory] conduct." The final report was less explicit than Christopher would have liked, but it tacitly endorsed Christopher's sanctioning theory of state action. According to the report, the 1948 Supreme Court decision *Hurd v. Hodge* held that the Fifth Amendment prohibited enforcement of a racially restrictive covenant and thus spoke to "the power of Federal tribunals" like the NLRB. A federal appellate judge had recently mused that *Hurd* might bar the Board from recognizing or enforcing racially discriminatory agreements, the report continued. Particularly promising for the NAACP, the report noted that in the railroad case *Betts v. Easley*, the Kansas Supreme Court had found that an exclusive representative was "an agency of the Federal Government."[15]

The committee's discussion of unions' membership policies emphasized that the NLRB had constitutional duties. In the 1940s, the Board had determined that it lacked authority to deny or revoke unions' certification based on their discriminatory membership policies. This determination turned partly on *Plessy v. Ferguson*'s separate-but-equal rule. In the intervening years, *Brown v. Board of Education* and *Bolling v. Sharpe* held unconstitutional segregated public schools in the states and Washington, D.C. Based on those cases, "No determination of a relationship which is controlled by racial considerations," the committee concluded, "will satisfy the Constitutional requirements." The report acknowledged Taft-Hartley's proviso protecting unions' membership policies and Senator Taft's promise that the act would not affect unions' racial exclusivity. Christopher nonetheless urged the NLRB to "refuse to certify a union that denies equal and full participation in the affairs of the organization solely on the basis of race." His fellow committee members agreed.[16]

The Board's recent decisions also boded well. When Christopher's boss, NLRB chairman Guy Farmer, joined the Board in 1953, he was the first Republican to hold the post. Farmer was determined to correct a perceived prolabor bias in board policy. As President Eisenhower and a Republican-controlled Congress filled the NLRB with allies ranging from management-side moderates to self-avowed "union busters," Farmer gradually assembled a majority for his reforms. By 1954, he had implemented a number of controversial policy changes, including strengthening protections for employer free speech and broadening the definition of an illegal striker. Farmer included racial discrimination among the areas in which the NLRB had been too easy on labor. In 1955, the Board for the first time decertified racially exclusive unions that had discriminated in their representation of black workers. Notably, it did so even though the accused unions had subsequently negotiated contracts that covered the excluded African Americans, a correction that would have earned the unions a pass in the past.[17]

The Board's vigilance was less surprising for a Republican-dominated and right-leaning agency than it might seem. Republican support for civil rights strengthened in the 1950s as America competed with the Soviet Union for the allegiance of African and Asian nations. Domestic politics also favored NLRB action. Bipartisan legislative proposals in 1953 and 1954 would have authorized the Board to issue unfair labor practice orders for racial discrimination. Some Republican sponsors were among the minority that had long supported fair employment legislation. But Barry Goldwater, a new senator from the right-to-work state of Arizona, represented the party's conservative edge. Like most Republicans, Goldwater opposed letting government agencies enforce fair employment laws. His anomalous support for the proposed unfair labor practice provisions arose from his right-to-work politics. Employers could wield these discrimination charges as a weapon against unions. Assigning the NLRB antidiscrimination powers would also erode its support among southern Democrats. The proposed amendments died in committee, but they showed that even conservative Republicans might be sympathetic to the NAACP's oil-worker cases.[18]

When the NAACP's complaints arrived in 1955, the Board had even greater responsibility to harmonize its policies with the Constitution's commands than in the 1940s. Cries that the NLRB wielded unconstitutional powers had reached a fever pitch when the Board established its race discrimination polices in 1946. That furor had since died down. Congress passed the Administrative Procedure Act in 1946, followed in 1947 by the Taft-Hartley Act. These laws imposed new due process and free speech restraints on the NLRB. Since then, the Court had largely stopped policing the constitutionality of agencies' actions. In the 1950s, public criticism of agencies shifted away from the constitutionality of their practices and toward their inefficiencies and backlogs, as well as to *capture*, the concern that agencies were overly friendly with, perhaps even controlled by, the industries they regulated. Without public or court scrutiny as a prod, the onus was on agencies to interpret their mandates voluntarily in light of constitutional constraints.[19]

The NLRB also had more room to maneuver politically than it did in 1946. The 1952 elections that put Eisenhower in the White House also handed Congress to the Republican Party, creating an opportunity for Republican-led labor-law reforms. But Eisenhower was no anti–New Deal conservative. He proposed amendments designed to please both business conservatives and the Republican-leaning AFL, which predictably pleased no one and thus went nowhere. The NLRB could expect some latitude from a president with no clear reform agenda. When Republicans lost control of Congress in 1954, the divided government that resulted gave the Board even more leeway.[20]

The NAACP's complaint thus arrived at a particularly auspicious time. The NLRB had the political space and will to police union and employer discrimination more aggressively. Thanks to Christopher's committee, it also had a blueprint of its constitutional duty to disallow the job segregation challenged by the NAACP.

Therein lay the NAACP's tactical mistake or, from a different perspective, the cost of its close alliance with labor. The NAACP lawyers had filed unfair labor practice charges only and did not seek decertification of the oil industry unions. But Taft-Hartley had bifurcated the NLRB, vesting prosecutorial functions in a general counsel who answered to the president and Congress, not the Board. The NLRB retained exclusive jurisdiction over representation matters, including whether to certify or decertify a union, but Board members now heard only the unfair labor practice charges that the general counsel decided to bring. And unlike the Board, the general counsel was not open to the NAACP's complaint. President Harry Truman's general counsel had been skeptical that the NLRB could issue unfair labor practice orders for union violations of the duty of fair representation. His replacement under Eisenhower was closely allied with the administration's probusiness, anti–New Deal, and antilabor wing. Even if he was inclined to take a more expansive view of the NLRB's unfair labor practice powers, however, he had not been on the job long enough to implement such an important policy change.[21]

In 1955, the NLRB's regional offices investigated the NAACP's claims. The reports from the field were promising. The NLRB examiner informed an LDF staff member that "the matter was shaping up in accordance with the complaint." But that fall, the regional director notified Carter that he had not found sufficient evidence to pursue a case on the oil workers' behalf. Carter appealed the regional director's decision to no avail. The general counsel's office explained to Carter that the NLRB and its general counsel were "concerned solely with violations of the National Labor Relations Act." The evidence might constitute a legal violation of some kind, but it was not, in the general counsel's view, "conduct constituting an unfair labor practice." The counsel's office had no sympathetic Arthur Christopher and no interest in the workplace Constitution.[22]

The NAACP hoped that its complaint to President Eisenhower's Committee on Government Contracts would fare better. The PCGC had both the authority and the responsibility to address workplace discrimination; it also might do so in the name of the workplace Constitution.

The PCGC Tests Republicans' Fair Employment Approach

Soon after the NAACP filed its complaint, George Weaver was asked to help the PCGC resolve the oil cases. Weaver already straddled the divide between labor and government: in addition to his CIO duties, he helped the State Department battle Communist incursions into the international labor movement. Now he had an opportunity to influence the outcome of the coordinated actions he had helped instigate. As before, Weaver's primary goal was to secure changes not only at plants organized by the CIO's Oil Workers union but also those represented by AFL and independent unions. Weaver's involvement in the cases' resolution was just one of several signs that the NAACP's complaint might fare well at the PCGC.[23]

Eisenhower's contract committee was stronger than his predecessors'. He justified his committee in a constitutional register, explaining that "persons are entitled to fair and equitable treatment in all aspects of employment on work paid for from public funds." For the first time, contracting agencies were required to cooperate with the PCGC, and the PCGC could receive individual complaints and monitor contracting agencies' progress, creating new layers of committee oversight.[24]

Eisenhower's decision to put his vice president, Richard Nixon, in charge of the PCGC also augured well. Like all but the most liberal Republicans, Nixon "did not believe in Federal compulsion to assure equal employment opportunities," instead favoring voluntary fair employment laws that used education and persuasion to achieve workplace equality. But "in employment where federal funds are spent," Nixon "believe[d] … in [a] strong FEPC." He, too, seemed to think that federal funding, and by implication the Constitution, enhanced the government's fair employment responsibility.[25]

Nixon took the NAACP's oil industry complaints seriously. In May 1955, he appointed a special subcommittee that was designed to get things done. Leading the effort was John Minor Wisdom, a Louisiana native who practiced business law and played party politics in a Gulf Coast state dominated by the oil industry. Another member was a Howard law professor and NAACP collaborator renowned for his civil rights advocacy. High-ranking officials in the Department of Justice and the Department of Defense, which held contracts with the Gulf Coast oil companies, also participated. Given the delicate union politics involved, Nixon asked the secretary of labor to participate as well.[26]

Oil industry executives sensed that the PCGC meant business. Wisdom met in the summer of 1955 with executives from Esso and the Cities Service Refining, who expressed interest in changing their "employment policies ... toward minority group members." Shell Oil's Houston managers responded to Roberson King's PCGC complaint with intransigence, but the company's top executives forced them to the negotiating table.[27]

National labor leaders likewise pushed for change. Publicly, they insisted that black workers' limited job opportunities were "primarily the result of decisions by the employer who has sole responsibility for hiring." Behind the scenes, however, AFL and CIO leaders acknowledged that their unions negotiated the discriminatory contracts. In 1955, the AFL tried to bring its recalcitrant locals into line, and Weaver suggested that the implicated Oil Workers locals should express their support for change "off the record." Their parent union, the Oil Workers International, backed Weaver's efforts. Its general counsel had already distributed a memo warning its locals that "under the *Constitution* of the United *States* and *Federal Law, labor unions are liable for damages*, when they negotiate contracts that *freeze-off* promotional rights of employees, or when they *refuse to present grievances in their behalf*, primarily because such employees happen to be colored or of a particular race." The Oil Workers International now warned that it would "not ratify any collective bargaining agreements containing discriminatory provisions"; its general counsel asked to help the government resolve the Shell PCGC complaint, not the other way around.[28]

The PCGC produced results. In 1955, Shell abolished its segregated general labor department and integrated its lines of promotion. The agreement helped compensate for past discrimination by making some jobs available based on years of service to Shell ("plant seniority") rather than years of service in the department where the newly opened jobs were located ("departmental seniority"). The Baton Rouge Esso plant also opened all but professional and clerical jobs to African Americans and promised to promote twenty-five black workers to the newly opened jobs. In 1956, the Beaumont, Texas, Magnolia Oil plant, another of Wisdom's targets, agreed to promote thirty-two African Americans into previously whites-only jobs.[29]

Soon, however, change stalled. The first problem was the PCGC subcommittee's highly individualized approach. George Weaver urged the subcommittee in 1955 to gather the NAACP together with the offending companies and unions to hammer out an industrywide resolution. Wisdom rejected the idea. He favored a southern-liberal approach that would preserve white businessmen's control and tolerate their preference for gradual change. Wisdom negotiated privately with oil industry executives, excluding the complainants' lawyers (the NAACP, Wisdom insisted, was "anathema in the South" and would only frustrate his subcommittee's efforts), the implicated unions (their "attitude was a stumbling block"), and even his fellow committee members. Wisdom's plant-by-plant approach left cooperative unions vulnerable to raids by competitors who promised to restore the discriminatory status quo ante. By insisting on going it alone, he also made the process dependent on him. When he left the PCGC in 1956, the impetus behind the oil cases left with him.[30]

The efficacy of the PCGC's voluntarist approach was also inherently limited. Southern states that had progressed incrementally toward equality in the 1940s and early 1950s broke into open racial warfare in the wake of *Brown v. Board of Education.* Politicians across the South tried to outdo each other's adherence to white supremacy. States enacted laws designed to shut down NAACP activity, and national labor leaders fretted that White Citizens' Councils were infiltrating southern union locals. This was not a context that fostered voluntary integration of jobs.[31]

Employers began resisting change, blaming white supremacy. The Carbide and Chemicals Company's managers attributed their lack of progress to the "still pretty strong customs instilled in the minds of the run of the mill type of white employee." Even Esso stalled. Its previously sympathetic executives counseled that before further change could occur, the country needed to alter "the thinking of the younger white generation" by "timely education through our schools, churches, social and religious organizations, industry, press and the Government."[32]

Labor ceased pushing for change as well. AFL unions remained recalcitrant. At the Carbide plant, the union's leader publicly berated the black local for seeking the NAACP's help and claimed that its contract discriminated only against more-qualified white workers who could not get jobs in the all-black labor department. Oil Workers International officers also backed down in the face of angry white members. The Gulf Coast states all had right-to-work laws, making the Oil Workers unions particularly vulnerable to worker defection. The general counsel warned Weaver that the international union could no longer police its locals' progress, lest "already strained feelings ... be aggravated." The 1955 merger of the AFL and CIO into a single federation promised to bring union policy up to the CIO's interracial par, rather than down to the AFL's racially exclusive floor. But the new AFL-CIO's Civil Rights Department forced errant locals to change only in the rare instances when a union's discrimination attracted sufficiently embarrassing national attention. Unsurprisingly, Weaver got nowhere when he tried to sway the department to act in the oil cases.[33]

In 1957, George Weaver took stock of the oil industry plants that had desegregated their jobs, seniority, and promotions. In only one case, Shell Oil, did he find the PCGC's involvement "decisive," and there he credited a contracting agency attorney, not his subcommittee. Otherwise, Weaver attributed the changes to the unions or management. For instance, at Magnolia Oil, Weaver and the NAACP's Herbert Hill were involved long before Wisdom. And in many plants, nothing had changed. The PCGC's voluntary approach had succeeded only where change had already been likely, and then left the pioneering unions vulnerable to race-based raiding, just as Weaver had always feared. Before the PCGC, as before the NLRB, realizing the promise of the oil cases ultimately proved elusive.[34]

Labor and the Workplace Constitution

The oil cases might have increased labor's support for the liberal workplace Constitution even if they had failed before the NLRB and the PCGC. In 1954, the opinion of the Oil Workers' general counsel, Lindsay Walden, that unions had a constitutional duty to negotiate nondiscriminatory contracts, seemed destined to become the CIO's official position. Thanks to George Weaver's efforts, Walden's memo circulated within the United Steelworkers and the UAW, the CIO's two most powerful unions.[35]

Not all labor lawyers shared Walden's enthusiasm for the workplace Constitution, however. The child of Russian Jewish immigrants, Arthur J. Goldberg came of age in the 1920s among Chicago's garment trades, imbibing that industry's faith in industrial unionism and stable, mutually beneficial labor-management relations. Goldberg eventually became the Steelworkers' lawyer and later added the CIO to his list of clients. In the 1940s, before Goldberg took over, the CIO's Office of the General Counsel was dominated by leftists who were predictably open to broad state action theories. After World War II, when the NAACP challenged the constitutionality of union discrimination before the NLRB, it had the CIO's support. As the Cold War descended in the late 1940s, however, the CIO's lawyers were accused of Communist sympathies and departed the organization along with its left-leaning unions. Liberal anticommunists like Goldberg replaced them, taking the CIO in a different legal direction.[36]

The dominant liberal view of labor relations, an anti-statist strain of industrial pluralism that became known as "labor pluralism," did not incline adherents such as Goldberg toward the workplace Constitution. Like other labor pluralists, Goldberg favored creating and enforcing the law of the workplace through a private system of collective bargaining, arbitration, and grievances. Particularly "within the economic sphere," Goldberg opined, "the state does not prescribe action." Indeed, the "free society," Goldberg argued, "suffer[ed] a positive loss whenever a course of action is prescribed by governmental authority rather than left to the free play of private regulation." For labor pluralists, some regulations were worth this cost. These included the NLRA, which helped level the playing field between workers and employers and facilitated collective bargaining. Other regulations were not. "The protection of civil rights within the field of labor-management relations," Goldberg contended, was best achieved by safeguarding "the right to organize and bargain collectively with employers."[37]

Goldberg had no qualms about integrating union membership, but he rejected the workplace Constitution. He supported civil rights and had recently authored the CIO's amicus brief in *Brown*. Accepting that unions and employers were state actors subject to the Constitution's commands, however, would undermine labor pluralism's core tenets. Labor-management relations would no longer be the "system of voluntary government, not created by law or compelled by law, but created by free people ... as a matter of choice" that Goldberg prized. Collective bargaining and workplace governance would be riddled with the same constitutional limits as the political democracy from which Goldberg believed it should be distinguished. If focused statutory regulation of collective bargaining was only occasionally desirable, then subjecting unions to a panoply of constitutional duties and empowering workers, not to mention employers, to assert constitutional claims against them was anathema.[38]

Goldberg's views became the official CIO position. In 1954, instead of adopting Walden's memo on union discrimination, Goldberg wrote his own. It stayed predictably clear of unions' and employers' duties under the U.S. Constitution. Goldberg instead emphasized nondiscrimination obligations in *unions'* constitutions. He also pointed to unions' duty of fair representation but decoupled it from the Constitution, ascribing it only to the NLRA. This way, labor could advance African Americans' workplace rights without altering the "system of voluntary government" Goldberg held dear. At its 1954 annual convention, the CIO incorporated Goldberg's position into its civil rights resolutions, and his memo became the template for other international unions' advice to their membership.[39]

Robert Carter, George Weaver, Roberson King, and the CIO's most racially progressive unions had advocated a liberal workplace Constitution, one that they believed would provide African Americans with decent jobs and a union voice, while also strengthening the labor movement. The CIO's labor pluralists were skeptical. In their opinion, the Constitution was a blunt instrument that would bludgeon the precious "free play of private regulation." For them, there was no such thing as a *liberal* workplace Constitution.

The 1950s opened with promise for African American workers and for the liberal workplace Constitution but ended with their prospects in shambles. Instead of producing a *Brown v. Board of Education* for the workplace, the coordinated litigation sowed disappointment, acrimony, and unease. The AFL-CIO's lack of action angered the NAACP. In 1958, Herbert Hill publicly criticized the labor organization's Civil

Rights Department, calling its approach "totally inadequate" and urging a "direct frontal attack against segregation and discrimination within trade unions." At the same time, Robert Carter's advocacy for the workplace Constitution risked alienating such union allies as Arthur Goldberg. The NLRB fretted about its constitutional duties, but its power to implement them was constrained. President Eisenhower's Committee on Government Contracts ran up against the limits of "voluntarism," the fair employment approach favored by the Republican Party and many state fair-employment committees.[40]

The bitterest disappointment was felt by the oil workers, however. Even the agreements adopted by sympathetic employers and unions created little change in African Americans' job prospects. The Shell Oil agreement, which Weaver touted as "a model" for the industry, had little actual effect. The jobs it opened had educational requirements and qualifying tests that few if any black employees could satisfy. Only at Esso, where the company set aside twenty-five skilled jobs for African Americans, a "quota" in today's parlance, did substantial promotions occur. Once the quota was filled, however, the change stopped. In 1957, a recession hit and Gulf Coast oil refineries began laying workers off. Esso shed more than a third of its workforce over the four years following the NAACP's complaint. When contract agency investigators came knocking, Esso blamed its lack of further promotions on the economic downturn. This could not explain Esso's persistent unwillingness to open white-collar jobs to black workers, however. Even the promotions that occurred left a bitter taste. Esso complainant Thomas Davis applied but was not among those promoted. Although the college-educated Davis was otherwise qualified, according to Esso management he "was too sensitive about [his] race and ... did not show respect for the white people." Being the kind who would win change, however meager, also meant being the kind who would be denied its benefits.[41]

Despite the overwhelming sense of defeat, however, the decade was not all negative for the workplace Constitution. Although invisible to outsiders, the concept had taken firmer root at the NLRB and gained a foothold at the PCGC. For the first time, administrators joined advocates in understanding it not only to require fair representation but also to bar segregation. The NAACP also developed a new "sufficiency of contacts" theory of state action, which at least one federal judge adopted (albeit in dissent) in Roberson King's Gulf Oil case, providing new nutrients for the workplace Constitution's administrative roots.[42]

Even as the workplace Constitution gained support, however, its liberal potential was threatened by more than labor pluralism. As Arthur Goldberg found out in a 1955 debate with a prominent right-to-work lawyer, Carter and his union allies were not alone in arguing that government-certified unions were state actors.

6

Conservatives Pursue the Workplace Constitution in the Courts

"Their individual rights and liberties as free men"

Complaint, *Ward v. Seaboard Air Line Railroad Co.*

In 1950, Congress debated amending the Railway Labor Act to allow union shops, ones in which eligible workers were required to join the union to keep their jobs. "I and my co-workers ... believe in the necessity of unions," Kentuckian William T. Harrison wrote several southern Congressmen, but "forced membership in either a union, club, lodge, church or anything else ... is Un-American and should be left to Russia." As an official of the Brotherhood of Railway Clerks, Harrison's prounion stance was sincere. His opposition to "forced membership" was equally heartfelt. It stemmed not only from patriotic anticommunism but also racial politics. The national labor leaders who pushed for union shops, Harrison objected, "seek such power to further their political ideas, which for the great part are of the F.E.P.C. and other civil rights programs of the North and East variety." To Harrison's chagrin, in 1951 the union shop amendments passed and his union suspended him for publicly opposing them.[1]

The Railway Labor Act amendments transformed the right-to-work movement. Most notably, they channeled the movement's strategy back into the courts. As discussed in Chapter 3, Hollywood mogul Cecil B. DeMille had decided that influencing public opinion was the best way to achieve a Supreme Court victory for the his cause. Instead of funding litigation, he lobbied states to adopt right-to-work laws. Individual workers still occasionally brought right-to-work suits but they were not part of any larger Supreme Court strategy. The Railway Labor Act's amendments overrode (in legal terms, "preempted") state right-to-work laws, however, foreclosing the state-law antidote and sending the movement back to court. Generating litigation, it turned out, was only one of several ways the amendments transformed the right-to-work movement.

The Movement Finds Its Workers

The 1951 amendments spurred vehement and newly coordinated worker opposition. In a letter to the editor, a writer who signed as "Disgusted Railroad Worker" called union shop agreements "the bludgeoning of the independent worker into an organization which he despises with good cause and distrusts with even greater reason." The union shop, urged a West Coast railroad employee, empowered a union to "deprive one of an essential of 'life' (his earnings), an essential of 'liberty' (his freedom to work) and an essential of 'property' (the sale of his labor)." These mobilized workers changed the face and tactics of the right-to-work movement.[2]

The railroad brotherhoods' embrace of the union shop went against tradition. The independent, wealthy, and highly exclusive "operating" unions – engineers, firemen, brakemen, trainmen, and hostlers – competed fiercely for members, owing to their overlapping jurisdictions. The operating unions also distrusted the mostly AFL-affiliated nonoperating unions that represented the vast majority of railroad workers. They all united, however, in their desire to eliminate company-dominated unions, which employers established to keep the railroad unions out. This desire had fueled their support of the NLRA-like 1934 Railway Labor Act and its ban on union shops, which labor leaders feared would be a boon to company unions. By 1951 the calculus had changed. Company unions were mostly gone, making the union shop option safe. A new threat had also appeared: the CIO. The railroad brotherhoods had fended off industrial unions, which organized workers across the brotherhoods' carefully drawn craft lines, since the late nineteenth century. In the 1940s, however, a CIO-affiliated industrial union made inroads. Despite their voluntary membership levels at upward of 90 percent, the brotherhoods felt threatened and backed the union shop to keep the CIO out.[3]

The 1951 amendments instead *spurred* industrial unions and opposition to the union shop. Immediately following their enactment, the United Railroad Operating Committee (UROC) organized operating and nonoperating workers together in a single union. Among its core precepts were greater democratic accountability and opposition to the union shop. Before the year's end, UROC had nearly 14,000 members. The CIO also benefited from the amendments. When most railroad companies finally gave up their fight against union shop agreements in 1952, the CIO won an agreement covering nonoperating workers on the Pennsylvania Railroad. Unionists claiming the support of several thousand workers protested against this and formed the National Committee for Union Shop Abolition. William T. Harrison became their leader.[4]

The National Committee and UROC rekindled right-to-work litigation and fomented worker support for the movement. Picking up where DeMille had left off, the National Committee adopted the credo, "The right to earn a living, with or without benefit of union membership is an inherent Constitutional right of every citizen of the United States." Its primary goal was to get the Supreme Court to "once and for all declare the Union Shop to be in conflict with the Bill of Rights and therefore un-Constitutional." When the railroad brotherhoods thwarted UROC's efforts to win recognition from the federal labor boards, its dwindling members switched from trying to win representative status to joining the National Committee's lawsuits.[5]

The politics of UROC and the National Committee were slippery. UROC was a legitimate union that grew out of genuine struggle among railroad workers over how to organize. It had idealistic leaders and notable support among workers (although its members were a small fraction of the railroads' employees). It also sought CIO affiliation – an ally of radical labor leader Harry Bridges even edited its newsletter. Its members simultaneously believed in unions and opposed the union shop.[6]

The National Committee's bona fides were more questionable. By the 1950s, anti–New Deal conservatives had built an intricate network of activists, funders, and organizations that deepened and broadened support for their cause. They also developed a rigorous intellectual defense, and imprimatur, for their free-market advocacy. Austrian economists Friedrich von Hayek and Ludwig von Mises challenged the dominant Keynesian arguments in favor of government-primed and regulated markets. *Unfettered* markets, Hayek and Mises countered, better advanced the freedom and material well-being of all. In their view, markets were so complex that government regulation inevitably mangled them, restricting liberty and inviting tyranny. These ideas were refined through Hayek's Mont Pelerin Society, an exclusive international salon, and disseminated by think tanks such as the American Enterprise Association (later the American Enterprise Institute).[7]

Religion also fueled anti–New Deal conservatives' fight against creeping socialism and helped generate mass support. In Los Angeles, Spiritual Mobilization, a group formed by Reverend James Fifield, the entrepreneurial pastor of the city's booming First Congregational Church, promoted theological arguments against the New Deal regulatory state. Fifield sent copies of Hayek's wildly popular 1944 book, *The Road to Serfdom*, to fellow ministers; established "Freedom Clubs" around the country; and preached to southern California's conservative housewife-activists. Clarence Manion, a devout Catholic and former dean of Notre Dame Law School, was a Democrat who converted to the anti–New Deal cause. Manion had a weekly radio show during the 1950s on which he railed against the federal income tax, government spending, and labor "czars." He was one of many Catholic priests, academics, and popular writers who made a vigorous ecclesiastical case during the 1950s against the New Deal state and for the right to work.[8]

Free-market economics and religion dovetailed with anticommunism, the grassroots engine of 1950s conservatism. The Cold War Soviet threat united conservatives across their ideological divides and transformed what had been an avowedly elitist movement into a populist one. The threat provided a common framework for conservatives ranging from Spiritual Mobilization's housewife-activists to southern segregationists, such as Senator Strom Thurmond of South Carolina, to the founding members of the ultraright John Birch Society. It also gave anti–New Deal conservatives a broadly appealing language in which to decry creeping socialism at home and the growing power of labor.[9]

Harrison's National Committee was embedded in the right-to-work corner of anticommunism's religiously infused free-market wing. Harrison, who also belonged to the DeMille Foundation, created connections between the two organizations. The committee's main funder was the National Labor-Management Foundation, which argued that the "Golden Rule of Jesus Christ" was the cornerstone of good industrial relations. Maurice Franks, a longtime union member and former railroad union agent, was the Labor-Management Foundation's public face. Closed shops, where employers could hire only union members, Franks charged, subjected workers to a "dictatorial system" akin to those the Allied forces fought in World War II. They reduced members to subjects, the antithesis of the independent, virile white manhood union members were supposed to represent. Franks was equally opposed to union shops, which were "nothing less than the black cat of the closed shop dyed white."[10]

The Labor-Management Foundation and the National Committee for Union Shop Abolition were at the epicenter of Rust Belt right-to-work politics and Christian anti–New Deal activism. Foundation board member Alfred P. Haake was a labor economist who consulted for corporations and business groups. In the 1940s, he debated Socialist Norm Thomas about whether capitalism would survive the war (yes, if people followed Haake's motto about postwar deregulation: "When in doubt, kick the government out!"). In the 1930s and 1940s, Haake had criticized the New Deal in increasingly Christian and anticommunist terms, eventually becoming a leader in Spiritual Mobilization and forming a consulting business with Clarence Manion. A second foundation board member, Father Edward Keller, taught economics at Notre Dame, collaborated with the DeMille Foundation, and was also a partner in Haake's consulting firm.[11]

In 1953, Harrison's National Committee challenged the union shop's constitutionality. Dozens of railroad workers in right-to-work states across the South and the upper Midwest filed lawsuits seeking to block union shop agreements. Such agreements, their complaints alleged, were "an invasion of their individual rights and liberties as free men under the American way of life and civilized government." These were highly coordinated "test cases": most were filed within days of the others, often using identically worded complaints. The onslaught of cases dwarfed civil rights and labor advocates' simultaneous pursuit of a liberal workplace Constitution and rivaled the scale of the NAACP's challenge to public school segregation. The cases were organized and financially supported by Harrison's National Committee, the Labor-Management Foundation, and UROC. The DeMille Foundation trumpeted what it called the "court test of the right to work," predicting that "sooner or later one or more of these suits will probably reach the Supreme Court."[12]

The Movement Finds Its Lawyer

Fred G. Gurley, president of the Atchison, Topeka and Santa Fe Railway and cofounder of the DeMille Foundation, addressed a meeting of the Academy of Political Scientists in 1954. "The proposed [union shop] agreement contemplates we would use the power of an employer to deprive individual men and women of a freedom which is theirs as an unalienable right," Gurley decried. *Fortune* magazine had recently dubbed the Santa Fe the "nation's number one railroad." Significant credit went to Gurley, who had presciently adopted the new diesel electric engine and developed rail service to the Sun Belt's booming agricultural and manufacturing sectors. He was equally enmeshed in the Sun Belt's conservative politics. By the mid-1950s most railroads had capitulated to labor's union shop demands. Not Gurley. His Santa Fe Railway instead joined a suit to block proposed union-shop agreements that was brought in the Texas courts by thirteen of its employees. "We are asked to fire people for exercising their rights," Gurley roared, rights that he insisted were fundamental to the Declaration of Independence and enshrined in the Fifth Amendment of the U.S. Constitution. Gurley's suit, *Sandsberry v. Gulf, Colorado & Santa Fe Railroad*, produced the movement's first legal star, one who perceived, in a way DeMille's lawyers had not, the importance of state action and the links it created between the liberal and conservative workplace Constitutions.[13]

During the late 1940s and the 1950s, many American businessmen got off the sidelines and became active in the conservative movement. Business executives representing smaller enterprises, as well as corporate giants such as General Motors, invested in rolling back the New Deal state. They bankrolled Hayek's Mont Pelerin Society, the American Enterprise Association, and dozens of smaller free-market groups. They also fed the movement's grass roots by underwriting Spiritual Mobilization and disseminating their free-market, antiregulatory beliefs to their professional contacts, shareholders, and workforce. Gurley was no different. In addition to remaining active in DeMille's foundation, he educated his middle managers in the "philosophy and goals of the American system of free enterprise."[14]

Gurley also invested in the law. His most valuable asset was the railroad cases' legal mastermind: Santa Fe Railway vice president and general counsel Jonathan C. Gibson. A Virginia native, Gibson had served on the Interstate Commerce Commission and practiced in the Washington, D.C., office of a New York tax firm before decamping to Chicago during the Depression to work for the railway. When Gurley joined his employees in their suit, the task of making the plaintiffs' case fell to Gibson.[15]

Thanks to *Sandsberry*, Gibson became the right-to-work movement's legal spokesperson. The trial allowed Gibson to make his case to the nation. In early 1954, the jury found facts largely in the plaintiffs' favor and the judge endorsed Gibson's constitutional theories. Texas judge E. C. Nelson found that the union shop violated the plaintiffs' First Amendment free speech and association rights as well as their Fifth Amendment right to work. Citing the Declaration of Independence, whose "spirit is breathed into and permeates every part of" the Constitution, Judge Nelson called the union shop "repugnant to the idea of human worth and to man's freedom of choice." The *Sandsberry* trial was widely reported, owing to the Santa Fe Railway's prominence and its close ties to the press, particularly the *Los Angeles Times* and the *Chicago Daily Tribune*. Gibson became a sought-after speaker, "the nation's foremost authority on voluntary unionism." Whether debating prominent labor lawyer and CIO general counsel Arthur Goldberg, appearing on television, or speaking to gatherings of lawyers and businessmen, Gibson made the constitutional case against the union shop.[16]

Gibson quickly learned the significance of the state action barrier. In late 1954, the Texas Court of Appeals reversed Judge Nelson, in significant part because it found that no "governmental action was taken on behalf of the unions by [the] congressional enactment." On appeal to the Texas Supreme Court, the state action issue moved front and center.[17]

Gibson's state action arguments drew right-to-work suits closer to African Americans' claims to a liberal workplace Constitution. Gibson argued briefly that state action was present because the union shop amendments preempted Texas's right-to-work law, an argument peculiar to conservative claims to a workplace Constitution. But his arguments mainly resembled those made by liberal advocates of a workplace Constitution. Gibson insisted that mere government permission or sanction "has been held by the Supreme Court to be governmental action." In support, he cited the First Amendment cases *Public Utilities Commission v. Pollak* and *American Communications Association v. Douds* as well as the Court's white-primary cases. Gibson also contended that the white-primary cases, along with *Steele* and *Betts v. Easley*, "unmistakably recognized that when a legislative body like Congress vests power and authority in groups or associations like appellant unions, the actions of the latter are to be judged as tantamount to those of the legislature." Colloquially, Gibson explained that "labor relations are so regulated by law today that compulsory union membership is ordinarily possible only by governmental permission and it is usually imposed by union leaders using as a weapon the great complex of powers placed in their hands by modern labor law."[18]

The Texas Supreme Court would not decide the merits of Gibson's state action theories, however. While *Sandsberry* was pending, the U.S. Supreme Court granted review to another railroad case, *Hanson v. Union Pacific Railroad*. The Nebraska Supreme Court had found sufficient state action in the Railway Labor Act's preemption of state right-to-work laws and ruled that the union shop amendments violated plaintiffs' Fifth Amendment right to work and First Amendment freedom of association. *Hanson* became the right-to-work movement's great hope, replacing *Sandsberry* as the subject of DeMille Foundation bulletins.[19]

Storming the Court

DeMille's foundation was "in constant touch with Right-to-Work groups in the various States," but DeMille found "it [a] better strategy to let the publicity accrue to the local groups while we remain in the background." The foundation shrouded its role in right-to-work campaigns to steer credit not only to the state organizations but also to the ordinary citizens and workers the foundation wanted in the movement's forefront. As its secretary advised one state Chamber of Commerce, "Powerful individual and corporative interests must be enlisted in any such [state right-to-work] campaign as the 'anonymous quarterbacks.'" They would "determine the policy and call the turns," but these should "be executed by citizens less associated in the public mind with employer interests."[20]

DeMille tried to ensure, with mixed success, that the *Hanson* litigation proceeded according to his workers-first precepts. Foundation staff mobilized an array of amici for the *Hanson* plaintiffs, especially targeting the attorneys general of right-to-work states, and promoted Gibson's legal arguments as a model for activists and lawyers alike. Neither DeMille nor his foundation filed a separate brief, however. As for other right-to-work organizations, DeMille's staff was confident that "all the fairly prominent state Right To Work Committees ... agree thoroughly with our position," but they worried about a newcomer to the right-to-work scene.[21]

The National Right to Work Committee held promise and peril, in DeMille's eyes. Conceived in 1954, its organizers told DeMille that they planned "to work at the national level for the same objective as your Foundation." As right-to-work advocates contemplated promoting a federal right-to-work law and participated in coordinated Supreme Court litigation, national representation made sense. The number and fractiousness of the state campaigns compounded the need for coordination. But the Right to Work Committee made former congressman Fred Hartley of Taft-Hartley fame its president. His concurrent work as a spokesperson for employer groups further violated the DeMille Foundation's workers-first credo. To make matters worse, the committee's board chairman was a southern businessman fresh from a bitter but successful fight against unionization. Much to DeMille's relief, the Right to Work Committee recognized the problem. William Harrison soon replaced Hartley as its public face and its operating force.[22]

The *Hanson* litigation was one of Harrison's first undertakings. His Right to Work Committee filed a brief and helped Gibson and DeMille's foundation coordinate those from the state attorneys general. Eight out of the seventeen right-to-work states ultimately filed briefs. Although DeMille preferred that employer groups stay in the background, the National Association of Manufacturers, United

States Chamber of Commerce, Southern States Industrial Council, and American Farm Bureau Federation each filed substantial briefs. But there were plenty of employees represented as well. Workers in two of the other railroad cases filed briefs, including Gibson's one-hundred-plus-page behemoth on behalf of the *Sandsberry* plaintiffs. Also notable was a brief signed by approximately five hundred railroad workers, several of whom were Right to Work Committee board members and probably all of whom were affiliated with UROC.[23]

The right-to-work briefs mostly mimicked Gibson's arguments to the Texas courts, cementing the links between the liberal and conservative workplace Constitutions. Respondents and about half of the amici argued that the railroad unions, as exclusive bargaining representatives, were state actors. Nearly all right-to-work filers also argued that something shy of government compulsion sufficed to trigger constitutional protections. A number even argued that mere government permission or "sanction" was all that was needed.[24]

The briefs by Gibson and Harrison's Right to Work Committee were nonetheless broader and more innovative than the others, pulling the movement closer to the minority rights arguments associated with postwar liberalism. Gibson, like DeMille before him, looked beyond freedom-of-contract precedents to support the right to work. He cited not only the Declaration of Independence, natural law, and the Ninth Amendment, but also the 1949 United Nations Declaration of Human Rights. Harrison, in contrast, all but ignored the right to work, emphasizing instead First Amendment speech and association claims. Gibson and Harrison also challenged most fundamentally labor's primary defense of the union shop. Unions argued that union shops were necessary to prevent "free riders," workers who benefitted from union contracts without sharing their costs. Most right-to-work amici challenged this argument at its margins, contending that mandatory support of unions' political activities or welfare programs exceeded what was necessary to eliminate free riders. Gibson and Harrison challenged the free-rider argument's very premise. Unions had fought to have the labor laws grant them exclusive representative status, they observed. Having succeeded, the fact that unions now had to bargain on nonmembers' behalf was a privilege, not a burden. The true problem was thus constitutionally wronged "forced followers," they insisted, not cheating "free riders." Gibson and Harrison also urged the Supreme

Court to abolish union shops in their entirety. Their arguments against it, they stressed, applied not only to right-to-work states like Nebraska but also to states without right-to-work laws, and to unions organized under the National Labor Relations Act as well as those organized under the Railway Labor Act.[25]

Making Lemonade

Right-to-work advocates lost. In 1956, the Supreme Court unanimously reversed the Nebraska Supreme Court in *Hanson*, leading lower courts in which test cases were pending, including *Sandsberry*, to lift their injunctions. A *Los Angeles Times* columnist and Santa Fe ally predicted that the Court's decision "could lead to tight union control of untold numbers of workers in many industries where union membership is not now requisite to holding jobs." DeMille fretted that the case might destroy the National Right to Work Committee. The committee survived, but the movement's miseries were compounded in 1958 when voters in California, Colorado, Idaho, Kansas, Ohio, and Washington weighed right-to-work laws and rejected them in all but Kansas. In a symbolic as well as material loss, Cecil B. DeMille died several months later, and his foundation, convinced that "no one can take Mr. DeMille's place," disbanded. Right-to-work leaders gathered in Kansas City in June 1959 to lick their wounds. The invitees assembled under the bland name the E. M. Greb Meeting to deflect scrutiny. Gibson presided over the reeling movement's clandestine affair. Desperate to map a new way forward, and troubled that the AFL-CIO had so effectively recast their legislative proposals as "Right to Wreck" laws, attendees at the Kansas City meeting even considered rebranding themselves the "freedom of association" movement.[26]

Perhaps imperceptible through this haze of defeat, however, were some glimmers of hope for the railroad cases and the movement more broadly. The *Chicago Tribune*'s editors called *Hanson* "the complete negation of classic liberalism that concerned itself with the liberty of the individual." The decision was instead "typical of the new liberalism" according to which "if a thing seems good for the majority ... the individual has no right to protest." But there was more life in classical liberalism than the editors granted. Justices Douglas and Black epitomized the "new liberalism." Yet in a recent dissent, they had called the right to work "the most precious liberty that man possesses," sounding like "something copied from one of the pamphlets of the DeMille Foundation," a right-to-work ally observed. These two justices held the deepest but not the only concerns about minority rights in new liberalism's majoritarian regime. Courting their sympathy might provide the right-to-work movement a path forward.[27]

Read closely, *Hanson* was also a more favorable decision than it first appeared. *Hanson* was "a simple case," Chief Justice Warren insisted when the justices discussed it privately in 1956. Every justice agreed that Congress had the power to provide for a union shop. But Justices Douglas and Black found the right-to-work litigants' constitutional claims compelling. Douglas's opinion for the Court reflected their sympathy. He agreed with the Nebraska court that the union shop contract was infused with sufficient government action to trigger constitutional protections. He also left it ambiguous whether this was because the amendments preempted Nebraska's right-to-work law or, as Gibson had argued, because they generally authorized the union shop. This was a blow to the unions, who had defended themselves exclusively on the grounds that the union shop agreements involved no state action and thus could not trigger constitutional protections. The Court easily dismissed the right-to-work claim (Douglas even observed that "trade unionism ... enhance[d] and strengthen[ed] the right to work"). But DeMille had nonetheless succeeded in "chang[ing] the mind of the Supreme Court": Douglas rejected the speech and association claims only for lack of evidence that the union would use workers' payments for anything other than collective bargaining activities. The constitutional issue might come out differently, Douglas cautioned, if they were instead "used as a cover for forcing ideological conformity or other action in contravention of the First Amendment."[28]

Activists built on the opening Douglas provided. The real concern was not the union shop, Gurley's *Los Angeles Times* mouthpiece soon urged, but unions' use of funds to "support a political party or candidate with whom some members are not in sympathy." The movement should pursue the political-freedom dimension of its cause, the *Times* advised, deferring for now its economic-freedom claims. This approach would "substantially [eliminate] the 'free-rider' argument, so effectively used in the campaigns against right-to-work proposals," while taking advantage of the individual-rights route Douglas opened in the new liberalism regime.[29]

As the movement made political coercion its mantra, it also revealed its partisan ambitions. By the late 1950s it was no longer taboo to attack unions' political influence. The Senate's lengthy and widely followed investigation of union corruption, which involved a star turn by right-to-work enthusiast Barry Goldwater, unearthed evidence of racketeering. Although the investigation also revealed that it did not pervade the labor movement as right-to-work advocates argued, labor's legitimacy was sufficiently damaged that a *Democratic* Congress passed the first NLRA reforms since Taft-Hartley: the 1959 Landrum-Griffin Act, a so-called bill of rights for union members. Right-to-work advocates now urged that limiting unions' collection of dues for political spending would protect not only workers' rights but also "the nation against the building of a vast political machine." In 1958, the Georgia Supreme Court enjoined a union shop agreement because the unions spent worker dues on political activity. Media outlets friendly to the right-to-work cause celebrated the decision as "a body blow to the rise of the Reuther Social Democrats" and to the AFL-CIO's Committee on Political Education, which had so effectively defeated right-to-work laws and antilabor candidates in the 1958 elections. If the Supreme Court affirmed, it could free labor's "captive Congress."[30]

The railroad cases also showed right-to-work advocates new ways to advance their cause before the court of public opinion. Like the other plaintiffs in the railroad cases, those in *Ward v. Seaboard Air Line Railroad Co.* asserted that their employer's union shop agreement was an unconstitutional "invasion of their individual rights and liberties as free men." Unlike the other plaintiffs, however, these five Richmond, Virginia, men were African American members of A. Philip Randolph's Brotherhood of Sleeping Car Porters. They wanted to be represented by Randolph's union and not the all-white operating brotherhood that had secured a union shop agreement. Instead of turning to the liberal workplace Constitution like their fellow members, the *Ward* plaintiffs turned to its conservative twin.[31]

At first blush, this seems an improbable turn of events. Right-to-work advocates generally did not ally themselves with African Americans even when they analogized union security to slavery and asserted that the right to work was a core civil right. Barry Goldwater supported a nondiscrimination amendment to the NLRA in 1952, but for right-to-work ends. And he used his frequent right-to-work amendments to civil rights bills as poison pills, bragging to DeMille's staff that his amendments had "stopped these eggheads in their drive."[32]

The right-to-work movement also remained closely linked with white supremacy. William Harrison's leadership was a case in point and UROC, the renegade railroad union that provided many of the railroad cases' plaintiffs, was white only. In the 1950s, southern Democrats built close ties with business conservatives. Influential North Carolina senator Sam Ervin's antiunionism rivaled his opposition to civil rights. South Carolina senator Strom Thurmond, a staunch segregationist, switched from being a New Deal supporter and labor ally to an anti–New Deal, right-to-work advocate as he courted business support. State right-to-work committees shared leaders with supremacist White Citizens' Councils.[33]

The fusion of right-to-work and anti–civil rights politics was not a purely southern affair. The housewife-activists who filled the pews of James Fifield's Los Angeles church fought against local school integration plans. When Fifield launched Spiritual Mobilization with the railroad cases' backer Alfred Haake, he spoke out against fair employment laws and criticized African Americans for "push[ing] in where they are not wanted." Northern conservatives made common cause across the Mason-Dixon Line over white supremacy as well as the right to work and business opportunities. Donald Richberg, a northern Thurmond ally who helped with Gibson's *Sandsberry* brief, was also an outspoken critic of fair employment laws, denying the existence of racial discrimination in the workplace.[34]

The *Ward* railroad case, filed in 1953, presaged a shift in movement strategy. Right-to-work proposals had succeeded primarily in the Sun Belt where unions were weak, but activists now looked north and west to union strongholds. During the mid-1950s DeMille's staff worked in states like Indiana, Ohio, Washington, and Massachusetts. When Indiana passed a right-to-work law in 1957, DeMille predicted that therefore "it can be done in other industrial States."[35]

As the targets shifted, so did the movement's politics. In these industrial centers, African Americans often held an important swing vote, giving northern right-to-work activists an interest in wooing black voters. Right-to-work laws would open jobs as well as shops, advocates argued. In 1953, a National Association of Manufacturers' official promised African Americans in Missouri that they would find their best opportunities if "competition is kept free from government control, or monopolistic group control by either management or labor." A 1958 pamphlet promoting the right to work in California featured a black railroad worker complaining of the brotherhoods' white-only membership policies. "Voluntary Unionism would eliminate discrimination against minorities and help safeguard their Constitutional rights as American citizens," the pamphlet promised.[36]

Focusing on union discrimination was an effective way to solicit black voters and simultaneously to alienate racial liberals' support for labor. In Ohio, state labor officials pleaded with the AFL-CIO to force a Cleveland Electrical Workers local to admit African Americans. "This matter is rapidly becoming a disgraceful scandal within the general community," the state official warned in 1956, "and is providing ammunition for the advocates of the 'right to work' laws." The Alton, Illinois, branch of the NAACP threatened in 1958 that if AFL-CIO officials could not persuade a local building-trades union to end its discriminatory practices, perhaps "Right to Work legislation ... [wa]s the solution." In Milwaukee, African Americans sued an all-white bricklayers' union. The Milwaukee press warned that the union's policy "invite[d] ... just what labor most deeply hates and fears – a 'right to work' law in Wisconsin." DeMille Foundation staff hoped their local committee would "be able to make use of" this case of union discrimination. Goldwater also touted the black bricklayers' case on the Senate floor to explain why his latest right-to-work amendment belonged in a pending civil rights bill.[37]

Take Two

In 1959 the Supreme Court agreed to review the Georgia Supreme Court decision striking down a union shop, giving right-to-work advocates a second chance to package their claims in terms the Court's new liberals might accept. Union shop opponents never knew it, but they came breathtakingly close to winning. When *International Association of Machinists v. Street* was argued in 1960, the railroad workers framed their claims in minority-rights terms. It worked. Justice Black initially won the support of all but Justices Frankfurter and Harlan in finding that the Railway Labor Act was "being used ... to exact money from these employees to ... win elections for parties and candidates they are against" and therefore "violate[d] the freedom of speech guarantee of the First Amendment."[38]

This right-to-work victory was not to be, however. The Court had overlooked notifying the solicitor general that the constitutionality of the act was in question, which it was required to do. The justices gave the solicitor general a chance to participate and set the case for reargument. He implored the Court to avoid the constitutional issues, either by reversing based on *Hanson* or by interpreting the Railway Labor Act to disallow any constitutionally questionable union expenditures. Black's majority splintered. The chief justice determined that at least some of the union expenditures should be barred, but that the constitutional issues should be avoided. Warren assigned the opinion to the like-minded Justice Brennan.[39]

During the spring of 1961, Brennan struggled to cobble together a majority holding that the Railway Labor Act barred unions from expending members' dues to support "political and economic doctrines" with which they disagreed. Douglas and Black insisted that this be determined on First Amendment grounds, while Justice Whittaker now joined Justices Harlan and Frankfurter, who concluded that the expenditures were legal under both the Railway Labor Act and the Constitution. In June, Brennan gave up and redrafted his opinion, affirming on the only ground that commanded a majority: the First Amendment. Notoriously persuadable, Justice Whittaker shifted once again, however, and endorsed Brennan's statutory approach, giving it a bare majority.[40]

These background machinations were invisible to right-to-work activists, however. All they knew was that when the Court issued its decision several days later their victory seemed Pyrrhic. There were some positives. The Court found that the Railway Labor Act denied unions "the right, over the employee's objection, to use his money to support political causes which he opposes." Brennan's opinion even adopted the activists' derogatory term for the union shop, "compulsory unionism." Justices Black and Douglas also wrote separately, arguing that dissident workers had a constitutional right not to pay for political activities they opposed.[41]

Right-to-work advocates nonetheless saw *Street* as a loss. The Georgia courts had enjoined enforcement of the union shop agreements until the unions could show that they were no longer using member dues for disallowed purposes. Advocates hoped this would "sharply curtail the flow of money into union political war chests"; perhaps even "render most present union shop agreements unenforceable." From this perspective, Brennan's opinion in *Street* was a half-empty glass. He reaffirmed the constitutionality of the union shop and rejected the Georgia court's remedy because it gave too little weight to the *union majority's* free-speech rights. Brennan also required dissenting members to opt out of paying for political speech. Activists hoped for a regime in which union members would have to opt *in*, convinced that it would have a far greater impact on union coffers. Speaking for the National Right to Work Committee, William Harrison called *Street* "disappointing ... [and] harmful to the interests of workers."[42]

Labor advocates agreed that they had emerged from *Street* relatively unscathed. "High Court's Ruling Leaves Labor Calm," the *Washington Post* reported. Yes, "the gloomiest ... labor lawyers worr[ied] that Justice Hugo L. Black's one-man dissent [which protected dissenting workers from paying any dues at all] may at some distant day become the law for all unions." Yes, they anticipated "a minor rash of harassing suits, some covertly financed by antiunion employers and others promoted by genuinely dissident factions." Sure, this would "cost some unions legal fees, a little prestige, and minimal amounts of refunds." But "the Court's holding as it now stands will change nothing in the unions' way of life," labor experts contended. Nor was it likely that the Court would ever similarly interpret the NLRA to limit workers' obligation to support unions' political activities, leaving the vast majority of union shops untouched.[43]

Five months after *Street*, Alfred Haake died of a heart attack midway through a speech he was giving in Atlanta. Like DeMille, whose death also followed a major loss by the right-to-work movement, Haake traced his roots back to the nineteenth century. Their generation of activists had come of age during the freedom-of-contract era and struggled at midcentury to synthesize those commitments with the nation's strange brew of "new" liberal majoritarianism and "old" liberal individual rights.[44]

Haake and his allies had made tremendous progress, even if they did not recognize it. The 1950s are generally viewed as a decade in which labor and management reached a truce, or at worst a draw. The railroad cases demonstrated, however, that the work of activists like DeMille on popular perception and of right-to-work lawyers like Gibson on legal claims had forged a modern First Amendment challenge capable of commanding, at least behind closed doors, a majority of the Court. The railroad cases also showed the movement there was a way to build on the similarities between the liberal and conservative workplace Constitutions politically as well as legally. Right-to-work advocates increasingly urged it was the open shop, not union rights, that best protected black workers from discrimination.

In what direction would the next generation of right-to-work leaders take the movement? What mix of popular mobilization, state and federal legislative action, and litigation would it pursue? And how would the increasingly interconnected liberal and conservative workplace Constitutions affect each other?

PART III

ADMINISTERING THE LIBERAL
WORKPLACE CONSTITUTION
IN THE LONG 1960S

7

Agencies Recognize the Liberal Workplace Constitution in the New Frontier

"Stator v. Privatus"

Archibald Cox

Writing one's name can be the most mundane of acts, but for Ivory Davis, it was an act of resistance. It was 1962 and Davis was a leader in the all-black local of the Independent Metal Workers Union. For decades, Davis's employer, the Hughes Tool Company in Houston, had confined African American workers to the least-skilled, lowest-paying jobs. In the latest round of contract negotiations, Davis's local had refused to sign any contract "unless it provided equitable opportunity and job advancements for *all* employees." The company and the whites-only local instead renewed the existing racially stratified contract and, salting the wound, created six new apprenticeship positions for the higher-paying and still all-white tool and die department. When the company asked for applicants in February 1962, Ivory Davis signed up. His local insisted that its members deserved "to be treated like all other Americans" and should be "eligible to fill the [apprenticeship] jobs." The company did not award Davis an apprenticeship, however, citing the contract's terms, and the white local refused to help Davis challenge (or "grieve") the company's decision. Davis and his local took their protest to the National Labor Relations Board instead.[1]

By the time Davis's local filed its unfair labor practice charges in 1962, African Americans' freedom struggle was consuming the nation's attention. The 1960 decision by four black college students to ask for service at a Woolworth's lunch counter in Greensboro, North Carolina, had sparked a sit-in movement that rippled across the South and inspired mass actions on an unprecedented scale. Best known are the southern Freedom Rides, the rural Mississippi voter registration drives, and Martin Luther King Jr.'s marches down the streets of Birmingham, Alabama. Less well known are the protests by angry picketers in cities across the Rust Belt who demanded jobs for black construction workers, and the complaints black workers like Davis made to the NLRB in cities from San Francisco to the Southeast.[2]

The era's mass actions spurred debates over the state action doctrine's proper bounds, revealing key tensions within postwar liberalism regarding the proper balance between individual rights and majority rule, between equality and liberty, and between private rights and public duties in an era of big state, big business, and big labor. The NLRB's response to Davis's charges would turn on how these tensions were resolved, as well as on how the Board members viewed administrative agencies' obligations to the Constitution, Congress, and the Supreme Court.[3]

Union Democracy at the NLRB

"The discrimination, if any, by [the all-white Metal Workers] Local 1 against Davis was not based on Union considerations, but was at most racial discrimination," an NLRB investigator concluded. As a result, there was no basis for Board action. The head of the regional office agreed. In his view, neither the employer's failure to consider Davis for the apprenticeship nor the white local's failure to process his grievance was an unfair labor practice. Davis's charges seemed doomed to meet the same fate as those filed in the 1950s by the Gulf Coast oil workers.[4]

Davis and his local received a boost from an unlikely quarter, however. Since the 1940s, civil liberties–minded labor law scholars had warned about big labor's repressive potential. These scholars favored unions and the New Deal labor laws, but brought to them a concern for *union democracy*: protections for individuals and minority groups within unions similar to those the Constitution guaranteed for members of the polity. They argued that all workers should have a say in the governance of the union that represented them and be free to criticize or oppose union officials without facing reprisals. They were sympathetic to the union members DeMille's Foundation popularized: workers beaten up for refusing to strike or penalized for publicly opposing the union shop. These early union-democracy proponents favored deeming large corporations or unions state actors and subjecting them to court scrutiny.[5]

During the 1950s, labor pluralists took up and transformed the call for union democracy. The Supreme Court clarified that the duty of fair representation applied to matters other than racial discrimination, and Congress passed a union members' bill of rights, creating new legal remedies for undemocratic unions and bestowing new prominence on the issue. Leading labor law scholars now joined the call for union democracy. Yet they brought to this topic their labor-pluralist distrust of the state and their New Dealer preference for agency over court supervision. They argued that the NLRB was best suited to police union democracy. A Board member "is a specialist" with "a learned staff" that would be able to develop standards that "protect minorities without constricting normal negotiations." The Board was more flexible than courts since its precedents were "easier to distinguish and even to overrule." And the NLRB's general counsel prosecuted most charges, relieving injured workers of litigation costs. By 1962, when Davis's local filed its charges, scholars were arguing that the Board could issue unfair labor practice orders to remedy unions' racial discrimination. Unless the general counsel, who was the gateway to such charges, was willing to test these ideas, however, they would go nowhere.[6]

In 1962, Stuart Rothman was three years into a hard-charging term as the general counsel for the NLRB. A Jewish Republican from St. Paul, Minnesota, Rothman was used to confounding expectations. He earned a reputation for being "all work and no play" because of the grueling schedule he kept as Labor Department solicitor under President Eisenhower. Rothman was associated with the labor-friendly wing of Eisenhower's administration, and his 1959 nomination to be the Board's general counsel was opposed by conservative Barry Goldwater. Owing to Rothman's "strong union sympathies," the right-to-work–allied *Los Angeles Times* predicted that he "might ruin the NLRB." Once in office, however, Rothman countered violence during

labor conflicts, targeted racketeers, sped up case processing, and implemented the union members' bill of rights. Even before Davis filed his
charges, Rothman had decided to test the scholars' proposals. All cases
that "bear on the duty of equal representation," he directed, were to be
forwarded to his office.[7]

Thanks to Rothman, Davis's charges were rescued from the dustbin
that had claimed the oil cases. "In accordance with SR-471" (bureaucratic shorthand for Rothman's directive), regional officials sent Davis's
charges to Washington. In August 1962, Rothman announced that he
would pursue Davis's case, noting that it would be a first "in the 27-year
history of the National Labor Relations Act." Davis had complained
about his *employer* as well as his union, but Rothman focused on one
issue only: the white union's "refusing to process, because of his race,
the grievance of a negro employee in the bargaining unit." Rothman
wanted the Board to "have the opportunity to decide whether such
conduct is an unfair labor practice and not merely a basis for revoking
the certification of such a union." But the case the Board heard would
not be so narrow.[8]

Labor and the NAACP's Workplace Constitution

In October 1962, the NAACP announced that it was launching a
"frontal attack on barriers to Negro employment and job promotion" by taking legal action "designed to halt racial discrimination"
by unions and employers. At the request of Davis's union, its NLRB
action would be part of what the NAACP called its "legal attack on
trade union bias." *Brown v. Board of Education* had been a significant
achievement, NAACP general counsel Robert Carter granted, but "the
right to equality in job opportunity is equally as basic, if not more so,
as the right to an unsegregated education." Carter planned to transform Davis's case into a more powerful vehicle for achieving this basic
right.[9]

The NAACP's newly contentious relationship with the labor movement created an opening for its legal attack. After the disappointments
of the 1950s and the mass actions of the early 1960s, the NAACP
began confronting labor more boldly. NAACP executive secretary
Roy Wilkins and AFL-CIO president George Meany argued publicly
over the exclusion of black workers from prominent federal building

projects in the nation's capital. Labor Secretary Herbert Hill chastised the AFL-CIO's Civil Rights Department. Its "major function is to create a 'liberal' public relations image," Hill charged, "rather than to attack the broad pattern of anti-Negro practices within affiliated unions." Hill even called for a congressional investigation into discrimination by the International Ladies' Garment Workers' Union, which many (including the union's leadership) thought of as a civil rights exemplar.[10]

Carter's amendments to the Davis case contributed to the NAACP's newly aggressive image and further strained its relationship with labor. Carter significantly broadened Davis's NLRB challenge. For instance, he asked the Board to decertify the Metal Workers altogether. In the past, the NAACP had disfavored such charges because, if successful, they would leave black workers with "no union ... and, therefore, no protection whatsoever against discrimination by the employer." But a more racially progressive union, the United Steelworkers, was eager to take over Davis's shop, so his case offered an opportunity to set Board precedent without risking worker representation. At the hearing, Carter surprised everyone by also proposing new grounds for the unfair labor practice charges: the union's negotiation and approval of discriminatory contracts. Only a union could be guilty of a failure to grieve, but both unions and employers engaged in collective bargaining. In the long term, Carter's end run could lay the groundwork for future unfair labor practice charges against employers.[11]

Carter's amendments infuriated the NAACP's labor allies. Walter Reuther's United Auto Workers had previously "t[aken] the NAACP to task" for not "condemning management and employers' organizations for continued discrimination at the hiring gates." And although labor law scholars welcomed NLRB remedies for union discrimination and undemocratic practices, labor leaders did not. The AFL-CIO's legal counsel warned that if the Board issued unfair labor practice orders for duty of fair representation violations, it would be "seriously adverse to labor." The Civil Rights Department's staff also worried that it "could present serious problems for the entire trade union movement" if the NLRB made good on its threats to decertify discriminatory unions. The NAACP's attacks, said one advocate, advanced the right-to-work cause. "Employers or anti-union elements" might "trump up charges of discrimination to remove ... union protection from its members." Meanwhile, a pro–right-to-work newspaper cited the NAACP's accusations as proof that labor unions were responsible for African Americans' economic woes.[12]

Carter also promoted controversial quota-like remedies. With African Americans making up only 20 percent of the bargaining unit, the members of Davis's local worried that an integrated union "could stifle the votes of the colored employees." Carter sought to protect his clients from this outcome. When the two locals discussed merging in an effort to settle the dispute, Carter demanded that the white local provide concrete "ways and means of assuring that the entrance of Negroes ... will be accompanied with their having a voice in the conduct and affairs of the Union." The white local ultimately agreed to amplify African Americans' voice by giving them half the seats on the important executive, negotiating, and grievance committees.[13]

This sort of race-conscious remedy was already a sore topic between the NAACP and labor leaders. The plantwide seniority the NAACP had promoted in the 1950s did not help new employees. Still at the end of the seniority line, when recently opened jobs dried up in the late 1950s, they were the first to be fired. Waiting lists for apprenticeships served a similar function. As the NAACP learned in the oil cases, integrated seniority and promotion did little good if black workers lacked the skills needed to qualify for jobs. By the 1960s, the NAACP argued that unions should "[undo] the effects of past discrimination" by awarding black workers "super seniority" dating back to the union's first discriminatory exclusion, or by setting aside their apprenticeship lists. These lists were integral to organized labor, however, constituting a quasi-property that members earned and, in the case of apprenticeships, could pass down to the next generations. Union leaders were willing to end racial exclusion and segregation, but not to alter these lists. Opposing super seniority, labor leaders asserted, was a "sound trade union position," as was protecting the "father-son method of selecting apprentices."[14]

Carter injected the Constitution into Davis's charges as well. Noting that the Metal Workers derived its exclusive bargaining rights from the NLRA, Carter argued that it "is thus bound by the Fifth Amendment not to violate the rights of Negro employees it represents." Carter also argued that the NLRB itself was "governed by the Constitution." Carter contended that "the Federal government and its agencies may not, either by action or inaction, foster or sanction unlawful conduct on the part of" exclusive bargaining representatives. Carter relied on the white-primary cases and more recent decisions finding the government responsible for discrimination by those it empowered or with whom it was "intertwine[d]." If the Board failed to decertify a discriminatory union, Carter insisted, it would "violate the Fifth Amendment."[15]

Circa 1962, introducing the liberal workplace Constitution was sure to raise the hackles of powerful labor pluralists. Arthur Goldberg, who maneuvered the CIO away from the workplace Constitution in the 1950s, was now President Kennedy's secretary of labor. A fellow pluralist, Archibald Cox, served as Kennedy's solicitor general. For them, the liberal workplace Constitution was still anathema. Cox had argued in 1957 that violating the duty of fair representation was an unfair labor practice, but he had studiously avoided the Constitution, arguing that the duty resulted exclusively from "fusing common law [agency principles] and legislation."[16]

Right-to-work litigation further complicated matters, highlighting the risks the workplace Constitution posed to labor. A 1961 article put the stakes most clearly. "Only a slight doctrinal extension from existing case law is needed ... to bring the Constitution to bear on union conduct," the labor law scholar conceded. But "extension of the governmental action doctrine to help" black workers excluded from membership, he cautioned, would make it "impossible to justify failure to extend it to the ... [right-to-work] problem." Much better to interpret the labor laws to bar racial discrimination, the scholar urged, and leave Congress to determine what (if any) protections dissenting union members deserved.[17]

Finding an Executive Branch Ally

While labor leaders debated the wisdom of Carter's amendments, Davis's charges were swept up into executive branch politics. As a senator, John F. Kennedy was better known for investigating corrupt unions than supporting civil rights. On assuming the presidency, however, Kennedy embraced "the constitutional obligation of the United States Government" to ensure civil rights and launched a "quiet, steady campaign for effective executive action." Thus far, the Justice Department's Civil Rights Division, the office charged with enforcing civil rights laws and advising the government about civil rights issues, had focused on schools, transportation, voting rights, and police brutality, not employment discrimination. But in February 1963, on the 100th anniversary of the Emancipation Proclamation, President Kennedy delivered a "Special Message to Congress on Civil Rights." His action plan for employment was to "direct the Department of Justice to ... urge the National Labor Relations Board to take appropriate action against racial discrimination in unions." NLRB action, the president predicted, would "make unnecessary the enactment of legislation."[18]

Davis was unlikely to become part of the president's campaign, however. An NLRB trial examiner released a dramatically timed decision in Davis's favor the same day that Kennedy delivered his message to Congress. That the trial examiner granted the unfair labor practice charge was unsurprising; the Board had recently issued such orders for a nonrace duty of fair representation violation. But the examiner amplified the case's significance. The general counsel had filed a charge under only one unfair labor practice provision and had targeted the union's failure to grieve. The trial examiner instead found that the failure to grieve violated all three possible unfair labor practice provisions and justified his findings in terms that could encompass Carter's additional allegations. The examiner also "incline[d] to the view that" the Board "cannot constitutionally accord certified status to a union which discriminates on racial grounds." However, he decertified the segregated union based instead on a duty of fair representation that he said was informed by *Brown* but emanated from the statute. Remarkably, he found the union's segregated membership, in addition to its racially segregated contracts, violated that duty. For the first time since Frank Bloom's 1945 *Larus & Brother, Co.* report, a federal judge (albeit, again, an administrative one) embraced African Americans' full and equal access to union membership – or, in the words of the *New York Times*, their "union rights" to voice and participation.[19]

Burke Marshall, the head of the Civil Rights Division, concluded that it would be unwise to intervene in Davis's case. "Our overall impression," the division reported, "is that the problem we are dealing with is extremely complex." Even the experts they consulted were not "able to offer any easy solutions." Participating in *Hughes Tool* would implicate "policy matters of vast importance" that the Justice Department was unprepared to parse, given that it was "so completely inexperienced in this area." If the department wanted to do something "dramatic and far reaching," division staff urged, the attorney general should petition the NLRB to issue rules denying unfair labor practice orders and certification to unions that violated the duty of fair representation. Agency rules were like statutes, allowing agencies to set policy that was prospective and binding on all parties. The Board had never issued rules, always setting policy case by case in adjudications like Davis's. But the Civil Rights Division thought rules had clear advantages. The public had a right to comment on proposed rules. Given the many groups that would participate, the process would "highlight the problems in this area," generate voluntary compliance, and "stimulate complaints," of which there was a "dearth."[20]

The White House agreed regarding *Hughes Tool* but wanted the Justice Department to participate in another NLRB action. In *Miranda Fuel*, a closely divided Board had issued an unfair labor practice order for a *non*-race duty of fair representation violation. Now the Board had asked a federal court to enforce its order. If the court "should agree with the dissent[ing Board members] ... it would have a substantially adverse effect upon the 8(b)(1)(a) [unfair labor practice] allegations in *Hughes Tool*," a White House aide warned. Marshall set his staff to researching the rulemaking option and preparing to participate in *Miranda Fuel*.[21]

Hughes Tool's all-white Metal Workers local would not let this sleeping dog lie, however. In April 1963, it appealed the trial examiner's decision in its case to the Board. According to the white local, the examiner's decertification recommendation was vindictive, his unfair labor practice recommendation lacked a statutory basis, and the constitutional antisegregation cases he cited were irrelevant, given that "there is no authority to find that internal union affairs are state action." The Civil Rights Division changed course. In May, the attorney general asked to participate in *Hughes Tool* because of its "widespread significance for the protection of Negro workers from racial discrimination by labor unions."[22]

The Justice Department's State Action Debates

"The Solicitor General's Office: Two Years of Obstructing Civil Rights Progress," Howard Glickstein titled an indignant memo. Glickstein joined the Civil Rights Division with more expertise in management-side labor law than civil rights. Although initially cautious about creatively using the Constitution to advance civil rights, Glickstein became one of the division's most ardent advocates. "Civil rights ... are problems of unprecedented magnitude and unprecedented action – and thinking – is required to deal with them," Glickstein insisted. "At best, it can be said that the Solicitor General's Office has not fully understood the significance of these problems," Glickstein charged. "At worst, their attitude has been one of indifference, if not hostility." Glickstein's jeremiad was the latest in a volley of memos between the Civil Rights Division and the Solicitor General's Office. The Justice Department's position in *Hughes Tool* would turn in part on which office formulated it.[23]

The core of their dispute was how broadly to argue state action. Debate centered on whether and how to invoke the Court's first sit-in decision, *Burton v. Wilmington Parking Authority*. The decision suggested that the Court was not averse to extending state action but was growing wary. *Burton* involved a restaurant located in a publicly owned building. The Court found that the public funding, upkeep, and benefits the city provided to or accrued from its lessee restaurant "indicate[d] that degree of state participation and involvement in discriminatory action which it was the design of the Fourteenth Amendment to condemn." The Court even held that the Parking Authority's failure to require its tenants to provide integrated services was unconstitutional. "By its inaction, the Authority, and through it the State, has ... place[d] its power, property and prestige behind the admitted discrimination." At the same time, the Court cautioned that it had "by no means declared ... universal truths" but merely found state action on the case's particular facts.[24]

Glickstein's boss, Burke Marshall, embraced broad readings of the Court's state action decisions. Marshall was not known for civil rights activism, having spent nearly a decade as an antitrust lawyer at a prominent Washington law firm. But as a liberal concerned that big business threatened the nation's constitutional and liberal democratic order, he was open to broad state action arguments. In a case challenging discrimination against black patients and medical providers, Marshall and Glickstein argued that the defendant nonprofit hospitals, which were publicly funded and regulated, were state actors. In support, they relied on *Burton*, likened the hospitals to certified unions, and treated

Steele as one of the decisions "in which ostensibly private actions have been found to have sufficient nexus with governmental action to justify use of the Constitution as an instrument of control." In the sit-in cases, Marshall urged the government to adopt the protesters' position that the state, by arresting and convicting them, engaged in *Shelley*-like unconstitutional enforcement of private discrimination.[25]

The Solicitor General's Office, in contrast, was cautious about such arguments. From the start, the office's lawyers warned that these broad state action arguments, if adopted by the Court, would "wipe out all meaningful distinctions between state action and private action." Were the Court to use even the narrowest of the broad theories, it would "affect our entire approach to government in this country," one lawyer warned. "A free pluralistic society has between the individual and his government numerous other groups such as clubs, unions, corporations, churches, and the like." Broad readings of *Shelley* and *Burton* would eliminate these mediating institutions and create "a statist, almost totalitarian, concept of the relationship between the individual and the state."[26]

These divisions within the Justice Department were attributable in part to the offices' respective roles. The Civil Rights Division was charged with enforcing the laws and advancing a particular issue. Glickstein argued that the Justice Department's primary duty was to the "nearly 19,000,000 Negro American citizens who every day suffer the indignities, the abuses and the unequal treatment that the sit-in cases represent." The solicitor general defended the government when agencies were sued or federal laws challenged. As a defendant, it need not "worry about whether [its position] would be the right decision for the Court to make." But the solicitor general also advised the Supreme Court as an amicus, earning him the moniker the "tenth justice." As one staff member put it in a note, the solicitor general was the "conscience of the Govt in the Sup Ct." When acting as amicus, the solicitor general had to "be very careful" not to put forth a theory that he thought "would be bad constitutional law for the Supreme Court to adopt." This was the role he had in the sit-in cases and it inclined lawyers in his office to narrow, incremental approaches.[27]

But who occupied the position of solicitor general was also key. Eisenhower's solicitor general, J. Lee Rankin, had overridden his staff's concerns and adopted the Civil Rights Division lawyers' broad state action arguments. Indeed, *Burton*'s broad reasoning and language followed closely from Rankin's briefs. The man Kennedy replaced him with in 1961, the committed labor pluralist Archibald Cox, opposed the liberal workplace Constitution. A Harvard labor law scholar, Cox harbored long-standing concerns about the rights of workers within unions, but he believed that, absent gross injustices, the government should confine itself to facilitating collective bargaining and ensuring workers' right to self-organization. He found arguments that government-empowered unions were state actors "highly dangerous." Cox recognized that there had "been few more stirring displays of idealism and quiet courage" than the sit-ins. But "the role of government has been steadily widening, ... blurring the distinctions between ... 'State action' ... and private decision-making." In the sit-in cases, "the pressure to expand the notion of State action is strong" but their resolution, Cox warned, "may have a profound effect in determining how far the decisions of large private groups who perform public, if not governmental, functions are to be subjected to constitutional review." It would be unwise, Cox urged, to constitutionalize labor unions' admissions decisions or impose "rigid ... employment policies o[n] the steel companies in Pittsburgh and the auto companies in Detroit."[28]

Cox's labor pluralism ultimately led him to take a narrow position in the sit-in cases. Nothing expresses his thought process as concretely as the Socratic dialogue he penned. Across nearly seventy pages, two characters, "Stator" and "Privatus," debated the "broad" arguments. Cox wrote the dialogue when a third round of sit-in cases increased the pressure to expand state action. Thus far he had filed only narrow arguments, but now none of them seemed available. The exchange was both heated and collegial (the characters shared three bourbons before the night was over). On paper, it seemed Stator had worn his opponent down, but Privatus ultimately won out: Cox filed yet another narrow brief.[29]

The Justice Department's position before the NLRB reflected its internal divisions over the state action doctrine. Cox could dictate the government's arguments before the courts, but before the Board he held less sway. Civil Rights Division head Burke Marshall's brief in *Hughes Tool* went far beyond the position Cox favored. But Cox, who drafted passages for the brief (but did not sign it), likely limited its scope. Marshall made no broad state action arguments. Contrary to his treatment of *Steele* elsewhere, he emphasized that "the duty of fair representation is the safety valve which has enabled the Supreme Court to *avoid* constitutional issues implicit in" exclusive representation.[30]

The NLRB was an independent agency, partially insulated from White House pressure. Receiving a Justice Department brief and being the subject of a presidential address was highly unusual. All eyes turned to the Board to see if its decision in Davis's case would prove "an important 'sleeper' in President Kennedy's civil rights program."[31]

The NLRB's Boss: Congress or the Constitution?

From 1949 until his 1961 appointment to the Board, Chairman Frank McCulloch had been a staffer for Senator Paul Douglas, a liberal Democrat from Illinois. During that period, McCulloch had tried to repeal parts of Taft-Hartley and worked on the union investigations leading to the 1959 Landrum-Griffin Act and its bill of rights for unions, but he was no labor law expert. He thought President Kennedy selected him for the job due to a "feeling that I had independence and perhaps a degree of integrity that they wanted." Exactly whom Board members were supposed to be independent from and to whom (or what) they owed a duty proved a contentious and determinative question as the Board considered *Hughes Tool*.[32]

For McCulloch, Congress and, to a lesser extent, the Court, were the Board's lodestars. In his view, nearly every argument the Justice Department made lacked merit. McCulloch would decertify the union for its discriminatory contracts and failure to grieve, but insisted that the Board could not reach the union's membership practices. It would be incongruous, McCulloch argued, "for the legislature to stress the fact that a union had complete power over its membership policies" in one provision, if it "meant at the same time that the union could be decertified by the Board for the same conduct." McCulloch also dismissed all the unfair labor practice charges as inconsistent with the statute, its history, and its interpretation by the Court.[33]

The Constitution could constrain Board policy but could not countermand the statute, McCulloch insisted. McCulloch accepted a sanctioning theory of state action and used it to determine NLRB policy. Ordinarily, once a union executed a collective bargaining agreement, the Board applied a "contract-bar rule" that disallowed rivals from petitioning to replace the union for one year. McCulloch had recently held that the NLRB could not grant this protection to union contracts that segregated black workers. "Governmental sanctioning of racially separate groupings [i]s inherently discriminatory," his Board explained, citing *Brown* and *Burton*. The NLRA allowed but did not dictate the contract-bar rule, and McCulloch felt free to modify it based on his understanding of the Board's constitutional duties, so long as the result did not contradict the NLRA. But McCulloch did not think *Brown* could trump Taft-Hartley's explicit exemption of union membership from one of its unfair labor practice provisions. Where the statute spoke, McCulloch instructed, the Board had to "assume [its] Constitutionality" and do "what Congress intended."[34]

President Kennedy's pathbreaking appointment of Howard Jenkins Jr. to the NLRB upended McCulloch's plans for *Hughes Tool*. Given current alignments on the Board, Jenkins would have the deciding vote. Jenkins was a liberal Republican who had taught labor law at Howard Law School during what he described as "the golden years of 1946–'56" when he and his colleagues were "intimately involved in all of the social engineering that was going on in the Supreme Court, having to do with race relations." Jenkins had since served a number of years in the Labor Department. The first African American member of the Board, Jenkins emphasized the connection between civil and labor rights at his swearing in, symbolically scheduled for the day after the massively attended August 1963 March on Washington for Jobs and Freedom. There were parallels, he urged, "between the protest picketing for civil rights and the picketing for job rights." Jenkins would seek "to translate the is" of labor policy on these intersecting issues "to the ought."[35]

Like McCulloch, Jenkins ignored most of the Justice Department's arguments, but he thought the Constitution, not Congress, controlled the question. "The race basis of ... membership" as well as the Metal Workers' other racially discriminatory practices "*per se* violate the Constitution," Jenkins insisted. "Every provision in the Act must be read to be consistent with the Constitution," he argued. Jenkins thought this justified issuing all three types of unfair labor practice orders. He also thought the Board should decertify the segregated locals. According to *Shelley*, "the Board is without power or authority ... to assist a union to function in violation of the Constitution," he explained, and under *Brown* "'separate but equal' union membership ... is inherently unequal." Congress's intent barely entered into the equation.³⁶

Jenkins thought the Constitution could also assuage the policy concerns that would be raised if the Board issued unfair labor practice orders for duty of fair representation violations. Labor liberals like Cox and McCulloch were especially worried about the implications of doing so in nonrace cases like *Miranda Fuel*. Jenkins acknowledged that expanding the Board's unfair labor practice authority might intrude "the Board's judgment into the legitimate judgment areas of the unions" and could "encourage much unjustified individual ... litigation from ... disgruntled employees." But the NLRB need not open the door as far as *Miranda Fuel* in order to decide cases like *Hughes Tool*, Jenkins contended. In race cases, "the Board is not called on to make any determination of unfairness or inequity in the union's action; that has already been done by the Constitution," he reassured.³⁷

Hammering out where the Board majority would fall between the polar-opposite views of McCulloch and Jenkins did not prove the highest hurdle to reaching a decision. Instead, events in Congress nearly derailed Davis's case.

Rejecting Broad State Action: Congress and the Executive Branch

In June 1963, on the same day that governor George Wallace defied a desegregation order by standing in the University of Alabama's door, President Kennedy declared that "this Nation, for all its hopes and all its boasts, will not be fully free until all its citizens are free." He ticked off the economic disadvantages African Americans faced – twice the rate of unemployment, one-third the chance of getting a white-collar job, one-seventh the chance of earning $10,000 a year. Yet his proposed legislation did not include fair-employment provisions, as he deemed them too politically explosive. His civil rights bill got entangled with *Hughes Tool* and the NLRB, nonetheless.³⁸

After liberal House Democrats added a fair-employment title to Kennedy's proposed bill, *Hughes Tool* ground to a halt. Jenkins circulated his views in November 1963 and the Board reached a decision in early 1964. By then, however, the Justice Department was getting cold feet. Marshall believed that "it would be better to have [fair employment] legislation than to have the NLRB do this." He was concerned that the Board's decision might thwart the passage of what is now known as Title VII. Southern Democrats in the Senate, where the civil rights bill faced its greatest challenges, argued that "if the NLRB already has that power – which its attorneys believe it has – why do we need an FEPC"? McCulloch, with Jenkins's blessing, decided to hold the decision until Title VII's fate was resolved.[39]

Meanwhile, debates over the bill's public accommodations provisions cast doubt on Jenkins's broad state action theories. President Kennedy's bill said the Fourteenth Amendment, in addition to the Commerce Clause, gave Congress authority to enact these provisions. Liberal Democrats in Congress added a Jenkins-like definition of state action, stating that the provisions would reach businesses where the state licensed (akin to certified) or sanctioned their discrimination. Attorney General Robert F. Kennedy urged Congress to reject this approach. "Passing and upholding a bill solely upon the licensing theory or some variation would have vast Constitutional implications," he counseled, as it would unwisely convert a range of traditionally private entities, from charitable organizations to licensed professionals, into state actors. Instead Congress should bar states only from actively supporting or enforcing discrimination. Soon the public accommodations provisions featured only a narrow definition of state action.[40]

Rejecting Broad State Action: The Supreme Court

Congress was not the only institution debating broad state action theories, however. While the NLRB waited for a politically opportune moment to issue *Hughes Tool*, the Supreme Court engaged in its most searing debates yet on the state action question. Angered by African Americans' persistent "street parades," in 1963, Justice Black snapped that "it was high-time the Court handed down a decision against the Negroes." Black sounded ever more like the southern patrician angry at African Americans for wanting more than paternalistic whites were ready to provide. Thus far the justices had managed to overcome their differences and reverse the sit-in protesters' convictions on narrow due process or state action grounds. But the remaining cases divided them bitterly.[41]

Justices Douglas and Black, who had been inseparable allies during the 1950s, now disagreed over the private right to discriminate. Justice Black was prepared to overrule *Shelley* to affirm the remaining cases. "Once the barrier of privacy is broken down," he warned, "there is no stopping." For Black, private property and the privacy of the home meant the difference between liberalism's freedom of association and Hitler's fascist regime. Justice Douglas was in "diametric opposition." Although he agreed that "a man's home is his castle," in Douglas's view restaurants were different. A state's license to a restaurant, Douglas insisted, no less than the lease at issue in *Burton*, transformed those restaurants into "an instrumentality of the State," prohibited from running "on the basis of *apartheid*."[42]

In early 1964 Black mustered a bare majority to affirm the trespass convictions and business owners' constitutional right to discriminate. Black was joined by Justices Clark, Stewart, and Harlan, and Justice Whittaker's recent replacement, Byron R. White, who had previously done civil rights work in Kennedy's Department of Justice. Extending *Shelley* to the present case would "severely handicap a State's efforts to maintain a peaceful and orderly society," Black warned. To endorse the licensing theory of state action, his draft opinion added, would "be completely to negate all our private ownership concepts and practices." The Court would not say "that the Constitution compels either a black man or a white man running his own private business to trade with anyone else against his will." Invoking a trope of anti–New Deal conservatism, Black insisted that "if free enterprise means anything, it means that." The remaining justices lined up behind the Court's newest justice, labor pluralist Arthur Goldberg, who had steered the CIO away from the workplace Constitution in the 1950s before serving as Kennedy's secretary of labor. Goldberg's fiery dissent advocated reversing the convictions on equal protection grounds and accused Justice Black of writing an "apologia" for segregationists.[43]

As the two sides dug in, Justice Brennan made a play to break Black's majority. Having stood thus far with the dissenting justices' broad state action theories, now Brennan insisted that "well-settled principles" required the Court to avoid the broad constitutional questions. Brennan's tactic seemed to work. Within a week, the chief justice and Justice Goldberg had joined his opinion. Then, in a major coup,

Brennan peeled Justice Tom Clark away from Black's majority, flipping the Court from affirming the convictions on the broadest grounds to reversing them on the narrowest.[44]

Or so it seemed. Justice Douglas was adamant that principle, not pragmatics, must govern. "Oh, shit!" the justice is said to have shouted when he learned of Clark's switch. Douglas urged his brethren that the Court was under no obligation to avoid the broad questions. It was ludicrous to protect associational freedoms or to ascribe such an individualized notion as "personal prejudices" to the modern chain restaurant, Douglas argued. He declared that he would not join any opinion that did not hold that the commercial sphere of the 1960s was public rather than private.[45]

Douglas set the whipsaw in action again, only to be thwarted, in Douglas's opinion, by Brennan's bruised ego. Clark was assigned the task of drafting the new majority's opinion. In a surprising move, he circulated an opinion that reversed the convictions on both a broad *Shelley*-like enforcement theory and a *Burton* significant-involvement approach. Clark thus became the fifth justice to declare himself ready to reverse the cases on broad equal-protection grounds. Justice Stewart fought back. Brennan would be a hypocrite if he joined Clark's opinion, he argued. If "well-settled principles" dictated avoiding the broad questions when the Court was about to affirm the convictions, should they not also do so now that a majority was prepared to reverse? According to Douglas, Stewart's comment "hit Brennan pretty deep." Brennan soon declared that his pragmatic strategy was a principled stance: it would be narrow grounds or no grounds.[46]

The justices realigned once again, this time around Brennan. Douglas still refused to join, but this did not defeat Brennan's majority now that he had Stewart. On June 22, 1964, the Court handed down its opinion in this pivotal round of the sit-in cases, reversing all the convictions on Brennan's narrow grounds. To those who counted the concurrences and dissents, it was clear that the Court was deeply riven over the state action doctrine. Chief Justice Warren, as well as Justices Douglas and Goldberg, stood ready to broaden state action's scope, while Justices Black, Harlan, and White opposed any expansion. But for the Board members sitting on their *Hughes Tool* decision, a more subtle feature might have stood out: no justice, not even Douglas, embraced anything close to Jenkins's sanctioning theory of state action.[47]

The NLRB's Distinctive Constitution

After the Court's decision came down, the Senate logjam on the Civil Rights Act broke. On July 2, 1964, the very day President Lyndon Johnson signed the act into law, the NLRB released Jenkins's opinion in *Hughes Tool*. It was a stunning victory. A three-member majority held that the white local's failure to grieve Davis's exclusion from the apprenticeship program was an unfair labor practice under all three provisions. The majority stated that it would now issue such orders against unions that negotiated discriminatory contracts as well. The Board also declared segregated membership grounds for decertification and probably unfair labor practice orders. The Board majority embraced Jenkins's sanctioning theory despite the doubt cast on it by the Court, the attorney general, and Congress. "Racial segregation in membership, when engaged in by such a[n exclusive] representative, cannot be countenanced by a Federal agency," the majority reasoned, nor, after *Brown* and *Shelley*, can the Board "validly render aid" to a discriminatory union.[48]

The NLRB's *Hughes Tool* ruling made the front page of the *New York Times*, a space it shared with the 1964 Civil Rights Act. The NAACP's Robert Carter "called the decision 'almost revolutionary.'" The NLRB ruling was "more sweeping" than the Civil Rights Act because it was "effective immediately, subject only to judicial review," the *Wall Street Journal* surmised. The Civil Rights Act's Title VII, the new employment law, would not go into effect for a year and, when it did, it would require the government first to seek voluntary compliance and then to exhaust state antidiscrimination machinery before the courts could intervene.[49]

The day after the Board issued its order, Jenkins traveled to Houston, home to the Hughes Tool Company, Ivory Davis, and the Metal Workers locals. There, he gave a speech likening *Hughes Tool* to *Brown v. Board of Education*. Meanwhile, Carter celebrated this "landmark decision in the field of labor law," and Roy Wilkins, the NAACP's executive secretary, hailed the decision as a "key advance." Carter urged all NAACP branches to broadcast this new "formidable weapon" with which "to eliminate employment discrimination." Carter's office stood ready to "spend a major part of [its] time in assisting employees who desire representation before the Board." Once there, Jenkins promised, the Board would strive to harmonize workers' civil and labor rights.[50]

Hughes Tool validated administrative agencies' central role in implementing a liberal workplace Constitution, inspiring regulators and advocates alike. In its wake, even as the court-enforced Title VII struggled to get off the ground, the workplace Constitution blossomed in the post–New Deal administrative state.

8

The Liberal Workplace Constitution
on the Air and over the Wires

"A constitutional requirement to serve the community"
Howard Glickstein

"The tide of black revolution has begun to beat against the television establishment," the industry magazine *Broadcasting* reported in the fall of 1969. During the 1960s, militant African American activists targeted the Federal Communications Commission, a staid and powerful regulatory agency not generally associated with the civil rights movement's nationalist turn. A new organization called Black Efforts for Soul in Television, or BEST, had recently petitioned the FCC, seeking to block a Washington, D.C., station from renewing its license to broadcast over the government-controlled airwaves. BEST's chairman announced the challenge wearing an African-style dashiki, short Afro, and the thick-rimmed glasses signifying the black radical intelligentsia. WMAL-TV was the "supreme racist" of Washington-area stations, BEST charged: the staff was mostly white, half its black employees worked in custodial positions, and its programming "misrepresented blacks and the idea of blackness in a derogatory and insulting manner." Television, one petitioner claimed, did not "portray blacks in a way that was meaningful either to the blacks themselves or the whites in the 'golden ghetto' of the suburbs."[1]

The liberal workplace Constitution was transformed following the National Labor Relations Board's 1964 *Hughes Tool* decision. *Hughes*

Tool and the legal theories on which it rested spread quickly among activists and government officials, eventually taking root at the FCC and facilitating BEST's petition. Meanwhile, Title VII of the 1964 Civil Rights Act, which had prohibited employment discrimination, both spurred the workplace Constitution along and complicated its path. Regulatory agencies now struggled not merely with the relationship between their statutes and the Constitution, but also with how Title VII should affect their calculations. As officials and activists sorted out these relationships, they expanded the liberal workplace Constitution's reach: They contended that it barred statistical underrepresentation like that at WMAL-TV. They also asserted that it was an essential component of the "public interest" that agencies like the FCC and their licensees were obligated to serve.

Liberals Embrace Diversity in Broadcasting

"News and entertainment media which cater to the diverse interests and tastes of [America's] many publics," intoned the *Washington Post* in 1970, can best foster "[p]luralism ..., the genius of American society." By then, pluralist theory, which had long held that the jostling of discrete interest groups would produce a well-functioning democracy, had taken some knocks. Intellectuals and activists contended that interest groups' influence in government was part of the problem, not the solution. As interest groups lost favor, however, liberal faith in a different sort of pluralism gained ground, the identity-group pluralism touted by the *Post*'s editors. During the 1960s, liberals tried to stimulate an FCC foray into civil rights policy by arguing that to ensure that television served the entire community, as the agency had held that its public interest duties required, the FCC needed to nurture identity-group pluralism.[2]

Identity-group pluralism was, in part, a response to the increased political turbulence and discord that arose in the years following *Hughes Tool*. Violent clashes between civil rights protesters and southern police forces continued to occur, none more salient than "Bloody Sunday," a particularly brutal confrontation that took place in 1965 outside Selma, Alabama. These were mirrored in 1966 by the vicious reaction of whites to Martin Luther King Jr. when he took his campaign north to Chicago. Urban riots from Los Angeles to Detroit grew out of simmering frustration with inner-city poverty, neglect, and repression, leaving in their wake burned-out blocks and a palpable sense of crisis. Young African Americans increasingly turned from the fight for integration to black nationalism, with its message of self-help and, in the case of the Black Panther Party, armed self-defense. Identity-group pluralism offered a way to integrate these separatist groups into the plural whole, stemming their radicalization and, it was hoped, quelling the violence.[3]

The liberal establishment quickly identified television as part of the problem. Sales of TV sets had exploded after World War II. By the late 1960s, a majority of American families reported adjusting their eating and sleeping habits to accommodate the nearly six hours a day they spent with their TVs on. This cultural transformation knew no color or class line: televisions were termed "the universal appliance in the ghetto" and were found in nearly 90 percent of African American households. Television had also facilitated the decade's upheavals. Protesters in the South used it to beam themselves into sympathetic living rooms in the North and West; news footage of the urban riots inspired empathy in some viewers and outrage in others. The bipartisan and widely regarded Kerner Commission, assembled by President Johnson and charged with diagnosing the riots' cause and cure, reported in 1968 that television "contributed to the black-white schism in this country" in more mundane ways, as well. In particular, by overlooking "the degradation, misery, and hopelessness of living in the ghetto," as well as "Negro culture, thought, or history," TV programming fed "Negro alienation and intensif[ied] white prejudices."[4]

Liberals hoped television could nonetheless help resolve the nation's racial conflict by promoting identity-group pluralism. Programming should "treat ordinary news about Negroes as news of other groups is now treated," the Kerner Commission urged, and "report the travail of our cities with compassion and in depth." Broadcasters also should "integrate Negroes into all aspects of televised presentations." Doing so would make "a contribution of inestimable importance to race relations in the United States," the commission contended.[5]

The FCC offered liberals a way to enlist television in their pluralist project. In the early 1960s, the United Church of Christ (UCC) had tried to stop the FCC from renewing the license of a Jackson, Mississippi, station. To fulfill its duty to regulate in the public interest, the FCC required stations to provide balanced programming about controversial issues. The UCC charged that because the station's programming leaned heavily toward white supremacism and was devoid of civil rights coverage, it failed to meet the needs of its African American viewers. The UCC acted at the intersection of the civil rights protest movement, which it supported financially, and a reenergized consumer rights movement that challenged agency capture by industry. In 1966, the federal courts took the FCC to task for rebuffing the UCC. "Responsible and representative groups" like the UCC had a right to participate in FCC proceedings, the court held. Eager to make use of this opening, the UCC trained community residents to monitor local programming for bias. A liberal think tank published a "virtual how-to manual" for challenging broadcasters' licenses. Groups like BEST cropped up in towns and cities across the country to challenge local stations' biased programming.[6]

Liberals wanted to use the FCC to change the racial makeup of those behind the TV cameras as well as in front of them. Proponents of identity-group pluralism assumed that diverse staffing was a necessary predicate and guarantee of diverse programming. One reason the "media report and write from the standpoint of a white man's world," the Kerner Commission contended, was the industry's "shockingly backward" employment record: fewer than 5 percent of news editors and fewer than 1 percent of all editorial and supervisory staff were African Americans, most of whom worked for the black press. To heal the racial divide, the Commission prescribed, broadcasters needed to "employ, promote and listen to Negro journalists" as well as "Negro editors, writers and commentators." But the FCC's existing policies addressed programming only, not broadcasters' employment practices.[7]

In April 1967, the UCC again led the way, petitioning the FCC for a rule requiring broadcasters to demonstrate annually that they did not discriminate in employment. Anyone could petition an agency for a rule, and the agency was required to solicit public comments on those it proposed. Rulemaking thus seemed to unlock businesses' hold on regulators and created avenues for new constituencies to assert themselves. Generally thought to be more fair and efficient than case-by-case adjudications, rulemaking was soon the favored policy tool of administrators and advocates. The UCC's petition argued that the FCC could fulfill its statutory duties only if it regulated the racial composition of broadcasters' workforce as well as their programming. The success of rulemaking petitions turned on the agency's interest in them, however, and it was by no means clear that the FCC would respond sympathetically.[8]

The FCC Weighs In

The FCC's new chairman, Rosel Hyde, "doesn't belong to the boat-rocking school of federal regulation," one commentator observed wryly. Hyde, who had been an FCC commissioner for twenty years when President Johnson elevated him to chairman in 1966, wielded considerable agenda-setting power. His "conservative, pro-broadcaster views" and belief that "the least regulation is the best regulation" were well established. As a Republican, Hyde might seem an unlikely choice for Johnson, but his extensive experience and reputedly "restraining hand" could steady the agency during the decade's upheavals. Besides, Johnson's family owned many television stations, which may have tempered his interest in aggressive broadcast regulation. Whatever the reasons for Hyde's appointment, however, it was inauspicious for the UCC's pathbreaking petition.[9]

The UCC faced institutional obstacles as well. The FCC began the 1960s plagued by scandals, from illicit pay-for-play deals to rigged game shows. President Kennedy's provocative chairman had declared television a "vast wasteland" in 1961 and roiled his fellow commissioners with internal reforms. Divisions over the emerging cable TV industry and regulation of programming content further mired the FCC in controversy. In the late 1960s, lawmakers debated abolishing the agency altogether. The FCC also had a reputation for tepid enforcement of its existing policies. Whether because it was "a captive of the very industry it is purportedly attempting to regulate," as one liberal commissioner charged, or was merely too understaffed to police its more than 7,000 radio and TV-station licenses, the FCC rarely investigated and almost never revoked a license.[10]

The FCC seemed particularly unlikely to deliver aggressive civil rights policy. After chastising the FCC for rejecting the UCC's intervention in the Mississippi TV-station case, the D.C. Circuit Court of Appeals remanded the issue to the agency. In 1967 an FCC hearing examiner found that the UCC had "woefully failed" to prove its allegations, offering evidence that was "so speculative and doubtful that it could not bear scrutiny." The next year, Chairman Hyde, writing for a five-member majority, adopted the hearing examiner's decision. Two dissenting commissioners charged that Hyde's decision, "obstruct[ed] ... the efforts of the American government to establish confidence among Negro and other citizens who have been victimized by discrimination." But they were a small minority on a seven-man commission.[11]

The FCC's order and proposed rulemaking, issued the next month in response to the UCC's petition, signaled a new direction for the agency. Broadcasters argued that Congress in Title VII delegated "regulatory power over civil rights" to a newly created agency, the Equal Employment Opportunity Commission (EEOC), not the FCC. The FCC disagreed. Before granting or renewing a broadcast license, the FCC noted, its governing statute required it to determine that the license would serve the "public interest, convenience, and necessity." This included "tak[ing] into account ... whether the applicant has violated ... [Title VII of] the Civil Rights Act or a pertinent State law in this field." The "national policy against discrimination in employment" was "particularly embodied" in Title VII but was not limited to that law's provisions, the agency continued. Thus, "even where no violation of a specific [antidiscrimination] statute is established or alleged," discrimination "allegations may raise serious public interest issues." Because broadcasters used publicly owned airwaves to provide a "service to the public which is based entirely on a Federal license under a public interest standard," the FCC could not license a broadcaster that was violating this broader national policy. Broadcasters were like government contractors, the FCC reasoned, and, like them, should be subject to fair employment requirements.[12]

What sparked the FCC's new approach? There were a number of likely causes. Hyde often described the FCC as "an arm of Congress," so its commissioners probably listened when a handful of congressmen urged the FCC to grant the petition. One of the representatives even served on the House Commerce Committee, among those with greatest influence over the agency. Even more consequential, at least by the FCC's own accounting, was the guidance and encouragement it received from the Department of Justice and the EEOC. The head of the

Civil Rights Division, Stephen J. Pollak, assured the FCC that Title VII did not "circumscribe the authority of Federal agencies ... to regulate employment practices." Given its backlog and lack of enforcement powers, the EEOC "welcome[d] the adoption of the proposed rule," as did the Justice Department, whose ability to enforce Title VII was "limited by the need to prove discrimination and obtain relief on a case-by-case basis."[13]

The workplace Constitution also may have influenced how the FCC understood its authority and duty. Arguments that equal protection compelled the FCC to regulate broadcasters' employment practices had percolated within the FCC since at least 1963. These arguments also cropped up in comments the agency received on the petition and were addressed in the Civil Rights Division's "especially" helpful opinion. The FCC's decision to append the division's opinion to its order, constitutional argument and all, quickly moved the workplace Constitution to the center of the rulemaking proceedings.[14]

Making a Constitutional Case in the Title VII Era

"The Commission is under a statutory duty, backed by ... Constitutional requirements, to ensure that the programming of licensees serves the needs of all portions of the community," Howard Glickstein insisted in a comment on the FCC's 1968 proposed rule. Glickstein, the ardent Civil Rights Division lawyer who promoted broad state action theories in the early 1960s, was now a top administrator at the United States Commission on Civil Rights. Glickstein's commission lacked enforcement powers but it held hearings, issued reports, and conducted intragovernmental advocacy. The FCC was inundated with arguments like Glickstein's. These comments and the constitutional claims already before the agency reflected the growing influence of *Hughes Tool* and the state action theories on which it rested. They also indicate how Title VII changed proponents' understanding of the workplace Constitution.[15]

Commentators argued that Title VII and the "national policy against discrimination" the FCC was obligated to enforce implemented the workplace Constitution. Pollak, of the Civil Rights Division, cited Title VII and President Johnson's government contract committee, the Office of Federal Contract Compliance (OFCC), as evidence of

a national policy against discrimination and asserted that all three
derived from the Constitution. An OFCC spokesman also cited "the
constitutional principle underlying" his office's charge and linked the
principle to "the clearly established Federal policy against discrimination in employment." These arguments squared with FCC attorneys'
1963 position that the "policy of the United States Government against
racial discrimination" derived from the Constitution.[16]

According to commentators, the Constitution also explained the
FCC's obligation to implement this national policy. The FCC's 1968
order claimed that its public interest duties required it to do more than
ensure compliance with existing fair-employment laws. In 1963, FCC
lawyers had used the Constitution to explain why. They insisted the
FCC could not find that broadcasters whose employment practices
violated equal protection satisfied the public interest. To avoid "sanctioning ... discriminatory practices," they argued, the FCC must also
bar employment discrimination by broadcasters. Pollak's 1968 opinion, as well as comments on the proposed rule by the NAACP's Robert
Carter, similarly invoked a sanctioning theory of state action to establish the FCC's duty. If the FCC failed to "enforce the Constitutional
requirement" of nondiscrimination, Glickstein concurred, it "would
be participating in [its licensees'] unconstitutional conduct." And as
the UCC insisted, "Conduct permitted by the Commission is" state
action.[17]

Broadcasters, not only the FCC, had constitutional obligations that
justified the UCC's proposed rule, commentators urged. FCC attorneys
had contended in 1963 that, because of their federal licenses, broadcasters must "be measured by the standards of the Constitution." The
Civil Rights Division's 1968 opinion likewise argued that broadcasters' use of the airwaves gave them "enough of a 'public' character" that
the FCC could require them "to follow the constitutionally grounded
obligation not to discriminate." Title VII's complaint-by-complaint
approach, the UCC contended, "reflect[s] a caution in the exertion
of Federal authority over purely private businesses which is unnecessary and inappropriate in dealing with Federal licensees." Glickstein
relied instead on a sweeping interpretation of *Burton*. According to
Burton, constitutional duties did not devolve on private actors "unless,
to some *significant* extent, the State ... has been found to have become
involved in it." But Glickstein argued that the Constitution applied "to

all private action that has a *substantial tinge* of governmental involvement." This tinge, Glickstein asserted, was measured by the government's contacts with the "private act of discrimination, or ... [with] the private actor." Anywhere a private entity served a public interest and a government body regulated its conduct, Glickstein assured, there were "sufficient [contacts] to render the Constitution ... applicable."[18]

Commentators argued that the Constitution demanded more proactive measures than in the past. NLRB and court actions relied on a complainant's stepping forward. Commentators contended that the Constitution required the FCC to do more. "Passive non-discrimination," the OFCC counseled, "does not fulfill the requirements of Federal law." Glickstein concurred: "Waiting for complainants is not an appropriate way ... to fulfill the Commission's statutory and Constitutional obligation."[19]

But what sort of active steps did employers or regulators need to take? During the 1960s, legislators, courts, and federal administrators embraced statistics as an effective way to diagnose discrimination in public schools and voter rolls. In 1966, the EEOC joined in, requiring companies with 100 or more full-time employees to file annual reports on their workforce demographics. Significant disparity between minority representation in the labor pool and in the firm, the EEOC argued, was presumptive, maybe even conclusive, evidence of discrimination. Courts and administrators also used statistics to remedy discrimination, setting numerical goals for integrating schools and voting rolls, while the OFCC's "Philadelphia Plan" required government contractors to hire minorities "in every trade [and] in every step of the construction" of government buildings.[20]

Commentators argued that the workplace Constitution placed similar demands on state actors. Virtually no radio stations and only 15 percent of television stations had enough employees to fall under the EEOC's reporting requirement. But commentators insisted that the Constitution extended further than Title VII's reach. The ACLU declared that "the full realization of the Constitutional freedom from discrimination requires that the FCC" compel all broadcasters to annually report on the "racial composition of their staffs and describe their plans for recruitment from minority groups." The FCC's 1968 order had declared that the racial proportionality of a broadcaster's workforce alone could not prove discrimination. Glickstein countered

that the FCC's constitutional obligations "extend far beyond the
simple duty not to discriminate imposed by Title VII." The FCC
instead had a constitutionally derived duty to require that licensees
utilize "representative numbers of ... minority groups at all levels of
employment."[21]

The FCC's Workplace Constitution

The FCC's "flaccid image has now changed," *Newsweek* magazine
reported in March 1969, thanks to "a [recent] handful of portentous
FCC decisions and proposals." Hyde, portrayed as a do-nothing who
doodled his way through commission hearings, had surprised everyone. He insisted that the FCC had "a certain responsibility" to ensure
that those it regulated fulfilled their "duty to the public," even though,
the "southern commissioners ... were very unhappy with" his position. In a series of orders between June 1969 and December 1971, the
FCC strengthened its equal employment policies and extended them
to common carriers (primarily telephone and telegraph providers).
Remarkably, the FCC did this despite President Nixon's election and
an influx of conservative Republican commissioners. The agency suggested that the workplace Constitution demanded no less.[22]

Political pressure on agencies to assume a constitutional mantle
had waned since the UCC filed its petition in 1967. Persistent urban
riots strengthened racially coded calls for "law and order." The war
in Vietnam consumed Johnson's White House and dominated student
protests. The civil rights movement also fragmented: Martin Luther
King Jr. emphasized a global struggle against economic oppression,
while the student groups that led the sit-ins embraced black nationalism. The 1968 assassinations of King and Robert Kennedy brutally
marked the end of a more hopeful era. Republican candidate Richard
Nixon secured a narrow win in the 1968 presidential election. His successful mix of free-enterprise conservatism and subtle race-baiting did
not bode well for an expanded workplace Constitution.[23]

Yet the FCC adopted more far-reaching, aggressive policies. It would
delay licenses, for example, if complaints demonstrated "a pattern of
substantial failure to accord equal employment opportunities." But it
agreed with commentators that outright "denial of a license may sometimes be so severe a remedy that it becomes useless" and so offered less

drastic responses as well. Commentators also convinced the commissioners that addressing individual complaints would not enable the FCC to "cope with general patterns of discrimination developed out of indifference as much as out of outright bias." Employment statistics, the FCC concluded, could usefully show "industry employment patterns and ... raise appropriate questions as to the[ir] causes." Accordingly, it required a far broader swath of broadcasters and common carriers than fell within the EEOC's requirements to report their employment demographics. All regulatees also had to adopt and periodically assess "affirmative equal employment programs" that required "positive recruitment, training, job design, and other measures."[24]

The Constitution influenced the FCC's approach. The agency did not openly embrace broad state action theories, but the Fifth Amendment transformed the agency's statutory *can* into a constitutional *must*. In 1963, FCC attorneys recommended that the agency "avoid ... serious constitutional questions" by interpreting its public interest standard "to prohibit discrimination by licensees." In 1969, that is precisely what the FCC did. "A substantial case has been made," the FCC observed, "that because of the relationship of the Government ... to broadcast stations, the Commission has a constitutional duty to assure equal employment opportunity." But the FCC found that "its independent responsibility to effectuate" the national policy against discrimination let it avoid the issue. The agency nonetheless justified its rules in state action terms, contending that it would be "intolerable [for the FCC] to countenance discriminatory employment practices" by common carriers. Government lawyers had previously argued that businesses with a government-granted monopoly were state actors. The FCC made a similar claim: common carriers' "monopoly or semimonopoly positions" gave them "a unique and peculiar public interest role," even if the Communications Act did not expressly impose one.[25]

Remarkably, these equal employment rules received stable bipartisan support among the FCC commissioners. Hyde and another antiregulatory Republican joined three liberal commissioners in favor of the first order. Robert T. Bartley, a Texas Democrat, dissented, along with a Republican Eisenhower appointee. Surprisingly, the commissioners continued to issue equal employment rules even after the majority's Republicans were replaced by Sun Belt conservatives. Dean Burch, Nixon's pick to replace Hyde as chairman, was an Arizona attorney and protégé of Barry Goldwater who was known as "one of the Republican Party's most loyal workers." At Burch's Senate confirmation hearings, a representative of BEST, the group formed to challenge discrimination in broadcasting, called Burch a "rich, white racist" who would make the FCC "more antithetical to black progress and more opposed to integrated programming." Burch, however, surprised his opponents once he assumed office. Without him, the FCC would have lost a majority for anything beyond its initial, complaint-only approach.[26]

Burch's conservatism most likely explained his stance. A self-proclaimed "free enterprise advocate," Burch was a foe of the liberal and moderate Republicans who had driven his party's support for the 1960s civil rights statutes. Granted, he served a president who had endorsed and promised to enforce the new civil rights laws during his campaign. As president, Nixon also supported the OFCC's enhanced Philadelphia Plan, which required government contractors to set minority hiring goals and timelines for achieving them. But Burch disclaimed any White House influence. His position resonated, however, with those taken by his longtime mentor Barry Goldwater.[27]

Goldwater supported antidiscrimination laws only insofar as they furthered his right-to-work ends. In the early 1960s, Goldwater led a conservative insurgency in the Republican Party, running as its presidential candidate in 1964. He had previously supported two weak civil rights statutes but offered poison pills to federal fair employment bills. During his presidential campaign, he opposed Republican strategists who wanted to expand the party by recruiting African Americans rather than southern whites. Still a senator during his campaign, he also cast a dramatic vote against the 1964 Civil Rights Act. Goldwater insisted he was "unalterably opposed to discrimination or segregation on the basis of race, color, or creed." He nonetheless objected to Title VII because it "would embark the Federal Government on a regulatory course of action with regard to private enterprise" for which there was "no constitutional basis." Yet Goldwater took an entirely different approach to antidiscrimination laws that targeted unions only. He praised *Hughes Tool* on the Senate floor and sought to codify its ruling in the National Labor Relations Act. He justified his divergent approach on constitutional grounds: "The right of exclusive representation" was a "special privilege ... enjoyed by no other element in our society," he argued. "In granting unions this right," he contended, "the Federal Government ... bestowed upon them the power of government itself." But Goldwater had long used support for NLRB antidiscrimination powers to advance the right to work, even as his movement allies increasingly highlighted union discrimination to the same end.[28]

Burch likely supported the FCC's equal employment policies for similar reasons. Burch served as Goldwater's close aide in the 1950s and became known as "Goldwater's grassroots man" during the 1964 campaign. After Johnson trounced Goldwater in the election, Burch remained a member of Goldwater's "Arizona Mafia," a main artery of the Sun Belt's free market and right-to-work politics. Although the impact of the FCC rules on unions was less direct than Goldwater's favored NLRB policies, labor leaders viewed them with similar concern. Labor had long opposed antidiscrimination measures that bypassed union seniority or apprenticeship waiting lists and decried Nixon's use of goals and timetables as antiunion. His enhanced Philadelphia Plan, a black labor advocate charged, was "part and parcel of a general Republican attack on labor." When the unions that would be affected by the FCC's proposed rules joined employer groups in arguing that the rules would adversely insert the agency into labor-management relations, concerns about seniority lists lay just below the surface. In rejecting their concerns, Burch's commission put the onus for discrimination on unions. "The fact that ... [discriminatory employment practices] may exist in some unions, with management acquiescence," it tartly noted, "does not justify our disregard of such improper practices."[29]

Enforcing the FCC's Rules

"The FCC is constitutionally prohibited from conferring public benefits ... upon a company which maintains blatantly discriminatory employment practices," the NAACP charged. The NAACP's 1971 petition was one of hundreds that the FCC received after issuing its rules. Most accused broadcasters of failing to hire enough minorities. But the FCC's late addition of sex discrimination to the hiring practices the agency would scrutinize opened the agency to additional claimants. The NAACP's challenge, for instance, was joined by the National Organization for Women (NOW). In resolving these complaints, the

FCC relied on statistics to identify discrimination, despite having previously disavowed this approach, and imposed de facto numerical goals on its regulatees. As a result, during the 1970s, the workplace Constitution, as implemented by the FCC, demanded the most controversial affirmative action practices, was on the cutting edge of sex discrimination remedies, and dramatically changed the broadcast and common carrier industries.[30]

The FCC's broadcast rules were met by an outpouring of advocacy from the grassroots to the grasstops. BEST trained citizen groups in major U.S. cities to monitor local stations and file petitions like its challenge to the Washington, D.C., station's license. The UCC, flush with Ford Foundation funds, set up similar groups in the South and teamed up with the NAACP Legal Defense Fund to "break ... down barriers to fair employment in ... local radio and television stations." The rules had an impact on groups other than African Americans. The Mexican-American Legal Defense and Education Fund planned an ambitious challenge to employment discrimination by the major TV networks. NOW and groups such as the Japanese American Citizens League, the Oakland Chinese Community Council, and Spanish-Surnamed, Inc., challenged everything from local stations to an entire state's broadcasters.[31]

The FCC wrought remarkable changes, including in businesses too small to fall under Title VII. By 1975, the agency had reviewed more than 1,000 stations, had conditioned the renewal of more than 150 stations' licenses on strengthened affirmative action policies, and had even denied renewal altogether for some. Focusing only on formal FCC action understates the rules' impact, however. The FCC often took several years to decide petitions and considered changes made *after* challenges were filed. During this time many stations added enough women and minorities to avoid further action. WMAL-TV in Washington hired nearly half again as many African Americans after BEST's petition; African Americans made up 20 percent of post-petition hires by Columbus, Ohio, stations. In the three years that a San Francisco CBS affiliate remained under examination, minority employees increased from 10.9 percent to 18.3 percent of its workforce. The FCC also required more than improved *overall* numbers. Stations in Massachusetts and in Richmond, Virginia, received further scrutiny because minorities and women were underrepresented in the four highest job categories. Even the threat of FCC action brought changes. A San Diego station more than doubled its "Spanish-surnamed employees" after the FCC rules were adopted but before any petition was filed.[32]

The FCC did not accept lack of applicants as an excuse. "The affirmative action concept is meaningless unless positive action is undertaken to overcome the effects of past discrimination, however inadvertent," the FCC instructed. In response, stations formed "Broadcast Skills Banks" that claimed to have "doubl[ed] the employment of black people in the Columbus broadcast industry" alone. Others, including the San Francisco CBS affiliate, added internal recruitment, training, and promotion pipelines.[33]

The FCC's common carrier rules allowed for a nationwide attack on the country's largest corporation. American Telephone & Telegraph (AT&T) had the most assets and employees; as of the late 1950s, if it had been a state it would have been the thirteenth largest in the nation. A conglomeration of local monopolies, AT&T had thus far been impervious to fair employment efforts.[34]

Almost everything about the FCC's 1970 action against AT&T was unprecedented. For starters, it was initiated by the EEOC, which hoped to harness the agency clout and administrative enforcement powers it lacked. EEOC chairman William H. Brown III, a Republican and former litigator at an all-black Philadelphia law firm, took the unusual step of recruiting a former EEOC lawyer to organize similar challenges by civil rights groups in case the FCC rejected the EEOC's petition. Initially begun as a challenge to AT&T's request for a rate increase, the FCC treated the action as the maiden petition under its common-carrier equal employment rules. In December 1971, the EEOC submitted a 20,000-page report replete with statistical analyses supporting its claim that "AT&T's operating companies have historically excluded and segregated and continue to exclude and segregate women, blacks and Spanish-surnamed Americans." The next summer, the FCC held eye-catching public hearings in New York and Los Angeles featuring Spanish-speaking customers complaining about English-only operators and AT&T employees accusing their employer of being a "racist monopoly."[35]

Most extraordinary was the settlement the EEOC reached with AT&T in January 1973. Brown justifiably called it "the most

significant legal settlement in the civil rights employment history."
Some provisions were familiar. The agreement set hiring goals and
timetables for their fulfillment. Mirroring Title VII remedies, it opened
management training to women and made the qualifications for jobs
that had traditionally been held almost exclusively by white men more
job-related and less exclusionary. The agreement's fifty-million-dollar
payout, however, was pathbreaking, providing the largest ever back-
pay award, unprecedented restitution for employees who would have
been promoted sooner or earned more, absent company discrimination, and incentive payments to workers, male and female, to move
into nontraditional jobs.³⁶

The FCC action changed businesses other than AT&T. The EEOC's
"comparatively low profile ... was strikingly altered" by the settlement. The case also attracted the attention of the business community. Equal employment consulting firms multiplied, serving worried
employers looking for advice. They had reason to be concerned. "After
the A.T.&T. settlement, it's clear that a number of employers are going
to be held responsible for past actions – and it's going to cost them a
lot of money," one article predicted. "There is a lot of teeth-chattering
going on around here," a vice president of a large retail chain observed.
In March 1972, Congress gave the EEOC the authority to bring lawsuits challenging a private employer's "pattern or practice" of discrimination. During the summer of 1973, the EEOC filed 150 cases against
major corporations and assembled a national team of lawyers to "do
the same thing as AT&T [*sic*] all over again," only this time in the
courts.³⁷

The FCC actions against broadcasters and common carriers transformed the workplace Constitution even as they were informed by it.
Most notably, the workplace Constitution expanded to encompass
sex discrimination. Earlier actions had occasionally involved women,
but race rather than gender was the focus. After World War II, women
in the civil rights and labor movements pressed for sex equality as
well as racial equality but made little headway. In the 1960s their
efforts were buoyed by a new generation of "second-wave feminists"
who set their sights on combating what legal scholar Pauli Murray
termed "Jane Crow." During the early 1970s, marchers across the
country advanced constitutional claims in a Women's Strike for
Equality, Congress debated bills that advanced women's rights in the

name of the Constitution, and legal strategists sought constitutional test cases.[38]

The FCC actions inserted the workplace Constitution into the fight for sex equality. The multiple broadcasting petitions filed by NOW, the preeminent feminist advocacy group, were implicitly linked to the Constitution. The AT&T action made the connection explicit. Thanks to the efforts of a young feminist staff lawyer, the EEOC's AT&T brief connected Title VII's prohibition on sex discrimination to the Constitution. The EEOC argued that AT&T's sex discrimination, no less than its race discrimination, violated the company's and the FCC's constitutional duties. At a time when the Supreme Court had yet to strike down an instance of sex discrimination and still considered sex a reasonable basis for different treatment, the EEOC's brief was pioneering. When paired with the settlement's challenge to gender norms in the workplace, the brief presaged feminist litigators' subsequent use of the Constitution to break down sex stereotypes as well.[39]

The FCC's equal employment actions also cemented the connection between the workplace Constitution and affirmative action, particularly in the form of numerical goals. In the early 1970s, the meaning of affirmative action was unclear. The term had been in the federal employment policy lexicon at least since President Kennedy used it in his 1961 Executive Order on fair employment. Some, including employers eager to preserve control of hiring and unions concerned with protecting seniority, contended that it should require no more than recruiting and training underrepresented workers. Others, including Howard Glickstein, argued that employers should be required to achieve statistically proportional workforces. The FCC started out in the former camp. In cases like WMAL-TV, where African Americans made up less than 1 percent of the workforce even after improvements, the FCC insisted that this disproportionately low representation alone would not trigger further scrutiny. Over time, however, the agency relied increasingly on comparing a station's workforce demographics with those of the local labor market. If the differences fell outside what the FCC termed a "zone of reasonableness," the agency would require the broadcaster to "locate and encourage the candidacy of qualified protected persons," or even to set goals and timetables. The zone of reasonableness was broad – a minority hiring rate of 15 percent in a labor market that was 25 percent minorities was acceptable – but the very existence of the zone imposed a de facto goal as broadcasters eager to gain or keep licenses strove to fall safely within it.[40]

The Affirmative Action Debates

As agencies implemented the workplace Constitution with growing breadth and vigor, however, labor unions started to challenge the liberality of these efforts. Labor leaders had long worried that hiring goals, let alone quotas, harmfully pitted white and black workers against each other. It was "unrealistic to expect a white skilled worker to surrender his job because a black man needs it," the AFL-CIO insisted, especially because "white workers ... were not directly responsible for the discrimination against Negroes." Guaranteeing jobs for all, not quotas, was the labor movement's answer to African Americans' limited job opportunities. The AT&T action brought simmering debates over "hard" affirmative action remedies like hiring goals to the workplace Constitution, as civil rights advocates insisted that such remedies vindicated equal protection while labor advocates argued that they violated it.[41]

The liberal coalition carefully avoided open disagreement over the affirmative action issue until the summer of 1972, when the fissure cracked wide. A number of the country's most prominent liberal Jewish organizations, including longtime supporters of workplace civil rights, spoke against the type of remedies subsequently adopted in the AT&T settlement. "The concept of group rights [on which proportional representation relies] is totally alien to our constitutional system," the head of the American Jewish Committee declared. Critics insisted that they supported affirmative action and equal opportunity but saw hiring quotas as reverse discrimination (or "Crow Jimism," as one commentator put it). In response, the NAACP considered censuring its longtime allies. Striking a more conciliatory note, the head of the Urban League lamented that the "real obscenity here is that groups have been set squabbling amongst each other for the scraps from the table of the affluent society." With unemployment rising and the economy stalling, however, the supply of scraps was dwindling and the squabble escalated.[42]

The relationship between hiring goals, like those found in the FCC actions, and quotas was contested. Nixon's administration, including the FCC, rejected quotas but accepted goals. The Civil Service

Commission, which oversaw government hiring, defined a goal as a "realistic objective which an agency endeavors to achieve on a timely basis within the context of the merit system of employment." Goals should be "reasonable and flexible," crafted so that "they will probably be met," but open to revision if they were not. Quotas, in contrast, "restrict employment ... opportunities to members of particular groups by establishing a required number or proportionate representation" that must be "attain[ed] without regard to merit." To opponents of quotas, this definition drew a distinction without a difference. They thought that goals often functioned as "de facto quotas," as happened under the FCC's broadcasting rules. Even more fundamentally, however, many critics opposed *any* departure from meritocratic hiring. From this baseline, goals that "will probably be met" were no better than quotas that "managers are obligated to attain."[43]

The AT&T settlement's goals and timetables were ensnared in these conflicts. A 1973 *Fortune* article titled "How 'Equal Opportunity' Turned into Employment Quotas" used the case to critique preferential hiring generally. An artistic yet stereotyped graphic set up the problem: bland, anxious white men watched their share of the workforce steadily erode as they were joined by equally grim-faced Asian women, almost smiling black men, and swarthy Latinos. The article recognized the limited opportunities many African Americans faced but concluded that remedies like those adopted at AT&T amounted to reverse discrimination. They not only hurt white men but also "undermined ... old-fashioned notions about hiring on the basis of merit" and "denie[d] minority-group members who have made it on their own the satisfaction of knowing that."[44]

AT&T's unions agreed. Immediately after a court approved the settlement, AT&T's unions sued to stop it from taking effect. They were not opposed to antidiscrimination efforts; indeed, one of the unions had recently accused AT&T of discriminating against its pregnant workers. They were, however, opposed to affirmative action policies that circumvented the seniority provisions in their collective bargaining agreements. The unions claimed that the settlement's seniority override violated the Fifth Amendment because it "confer[red] a preference on individuals that is based on their race, sex, or national origin."[45]

The courts easily dismissed the unions' claims. In 1976, a federal district court upheld the settlement's preferences, finding that they were constitutional because they were conferred to *remedy* a history of discrimination. The court further rejected the argument that, even if remedial preferences were generally constitutional, those that "incorporate numerical ratios" were not. The court of appeals quickly affirmed. The appeals court found, however, that preferential remedies were not categorically constitutional and "must be held invalid under the ... Fifth Amendment unless it can be shown that the interest in making the classification is ... substantial." Additionally, "the use of the classification must be necessary" to safeguard that interest. In the appeals court's judgment, the AT&T seniority override met this test.[46]

During the first four years the FCC's rules were in effect, women's share of the broadcasting workforce rose from 23 to 26 percent and the percentage of minorities climbed from 9 to 13 percent. The FCC's rules also ushered in the industrywide approach George Weaver first called for in the 1950s. The EEOC's action against AT&T accomplished in one stroke what had required hundreds of individual complaints under Title VII. After AT&T, the government negotiated a sweeping consent decree with the steel industry under Title VII. Even then, the AT&T settlement remained "the largest court-ordered settlement made in an employment discrimination case."[47]

Yet the FCC actions also raised new doubts about the workplace Constitution's liberal potential. Most obviously, they aggravated the disfavor in which labor leaders held it. The appellate court decision upholding the AT&T settlement signaled a different way in which affirmative action could erode liberal support for the workplace Constitution: "The use of employment goals and quotas," the court warned, "involves tensions ... inherent in the due process clause of the Fifth Amendment." In the future, when the pattern of discrimination was neither as "particular" nor "identifiable" as it was at AT&T, courts could hold that cherished affirmative action remedies violated rather than vindicated the Constitution. Then civil rights advocates' support might evaporate, at least for court-based claims to a workplace Constitution. How would the NLRB's members, the first administrators to adopt the workplace Constitution, wend their way through its promises and perils?[48]

9

The NLRB Expands the Liberal
Workplace Constitution

"To fulfill the constitutional guarantees against racial discrimination"
Howard Jenkins

On May 24, 1968, NLRB member Howard Jenkins strolled with
President Lyndon Johnson through the White House Rose Garden.
A personal meeting with the president was a rare honor. Decades later,
Jenkins recalled the president's praise for Jenkins's 1964 *Hughes Tool*
opinion, issued on the same day Johnson signed the Civil Rights Act into
law. *Hughes Tool* decertified a racially segregated union and, for the
first time, found discrimination to be an unfair labor practice. Equally
important, Jenkins had argued that the Constitution required this outcome. As they walked among the spring blooms, Jenkins assured the
president that "if the Board had faced up [earlier] to its obligation to
properly interpret the Constitution" and the National Labor Relations
Act, Title VII of the Civil Rights Act would have been unnecessary. In
Jenkins's opinion, the NLRA held even more promise than Title VII,
although he did not share this with the president.[1]

Commentators agreed with Jenkins that the NLRB might be superior to Title VII. One author lauded the board's well-established administrative machinery, experienced staff, and swifter, more economical
approach. The Board had "sharper enforcement teeth than Congress
has provided minority workers in recent civil-rights legislation,"
another observed. The NLRB's general counsel provided free legal

services and the Board, unlike the Equal Employment Opportunity Commission, held public hearings, all of which could draw complaints away from the EEOC, he predicted. Indeed, African Americans were reportedly "claim[ing that] their demands for equal job opportunities have been frustrated under both the law [Title VII] and agency [EEOC] specifically created by Congress to deal with race bias." One government official even predicted that the Board "could put the [EEOC] ... out of business."[2]

To Jenkins and his fellow Board members, *Hughes Tool* only began to fulfill the NLRB's statutory and constitutional duties. In the following decade, the Board broadened steadily the scope of its antidiscrimination policies. The NLRB's embrace of the workplace Constitution raised as many questions as it answered, however. After *Hughes Tool*, its members struggled over the parameters of the Board's statutory and constitutional obligations, how to resolve tensions between them, and how they were affected by Title VII.

Race, Labor, and the Republican Party

Labor relations was "not a battle to be won," Edward Miller liked to say, "but a problem to be solved." His advice for keeping unions out? Be a good boss. President Richard Nixon appointed Miller as Board chairman in 1970. A longtime management-side attorney from Chicago, Miller's candidacy was a compromise between the Republican Party's warring conservative and liberal wings. He had a reputation as a "soft-spoken, dispassionate" attorney who was "fair-minded, trustworthy and understanding of labor's position." Labor opposed him, but only perfunctorily. The real losers were business groups and right-to-work advocates who had hoped for a more like-minded chairman.[3]

During the 1960s, the right-to-work cause became more mainstream within the Republican Party. In the 1950s, southern Democrats and conservative Republicans from right-to-work states had led the charge in Congress. In the 1960s, the dynamics shifted: conservatism itself became more influential, as reflected in Goldwater's 1964 presidential candidacy, tugging the party to the right. Right-to-work supporters who defied easy categorization also rose to prominence. Senator Everett Dirksen, for example, was from Illinois, which, while not a right-to-work state, was home to some movement power brokers. Dirksen recruited Goldwater to run for the Senate in 1951 and supported a federal right-to-work law later in the decade. Dirksen's 1959 elevation to the powerful position of Senate minority leader gave the issue new legitimacy. During the 1960s, he cut the deals that won Republican support for the decade's civil rights laws, further tempering the right-to-work movement's far-right image. At the same time, moderates such as Michigan's Robert Griffin joined the fight. By the 1968 elections, the issue had won sufficient support that Republicans in Congress attacked the NLRB for its prolabor bias, and party leaders planned to rewrite the NLRA if they won control of Congress.[4]

The NLRB's race policies were entwined with right-to-work advocates' attacks on the Board and on union power. Between 1965 and 1971, Colorado's junior senator, Peter Dominick, repeatedly introduced legislation titled a "Laboring Man's Bill of Rights." This slate of NLRA amendments mixed right-to-work protections, such as barring unions' use of dues for political purposes, with Board penalties for racially discriminatory unions. Griffin as well as the mainstream Republican Policy Committee also proposed curing the Board's "pro-union, anti-employee and anti-management bias" with a blend of right-to-work and union discrimination amendments. Even the Harlem Democrat Adam Clayton Powell linked the right to work, NLRB policy, and union discrimination. In 1965, labor backed a bill repealing the Taft-Hartley provision allowing state right-to-work laws. Powell refused to move it through his committee until "leaders in labor do more about discrimination in some unions." He even threatened to hold hearings in right-to-work states to publicize his argument that the repeal could hurt black workers by enhancing discriminatory unions' control.[5]

These strategies fit well with Republicans' broader use of fair employment to target unions. Some pioneering businessmen had employed this strategy since at least the 1920s. By the 1960s, opposing employment discrimination was a mainstream business position. So was blaming such discrimination on unions. The Republican Party adopted this tactic. The party's platforms recognized, in more or less fulsome terms, the legitimacy of the post–New Deal collective bargaining regime. But fair employment, or equal opportunity, as it became known in the 1960s, provided a seemingly moderate, even liberal way to critique organized labor. During the 1960 presidential campaign, Republicans proposed federal legislation barring discrimination by unions only. In

1965, after the enactment of Title VII's ban on employer *and* union discrimination, the mainstream Republican Policy Committee maintained that union discrimination was the bigger problem. This position was amplified in the media campaign that accompanied Republicans' 1968 attack on the NLRB. For instance, a bluntly titled article in *Fortune*, "The Case against the Unions," placed primary blame for workplace discrimination on unions.[6]

At first Nixon made this politics his own. During his 1968 campaign, he named well-known antiunion employers from right-to-work states as his economic advisers and announced that it was time to "completely reappraise" the Board's administration of Taft-Hartley. In 1969, he defended the controversial Philadelphia Plan, which required government contractors to adopt goals and timetables for minority hiring, despite stiff union opposition. He also dropped plans to make Howard Jenkins the NLRB chairman. One Republican supporter had praised Jenkins's race decisions because they had "driven the CIO crazy" by exposing unions' "fake civil rights position." But Nixon changed his mind under pressure from right-to-work supporters and business groups who had labeled Jenkins a "liberal ... bearing labor's stamp of approval."[7]

After 1969, however, Nixon switched course. In 1964 and 1968, Alabama governor George Wallace, a populist and staunch segregationist, had garnered support for his quixotic presidential runs not only in the South but also among northern and midwestern working-class white ethnics, who responded to his antielitism as much as his race-baiting. Nixon had barely won the 1968 election and was already eying warily his reelection campaign. In 1969, an adviser predicted that a more secure "emerging Republican majority" could be cobbled together out of Wallace's traditionally Democratic constituency; Nixon was sold. Over the next two years, he set about "build[ing] our own new coalition based on Silent Majority, blue-collar Catholics, Poles, Italians, Irish." Despite advice to the contrary, he did not follow the right-to-work playbook, which would have had him insert the Republican Party between working-class voters and organized labor. Instead, he courted union leaders. Nixon distanced himself from the Philadelphia Plan and declared that there would be "no more rhetoric from the Administration [that] contained any kind of anti-union implications." The party platform for his 1972 reelection "strong[ly] endorse[d] Organized Labor's key role in our national life." Nixon's strategy also brought the moderate Miller to the Board's helm.[8]

The Workplace Constitution Unites *and* Divides the NLRB

To Miller it was "plain as a pikestaff" that the duty of fair representation and the NLRB's obligation to enforce it were "not merely statutory, but are constitutional in origin." During his term Miller led the Board to expand its antidiscrimination policies and embraced the workplace Constitution as vigorously as Jenkins, even agreeing that conflicts between the Board's statutory and constitutional duties should be resolved in the Constitution's favor.[9]

Board members embraced the workplace Constitution more publicly and explicitly than other federal administrators. Jenkins insisted that the Board "lack[ed] the power under the ... Fifth Amendment to give effect to or to aid in the implementation of arrangements or agreements which are discriminatory or unlawful." Miller agreed. The board "had no *constitutional* power to confer, condone, or enforce exclusivity of representation," Miller insisted, where it was "being exercised in a discriminatory manner." A third Republican, Ralph Kennedy, joined the Board in 1970; he too agreed that the NLRB was "precluded by the Constitution from directly or indirectly sanctioning the private exercise of discrimination." Both Miller and Jenkins thought the Constitution also constrained certified unions and employers. Even the Board's remaining Democratic members, including one of the *Hughes Tool* dissenters, conceded that the duty of fair representation "may be constitutional as well" as statutory.[10]

How best to implement these constitutional duties remained contentious, however. Questions remained, Miller observed, as to "the proper procedural points at which the Board should or must permit this essentially constitutional issue to be litigated." Board members must not "invite frivolous litigation or ... compound the inevitable but lamentable delays that are built into our decision-making structure," Miller insisted. The Board thus had to decide "at what point may or must these issues [of racial discrimination] be raised? How must they be pleaded? Where should the burden of proof lie; and, correlatively, how much investigative time of the Board must, constitutionally, be

devoted to these questions?" These were the hard questions about how
to translate constitutional commands into concrete policies.[11]

The resulting debates demonstrated how difficult properly weigh-
ing and harmonizing the NLRB's statutory and constitutional obligations could be. In April 1972, Miller and Jenkins engaged the Board
in designing a process for handling claims of union discrimination.
"The major problem," the NLRB's solicitor mused, "is to establish
a procedure that will weed out the 'pretext' cases from the meri-
torious ones." The Board and its legal staff agonized over how to
prevent employers or rival unions from using its new procedures to
stall elections. Board members also worried about how to meet their
constitutional obligations without increasing their backlog or giving
employers free license "to engage in a wild fishing expedition" into
a union's records.[12]

Board members were hopelessly divided. Miller wanted the NLRB
to join the rulemaking craze and thought its union discrimination policies provided a perfect opportunity. He hoped to address systemati-
cally how the Board would entertain racial discrimination charges in
everything from initial representation petitions to unfair labor practice proceedings. But after more than a year of extensive deliberation,
Miller was unable to get the Board members to agree how to translate
their constitutional duties into answers to the procedural questions
he had posed. Without consensus, there could be no rule. The agency
instead set policy by issuing decisions in individual cases, an approach
that was more incremental and vulnerable to reversal.[13]

The Board's splintered 1974 decision in *Bekins Moving & Storage
Co.* encapsulated the members' disagreements. *Hughes Tool* had
decertified a union with a record of discriminating against the workers
it represented. *Bekins* addressed whether the board could deny exclusive representative status in the first instance based on the likelihood
that an otherwise qualified union would discriminate *in the future*.
The employer argued that the Teamsters local petitioning to represent
its Floridian workers "discriminates against minority groups upon
the basis of race" and thus "cannot evoke the process of the National
Labor Relations Board." To support its claim, the employer asked
for the demographics of the national union's members and leaders as
well as any discrimination charges filed against it or any of its locals
since 1964.[14]

One contentious issue was what constituted government sanctioning of union discrimination. The NLRB's three Republicans favored entertaining claims of union discrimination after an election but before the Board certified the union. The Democrats would let employers raise these claims only as a defense to a certified union's charge that the employer was not bargaining in good faith, an unfair labor practice under the NLRA. The Republicans found this remedy acceptable but inadequate. The dispute turned in part on whether certification actually sanctioned union discrimination. Forming a majority in *Bekins*, the Republicans found that certifying the Teamsters was state "action which would have the clearly foreseeable effect of supporting or assisting" a discriminatory union and was therefore unconstitutional. The Democrat dissenters responded that, far from "aiding and abetting the union's discriminatory policies," certification helped *remedy* them. Certification, they observed, imposed a duty of fair representation on the union and subjected it to unfair labor practice orders if it engaged in racial discrimination. Further, if constitutional problems arose from government involvement with discriminatory unions, the dissenters contended, this should bar the Board not only from certifying such unions, but also from overseeing their elections.[15]

Determining what kinds of discrimination the NLRB was constitutionally required to police further divided its members, even turning the majority Republicans against each other. Miller and Jenkins understood "the duty of fair representation to be rooted in the Constitution as well as the statute." The Board must therefore refuse to certify unions with "a propensity to fail fairly to represent employees." Ralph Kennedy viewed "the duty of fair representation ... as an obligation imposed [only] by statute" and only on unions that were already certified as exclusive representatives. As a result, the Board was *not* constitutionally obliged to entertain claims that unions violated this duty prior to certification. He would instead limit the Board's pre-certification inquiry to whether a union's membership policies were discriminatory. The Republicans divided over sex discrimination as well. Jenkins and Miller treated sex and race discrimination as constitutionally commensurate. Kennedy pointed to a recent Supreme Court decision finding that sex classifications were not subject to the heightened judicial scrutiny accorded race discrimination. He therefore did

"not regard precertification allegations based on sex discrimination as
a constitutional issue."[16]

The NLRB splintered over how to resolve conflicts between its statutory and constitutional duties as well. The Democrats insisted that
"the withholding of a certification from a union which has won a
fairly conducted valid election is beyond the power of the Board"
given that the NLRA mandated that the Board "shall certify" such a
union. And if "the act of certification [indeed] places the sanction of
government upon the offending discriminatory practices," they countered, the Board should conduct the inquiry into union discrimination
during the statutorily required *pre*election hearing. Due to subtleties in
the NLRA's phrasing, this approach avoided a conflict between what
Congress told the agency it "shall" do and what the agency thought it
was constitutionally required to do.[17]

The Republican majority acknowledged the NLRA's mandatory
language but contended that it must "be construed in harmony with
these ... constitutional requirements." They sought to mitigate the
constitutional incursion into the Board's statutory mandate. They preferred, for instance, the postelection, precertification juncture for hearing discrimination claims because it husbanded agency resources (the
NLRB wasted no time on claims against unions that lost their elections) while also preventing election delays, which all members agreed
were counter to the statutory purpose. Kennedy further favored limiting the precertification inquiry to race-based membership discrimination, lest it become "impossible for us to devote adequate attention
to those Federal policies which we were created to implement." But in
the majority's view, the Constitution could trump the statute if the two
conflicted. "What the Board lacks," they insisted, "is not the statutory
power to withhold the certificate, but rather the constitutional power
to confer it."[18]

Bekins established that the NLRB would not only decertify discriminatory unions but would also deny certification in the first instance
to unions with a "propensity" to discriminate. But *Bekins* also displayed how internally fractured the Board was over these policies.
Translating constitutional principle into administrative procedure was
no simple task. Just as in *Hughes Tool*, what precisely the workplace
Constitution required of the Board and how this was shaped by the
NLRA were among the thorniest questions the agency faced.

Adding Title VII to the Mix

Title VII, which came into play after *Hughes Tool*, could affect how the NLRB implemented the Constitution. "The Board was not created to resolve all problems of discrimination," a former trial examiner insisted when Chairman Miller sought the organized bar's view of his proposed rules. "Experience under Title VII ... shows how complicated, costly and time consuming" adjudicating discrimination claims could be, indicating that these problems should be left to the EEOC and the courts. His colleagues on the American Bar Association's NRLB-focused committee agreed. Miller replied that he was "astounded at the totally negative attitude evinced" by the committee and warned that he was uninterested in arguments that the Board ought to avoid "problems of discrimination." Miller may not have felt precluded by Title VII, but he also did not feel bound to implement it. Like most Board members, Miller thought that preserving the NLRB's statutory mission justified implementing narrower antidiscrimination policies than Title VII required.[19]

Since 1964, Title VII had won over critics allied with worker plaintiffs and employer defendants. After enactment, the liberal coalition that secured Title VII's passage sought repeatedly to empower the EEOC, like the NLRB, to adjudicate charges and enforce remedies. By the late 1960s, however, civil rights and labor advocates' agendas diverged. Court successes and EEOC disappointments had convinced civil rights groups that a hybrid of court and agency enforcement was preferable. In contrast, labor remained committed to agencies enforcing Title VII exclusively. Pressure to reform the law persisted after Nixon's election, producing in 1972 amendments that kept enforcement in the courts but gave the EEOC power to bring suits targeting systemic discrimination. The 1972 amendments also extended Title VII to state and local government employers and lowered the threshold for coverage from twenty-five employees to fifteen. Significantly, this time the law was signed by a Republican president, with the support of the preeminent employer group, the National Association of Manufacturers.[20]

To the Board's members, Title VII indirectly legitimized the NLRB's race policies. While considering the 1972 changes to the law, senators rejected an amendment designed "to eliminate [discrimination] actions brought before agencies or forums such as the NLRB ... and FCC." Because Congress rejected the amendment, Chairman Miller declared that Title VII "had not ... limit[ed] the Board's duty or authority in this area." Jenkins went a step further, contending that the law had in fact *affirmed* the Board's obligation to police racial discrimination. In Jenkins's view, the same constitutional policies that animated Title VII also constrained the Board. Even the NLRB's Democratic members supported at least some antidiscrimination policies, despite Title VII's enactment.[21]

But that did not mean that Board members agreed on how Title VII affected their statutory and constitutional obligations. Most fundamentally, Jenkins and his fellow members disagreed over whether Title VII set the standard for the Board's antidiscrimination policies. Jenkins argued that the NLRB had a duty to implement the principles expressed in Title VII. Miller, in contrast, was willing to depart from Title VII to preserve the Board's core statutory mission. Miller worried that if the Board's policies were coextensive with Title VII, it would be "so inundated with cases that its procedures would bog down in a hopeless morass." The majority followed Miller, not Jenkins, in deciding not to import all Title VII standards into Board policy.[22]

The NLRB members' decisions about when to penalize employers' discriminatory practices illustrated their dispute over Title VII's impact. In 1968, before Miller's arrival, the *Hughes Tool* majority issued an unfair labor practice order against Farmers' Cooperative Compress, a Texas employer, for failing to bargain in good faith about discriminatory practices. Remarkably, the decision extended the Board's race discrimination policies to include penalties against employers, not only unions. Even more remarkably, in enforcing the Board's order, Judge Skelly Wright held that employers who had a "pattern or practice" of racial discrimination (a phrase lifted straight from Title VII) could also be subject to an unfair labor practice order for "interfer[ing] with, restrain[ing] or coerc[ing] employees in the exercise of their rights" to self-organization and concerted action under the NLRA. The Board could issue this type of order regardless of whether an employer's business was unionized. At a time when efforts to give the EEOC enforcement powers were failing, one court watcher predicted that Wright's approach could make the NLRB the leading agency for employer discrimination charges.[23]

Miller was not interested in taking on that job. Wright remanded the case to the Board to determine whether the employer had a pattern or practice of racial discrimination. Miller found that the employer did not, obviating the need to take a position on Wright's expansive interpretation of the Board's powers. In a subsequent case, Miller protected his agency against the barrage of complaints he feared Wright's interpretation would produce. Wright had found that employers' racial discrimination interfered with workers' right to organize by "set[ting] up an unjustified clash of interests between groups of workers" and by "creat[ing] in its victims an apathy or docility which inhibits them from asserting their rights" under the NLRA. In *Jubilee Manufacturing Co.*, a dispute involving allegations of sex discrimination at an Omaha maker of automobile horns and alarms, Miller countered that a "continued practice of discrimination may" just as likely spur militancy and "cause minority groups to coalesce." He thus rejected Wright's suggestion that *any* pattern or practice of discrimination would be grounds for an unfair labor practice order. Instead, the Board would issue such orders only where there was a "direct relationship between the alleged discrimination" and workers' exercise of their rights under the NLRA. Jenkins dissented. He too rejected Wright's reasoning. But Jenkins argued that all "pattern or practice" discrimination warranted an unfair labor practice order nonetheless, because workers wasted "time, effort, and money" battling the discrimination that they could have spent on collective action.[24]

Miller also defined discrimination more narrowly than under Title VII. By 1971, the EEOC and the courts had applied Title VII to workplace policies that resulted in racial imbalance, regardless of whether those policies were intended to hurt protected workers. Miller rejected this approach. *Mansion House Management Corp.* grew out of a unionization drive by painters working for a St. Louis building management company. Miller joined two Democrats to rule that racial imbalance alone in a union's membership did not prove that it discriminated. Miller maintained this position even after the Eighth Circuit Court of Appeals directed the agency to consider statistical disparities between unions' membership and the general workforce. He also did so even though the appellate court (like other federal courts during the early 1970s) assumed that successful claims under the Constitution's equal protection guarantees, like those under Title VII, could rest on these statistics. Absent evidence to the contrary, the Board reasoned, it "must assume that the employers in the area exercise the true control over the selection of the work forces" and thus "who ... may become" a union member.[25]

Miller's NLRB also rejected the Title VII approach when assessing employer discrimination. On remand, a Board majority found that Farmers' Cooperative Compress did not discriminate, despite the fact that African American and Latino workers were concentrated in the least skilled, lowest paid jobs. "More than just numbers are relevant" to determining whether the company had a pattern or practice of discrimination, Miller's majority cautioned. Nor was anything wrong with company policies that benefited white workers and disadvantaged nonwhite ones, such as a transfer policy that perpetuated the concentration of black and Latino workers in lower-paying jobs.[26]

Jenkins thought Miller used formal equality to paper over real injustice. Finding no discrimination because Farmers' Cooperative Compress applied its racially disadvantaging transfer policy "to all three racial groups" (Anglo, African American, and Latino) upheld the kind of equality "which forbids the rich and poor alike to sleep under bridges," Jenkins scolded. But he was alone in his opinion.[27]

Was the Board's a *Liberal* Workplace Constitution?

After *Hughes Tool*, NAACP general counsel Robert Carter insisted that his support for black workers pursuing NLRB charges against discriminatory unions was "not based on hostility to collective bargaining or self-organization" but was "concerned with developing true solidarity and cooperation on an equal basis between workers of both races." Yet the strongest supporters of the Board's antidiscrimination policies proved to be Republicans, while their strongest detractors were Democrats. This raised the gnawing question of whether the workplace Constitution that the NLRB implemented was the liberal one that Carter described.[28]

There is no indication that the Republican members used the Constitution as a Trojan horse for a right-to-work agenda. Miller's reputation for evenhandedness, his narrow definition of union as well as employer discrimination, and his promotion of unfair labor practice orders for employer discrimination belied this explanation.

Ralph Kennedy was the Board member most closely associated with antiunionism; critics insisted that no director of an NLRB regional office (his prior post) was held in lower esteem by labor. Yet Kennedy defined most narrowly the grounds for precertification charges of union discrimination, a position more favorable to organized labor than that taken by Jenkins and Miller.[29]

Jenkins adhered to the liberal ideal for the workplace Constitution. True, he had close ties to right-to-work advocates. His wife campaigned for Goldwater, and the senators from his home state of Colorado, whose support was critical to his reappointment, were right-to-work proponents; one had even authored the oft-proposed "Laboring Man's Bill of Rights." But no one, including his supporters, mistook him for a management ally, and business groups opposed his bid for the chairmanship. Jenkins was deeply concerned about African Americans' economic plight. He was horrified that African American men's median earnings were only about half that of white men, and that 25 percent of young African Americans were unemployed. He warned that two-thirds of African Americans worked in the low-skilled jobs that "automation is eliminating ... at an extremely high rate" and called on the nation to rescue "the masses of Negroes from the economic oblivion to which they are otherwise consigned." In Jenkins's view racial justice and union rights were inseparable. He believed that "within the framework of free enterprise and a free labor movement there resides both the will and means to fulfill the constitutional guarantees against racial discrimination." Decrying the reigning spirit of "separatism and divisiveness" between labor and management, between labor and civil rights, as well as "within the ranks of each," Jenkins urged that the NLRB and all parties should "rededicate ourselves to the search for meaningful answers to the interrelated problems of race relations and industrial relations."[30]

The Board members' motivations could not control the use to which employers put NLRB policies, however. Although historians generally date business conservatives' coordinated attacks on labor to the mid-1970s, they were under way, if largely hidden from view, in the 1960s. Even in the 1950s, some employers aggressively thwarted unionization. During the 1960s, however, resisting unionization became a more mainstream business position. In 1963, the Washington Roundtable brought together industrialists for "monthly off-the-record meetings" with conservative issue groups such as the National Right to Work Committee. A "truly vast and unreported 'management movement'" formed to rewrite the NLRA in 1965. "Moderates as well as extreme conservatives" representing heavily unionized industry giants like AT&T, Ford, and U.S. Steel took the lead alongside right-to-work stalwarts such as the U.S. Chamber of Commerce, the National Association of Manufacturers, and the National Right to Work Committee. They were joined, according to one estimate, by "virtually all of the important, corporate labor lawyers in the United States." The *Wall Street Journal* reported in 1966 that "companies are putting up a real battle against the organizing attempts of unions." An instructional movie making the rounds of executive suites was described as "squeaky clean" because it avoided the traditional depictions of "the union organizer as a gorilla and unionization as forced labor or (south of Maryland) mongrelization of the races."[31]

Labor-friendly liberals were concerned that the Board's expanded antidiscrimination policies facilitated these business attacks on the agency and on unions. The Democratic dissenters may have earnestly interpreted the Constitution but they also were likely shielding the NLRB and unions from the inundation and delay they feared the Republicans' preferred policies would cause. The Board's regional officials certainly worried that Miller's proposed discrimination rules "might open a Pandora's box to those few legal technicians and obstructionists." Others complained that the rules "could result in the filing of numerous unwarranted and frivolous motions and thus unduly burden the workload of the Regions." Labor lawyers shared these concerns. Most worried about "motions from disgruntled employees who did not vote for the winning union" as much as they did pretextual employer charges. But union-side lawyers had a more pointed concern: the right-to-work movement. The Board's proposed rules, they warned, would open the door to "the many organizations now existing that would ... take advantage of such an opportunity to destroy collective bargaining in this country."[32]

Liberal labor law scholars likewise argued that the NLRB's policies were unwise and unnecessary. Leaving adjudication of labor union discrimination to Title VII and the EEOC, one scholar argued, would best accommodate "the national labor policy ... with the constitutional policy against racial discrimination." Congress, in passing

Title VII, had already "discharged any constitutional obligation to provide a remedy." If government had an affirmative constitutional duty to prohibit discrimination by the unions it empowers, another contended, "Title VII ... has fulfilled" it. Others said that proponents of the board's antidiscrimination policies wrongly assumed "the more remedies, the better." In these scholars' view, the NLRB should not erode workers' right to organize by adopting unnecessary antidiscrimination policies.[33]

The NLRB's decision in *Bekins Moving & Storage Co.*, issued in 1974, capped ten busy years during which the agency worked out the implications of the workplace Constitution for its policies. The Board never faced more than a trickle of discrimination charges. But no other agency embraced its constitutional duty to police union and employer discrimination so openly or fundamentally. As the NLRB discovered, however, an agency that took seriously its obligation not to sanction discrimination had a host of tough questions to answer. What constituted illicit sanctioning? What counted as discrimination? When, if ever, did the agency's statutory charge trump its constitutional duty (or vice versa)? How did Title VII affect these calculations? The Board members' varying answers to these questions made the workplace Constitution more secure but its boundaries less certain. Ultimately, the most powerful check on the scope of the Board's policies was the possibility that they would attract too many discrimination claims, a prospect Howard Jenkins would have welcomed.[34]

The NLRB's policies confounded political conventions. With a Republican majority on the Board implementing the workplace Constitution, it was difficult to ascribe the results to the liberal coalition. Labor liberals' persistent critiques of the Board's antidiscrimination policies fed this doubt. Then again, with free-market advocates outside the Board busily attacking the workplace Constitution and the broad state action theories on which it rested, it was equally difficult to attribute the Board's policies to conservatives.

PART IV

THE WORKPLACE CONSTITUTION IN
THE NEW RIGHT 1970S AND 1980S

10

Conservatives Reject the Liberal Workplace Constitution

"A primrose path on the 14th Amendment"
Chief Justice Warren Burger

In October 1972, conference goers gathered at an elegant five-star hotel on the pristine shores of Italy's Lake Como. William Taylor, the former staff director of the United States Civil Rights Commission, delivered a talk entitled "Problems in Developing and Enforcing Fair Employment Law in the United States." Despite some notable court-room victories under Title VII, Taylor contended, "there are still major limitations upon relying on law suits as the sole or even principal instrument of implementing fair employment policy." Agencies had a "great deal of expertise in the business practices of the industries they regulate," he observed. As a result, they were better than courts at evaluating whether employment qualifications that tended to exclude African Americans were justified. Additionally, lawsuits affected only a single employer, he pointed out, but "the mere issuance of regulations prohibiting employment discrimination" might "induce a great deal of voluntary compliance." Agencies' power to approve or reject rate increases or license applications gave them "enormous leverage" in reg-ulated industries "with significant equal employment problems," from airlines to banking, Taylor explained. The gas and utility companies overseen by the Federal Power Commission (FPC) alone, he noted, had "perhaps the worst record of any major industry in employing minorities."[1]

Taylor's talk was not idle; he and his allies had recently petitioned all the major regulatory agencies for equal employment rules. Taylor had long urged that "federal agencies ... are under a constitutional duty to prevent racial discrimination" by their regulatees. After graduating from Yale Law School in 1954, Taylor had worked on the Gulf Coast oil cases with the NAACP's Robert Carter. Later, he helped the Kennedy and Johnson administrations "be more inventive in the use of the law and government to fulfill the promise of the Constitution." Taylor left government in 1968 convinced that federal agencies would not "enforce civil rights laws without private monitoring and pressure," something he thought civil rights organizations failed to provide. To fill this gap, he founded the Center for National Policy Review at Catholic University and helped engineer equal employment rulemaking petitions.[2]

At the Federal Communications Commission and the National Labor Relations Board, President Nixon's appointees – including those drawn from the Republican Party's increasingly powerful conservative wing – sustained and even energized the workplace Constitution. The petitions by Taylor and his allies tested whether this pattern would hold.

The State of State Action

At first blush, a Supreme Court case decided in 1967 had little to do with Taylor's equal employment mission, yet *Reitman v. Mulkey* mapped the promise and peril of his administrative strategy. "This may well be the most important civil rights case of the decade," a member of the solicitor general's staff proclaimed, one with "far more importance in its potential consequences than all the 'sit-in' and 'protest' cases rolled into one." California had been one of twenty-four states that had a fair-housing law until its voters amended their constitution in 1964, returning to private property owners the unfettered choice of buyers and renters. California's highest court struck down the amendment, known as Proposition 14, on the grounds that it unconstitutionally *encouraged* private discrimination. Department of Justice attorneys supported this outcome. If Proposition 14 was allowed to stand, the solicitor general's staff member warned, "it will become a model for similar initiative measures in States throughout the Union" and will "doubtless throttle the last hopes for fair-housing legislation in this country." Justice Department lawyers worried that the U.S. Supreme Court's decision to review the case was "a bad omen" indicating that "those who espouse a narrow view of 'state action' ... may prevail." The ensuing debates among government attorneys and Supreme Court justices about the fate of Proposition 14 touched on the broad state action theories Taylor used to justify his proposed equal employment rules.[3]

Advancing the California court's encouragement theory of state action had strategic appeal. Justice Department lawyers were acutely aware of the Court's decision to avoid the broad state action arguments in *Bell v. Maryland*, the justices' most trying sit-in case. Department lawyers also worried about the vigorous dissent by Justices Black, Harlan, and White in *Bell*, in which they argued that the state could protect private discrimination through its trespass laws without triggering *Shelley*'s bar on state enforcement of private discrimination. The dissenters thought *Bell* came out differently than *Shelley* partly because there was no "official proclamation or action of any kind that shows the slightest state coercion of, or encouragement to" the restaurant's whites-only policy. Since *Bell*, Justice White had parted company with his fellow dissenters to find sufficient state action in a state law that merely permitted (rather than required) the complained-of discrimination. "Depart[ing] from a policy of strict neutrality," White reasoned in *Evans v. Newton*, "so involved the State in the private choice as to convert ... [it] into state action." Civil Rights Division lawyers wanted to convince Justice White that Proposition 14 had the same effect. Perhaps then he would join the four reliable votes for striking down the proposition. If he did, the Court would also nudge the state action needle closer to justifying administrators' implementation of the workplace Constitution.[4]

The encouragement rationale had its detractors, however. The solicitor general's staff declared the California Supreme Court's opinion "indefensible" and "flim-flammery." To them, Proposition 14 had merely repealed the prior fair housing law. Finding that a state could not repeal a law was tantamount to holding that it was obligated to pass the law in the first instance, some argued. "The basic distinction between 'state action' and private conduct demands that the State be permitted to abstain [from action]," one attorney insisted, or "else that distinction itself evaporates." Even if the encouragement rationale did not impose an affirmative duty to pass fair housing laws, another attorney pointed out, it improbably left "homeowners of California less free in choosing their vendees or lessees than citizens of other States," like Mississippi, that had never barred housing discrimination in the first place.[5]

The Civil Rights Division lawyers won out in the battle for Solicitor General Thurgood Marshall's approval. Unlike his predecessor, labor pluralist Archibald Cox, Marshall had not shied from broad state action theories during his time at the NAACP, even as he sought ways to harmonize the workplace Constitution with the New Deal labor regime. The government's brief to the Court argued that Proposition 14 "overstep[ped] the boundary of neutrality." By giving private housing discrimination "an official imprimatur," the brief stated, the proposition "invites and promotes," "facilitates," and "solemnly sanctions" it.[6]

Most of the justices' positions were predictable. In their private conference, Justices Harlan, Clark, Black, and Stewart voted to reverse the California Supreme Court. All four thought that Proposition 14 merely returned the state to the status quo ante. Justice Black put their position most bluntly: "We should not affirm merely to make it easier for minorities to get their way." Justices Douglas and Brennan easily voted to affirm without belaboring the reason why, while Chief Justice Warren and Justice Goldberg's liberal replacement, Abe Fortas, favored affirming but on a narrower basis than the California court's encouragement rationale.[7]

The Civil Rights Division lawyers had calculated well. Justice White voted to affirm the California court's decision. Proposition 14 "authorize[d] and encourage[d] discrimination on racial lines," he argued at conference, and his opinion for the Court found "no sound reason for rejecting this [the California court's] judgment." Proposition 14 had "embodied in the State's basic charter" the "right to discriminate on racial grounds." This, White contended, meant that "those practicing racial discriminations ... could now invoke express constitutional authority." The California court therefore justifiably found that the state "had taken affirmative action designed to make private discriminations legally possible," thereby unconstitutionally "involv[ing] the State in" them. White's opinion was the closest the Court had come to endorsing the broad sanctioning theories relied on by the NLRB and FCC. Yale law professor Charles Black predicted that the Court was even verging on holding that the Constitution required state actors to take affirmative steps to end racial discrimination.[8]

Justices Harlan, Black, Clark, and Stewart dissented vigorously. "State action required to bring the Fourteenth Amendment into operation must be affirmative and purposeful," they insisted, "actively fostering discrimination." Proposition 14 was "simply permissive of private decision-making." If this alone were sufficient, it would "tinge all private discrimination with the taint of unconstitutional state encouragement," since "every act of private discrimination [wa]s either forbidden by state law or permitted by it."[9]

Targeting the Administrative State

Three years later, civil rights advocates put *Reitman*'s line to the test. "The march toward full equality has bogged down in a morass of bureaucracy, lassitude, and indifferent leadership at the very heart of the American Government," the *New York Times* announced in October 1970, echoing a scathing report by the Civil Rights Commission. The report was the work of Howard Glickstein, the former Justice Department lawyer who had since replaced Taylor at the Civil Rights Commission. After canvassing all the major regulatory agencies, the commission concluded that only the FCC had taken meaningful steps to ensure that the industries it regulated practiced equal employment. Glickstein accused the FPC of foot-dragging and skewered other agencies for either failing to consider the issue or denying that they had the authority to act.[10]

Glickstein adopted a broad sanctioning theory of state action that crossed the line between encouragement and permission that Justice White tried to draw in *Reitman*. Regulatory agencies "are prohibited from permitting discrimination in their fields of regulation," the report argued, and even had "an affirmative duty to end any discriminatory practices (including employment) of ... all who deal with the agency." In place of the Supreme Court's requirement that a state significantly involve itself with private action, Glickstein's report insisted that equal protection was also triggered whenever there was "*some measure* of involvement or interdependence" between the state and otherwise private actors. Regulatory agencies' "pervasive presence ... in the most vital economic matters which a company must face," the report insisted, "should satisfy any test based on sufficiency of contacts."[11]

Glickstein's report inspired civil rights advocates. He was disappointed by his commission's ability to "get the Federal bureaucracy to move." The Civil Rights Commission was expert at developing reports but, he complained, "we ... then fall on our face when it comes to implementing them." Luckily for Glickstein, his former boss, William Taylor, had an intriguing proposal. Taylor was seeking funding for a center that would press the federal government to fulfill the report's blueprint for action. The commission, he hoped, would endorse his proposal. The commission's chairman was concerned about effectively outsourcing to "a private organization ... work that we should be doing," but he took Taylor's proposal seriously. Taylor simultaneously worked with the Leadership Conference on Civil Rights, an umbrella group of civil rights, labor, and religious organizations, to create a Federal Regulatory Task Force that he hoped could mobilize the conference's constituent groups to help in these efforts.[12]

Taylor achieved remarkable public-private collaboration. In March 1971, his liberal coalition petitioned the Interstate Commerce Commission for equal employment rules. Once the agency issued a notice of proposed rulemaking in June, comments flowed in from civil rights advocates inside and outside the government. The NAACP Legal Defense Fund, the Leadership Conference, and Taylor's new Center for National Policy Review argued that the Constitution mandated that the trucking industry eliminate employment discrimination and that the Interstate Commerce Commission adopt rules like those at the FCC. The Equal Employment Opportunity Commission and the Civil Rights Commission – even the Department of Transportation's general counsel – concurred. The Justice Department's Civil Rights Division, the Office of Federal Contract Compliance, and the Postal Service's Office of Equal Employment Compliance also urged the agency's statutory authority, if not its constitutional obligation, to act. Throughout, the Civil Rights Commission kept up pressure on agencies by issuing periodic assessments of their responses to its initial report.[13]

Civil rights advocates viewed federal agencies as a source of great hope as well as great disappointment. Advocates were generally unhappy with Nixon's civil rights efforts, which were sporadic, short-lived, and often fell short of advocates' demands. Indeed, the White House saw Glickstein's 1970 report as an indictment and tried to suppress it until after the fall elections. Title VII litigation had also increased civil rights advocates' faith in the courts. But they still pushed for agency enforcement of equal employment. Even the NAACP Legal Defense Fund, by now a strong proponent for court enforcement of Title VII, nonetheless sought agency-implemented equal employment rules. In part, this was an effort to acquire the enforcement powers the EEOC lacked; but it was also intended to reach beyond the limits of Title VII.[14]

Taylor's coalition targeted all the agencies outlined in Glickstein's report. Environmental groups requested equal employment rules in a petition to the Securities and Exchange Commission seeking environmental disclosure regulations. The Civilian Aeronautics Board requested comments on its authority to issue equal employment rules after being urged to act by the EEOC, the Civil Rights Commission, several congressmen, and a group of law students calling themselves Future Lawyers Investigating Transportation Employment, or FLITE. At the EEOC's request, Taylor's Regulatory Task Force organized the civil rights groups' petitions to the FCC in the EEOC's 1971 challenge to discrimination by AT&T. Finally, in the summer of 1972, Taylor's Center for National Policy Review petitioned the FPC on behalf of the Leadership Conference's diverse constituent groups.[15]

The Federal Power Commission Fights Back

Taylor's petition was the latest effort to influence the FPC. A California legal services organization had asked to intervene in a West Coast utility's license application as early as March 1969. The legal services lawyers objected to the requested license unless the utility rectified its allegedly abysmal minority hiring practices. Their petition was unexpected at this obscure and technical agency, which was accustomed to the attentions of only gas and electric executives or an insular community of energy industry lawyers. The FPC handled some of the "most controversial and convoluted subjects in the entire history of regulation in America," but was considered ineffective: "addled, lethargic," and beholden to the industries it regulated. During the 1960s, the agency took a more consumer-friendly turn, however, and it allowed the legal services lawyers to intervene. The chairman, Lee C. White, had worked previously on civil rights issues as a legal adviser to Presidents Kennedy and Johnson. He announced in July 1969 that the FPC ought to address the issues the legal services lawyers raised "in a general rulemaking proceeding of the type recently initiated by the" FCC.[16]

Utility companies held particular promise for minorities: they trained skilled workers in-house, avoiding trade unions' apprenticeship waiting lists. They also tended to have effective job ladders even for entry-level positions. And, crucially, they were located in or near urban centers. Industry had fled to the suburbs and the South since the 1950s, leaving behind many unemployed African Americans. In the 1960s and 1970s alone, northeastern cities lost 600,000 jobs while their suburbs gained 100,000 and the Sun Belt gained ten times that number. Utilities, because of their intensive capital investments and required proximity to their customer base or their natural resource, were not expected to move.[17]

Yet utilities lagged behind other industries in hiring and promoting women and minorities. In 1968, fewer than 4 percent of utility employees were African American, and nearly all of them were concentrated in the worst jobs. By 1970, the percentage of African American employees had risen slightly to 6 percent, but it was still the lowest rate among large industries. About half of the biggest utilities had no African American managers and a handful did not have a single black employee. Latinos were concentrated in laborer and service jobs, and women were employed almost exclusively in office and clerical positions.[18]

Utilities had long evaded federal efforts to remedy their hiring record. In the 1950s and 1960s, rather than agreeing to antidiscrimination terms in government contracts, utilities simply provided services without contracts. Even if they had signed the contracts and then failed to meet their antidiscrimination terms, canceling the utilities' contracts – the government's primary enforcement tool – was an unrealistic threat: the utilities were monopolies, so cancelation would effectively cut off power to the federal government. The NAACP Legal Defense Fund's early Title VII suits targeted southern utilities, but as of the late 1960s they had not borne much fruit.[19]

Under Lee White, the FPC prepared to act. In 1961, administrators at President Kennedy's Committee on Equal Employment Opportunity had argued that because utilities were government-licensed monopolies required to serve the public interest, they were constitutionally bound not to discriminate. Negotiations with the utilities had gone nowhere, however, and in April 1969 the FPC's legal staff turned back to the Constitution. The FPC's animating statutes required it to regulate in the public interest and to assure just and reasonable rates. Those public interest duties, FPC lawyers reasoned, obligated the agency to consider the national policy against discrimination when licensing or certificating utilities. Furthermore, because this national policy derived from the Constitution, the FPC could (and maybe had to) demand equal employment even from utilities that were not technically violating Title VII.[20]

President Nixon replaced White, however, leaving his rulemaking plans in limbo. The new chairman, John Nassikas, had grown up in New Hampshire, the only son of Greek immigrants. His father grew wealthy processing and distributing New England's dairy riches. Nassikas, who earned graduate business and law degrees from Harvard University, was a classic northeastern business Republican. Such Republicans' liberal reputation notwithstanding, Nassikas was "foursquare" with free enterprise and followed his father's example of "working your own way with your own talents," "initiative," and "nondependence on government." Nassikas spent much of his career fighting regulators on behalf of the banking, utility, and railroad industries, rising to prominence in the New Hampshire corporate bar. Nixon made good on his campaign promise to reverse Democrats' "heavy-handed bureaucratic regulatory schemes" when he selected Nassikas.[21]

It was not immediately clear whether Nassikas would end the FPC's exploration of equal employment. In January 1970, the FPC's new general counsel, R. Gordon Gooch, asked the Civil Rights Division for an advisory opinion on the issues the California legal services lawyers had raised. Meanwhile, the FPC granted civil rights groups permission to file briefs in support of the legal services lawyers' claims. Nassikas, when pressed during a Senate hearing, testified that the FPC would "try to assure" that utilities improved equal employment opportunity, although he declined to say if it had the power to demand that they do so.[22]

The significance of the FPC's change in chairmanship soon became clear. In November 1970, just after the release of Glickstein's report, the FPC denied the legal services lawyers' petition and granted the West Coast utility's license. In its order, the FPC acknowledged the "national policy that discrimination in employment is to be eliminated by all elements of our society, public and private." The FPC even recognized that this policy implemented the Constitution. But it decided that Congress had given the FPC no statutory command or even discretionary leeway to require equal employment from the utilities it regulated. The agency arrived at this last conclusion by applying a novel nexus argument. The FPC contended that employment discrimination was not sufficiently related to any of its regulatory purposes to fall within its jurisdiction. The agency promised that it would urge utilities to adopt equal employment policies and cooperate with the EEOC, but its primary job was to ensure equal provision of *services*, not of employment.[23]

The FPC's general counsel soon turned this nexus argument into a powerful limit on the workplace Constitution. Gooch had practiced oil and gas law for one of Houston's top firms until Nassikas, seeking a like mind, picked him to be general counsel. Gooch read a nexus criterion similar to that the FPC had recognized in the West Coast utility case into the Supreme Court's state action decisions. In cases such as the Washington, D.C., streetcar case, *Public Utilities Commission v. Pollak*, Gooch argued, the regulatees' challenged actions were found to be within the regulating agency's authority. Here, that authority was lacking. If the FPC could not regulate utilities' employment, it also could not devolve onto them a constitutional duty to provide employment without discrimination. In response to Gooch's earlier request for advice in the West Coast utility case, Civil Rights Division lawyers had opined that utilities were state actors based on a sufficiency-of-contacts theory. Gooch countered that what mattered was the nexus *quality* not the *quantity* of contacts between government and private entities. Gooch also dismissed arguments that the Constitution obligated the FPC to act, arguing that language to that effect in the early sit-in case *Burton* applied exclusively to leased public property.[24]

When Taylor and his team petitioned the FPC for equal employment rules in June 1972, they unwittingly gave the agency an opportunity to implement Gooch's approach. Taylor's petition made the usual statutory, policy, and constitutional arguments, including the sufficiency-of-contacts rationale from Glickstein's 1970 report. In less than three weeks, what the *New York Times* called "an eyeblink in regulatory time," the FPC denied the petition. The commissioners simply relied on the arguments Gooch had presented to them months before. "Executive authority and constitutional considerations do not provide the basis for Commission jurisdiction," the FPC insisted; only Congress could empower it to act. If the petitioners did not like what the FPC had to say, the order concluded, they should ask a court to intervene. The petitioners and the EEOC asked the FPC to reconsider. In another "eyeblink," the FPC denied their request. Taylor's team took up the FPC's challenge and asked the D.C. Circuit Court of Appeals for review.[25]

Strictly Constructing State Action

"The 'leopards' in law school and courts are trying to lead people down a primrose path on the 14th Amendment," Chief Justice Warren Burger warned in 1973. During his presidential campaign, Nixon had promised to appoint a "strict constructionist" to the Court, code words for a jurist who would reverse the Warren Court's expansive rights jurisprudence. Burger, whom Nixon appointed in 1969, fit the bill. A midwestern moderate Republican, Burger had worked in the Eisenhower Justice Department before being elevated to the D.C. Circuit Court of Appeals in 1955. During the 1960s, he was a frequent critic of the Supreme Court's criminal procedure decisions. After Nixon appointed three more justices between 1969 and 1971, court watchers expected a wholesale undoing of the Warren Court. But by 1973, the Burger Court had actually *expanded* protections in contentious areas like public school desegregation and added controversial new ones, such as abortion rights. The Burger Court became known as "the counter-revolution that wasn't." His Court's legacy looks quite different from the perspective of the state action doctrine and the workplace Constitution, however.[26]

The primrose path Burger worried about led to the licensing and sanctioning theories of state action that had gained traction during the 1960s. In 1972, Burger put the Court's newest justice in charge of contracting the state action doctrine. William H. Rehnquist was a self-described ultraconservative and strict constructionist steeped in the Sun Belt's right-to-work politics. Rehnquist had earned a law degree from

Stanford University then built his legal and political career in Arizona. He was an avid supporter of Barry Goldwater during his failed 1964 presidential campaign. In return, the senator helped Rehnquist secure a position at the helm of the Nixon Justice Department's elite Office of Legal Counsel. Rehnquist's civil rights record was as spotted as his free-enterprise qualifications were pristine. Known to use derogatory terms when referring to African Americans, he had urged Justice Robert Jackson, for whom he clerked, to uphold school segregation in *Brown*, formulated Goldwater's constitutional case against Title VII, and opposed Phoenix's public accommodations ordinance and school desegregation plans. Rehnquist insisted constitutional principle underlay these positions. In his view, strict constructionists were generally not "favorably inclined toward claims of either criminal defendants or civil rights plaintiffs." To Rehnquist, the Constitution protected freedom, including the freedom to discriminate.[27]

Rehnquist's 1972 opinion in *Moose Lodge v. Irvis*, issued just ten days before Taylor filed his FPC petition, threw into doubt the licensing theory of state action on which Taylor relied. *Moose Lodge* adopted R. Gordon Gooch's nexus requirement in a case involving a fraternal club. Over the dissents of Justices Brennan, Douglas, and President Johnson's last appointee, Thurgood Marshall, Rehnquist held that a liquor license did not transform a private club into a state actor prohibited from excluding African American guests. Like Gooch before him, Rehnquist reached this outcome by emphasizing the *quality*, not the *quantity*, of the state's involvement with the club. "However detailed ... regulation was," Rehnquist held, the state must have "significantly involved itself with invidious discriminations" for them "to fall within the ambit of the constitutional prohibition." Here, the licensing agency played "absolutely no part in establishing or enforcing the membership or guest policies." Rehnquist noted that the club was not a state-authorized monopoly, meaning that the Court might view the utilities targeted by Taylor's petition differently. Still, *Moose Lodge* was inauspicious.[28]

The next year, the Burger Court edged toward closing *Moose Lodge*'s loophole. The D.C. Circuit Court had found that broadcasters, by adopting a ban on controversial political advertisements, and the FCC, by allowing them to do so, had violated the First Amendment. In reaching its decision, the appellate court held that the FCC's extensive relationship with broadcasters converted them into state actors. The court also found that "specific governmental acquiescence, as well as specific approval" of discriminatory practices constituted state action. In *Columbia Broadcasting System v. Democratic National Committee*, the Supreme Court reversed the D.C. Circuit. Even assuming state action, a majority found no violation of the would-be advertisers' First Amendment rights. But six separate opinions in the case revealed that the justices were deeply, if oddly, divided over state action. Chief Justice Burger and Justices Rehnquist, Stewart, and Douglas wanted to reverse the lower court's state action analysis, while Justices Brennan, Marshall, and possibly White (his cryptic concurrence was hard to pin down) defended it.[29]

On further inspection, however, the various opinions and the wrangling that led to them suggested greater agreement than at first appeared. During the justices' internal deliberations, Burger, White, and Rehnquist rejected the D.C. Circuit's finding that government's "mere acquiescence" was sufficient to trigger constitutional protections. Not even the dissenters argued to the contrary. Also, only Justices Brennan and Marshall endorsed the licensing theory of state action. In a telling sign, its original champion on the Court, Justice Douglas, conceded that he had lost his fight. Instead of dissenting, he wrote a concurrence that favored reversing the D.C. Circuit's decision.[30]

Most justices also seemed ready to extend *Moose Lodge* to licensed monopolies. In a part of his opinion that lacked a majority, Burger determined whether broadcast licensees were state actors by analyzing "the *quality* and degree of Government relationship to the *particular acts in question.*" Even though only Justices Rehnquist and Stewart joined, most of the justices accepted this *Moose Lodge* standard. Even the dissenters argued that "the specific governmental involvement in the broadcaster policy," including the "obvious nexus" between the FCC's policy and the broadcasters' ban, cinched their state action finding.[31]

The case also revealed that Chief Justice Burger was a crusader when it came to state action. Burger circulated law review articles supporting his position to all the justices and made individual pitches highlighting the implications he thought most likely to persuade his colleagues. With most of the justices, Burger focused on the case's First Amendment implications and the sanctity of the press. Only with

his childhood friend Harry Blackmun did he allow that his deeper
concern was the state action doctrine's future. Like Burger, Blackmun
had spent his early career in Minnesota, joining the Eighth Circuit
Court of Appeals in 1959. Once elevated to the Supreme Court,
Blackmun referred to himself as "Old No. 3," since Nixon chose him
only after two prior nominees were derailed by their segregationist
ties. In his early years on the Court, Blackmun followed Burger's lead,
earning the nickname "Hip Pocket Harry." Eventually he struck out
on his own, however, including by declining to join Burger's state
action holding in *Columbia Broadcasting*. Burger responded in a private handwritten note with his dire "primrose path" warning. The
"wild eyed, expansive view of '14'" being peddled in some quarters,
Burger warned, "would open virtally [*sic*] all gov't decisions to judicial review." It was up to the Court, Burger urged, to steer the nation
off this dangerous course.[32]

Burger and Rehnquist soon had an opportunity to act more deci-
sively. The Court was presented with a case in February 1974 that
tested state action's outer limits. In *Jackson v. Metropolitan Edison
Co.*, an electric company had terminated Catherine Jackson's power
for failure to pay her bills. Her legal-services attorneys argued that the
termination violated her due process rights. The lower courts rejected
her claim and the justices initially voted to deny review. Justice
White, however, thought the state actor status of government licensees was too important a question to pass by. He drafted a dissent
to the Court's denial, which Justices Douglas and Marshall quickly
joined, winning a new vote. Thanks to Justice Brennan's joining
their side, the erstwhile dissenters secured the Court's review. As the
Court considered the case, however, Marshall, Brennan, and White
recommended dismissing the review as improvidently granted. Their
change of heart may have been in response to the way the Court was
coalescing. Justice Rehnquist urged his brethren that it would "defuse
all prop[erty] right[s]" to find that the utility was a state actor. He also
cautioned that if "mere passivity on the part of a regulatory agency is
sufficient to convert private action into public action, an entire area
of activity that up to now has been governed by contract law will
heretofore be governed by constitutional law." Justices Blackmun and
White were again torn, but ultimately all but Justices Marshall and
Brennan signed on to Rehnquist's opinion.[33]

Issued in December 1974, *Jackson* closed the remaining loopholes for regulatory theories of state action. The Constitution did not reach even state-licensed monopolies, Rehnquist held, unless there was "a sufficiently close nexus between the State and the challenged action of the regulated entity." Only then could the action "be fairly treated as that of the State itself." Before *Jackson*, commentators contended that the Supreme Court might accept the constitutional theories informing agencies' equal employment policies. After, that was no longer the case.[34]

Two months after *Jackson*, the combined impact of Nixon's appointments to the FPC and the Supreme Court hit the workplace Constitution with full force. The D.C. Circuit finally decided Taylor's appeal of his denied FPC petition, which had become far more adventurous given the Court's contraction of state action during the three years it was pending. The FPC lacked the statutory authority to adopt the petitioners' proposed equal employment rules, the court held. Sidestepping *Jackson* and the question of *whether* there was state action, the court ruled that even if there were, it would not have the effect Taylor claimed. The court reasoned that state action typically imposed constitutional obligations on an "ostensibly private entity." It might also oblige the government to terminate its relationship with the discriminating entity. But it would not require the government to "affirmatively regulate its private partner to insure that the latter discharges [its] constitutional obligations." Indeed, the court noted that the Supreme Court in *Columbia Broadcasting* had overturned the D.C. Circuit's only precedent supporting such an approach. "However we might resolve our difficulties with the proposition that the Commission is constitutionally required to adopt *some* anti-discrimination rule," the court asserted, "we are very sure that it is not required to adopt *this* one."[35]

Wishfully, Taylor called the D.C. Circuit Court's decision a limited victory. The court *had* found that the FPC could take utilities' discrimination into account when determining appropriate rate levels. "If the petitioners have been extravagant in their claims," the court scolded, "the Commission has been miserly in its response." But the court also held that the FPC was free to decline to act. Arguably, the decision also undermined the basis for agencies' existing equal employment policies.[36]

The D.C. Circuit had nonetheless gone too far for the FPC, which successfully petitioned the Supreme Court for review. When the NAACP, the named party in Taylor's original petition, predicted the "far-reaching consequences" that a Supreme Court decision could have for "all industries under governmental regulation," it must have been with trepidation.[37]

Deregulating the Workplace Constitution

When the Supreme Court granted review in October 1975, Taylor's prospects looked dim. "All in all, the emerging views of this predominantly conservative court indicate that it's getting 'more friendly to claims against government regulation,'" the *Wall Street Journal* reported in 1975. "These Justices don't show much sympathy to novel theories of government regulation," a Justice Department lawyer concurred. Experts attributed the Court's turn to factors ranging from the majority's "pro-business conservatism" to its strict constructionist "tendency to defer to Congress" rather than use the Constitution to remedy problems. In truth, however, by the mid-1970s there was nothing particularly conservative about antiregulatory politics.[38]

Economic woes were partly to blame. After the late 1960s, the economy had ground to a halt. Wages had dipped and national economic growth, which had averaged more than 4 percent a year since the 1940s, dropped nearly to zero in 1970 and averaged less than 3 percent in the following decade. At the same time, unemployment rose, reaching 9 percent in 1975, while inflation climbed to 8 percent in 1973 and passed 12 percent in 1974. The resulting "stagflation" confounded reigning economic theories, providing an opening for the free-market approach promoted by business conservatives and by scholars such as Friedrich Hayek since the 1940s. Now liberal as well as conservative economists promoted deregulating prices and even abandoning licensed monopolies altogether.[39]

Diminishing faith in government also played a role. In 1973 and 1974, the Watergate scandal engulfed the White House, raising concerns about government secrecy and dysfunction to new levels. Consumer advocates like Ralph Nader further tainted administrative agencies by issuing numerous reports charging that they had been captured by corporate interests. Meanwhile, the Republican Party

wooed disaffected white working-class voters with antistatist rhetoric, and business conservatives, after more than a decade mostly playing defense, launched new attacks on disfavored government programs. The antigovernment fervor translated into the policy arena. In 1975, Nixon's replacement, President Gerald Ford, proposed and Congress debated deregulating everything from natural gas prices to the airline industry. Congress simultaneously enacted legislation designed to shed disinfecting "sunshine" on distrusted agency activity. During the 1976 presidential campaign between Ford and Jimmy Carter, deregulation was *both* candidates' buzzword.[40]

The turn against the regulatory state threatened Taylor's equal employment vision. Most immediately, deregulation undermined the claim that regulated industries' employment practices involved state action. The political outcry might also sap many agencies' willingness to act and provide an excuse for others, like the FPC, that were disinclined to do so. As administrative agencies went from appealing levers for social change to beleaguered targets of political opprobrium, even civil rights advocates depicted them increasingly as part of the problem. The same organizations that had signed on to Taylor's petition in 1972 lined up in Congress in the mid-1970s to lobby for a bill that would promote court enforcement of civil rights laws. Litigation in the courts was more "flexible" and "efficient," they argued, than enforcement by underresourced, distracted, or uninterested agencies.[41]

When Taylor's case arrived at the Supreme Court its odds seemed long. Chief Justice Burger as well as Justices Powell and Rehnquist favored review, causing the justices' law clerks to surmise that the Court would focus on whether the FPC even had jurisdiction to consider its regulated industries' employment practices. "No one," the clerks concluded, was "very concerned with the rejection of the NAACP's claim that the FPC is constitutionally or statutorily *required* to promulgate rules." Longtime NAACP Legal Defense Fund ally and University of Pennsylvania Law School dean Louis H. Pollak offered Taylor a similar prediction, apologizing for his "doctrinal gloom." With Justice Marshall recused from the case and Justice Douglas retired, the Court seemed poised to restrict – if not eliminate – agencies' authority to address racial discrimination by their regulatees.[42]

At oral argument, the justices focused not on agencies' *obligation* to regulate employment discrimination but on whether there was *any basis* for an agency to do so. The FPC's lawyer asked the Court to "set the fences" between the nation's antidiscrimination and economic regulatory statutes. Agencies' oversight of utilities' employment practices, he argued, would draw the FPC into a "hopeless morass ... of litigation" it was ill equipped to handle. Glickstein countered that the FPC believed that it had the authority "to do [only] what is easy and not to do what is difficult." The justices seemed to agree with Glickstein. As Stewart said in their private conference, many of the justices thought that the "FPC overreacted here." Under the justices' questioning, the FPC admitted that it already prohibited utilities from passing on many costs to consumers, including those levied by a court judgment in an antidiscrimination lawsuit.[43]

The Court's May 1976 decision in *NAACP v. Federal Power Commission* was a modest win for Taylor's petitioners. The justices unanimously affirmed the D.C. Circuit's finding of some statutory authority. The FPC had a "duty to prevent its regulatees from charging rates based upon illegal, duplicative, or unnecessary labor costs," the Court held. The FPC should therefore disallow any costs that were "demonstrably the product of a regulatee's discriminatory employment practices."[44]

The decision was ruinous to the petitioners' ultimate goal of disseminating equal employment policies throughout the administrative state, however. Crucially, the Court held that statutory provisions requiring agencies to regulate in the public interest were not "a broad license to promote the general public welfare." As Gooch and Nassikas had long contended, the Court found that these provisions authorized only regulations that were directly related to the agency's statutory mandates. The Court gave the FCC's equal employment rules a reprieve, reasoning that the FCC's statutory duty to ensure that broadcasting "reflect[ed] the tastes and viewpoints of minority groups" provided the requisite regulatory nexus. But for other agencies, the Court rejected fifteen years of administrators' expansive understanding of their obligation to implement the "national policy against discrimination" and, implicitly, the Constitution from which it was derived.[45]

The Court's decision confused the news media. One headline read "Court Backs FPC Role on Job Bias," while another asserted "Agencies Needn't Curb Industry Job Bias, Court Says." In truth, they were both right. In the FPC's opinion, the Court had upheld its claim of limited

authority. In future rate proceedings, the FPC would ˪
auditing procedures to disallow the costs a court or agenc
resulted from a utility's employment discrimination, but it
adjudicate discrimination claims itself. The Civil Aeronautı
and the Interstate Commerce Commission had been waiting
what would come of the FPC's fight. Now, both agencies issued nᴺ
similar to the FPC's. The Court had decided in *NAACP* that agenc
statutes required very little of them.[46]

Taylor called the Court's decision "a victory, especially in light ot
the Court's mood in other civil rights cases." While his view was more
tempered after seeing the order the FPC issued in response ("It's better than nothing," he wrote, "but it sure ain't much"), Taylor nonetheless stressed the decision's potential. He suggested bringing to the
attention of lawyers fighting utility rate increases the "new arrow that
NAACP v. FPC puts in their quiver." The Center for National Policy
Review also forwarded the names of utilities charged with employment
discrimination to the FPC to ensure that the agency appropriately
discounted those costs.[47]

Despite Taylor's optimism, however, Nixon's conservative appointments – strict constructionists to the Court, deregulators to the agencies – had dealt a major blow to the workplace Constitution. Certainly,
there was nothing in the Court's decisions that said agencies could not
find themselves constitutionally obligated to ensure equal employment.
The Court's decisions from *Moose Lodge* to *Jackson* had focused on
when regulation converted private actors into state ones, and *NAACP
v. Federal Power Commission* did not decide agencies' own constitutional obligations. But it had been one thing for agencies to implement a broader notion of state action than the Court when the Court
was moving in the same general direction. It was an entirely different
matter for them to do so when the Court was clearly determined to
contract state action's scope. The Court's trajectory rendered agencies'
broad theories precarious should they be challenged in the courts. And
going forward, advocates would no longer have Supreme Court precedent to support their claims. If agencies continued to implement the
workplace Constitution, it would be increasingly clear that they did so
based on their own understanding of the Constitution's commands.

1 Charles W. Rice circa 1955. C. W. Rice Collection, MSS 0242–002, Houston
Public Library, Houston Metropolitan Research Center.

2 Charles Hamilton Houston (*center*) with Senator Robert F. Wagner, archi-
tect of the National Labor Relations Act (*left*), and Vincent Altmeyer (*right*)
at Marian Anderson concert on steps of Lincoln Memorial, January 1, 1939.
Thomas D. McAvoy/Getty Images.

3 Interracial members of the United Cannery, Agricultural, Packing, and Allied Workers of America talking before meeting in Tabor, Creek County, Oklahoma, February 1940. U.S. Farm Security Administration/Office of War Information, Library of Congress.

4 Cecil B. DeMille addressing St. Patrick's Day luncheon given by William M. Jeffers, president, Union Pacific Railroad, March 17, 1945, Omaha. DeMille Papers, Box 17, Folder 9, Item 4133, L. Tom Perry Special Collections, Harold B. Lee Library, Brigham Young University.

5 A. Philip Randolph (*center front*) and Joseph Rauh (*rear, third from right*) with (*from left to right*) Mathew Ahmann, executive director of the National Catholic Conference for Interracial Justice; Cleveland Robinson, chairman of the Demonstration Committee; Rabbi Joachim Prinz, president of the American Jewish Congress; John Lewis, chairman, Student Nonviolent Coordinating Committee; and Floyd McKissick, national chairman of the Congress of Racial Equality, at the Lincoln Memorial for the March on Washington for Jobs and Freedom, August 28, 1963. U.S. Information Agency Press and Publications Service, National Archives at College Park, Md.

6 A. R. Kinstley, vice president of the Oil Workers International Union (*seated left*), and George L. P. Weaver (*seated right*) with (*from left to right*) William H. Oliver, codirector of the Congress of Industrial Organizations (CIO) Committee to Abolish Discrimination, and James E. Turner, director of the United Rubber Workers of America's fair employment office, discussing the selection of Denver as the first city for the CIO's National Anti-Discrimination League campaign against racial discrimination, July 19, 1950. Denver Post/ Getty Images.

7 Robert L. Carter, NAACP Legal Defense and Education Fund, January 1, 1955. Hulton Archive/Getty Images.

8 Howard Jenkins Jr. in his office, Washington, D.C., July 24, 1963. "The first black person picked for the [National Labor Relations Board], if approved by the Senate, may open his career in his new job by having to make a decision as to whether racial discrimination is an unfair labor practice." Associated Press (text) and William Smith/AP Images.

9 William H. Brown III (*center*), with his wife, being introduced by President Richard M. Nixon as the new chairman of the Equal Employment Opportunity Commission, May 6, 1969, White House, Washington, D.C. Bob Daugherty/ AP Images.

10 Reverend Douglas Moore (*bottom at far left*), chairman of Washington's Black United Front, announcing petition to deny WMAL-TV's license renewal application; Absalom Jordan (*top left*), national chairman of Black Efforts for Soul in Television (BEST); William D. Wright (*top right*), director of Washington's Unity House, active in BEST and WMAL-TV petition. Reprinted with permission of New Bay Media LLC from "New Challenges from Every Side," *Broadcasting*, September 8, 1969, 25–27.

11 John Nassikas, chairman of the Federal Power Commission, at Senate hearings on the energy crisis, Washington, D.C., November 8, 1973. Henry Burroughs/AP Images.

12 Betty Southard Murphy, National Labor Relations Board chair, Denver, September 1975. Millard Smith, Denver Post/Getty Images.

13 Ernest C. Smith, 1973. Generously provided by National Right to Work Committee.

14 Reed Larson (*far left*), talking to group in National Right to Work Committee offices, circa 1973. Generously provided by National Right to Work Committee.

15 Jonathan C. Gibson (*center*) and Sylvester Petro (*right*), architects of the right-to-work movement's legal arguments, with Mike Merrill, circa 1970s. Generously provided by National Right to Work Committee.

16 Anne B. Parks (*left*), Bob Johnson (*center*), and Alberta Kyes (*right*), plain-
tiffs in *Abood v. Detroit Board of Education*, on steps of the United States
Supreme Court, Washington, D.C., 1976. Photo appeared on the cover of
Free Choice, April 28, 1978. Generously provided by National Right to Work
Committee.

17 Harry Beck testifying in favor of the National Right to Work Act, 1996, Washington, D.C. Generously provided by National Right to Work Committee.

11

Liberals Rethink the Workplace Constitution

"Neither mandated by the Constitution nor by the Act"
Handy Andy, Inc., 228 N.L.R.B. 447 (1977)

In 1976, only two years after the National Labor Relations Board decided to deny certification to unions with a record of discrimination, it called a hearing to reconsider the case of *Bekins Moving & Storage*. As the Board's announcement noted, the *Bekins* decision had garnered only a bare majority, and two of its supporters, Chairman Edward Miller and fellow Republican Ralph Kennedy, had since left the agency. At first glance, Miller's replacement appeared likely to support the *Bekins* majority. Republican Betty Southard Murphy was the first woman on the NLRB and the only female head of a major regulatory agency. A former international journalist and hard-boiled labor lawyer, Murphy had already smashed one glass ceiling at the helm of the Wage and Hour Division in Nixon's Department of Labor. Murphy was described as a "gingerly feminist": someone "who can recount years of indignities as a professional woman but who does not make a point of doing so." That said, she supported the Equal Rights Amendment and "civil rights and equal employment opportunity for workers." But the possibility that employers might accuse unions of racial discrimination simply to avoid recognizing them worried Murphy. Her upcoming hearing would reconsider *Bekins* in light of this concern.[1]

In the late 1970s, *Bekins*, and the workplace Constitution on which it rested, scrambled political alliances. Assigning labels like "liberal" and "conservative" was tricky. Those resisting unionization were a much broader, more ideologically diverse group than the anti–New Deal conservatives who gave birth to the right-to-work movement. Similarly, those defending workers' right to organize stretched beyond New Deal Democrats. Yet one thing was clear: nearly all who supported retaining *Bekins* made no pretense of seeking to harmonize civil and labor rights. More than ideology or politics, opposition to unions drove their support.

Avoiding Unions

"There is a movement on to stay non-union," Charlie Hughes told the audience at one of the weekly seminars he gave during the mid-1970s. Whether they worked in the booming service industry or the struggling manufacturing sector, in the Sun Belt or the Rust Belt, audience members' companies had paid hundreds of dollars for them to attend sessions on topics such as "How to Maintain Non-union Status" and "Winning Organizational Campaigns." Typically, Hughes played the behavioral psychology good cop to Alfred De Maria's tough, New York–lawyer bad cop. Hughes told the audience how to make their workers too happy to want a union; De Maria told them what they could legally get away with, as well as how to skirt and when to break the law. De Maria's basic lesson about fending off organizing campaigns: "Delay is crucial to your strategy." Delay bought employers time to turn their workers against the union and made unions seem ineffective. These seminars and the lawyers who taught them were on the NLRB members' minds when they decided to revisit *Bekins*.[2]

Hughes and De Maria were just two players in a booming "union avoidance" industry. They and possibly hundreds of other "high-priced consultants, most of them lawyers," worked for companies with bland names such as Modern Management Methods and Executive Enterprises, Inc., or for specialized law firms. The National Association of Manufacturers' more forthrightly named Council on Union-Free Environment aggregated and disseminated their tactics.[3]

This burgeoning industry was connected to, but not identical with, the right-to-work movement. In 1972, the secret "management movement" that had formed to rewrite the National Labor Relations Act in 1965 merged its organizations into the Business Roundtable and went public. By 1976 the Roundtable had been dubbed "Businesses' Most Powerful Lobby in Washington." The Business Roundtable, like its predecessors, included moderate as well as conservative executives. Similarly, the union avoidance industry's customers included putatively liberal institutions, such as nonprofit universities and hospitals, as well as movement-affiliated firms like U.S. Steel or the virulently antiunion textile company J. P. Stevens. Some customers explained their interest in the ideological terms of the right-to-work movement. Others invoked concepts like efficiency, flexibility, and competitiveness that resonated in an economy facing tough international competition and with a public that increasingly saw unions as sclerotic and self-interested.[4]

Unionization rates suffered as a result. By 1976, the proportion of the nonfarm workforce that was unionized had dropped by about a third, from its 1954 peak of 38 percent to 24.5 percent. Unions lost more elections too, with their success rate dropping from 80 percent in the NLRA's first ten years, to 62 percent in 1966, and down to 48 percent in 1976. At the same time, the number of unfair labor practice charges against employers, a proxy for the vigor of employers' antiunion campaigns, spiked, increasing sixfold between 1955 and 1976, from 7,451 to 42,802. In retrospect, the reasons for unions' decline also included everything from tectonic shifts in the economy to unions' strategic blunders to worker disaffection and complacency. At the time, however, social scientists attributed the decline primarily to employers' growing resistance.[5]

The *Bekins* line of cases fed concerns that employers were using the NLRB's antidiscrimination policies primarily to avoid unionization. Bekins's lawyer was a right-to-work activist and a leader of the National Right to Work Committee in the 1960s; his client was likely using its discrimination charges strategically. Alden Press which had an all-male supervisory staff and an all-female clerical staff, sought disingenuously to disqualify a union local from representing its workers "on the grounds that it engaged in discriminatory practices on the basis of sex." S. H. Kress & Company brought discrimination charges against the Poor People's Union of America, a multiracial union associated with Martin Luther King Jr.'s Southern Christian Leadership

Council. Such charges delayed unions' election petitions, which were supposed to be resolved speedily, often by over a year.[6]

Employers also raised discrimination charges as a defense when newly certified unions sought an order to bargain from the NLRB. In the 1973 case known as *Mansion House*, a federal appeals court held that the Constitution prohibited the Board from ordering an employer to bargain with a discriminatory union. *Mansion House* charges also fit neatly into the strategy of union avoiders. If a union managed to win an election, De Maria instructed, the employer should "bargain to the point of boredom over the next year." This would demonstrate the union's weakness and, it was hoped, force it into a support-sapping strike. But if the union sought a bargaining order from the Board, a discrimination defense bought the employer more time. Indeed, employers had since raised this defense in cases where their concern for discrimination seemed as unlikely as in *Bekins*. The Board would also consider the *Mansion House* rule at its 1976 hearing.[7]

Whose Workplace Constitution?

"It is just outrageous for an employer who was the discriminator" to be bringing these charges, a Teamsters' lawyer charged at the NLRB hearing. The Board members seemed to agree. In one of the cases under consideration, the employer claimed that a *union*'s sex discrimination barred it from representing the *company*'s all-male stationary engineers. Chairwoman Murphy and board member Howard Jenkins badgered the company's attorney into admitting that the company, not the petitioning union, was responsible for the unit's being all male. Another employer accused a Teamsters local that was organizing its all-white, all-male truck drivers of racial and sex discrimination. Jenkins asked the employer's lawyer if the Board should develop standards of proof that blocked employers from using *Bekins* "for purposes of delay and gamesmanship in order to buy time and perhaps avoid the evil name?" Murphy was also concerned that employers were raising discrimination claims that their minority workers did not support. The union lawyers' outrage and the Board members' skepticism were expected. More surprising was who did and did not advocate for the Board's antidiscrimination policies.[8]

Perhaps most remarkable was the absence of the NAACP. Robert Carter, who had led the association's constitutional advocacy before the Board since the 1950s, had left the NAACP in 1969. Carter's replacement was also committed to administering the workplace Constitution, but not before the NLRB. The NAACP was the lead plaintiff in the 1976 Supreme Court litigation demanding equal employment rules from the Federal Power Commission and brought charges under the rules already adopted by the Federal Communications Commission. The fact that these other agencies' rules targeted employers while the Board's policies had increasingly obvious antiunion potential probably explained the NAACP's choice. Tensions over affirmative action were already driving the NAACP apart from its union allies; even assuming the NAACP supported the Board policies, defending them might not have seemed worth the fight.[9]

And it would have been a fight: labor opposed *Bekins* and *Mansion House* on constitutional and policy grounds. The AFL-CIO's lawyer argued that Congress never intended the NLRB to police union discrimination and that it was not required to do so by the Constitution. Supreme Court authority never squarely supported the Board's analysis, he argued, and the Court's recent narrow state action decisions, *Moose Lodge* and *Jackson*, precluded it. "The state must be involved with the wrong, not simply empowering somebody to commit a wrong," he insisted. To the unions appearing at the hearing, the Board's policies were "simply another weapon in the [employers'] arsenal of delay."[10]

Another surprise came from the Chamber of Commerce. The Chamber's lawyer, Robert Thompson, was a management attorney from a right-to-work state, and the Chamber of Commerce, which Thompson also helped lead, was a longtime player in the right-to-work movement. Yet, Thompson informed the Board, "We find ourselves in perhaps the unusual position of being in agreement with the" AFL-CIO that *Bekins* and *Mansion House* "are wrong and should be repudiated by the Board." Here was a right-to-work attorney arguing *against* the workplace Constitution in an instance in which it was being used to hurt unions.[11]

On closer inspection, however, Thompson's position was less puzzling. Unlike the AFL-CIO, Thompson accepted that the Constitution barred the NLRB from sanctioning union discrimination. He simply argued that the Board's *post*certification remedies satisfied its constitutional responsibility. This fit with the movement's emphasis on exclusive representation (which followed from certification) as the linchpin in its state action arguments. Thompson also valued curbing the Board's authority more than expanding employers' "arsenal of delay." *Bekins* and *Mansion House*, he contended, were naked attempts by the NLRB "to extend by fiat its otherwise clearly limited jurisdiction." Thompson found his weapons elsewhere: instead, he contended, the Board should more liberally *de*certify discriminatory unions. Decertification was popular with union avoiders. If an employer failed to thwart unionization, decertification could undo it. As early as 1969, right-to-work activists were helping workers decertify their unions in Missouri and Kansas. Employers could not initiate a decertification, but, De Maria assured them in another of his workshops, there were ways to facilitate one, ways the Chamber of Commerce's prescription would make more readily available.[12]

That left only employers to defend *Bekins* and *Mansion House*. They did so with vigor, insisting that "the protection of individual rights ... get[s] lost in the shuffle in the Chamber's method." "I don't think there is any excuse for the Board shirking its clear obligation to withhold a license here from a discriminator," one employer contended. "That's the real meaning of *Bekins* and I think it was right then, and it is right now." Another argued broadly that "the Constitution deprives the Agency of the power to grant a request by any labor organization which practices invidious discrimination."[13]

The Supreme Court's Permission

The AFL-CIO urged the NLRB to delay its decision, pending the outcome in *NAACP v. FPC*. The Supreme Court's decision several months later, that agencies needed to implement antidiscrimination only if it was related to their primary statutory mission, went a long way toward "set[ting] the fences" between the nation's antidiscrimination and economic regulatory statutes. In a concurrence, Chief Justice Burger argued that Congress was wise to decide against diffusing enforcement of Title VII across federal agencies. Doing so, he contended, would create "inevitable potential for conflict between administrative agencies," would subject "regulated industries ... to the commands of different voices in the bureaucracy," and would result in "the agonizingly long administrative process grind[ing] even more slowly." *NAACP* was one of several mid-1970s Supreme Court decisions that set fences among regulatory statutes and between them and the Constitution. Together the decisions left the NLRB free to reject *Bekins* and *Mansion House*. Burger favored these fences for much the same reason the Chamber of Commerce opposed *Bekins*. He even cited an article with the provocative teaser, "Will the ACLU come to the rescue of businessmen whose civil liberties are trampled by government bureaucrats?" But the Court's fence-setting also had the support of its liberal justices.[14]

The first of these Supreme Court cases, decided before the Board's 1976 hearing, disentangled Title VII and the NLRA. In 1974, the Court bolstered *Bekins* and *Mansion House* by ruling that, although the NLRA allowed a union to bargain away a range of individual workers' rights, "Title VII's strictures are absolute" and could not be waived through collective bargaining. Court watchers thought the case affirmed "the primacy of Title VII rights over those rights provided by the NLRA."[15]

Then came *Emporium Capwell v. Western Addition Community Organization*. Emporium Capwell, a chain of department stores, had fired African American employees who had attempted to discuss charges of systemic racial discrimination with the company president and, when unsuccessful, picketed its San Francisco store. The workers charged that their termination violated their rights under the NLRA to concerted action, notwithstanding the fact that their union was prepared to grieve their complaints. In 1971, the Board found that the NLRA did *not* protect the workers' efforts to bypass their exclusive bargaining representative. The Supreme Court agreed. The workers' request would create "too big a hole" in the system of exclusive representation, Justice Brennan insisted to his brethren during their private conference. Justice Marshall, writing for all but Justice Douglas, recognized that the Board had to interpret the NLRA "in light of the broad national labor policy of which it is a part." This policy "embodies the principles of nondiscrimination as a matter of highest priority," Marshall recognized. But employees' right to be free from discrimination "cannot be pursued at the expense of the orderly collective-bargaining process contemplated by the NLRA," he insisted. The fact that Title VII may have protected the employees did not mean that the NLRA had to. Read most broadly, *Emporium Capwell* relieved the

Board of a duty to counter discrimination if doing so would frustrate its core statutory mission.[16]

The next year, the Court erected a similar boundary between the Constitution and Title VII. *Washington v. Davis* involved a charge that the Washington, D.C., police department used qualifications for officers that disproportionately excluded African Americans. At the time the case was filed, Title VII did not apply to the District of Columbia's employees, so the claim was brought under the Fifth Amendment only. The parties, the trial judge, and the court of appeals nonetheless used Title VII doctrine to determine the merits of this constitutional claim. Title VII deemed employment qualifications with a racially disproportionate impact illegal, even absent discriminatory intent, unless the employer could show that the qualifications were closely related to job performance. "Title VII and E[qual] P[rotection] are very different," Justice Rehnquist insisted when the justices discussed the case privately. Equal protection required not only "disparity" but also "intent." As the Court's opinion in *Davis* acknowledged, some of its previous cases had suggested the opposite. *Davis* clarified that Rehnquist now spoke for the Court. "We have never held that the constitutional standard for adjudicating claims of invidious racial discrimination is identical to the standards applicable under Title VII, and we decline to do so today," the Court ruled. Justices Brennan and Marshall dissented, but not to the Court's rending of Title VII from the Constitution's equal protection guarantees.[17]

These decisions, issued within two years and sandwiching the Board's hearing, showed remarkable consensus on the Court for setting fences among regulatory statutes and between those statutes and the Constitution. The liberals and conservatives on the Court likely reached their conclusions for different reasons. In *Davis*, Brennan and Marshall may have seen where the Court was headed on equal protection and decided that the best bet was to cut Title VII loose. Rehnquist, in contrast, was likely protecting equal protection from a more liberal Title VII standard. Similarly, in *Capwell*, Brennan and Marshall protected the New Deal collective bargaining regime. Justice Burger, who found a Title VII–inspired exception to exclusive representation "artificial and indefensible," sounded like the business conservative of his *NAACP v. FPC* concurrence. In other words, the liberal justices accepted the fences to preserve the New Deal administrative state, whereas the conservatives did so to contain it. Regardless, the Court's trio of decisions interrupted the chain that agencies had previously followed from the Constitution to Title VII (or a more amorphous national antidiscrimination policy) and on into their own statutes. The upshot was that the NLRB faced no pressure from the Supreme Court to implement the Constitution.[18]

Rejecting the Workplace Constitution

In February 1977, the NLRB repudiated *Bekins* and the *Mansion House* rule. Those policies gave employers "an incentive to inject charges of union racial discrimination into Board certification and bargaining order proceedings as a delaying tactic in order to avoid collective bargaining altogether rather than to attack racial discrimination," the Board asserted. "Neither [was] mandated by the Constitution nor by the Act," the Board concluded. Instead, they "significantly impair[ed] the national labor policy of facilitating collective bargaining, the enforcement of which is our primary function," and denied workers' right to a representative of their choosing. The Board also found it particularly "ludicrous to excuse the employer from its bargaining obligation" when the employer's *own hiring* often produced the evidence used to allege *union* discrimination. The Board was supported not only by the conservative justices' contraction of the state action doctrine, but also the fence-setting decisions accepted, even championed by the Warren Court's last liberal lions, Marshall and Brennan.[19]

The Board majority accused Jenkins and former NLRB chairman Miller of "misconstru[ing] the 'state action' doctrine" in *Bekins*. Government impermissibly involved itself with private discrimination only when it affirmatively enforced, required, authorized, or fostered the discriminatory practices, the majority found. Furthermore, there had to be "a sufficiently close nexus ... between governmental action and actual discrimination by a private party." According to the majority, Board certification and bargaining orders met none of these criteria. In fact, the majority contended, rather than *involving* the Board in discrimination, they triggered *remedies* for it. Certification imposed a duty of fair representation on unions, enforceable in the courts or by the NLRB. Other unfair labor practice orders were also available, as well as decertification and protections during representation proceedings.

To top it off, there was always Title VII. "It simply cannot be established that either the certification or the bargaining order makes the Union's discriminatory practices the actions of the Government," Murphy's majority concluded.[20]

Murphy's Board also rejected the notion that it could find that the Constitution trumped the NLRA. That statute stated that the Board "shall certify" a union "duly selected by a majority of the unit employees." In deciding otherwise, the *Bekins* majority had "arrogated to this Board the power to determine the constitutionality of mandatory language in the Act we administer," Murphy's majority accused. The Supreme Court, they quoted, had recently observed that "adjudication of the constitutionality of congressional enactments has generally been thought beyond the jurisdiction of administrative agencies."[21]

Jenkins dissented, but to no avail. "Direct commands in a statute are impliedly made subject to constitutional limitations," he countered. As a result, "an agency is not holding a statute unconstitutional when it decides to administer it in a constitutional manner." In fact, Jenkins charged, the majority inadvertently acknowledged that "the Board is required to interpret and apply the Act in a manner which will avoid offense to the Constitution." The various Board remedies on which the majority's analysis relied, he observed, were based on the Constitution. "My colleagues," Jenkins noted, thus "rely no less on constitutional requirements than they would if they held nondiscrimination to be a condition to certification."[22]

Having rejected any constitutional duty to deny certification or bargaining orders to discriminatory unions, the majority used the Court's fence-setting decisions to dismiss any statutory obligation to do so. *Mansion House* had assumed that Title VII established the standard for the constitutional protection it imposed. *Washington v. Davis*, Murphy's majority noted, separated the two. *Emporium Capwell* had recognized that the Board had to interpret the NLRA in light of "the national labor policy" but had rejected the proposition that its statute "should give way to the paramount value of combating racial discrimination." Finally, *NAACP v. FPC* had clarified that when implementing national antidiscrimination policy, "consideration must be given to whether such action promotes or runs counter to the [NLRA's] basic policies and purposes." The Board was thus free to reject the Title VII standards "the [*Mansion House*] court preferred." Also, *Bekins* and the *Mansion House* rule impeded the NLRB's "primary function" of "facilitating collective bargaining," the majority asserted. Any Board "responsibility for carrying out aspects of the broad national policy against invidious discrimination in employment," the majority concluded, was thus "best discharged by" rejecting those policies in favor of the NLRB's postcertification remedies.[23]

For Jenkins, such policy arguments were irrelevant: "The constitutional impediment to certification of a discriminating union," he argued, "forecloses consideration of policy reasons for adopting a procedure which ... postpones determination of disqualifying discrimination to a later date." He explained, "The [F]ifth [A]mendment does not permit a Government agency to provide the instrument for practicing discrimination merely because at some uncertain future date the Board may have an opportunity to terminate this discrimination." Jenkins, however, was alone in this view.[24]

In 1979, Judge David Bazelon, a leading liberal on the D.C. Circuit Court of Appeals, wrote for a panel upholding one of the NLRB decisions rejecting *Bekins* and the *Mansion House* rule. Bazelon found that the Board's statutory purpose gave it a role in countering discrimination that was "far greater than the role assigned to the" Federal Power Commission in *NAACP v. FPC*. He nonetheless found this obligation better satisfied by the Board's postcertification remedies, which were more effective and "consistent with the other policies of the" NLRA. Like the Board, Bazelon rejected a contrary constitutional duty. "The effect of certification is to achieve precisely what was lacking in *Burton*," Bazelon concluded. That early sit-in case had found that the state violated the Constitution because it *failed* to require its lessor restaurant to provide equal protection. The Board's postcertification remedies, Bazelon reasoned, provided the requirement missing in *Burton*. Bazelon's opinion secured a liberal imprimatur on the Board's rejection of *Bekins* and the *Mansion House* rule.[25]

The liberal workplace Constitution had come to look quite conservative. At the same time, buried in the record of the NLRB's hearing was a clue that the conservative workplace Constitution could likewise be used to liberal, even radical, ends. The decertification petition that spurred one of the cases before the Board, the record reveals, was filed by an African American who "doesn't like unions at all."[26]

12

Conservatives Unite the Workplace Constitutions

"The best hope for outlawing compulsory unionism"
Everett Dirksen

An "all Negro political party when first presented sounds very ridiculous, doesn't it?" Ernest Smith asked in January 1964. "But," he insisted, "we will begin to see that this is one of the most profound ideas that Negroes have had for their own salvation." In the 1940s, Smith had been a field organizer for the Cannery Workers, the interracial CIO union that organized Larus & Brother's tobacco plant. Now Smith was teaching at Detroit's Cody High School and was the campaign coordinator for the local Freedom Now Party. This new party was a vehicle for "all-black political action" in the spirit of contemporaneous movements toppling white colonial rule in Africa. Party leaders urged African Americans "to take our freedom" because "one hundred years of waiting for Democratic and Republican politicians to correct our grievances is too long." They supported black candidates and promoted "self-reliance," not revolution. Smith declared that no one "in his right mind could argue against the ideal of integration and equality." Nonetheless, he had abandoned the Cannery Workers' fight for interracial class solidarity. Because "the white majority does not favor integration," he explained, African Americans' "only salvation is to build and nourish our own institutions."[1]

Since the 1930s, African Americans outside the South had voted ever more reliably for Democratic candidates, making many worry that the party took them for granted. The Freedom Now Party wanted to elect black candidates, but it also hoped to increase African Americans' influence within the existing parties. "What would happen to the Democratic party," Smith asked, "if they woke up one bright November morn and found that the Negro vote was no longer in their hip pocket?" What if, he continued, the Republican Party "started winning elections because the Democrats no longer had the Negro vote?" If both parties started "seriously vying with each other for the Negro vote through 'The Freedom Now Party,'" Smith argued, the Democratic Party would fight for African Americans' interests far more vigorously.[2]

Democrats' delivery of the Civil Rights Act of 1964 and the presence of Senator Barry Goldwater, who voted against the act, at the top of the Republican presidential ticket meant that "most Negroes ... voted straight Democratic" in November 1964. This wave of loyalty killed the Freedom Now Party. Five years later, however, when the Detroit Federation of Teachers signed a union security agreement with Detroit's Board of Education, Smith used the same tactics he had advocated for in 1964, only this time as one of the lead plaintiffs in a lawsuit challenging the agreement's constitutionality. Smith's suit opened new frontiers in the fight for a conservative workplace Constitution, among them the prominence of its black and female plaintiffs.[3]

The Right to Work in the Public Sector

The Black Teachers Workshop, which Smith joined in 1967, was part of the broader black nationalist turn in Detroit politics during the late 1960s. That summer, riots, known in Smith's circle as the "July Rebellion," had ripped through the city, accelerating white teachers' flight from Detroit's predominantly African American schools. Rather than try to stop the outflow, the Black Teachers Workshop demanded that the city recruit nationally for more black teachers. "Quality education for black children," the group insisted, "depends upon black faculties ... who will give our children ... the sense of control over our communities and destiny which we are denied in all areas of this society." The connections between Smith's Teachers Workshop and the complicated union politics embroiling the Detroit schools provide a clue as to how he became a lead plaintiff in a right-to-work lawsuit.[4]

Traditionally, teachers like Smith were a mainstay of the black elite. In the early twentieth century, teaching was one of the few professions open to African Americans. Teachers were also valued trench soldiers in the campaign to edify and uplift the race. More generally, government employment often offered African Americans better opportunities than the private sector, especially for white-collar work. When government hiring spiked after World War II, the numbers of African Americans working in the public sector soared. These trends affected classrooms; the number of African American women working in "education service" more than doubled between 1940 and 1960. By 1967, when Smith joined the Black Teachers Workshop, teachers and other public sector workers were the backbone of a solid black middle class.[5]

The workshop's demand for more black teachers resonated not only with the goals of the Freedom Now Party but also with older debates over segregation and integration. Just as black workers debated in the 1930s and 1940s whether they were better off in their own unions or majority-white unions, black teachers had long agonized over school integration. Black teacher associations in the South had refused to endorse *Brown v. Board of Education* or to fight for desegregation in the 1950s. Not only were they worried about retribution for taking a stand or that desegregation would eliminate their jobs, they were also concerned that black students' education would suffer in desegregated schools.[6]

In the 1960s, similar debates divided northern African Americans and teachers of all races. For teachers, a transfer to a better school was one of the few perks of accumulated service. Indeed, Smith had tried to do just that in 1962. But activists who favored integration were concerned about keeping experienced white teachers in black neighborhood schools, not only about bussing black children to predominantly white schools. In contrast, black nationalists such as the founders of the Black Teachers Workshop argued that white teachers' flight was an insult to black students. Instead they called for "community control" of schools in urban centers from New York to Chicago. Debates over how best to educate African American youth divided black parents from community leaders, and staunch integrationists from black nationalists.[7]

Battles over school integration intermingled with teachers' debates about whether and how to unionize. In Detroit, as elsewhere, there were two main contenders, the National Education Association (NEA, or DEA for the Detroit affiliate) and the American Federation of Teachers (AFT, or DFT for Detroit's local). As its name suggests, the NEA envisioned its members as part of a professional elite, eschewing the union label and tactics. Because it also allowed school administrators to join, the AFT accused the NEA of being a company union. The NEA could sound more like a union opponent than a union alternative, warning, for instance, that teachers belonging to the AFT would "live under an 'Iron Curtain' of [the AFL-CIO's] labor control." The AFT, in contrast, attracted more militant leaders, and engaged in controversial strikes. The AFT was stronger in the North and in cities, the NEA in the South and in suburban and rural districts. In late-1960s Detroit, the DFT had 7,000 members to the DEA's 1,400.[8]

The NEA and AFT were involved in debates over community control in the late 1960s. The AFT had been an aggressive champion of integration, expelling locals that refused to integrate in the 1950s, filing an amicus brief in *Brown*, and supporting the student sit-ins of the early 1960s. The NEA, in contrast, allowed segregated affiliates up to the mid-1960s and did not endorse *Brown* until 1961. Yet the NEA's ethos was more in keeping with black educators' elite, professional identity. When the NEA merged with an independent association of black teachers in the 1960s, then elected its first black president in 1967, it further boosted its appeal to African Americans. Meanwhile the AFT's star plummeted when, in 1968, white union members struck a community-controlled school in Brooklyn. Formerly loyal black teachers crossed the picket line and the AFT alienated its civil rights allies. The strike, which drew national media attention, made white teachers seem like part of the inner-city schools' problem, not the solution. The NEA, in contrast, created an Urban Task Force and invited speakers associated with community-controlled schools.[9]

Growing acceptance of public sector unions put Detroit teachers' allegiances to the test. Public sector workers were not covered by the National Labor Relations Act; indeed many of the law's early supporters thought that public sector workers should not engage in collective bargaining. In the mid-1950s, however, minds started to change. Wisconsin passed the first public sector collective bargaining law in 1959, sparking an explosion in unionization by government workers. By the mid-1960s, when Michigan followed in Wisconsin's path, about a half dozen states had such laws and twice that many were considering them. The laws varied in how closely they tracked the NLRA; none, for instance, allowed unions to strike. The Michigan law created a system of exclusive representation, however, and in 1967 the DFT won an election and was certified to represent all of Detroit's teachers.[10]

The DFT's first contract with the city spurred Ernest Smith into action. The contract contained an *agency shop* provision, which required covered workers to pay dues to – but not to join – the union to keep their jobs. The AFL-CIO had fashioned the agency shop in 1960 as a way around state right-to-work laws, which generally banned making workers join a union to keep a job. Smith, along with fellow teacher Christine Warczak, urged Detroit educators not to pay their dues when the DFT's agency shop provision went into effect in January 1970. They also promised to fight the provision's constitutionality all the way to the Supreme Court. "Isn't the right not to join a union a 'civil right'?" Smith queried. He and Warczak had the backing of the DEA and its black president. The organization paying for Smith's campaign, however, was the National Right to Work Committee.[11]

The Right to Work Committee's Next Generation

Reed Larson was a child of the Depression who cut his political teeth during the 1950s as the leader of an organization called Kansans for Right to Work. Under the tutelage of the DeMille Foundation, Larson implemented a successful combination of grassroots mobilization, prolific advertising, and outreach to Democrats. He built a model organization that appeared to be "composed of housewives, farmers, small businessmen, professional people, wage earners – no big business industrialists." While right-to-work laws elsewhere in the country failed miserably at the ballot box in 1958, Larson secured a win in Kansas. His success catapulted him to the leadership of the National Right to Work Committee in 1959. It fell to Larson to steer the committee and the movement out of its doldrums and into the turbulent 1960s.[12]

Five years after taking the helm, Larson informed the committee's leadership that "the Right to Work cause has made important progress." The committee had thwarted labor's efforts to repeal state right-to-work laws and to make the NLRA deny states the power to adopt them. Mississippi and Wyoming had even passed new laws. The Right to Work Committee had new influence in the Republican Party as well. With right-to-work supporter Barry Goldwater on the ticket in 1964, Republicans gave the nod to the movement for the first time, promising in their platform "constant opposition to any form of unregulated monopoly, whether business or labor."[13]

Larson also touted progress in the courts. Whiteford S. Blakeney, a Right to Work Committee founder and board member, was a Charlotte, North Carolina, attorney who represented some of the country's most notoriously antiunion employers. In 1963, Larson reported, Blakeney had scored "a most significant legal advance" before the Supreme Court in the last of the Railway Labor Act cases. Larson's depiction was puzzling, however. In *International Association of Machinists v. Street*, the 1961 decision finding that the Railway Labor Act protected dissenters from funding unions' political speech, the Court had suggested remedies that Larson's committee promptly declared disappointing. In Blakeney's 1963 case, the Court converted those disappointing suggestions into binding law. Then again, a dissenting Justice Harlan contended that the 1963 decision gave *Street* "an expansive thrust which can hardly fail to increase the volume of this sort of litigation in the future."[14]

Keeping the door to litigation open was just what Larson wanted. Having worked on the Railway Labor Act cases in the 1950s, Larson was closely attuned to the right-to-work movement's litigation. An inveterate organizer and popularizer, Larson realized that a two-way street ran between litigation and political mobilization. The DeMille Foundation had organized politically to change how the courts decided cases. To Larson, lawsuits were also an excellent way to generate support for the right-to-work cause. Under his leadership, the Right to Work Committee made litigation a core part of its agenda. It then published articles about its cases in *Free Choice*, a newsletter targeted to workers.[15]

Litigation looked even more appealing as the decade progressed. The movement's state legislative campaigns stalled. Although right-to-work activists continued to block labor's attempt to outlaw state right-to-work laws and stopped Congress from allowing "compulsory unionism" in the Postal Service, their efforts to enact federal right-to-work protections went nowhere. Senate Minority Leader Everett Dirksen counseled that the "best hope for outlawing compulsory unionism in America must lie with our courts and their recognition of the Constitution as a shield between the working man and the union officials." The Right to Work Committee's Washington counsel, John Kilcullen, argued in 1967 that the Warren Court's solicitude for individual rights meant that it was "highly probable that if the compulsory unionism question were again presented to the Supreme Court," the Court would decide it in the movement's favor.[16]

These predictions prompted the committee in 1968 to create a new institutional home for its litigation campaign, the National Right to Work Legal Defense Foundation. The foundation pledged to represent "workers who are suffering legal injustice as a result of employment discrimination under compulsory union membership arrangements." Within a year, the foundation reported that it had received donations from nearly 11,000 individuals, corporations, and other foundations. Ernest Smith's suit against the Detroit Federation of Teachers was its most prominent case.[17]

Liberalizing the Right to Work

In 1967, Larson took the stage at the California Negro Leadership Conference. Given "your dedication to freedom of the individual coupled with the unchallengeable fact of union discriminatory practices," Larson urged his audience, the right-to-work movement, not the labor movement, was African Americans' most natural ally. In the 1950s, Larson had helped the right-to-work movement connect its cause with African Americans' fight against union discrimination. Under his leadership, the Right to Work Committee expanded those efforts, finding great opportunity in African Americans' nationalist turn. For Larson, Smith's fight against the agency shop was doubly valuable: it helped the committee not only to counter a dynamic new front in union activity – public sector unions – but also to liberalize the movement's image.[18]

In the 1960s, the right-to-work movement allied itself with African Americans' struggle for civil rights. Only months before Smith challenged the DFT's agency shop clause, the Right to Work Committee helped James Nixon, Smith's fellow city employee, sue Detroit and his union, the American Federation of State, County and Municipal

Employees (AFSCME). Nixon was a longtime member and former representative of AFSCME. But as AFSCME began to resemble a private sector union by winning exclusive representation and signing an agency shop contract, Nixon turned against it. After winning his committee-funded lawsuit in April 1969, Nixon founded Michigan Citizens for Right to Work, backed Smith's fight against the DFT, and fed Larson's newsletter articles such as "Free Choice: Another Area of Civil Rights That Jim Nixon Deeply Believes In."[19]

Larson found African American support outside of Detroit as well. Poultry worker Ruth Johnson, *Free Choice* reported in 1969, founded Missourians for Right to Work and helped oust her union and its union shop clause. "It's almost like a new kind of slavery," she charged in *Free Choice*'s pages. Ben Howard had been a steward for the United Automobile Workers. While other disillusioned African Americans led a nationalist insurgency *within* the labor movement, Howard joined the Black Workers Alliance, an organization that "combats compulsory unionism for black people." In 1968, the Los Angeles chapter of the Congress of Racial Equality, which Howard led, endorsed a proposed state right-to-work law. The combination of mandatory unionization and union discrimination, he explained, meant that the black worker was being forced "to pay the cost of actions which discriminate against him."[20]

Larson also put women at the movement's forefront. Women had served as right-to-work plaintiffs since the 1940s, yet the face of the movement had remained resolutely male. As late as 1958, DeMille asked, "Does man have the right to work?" Women appeared only as the long-suffering wives of the "individual working man." Under Larson, in contrast, a 1966 pamphlet featured a working-woman plaintiff, and a conservative magazine featured a picture of Dirksen with members of the Women's Organization for Right to Work. A Right to Work Committee film about a strike in Indiana, titled ... *And Women Must Weep*, opened with a woman explaining how the violent clashes depicted in the film caused her to renounce her union membership.[21]

The public sector union cases not only helped Larson promote the committee's problack, prowoman image but also linked the right to work with New Left critiques of ossified union bureaucracy. By the early 1970s, Larson's speeches to young audiences included comments such as, "The more consistent elements in the 'New Left' shar[e] a remarkably large number of positions with the more consistent conservatives." Long-haired, young, white men fighting the unions at their schools joined right-to-work lawsuits, bolstering these claims.[22]

In 1970, Ernest Smith traveled to Washington, D.C., to be recognized for contributions to "furthering the principle of voluntarism in union membership." Encapsulating the strange politics afoot, the speaker at Smith's award ceremony was the staunch segregationist and North Carolina senator Sam Ervin.[23]

Establishing Teachers' Right to Work

In September 1969, a small group of activists gathered to plan the Detroit teachers' agency-shop challenge. Leonard A. Keller, a local management-side lawyer, was "quite anxious to get involved." The suit would help his client, the Michigan Association of School Boards, limit teachers' new collective bargaining rights. He crafted the lawsuit and helped establish the Right to Work Committee–affiliated but seemingly local organizations that championed it: Ernest Smith's and Christine Warczak's Detroit Teachers Opposed to Compulsory Unionism ("Teachers Opposed") and James Nixon's Michigan Citizens for Right to Work ("Michigan Citizens"). George P. McDonnell, who ran a telemarketing firm with close ties to the Right to Work Committee, wrote fund-raising letters and press releases for the suit and used conservative activist Richard Vigeurie's mailing lists to distribute them. Nixon signed McDonnell's fund-raising letters, which went out on Michigan Citizens' letterhead. John Kilcullen, now the Right to Work Legal Defense Foundation's general counsel, was not at the September meeting, but he may as well have been. He vetted the local counsel's arguments and paid Keller's bills. Right-to-work leaders promised to "work very closely with Jim Nixon and Ernie Smith," but there was no question about who called the shots.[24]

Smith proved an effective organizer. By April 1970, he and Warczak had recruited more than six hundred plaintiffs, 5 percent of Detroit's teachers, to what had grown into two massive lawsuits that challenged the agency shop and were working their way through the Michigan courts. Consolidated as *Abood v. Detroit Board of Education*, the plaintiffs proclaimed their opposition to public sector collective bargaining and asked the court to find the agency shop, and the state labor law authorizing it, unconstitutional. After five years, two trial-court dismissals, and a legislative amendment explicitly allowing agency shops for Michigan's public sector unions, the Michigan Court of Appeals finally heard the teachers' case in 1975.[25]

The *Abood* plaintiffs benefited from the wait. Concerns about job security, particularly protections for workers' speech and associations, grew in the late 1960s and early 1970s. Cases challenging discharges were rarely brought and typically failed owing to the at-will doctrine, a legal rule that left employers free to fire or discipline employees for "a good reason, a bad reason, or no reason at all." Even public sector workers, unless protected by civil service laws, were employed at will. On this basis, the Supreme Court had regularly dismissed their constitutional challenges to employer actions. This time-honored approach had recently come under attack, however. During the 1950s, the Supreme Court addressed the constitutionality of laws authorizing the discharge of public employees who refused to take loyalty oaths or who had belonged to "subversive" organizations. Gradually the Court recognized – usually more in words than deeds – due process and First Amendment limits on such laws. By the 1960s, a closely divided Court wavered between striking down and upholding these laws. Then, in 1968 and 1972, two cases clearly established that the First Amendment and due process protected government employees, providing rights to contest termination and to speak out on matters of public importance. The decisions, which had nothing to do with subversive activities, were seen as a watershed for public employees' constitutional rights.[26]

During this same period, the right-to-work movement generated significant popular and political opposition to public sector unions. In 1973, a former staffer from the California Right to Work Committee started the Public Service Research Council. The council argued that unionization among government workers threatened to allow labor to control government. Similarly, during the early 1970s, Reed Larson's Right to Work Committee and Legal Defense Foundation charged that "compulsory unionism threatens the merit principle, strips [teachers and other public employees] of tenure, and threatens academic freedom." In 1975, American cities were hit by nearly five hundred strikes as public workers protested recession-induced budget cuts and wage freezes. The Public Service Research Council and Larson's committee capitalized on the backlash, gaining public support for their campaign against government unions. That year, Larson's committee pulled in fifteen thousand new members per month and the movement helped defeat a proposed federal public-sector labor law.[27]

These shifts worked to the Detroit teachers' advantage. The *Abood* lawyers wanted to do more than protect public employees from supporting political speech that they opposed. The lawyers asked the appellate court to instead adjudge "the 'agency shop clause' [itself] ... contrary to the Constitution of the United States." They emphasized the rights the Supreme Court had recently recognized, particularly public employees' "full constitutional rights of speech, association, and belief embodied in the First Amendment." They also contended that the Supreme Court's new decisions established that the government must have "a demonstrated compelling state interest" in order to justify infringing those rights, one that was not met by the "free rider" and labor peace arguments that the Supreme Court had accepted in the early Railway Labor Act case, *Hanson v. Union Pacific Railroad*.[28]

The appellate court's decision was a "partial victory." To the Legal Defense Foundation's disappointment, the court applied the older right-to-work cases, finding that the reasons that made the union shop constitutional then still justified requiring "support of the collective bargaining agency by all who receive the benefits of its work." Promisingly, the court found that because the Michigan statute allowed unions to use objectors' dues for political purposes, the agency shop agreement it authorized "could violate plaintiffs' First ... Amendment rights." The Michigan court did not strike down the statute as the teachers had hoped, however. Instead, it merely required, as in the Supreme Court's Railway Labor Act cases, that the union refund a portion of the objectors' dues. After the Michigan Supreme Court refused to review the decision, the Detroit teachers petitioned the United States Supreme Court for review.[29]

The Court Finally Decides

Abood troubled Justice Powell. The case's outcome, he warned his fellow justices, "will certainly affect the political power of the public sector unions, and particularly their power to persuade state and local governments (and perhaps even the national government) to endorse the right to strike against the public." In 1976, the threat of public sector strikes still weighed heavily. In a case decided earlier that year, a bare majority of justices took the unusual step of striking down a law imposing federal wage and hour laws on local governments. Opponents of the law had urged that if the justices found Congress could pass this law, it would suggest that Congress could also extend the NLRA, "including ... the right to strike," to public sector workers. This concern, as well as worries about local governments' fiscal health, influenced the decisions by Justices Powell and Blackmun as well as Chief Justice Burger to vote against the law. In its opinion, the Court explained that respect for states' sovereignty, which the Court had not relied on since the New Deal, required no less. *Abood* once again challenged public sector unions' growing power. Would the justices find that the Constitution countermanded sovereign states' employment policies, even though they had just found that Congress could not?[30]

The lawyers for the Detroit teachers put the threat posed by public sector unions in the starkest terms. The Legal Defense Foundation brought in Sylvester Petro, a former organizer for the Steelworkers' union turned libertarian law professor, to argue their case. In a 1973 law review article, Petro had claimed that public sector labor laws posed a mortal threat to state sovereignty. He filed a similarly dramatic brief in the 1976 wage and hour case, warning the Court not to issue a decision that supported "federal laws imposing ... [a] compulsory collective bargaining regime" on the public sector. Petro's *Abood* brief made equally bold arguments. *Everything* a public sector union did, Petro contended, was political: Agreements about salary and benefits were public policies that had an impact on budgets and taxes; public employers were also public servants of the workers with whom they negotiated, and thus saw contract terms as a way to win their employees' votes; unions lobbied over how to allocate public funds among different agencies; and so on. As a result, "even if the Union's partisan activities were to be eliminated," Petro insisted, "public-sector bargaining would remain an inherently political phenomenon."[31]

At first, it seemed Petro had failed miserably. Justice Stewart left the justices' private discussion of *Abood* thinking they had all agreed that the Court's Railway Labor Act cases governed: the agency shop was constitutional but political use of dues was not; the union, as a result, must refund that share to dissenting workers.[32]

The justices' unanimity fractured once pen was set to paper, however. The remaining Warren Court appointees, perhaps compelled by Michigan's adoption of the New Deal labor law regime, signed on to Stewart's opinion, their recent embrace of more robust First Amendment rights for public sector workers notwithstanding. Not so Justice Powell, who found Petro's arguments compelling. Before joining the bench, Powell had been a partner in a leading Richmond, Virginia, firm that had close ties to the antiunion tobacco industry and was located in one of the first right-to-work states. Just before his nomination to the Court in 1971, Powell had urged the U.S. Chamber of Commerce in a secret memo to counter what he termed liberals' "Attack on the Free Enterprise System." The business community must adopt a legal strategy, not only a public relations and political campaign, Powell insisted. "The judiciary," he emphasized, "may be the most important instrument for social, economic and political change." Now he wielded this power on behalf of the Detroit teachers.[33]

Powell wrote a concurrence that the teachers' lawyers contended was really a dissent. Powell agreed with Petro that "collective bargaining in the public sector is 'political' in any meaningful sense of the word" and that the First Amendment therefore protected *all* union dues. He also adopted the position right-to-work attorneys had advanced all along: that under the Court's more recent First Amendment cases, any infringement of those rights had to be justified by a "paramount" government interest, a tougher standard than was applied in the Railway Labor Act cases. *Abood*, Powell urged, should be remanded for the government to prove that the unions' collective bargaining expenditures furthered a sufficiently compelling interest. For his part, Powell thought it unlikely that they would succeed.[34]

Powell was not alone. Chief Justice Burger was no fan of Petro. Burger upbraided Petro from the bench for submitting lengthy and "overwritten" briefs; he also confided to his fellow justices that he wished the case could be reargued "with competent counsel." But Burger was convinced that "compulsory membership in a union or any compulsory payment of union dues ... as a condition of public employment is not simply unwise and against all of our traditions, but it is violative of the Constitution." He, along with Justice Blackmun, readily joined Powell's opinion.[35]

The Right to Work Legal Defense Foundation considered the Court's 1977 decision a "serious setback" but "not a total loss." The foundation praised Powell's concurrence and the Court for barring unions from using objectors' dues for political speech. In finding these political expenditures unconstitutional, the Court had squarely recognized the right Cecil B. DeMille first claimed in the 1940s, one the courts of his day had easily dismissed. But foundation lawyers were dismayed that the Court had upheld agency shops so long as dues were used for representational purposes. *Abood*, they lamented, "has jeopardized the freedom of millions of public employees nationwide."[36]

The case was an unmitigated success politically, however. In 1975, Larson's team established Concerned Educators against Forced Unionism, a new public face for the teachers' right-to-work fight. Susan Staub, its staff director, discussed *Abood* on conservative talk radio programs, generated outrage about objectors' dismissals through a newsletter, and worked to get right-to-work arguments into the nation's classrooms. Concerned Educators gave a faintly feminist spin to its cause. One 1978 cartoon showed a female teacher standing at the blackboard writing repeatedly, "I will pay dues, I will pay dues ..." while a male union boss twisted her arm painfully behind her back. Larson's committee also produced educational materials targeted to a "minority" audience and cultivated black columnists to write pieces in an effort to reach African Americans. Larson never generated the support among black workers that Concerned Educators seemed to have found among women. Nonetheless his publications continued to feature black public-sector litigants and articles such as one in 1976 titled "Unions Like 'Massah,'" which argued that right-to-work advocates were black workers' true friends.[37]

The right-to-work movement's visible support of African Americans and women was more important to Larson than their widespread support for his cause, however. Historians associate 1970s conservatives and the white working class they courted with opposition to the civil rights and women's movements. Larson instead argued that the right to work *advanced* the interests of working women and African American civil rights. This proved a shrewd calculation, one that helped right-to-work advocates gain cultural legitimacy and shed their "ultraright" reputation. By the mid-1970s, even opponents credited Larson "with dissociating the movement from the right wing generally and with appealing to liberals," in part by creating "right-to-work ads [that] featured women and blacks who had had union trouble."[38]

In another sense, however, *Abood* contained an overlooked warning. One Nixon appointee to the Court had defected from Powell's concurrence: William Rehnquist. This Goldwater Republican was among a new wave of conservatives who were charting a more absolute, rights-restricting approach to the Constitution. The Framers, Rehnquist insisted in a 1976 article, looked to Congress and the president, not a "freewheeling unelected judiciary" or "the Bill of Rights and the Reconstruction Amendments," to solve "the numerous and varied problems that the future would bring." In *Abood*, Rehnquist's adherence to this conservative constitutional principle outweighed his sympathy for the right-to-work cause. The majority opinion, Rehnquist contended, was inconsistent with the robust First Amendment rights the Court had recently found public employees possessed. But Rehnquist had criticized the Court for recognizing those robust rights. Sticking to his position meant rejecting Powell's concurrence in *Abood*, which relied on strengthened First Amendment rights, and instead joining a majority he thought appropriately diminished them. Rehnquist might as well have said that Larson, and Rehnquist's fellow conservative justices, should look to Congress, not the courts, for vindication.[39]

13

The Conservative Workplace Constitution
Divides the New Right Coalition

"The Administration's ... commitment to strict construction"

Howard Baker

"No person should be forced to pay servitude to any organization whose ideology is contrary to their beliefs just in order to feed their family," Harry Beck insisted. Square jawed and stocky, Beck grew up in the sleepy Chesapeake Bay town of La Plata, Maryland, where he took a working-class path through the tumultuous 1960s. After graduating from high school, Beck went to work at the local telephone company and happily joined the Communications Workers of America (CWA). In 1964, he returned to his job after a stint in the Air Force. This time, Beck was less happy with his union. He fought to wrest representation of outposts like his from large urban-based locals that he believed shorted small-town members on pay and protected a "radical element of the union hierarchy." As Beck told it, after being excluded from secret union meetings, rebuffed by the National Labor Relations Board, and losing his coinstigators to mysterious deaths, his rebellion dissipated in 1966. In prevailing accounts, during the 1960s and 1970s, blue-collar workers took their political turns left or right without straying from the union. Beck instead quit the CWA, joined the National Right to Work Committee, and spent the next two decades fighting his former union from the outside.[1]

In the 1970s, Beck and the National Right to Work Legal Defense Foundation extended the right-to-work movement's constitutional challenge against agency shops to the vast majority of workplaces governed by the National Labor Relations Act. Forty years earlier, Cecil B. DeMille had pioneered the right-to-work movement so as to "change the minds of the city Councils, the legislatures, the governors, and the Congress" and ultimately "change the mind of the Supreme Court." With conservatives' clout rising during the 1970s and the partial victory of *Abood* already achieved, the movement he spawned seemed poised to claim that prize. Unless, that was, the ties between right-to-work advocates' workplace Constitution and its liberal twin proved a liability rather than an asset, once conservatives came to power.[2]

From Public to Private Sector

Organizing the independent phone companies and "Baby Bells" that made up the AT&T monopoly was no easy task. During the 1930s and 1940s, telephone workers unionized in droves but also feuded over how strong their national federation should be and whether to affiliate with the AFL or the CIO. In 1946, the CWA was born of these battles; it threw its lot in with the CIO three years later. By 1975, CWA represented more than two-thirds of eligible workers in the Bell System and had recently achieved record-setting wage and benefit increases as well as something akin to nationwide bargaining with AT&T and its affiliates.[3]

The victory came at a price. Along the way, CWA replaced or absorbed scores of smaller local organizations, leaving disgruntled members of the old unions in its wake. CWA's support of the Democratic Party alienated other telephone workers. During the 1950s and 1960s, the dissatisfied could simply quit the union. When the CWA won agency shop agreements in the 1970s, however, even nonmember critics like Beck had to start paying union fees, turning them into active opponents of the CWA.[4]

The Legal Defense Foundation came to Beck's aid after his employer agreed to an agency shop in 1974. Beck had received an award from the National Right to Work Committee for organizing opposition to the proposed contract. Once the contract was adopted, Beck joined with nineteen other Maryland telephone workers to sue CWA, the AFL-CIO, and AT&T. The plaintiffs in *Beck v. Communication Workers of America* accused AT&T and the unions of conspiring to violate their free speech, due process, and equal protection rights by spending their agency fees on political speech and member benefits.[5]

By the time the Legal Defense Foundation filed Beck's suit in 1976, it was thriving. Since its founding, its staff had nearly doubled, it had developed a network of 100 cooperating attorneys, and it had represented more than two thousand employees in more than a hundred actions. During the same period, the foundation's supporters had climbed from just under 11,000 to nearly 200,000 and its annual budget had tripled to about three million dollars, 79 percent of which came from individual contributions averaging thirty-six dollars each. For its part, the Right to Work Committee grew from fewer than 50,000 to 300,000 members in 1975 alone.[6]

The organizations also gained legitimacy and power. Reed Larson was featured in glossy biographical articles, popular magazines wrote features on the Legal Defense Foundation's work, and the major national newspapers reported on its wins and losses. In right-to-work states, papers brimmed with favorable editorials. During the 1976 presidential campaign, Democratic candidate Jimmy Carter touted his support for the right to work in the South and the Republican Party endorsed states' authority to adopt right-to-work laws. Larson repeatedly proved his ability to turn out millions of citizen lobbyists in support of the movement's legislative agenda. Most promising for Beck, even with the Detroit teachers' case, *Abood*, still in its future, the Legal Defense Foundation had achieved a number of victories in court, including an early win against CWA on behalf of a worker fired for quitting the union.[7]

The Legal Defense Foundation's success fed and was fed by the "New Right," a coalition of Goldwater Republicans and next-generation conservatives. Gathering power throughout the 1970s, by 1976 the coalition had amassed sufficient strength that its presidential candidate of choice, California governor Ronald Reagan, nearly beat out President Ford for the Republican Party's nomination. Like the midcentury right-to-work movement, the New Right cultivated a populist image by focusing on "social issues, religious and cultural alienation, antielite rhetoric, lower-middle-class constituencies and plebiscitary opinion mobilization," according to chronicler and participant Kevin Phillips. The Right to Work organizations' defense of workers oppressed by big labor fit hand-in-glove with the New Right's mission to win working-class support for its conservative cause. At the same time, the New Right's climb to power infused the judiciary with judges sympathetic to the right-to-work cause and more generally boosted the influence of constituent groups such as the Right to Work organizations.[8]

Beck would benefit from the enthusiasm and dedication of a young Legal Defense Foundation staff attorney and New Right partisan, Hugh Reilly. Born in 1940 and raised in the waning railroad town of West Springfield, Massachusetts, Reilly decamped for Washington, D.C., after high school. He came of age during the Goldwater campaign, the conservative insurgency that gave birth to New Right politics. He earned his undergraduate and law degrees from American University, and joined the Legal Defense Foundation in 1972. He remained there for most of the next twenty years. Like all of the foundation's lawyers, Reilly had a "strong philosophical orientation toward individual freedom and the protection of employees against abuses of compulsory unionism." He was generally polite, if a bit didactic, but he bristled at perceived slights and nursed grudges against his opponents. Reilly brought his tenacity and conviction to Beck's case.[9]

In 1977, Reilly successfully used the Legal Defense Foundation's quasi-victory in *Abood* to the *Beck* plaintiffs' advantage. *Abood* affirmed that government action was involved in agency shop agreements made under the Railway Labor Act, but explained that this was due to the statute's preemptive effect on state right-to-work laws. This was a feature, the Court noted, that the NLRA did not share. Reilly nonetheless claimed in Beck's case that, after *Abood*, "there can be no doubt ... that the constitutional rights of public-sector and private-sector agency shop employees vis-à-vis the union are the same." The CWA barely resisted. "There was no constitutional finding as far as private employee non-plaintiffs are concerned," CWA's attorney rightly noted. But he did not point out the Court's dicta distinguishing the NLRA and the Railway Labor Act for state action purposes, and he conceded that the "Court said some principles apply in both the private and public sector."[10]

In 1979, the district court sided with Reilly. Citing *Abood*, the judge found that the CWA "violate[d] the [F]irst [A]mendment rights of plaintiffs" when it collected fees "beyond th[ose] allocable to collective bargaining, contract administration and grievance adjustment."

He ordered the union to refund past fees spent on impermissible activities and enjoined CWA from collecting such fees in the future. The court's ruling fell shy of the movement's ultimate goal: having the agency shop declared unconstitutional. The foundation was thrilled nonetheless that a federal court had extended this constitutional principle to workplaces governed by the NLRA. Thanks to *Beck*, the vast majority of workers had finally surmounted the state action hurdle already crossed by public sector and railroad employees.[11]

The conservative press declared Beck and his lawyers civil rights heroes; they also proved auguries. In *Beck*'s wake, the Legal Defense Foundation racked up more district court decisions that used broad state action theories to find that NLRA-covered unions violated dissenting workers' First Amendment rights. One judge found that the NLRA, by permitting union security agreements and making them enforceable in court, imbued them with government action. Reilly also scored a victory on behalf of eighteen New York Telephone employees turned right-to-work activists. By authorizing exclusive representation, their judge observed, the NLRA "extinguish[ed] the individual employee's power to order his own relations with his employer" and made union security agreements enforceable in court. Accordingly, he reasoned, "the federal government ha[d] affirmatively put its omnipresent weight and power ... behind the agency shop clause contained in the collective bargaining agreement." Another judge even adopted a bald sanctioning theory of state action, finding sufficient government involvement because "Congress not only tolerated but expressly authorized agency shop agreements."[12]

In 1983, *Beck* wound down before the district court after several unsuccessful CWA attempts to dismiss the case and battles over the proportion of CWA fees that were unconstitutional. As the parties prepared their cross-appeals to the Fourth Circuit Court of Appeals, right-to-work advocates had reason to hope that the 1980s could be for the conservative workplace Constitution what the 1960s had been for the liberal one.

A New Right Twist on the Workplace Constitution

In September 1982, President Ronald Reagan's counselor, Edwin Meese, told a predominantly black audience of New Right conservatives that

"President Reagan has called for a new Emancipation Proclamation." Meese's speech capped a one-day program in the D.C. suburbs titled "Rethinking the Black Agenda." The nine-year-old Heritage Foundation, a conservative think tank founded by New Right stalwarts Paul Weyrich and Joseph Coors, cosponsored the event with the more recently minted New Coalition for Economic and Social Change ("New Coalition"). New Coalition, in turn, traced its roots to the Fairmont Conference, a December 1980 gathering in San Francisco of black conservatives who wanted to create a conservative alternative to the NAACP. "We believe the answer to black poverty lies in our black communities, and depends for success on our individual initiative and independent action – not on government," New Coalition asserted. Emancipation from government was precisely what President Reagan promised, Meese told his New Coalition audience.[13]

Right-to-work advocates had triumphed in politics as well as the courts during the early 1980s. Ronald Reagan, like Beck a former union member turned right-to-work spokesperson, was elected president in 1980. Although Reagan did not campaign on the right to work, once in office he appointed Donald L. Dotson his assistant secretary of labor for labor-management relations. A former NLRB attorney who later became a management-side lawyer, Dotson blamed big labor for the country's economic woes. Once in office, he tapped Reilly, Beck's attorney, to be his executive assistant. The next year, when Reagan appointed Dotson chair of the NLRB, Dotson made Reilly the Board's solicitor. Democratic critics argued Dotson had proved his antiunion bias by taking this "hired gun from the Right to Work Committee and put[ting] him in charge of the chicken coop."[14]

Larson had also seen Reagan's New Right administration adopt tactics his organizations had been testing since the 1950s. In the 1960s and 1970s, Larson had wooed black conservatives as well as black nationalists and civil rights activists, building ties to the leadership Meese courted in his 1982 speech. Like Larson before him, Meese sought black conservatives' support for a workplace Constitution, albeit to different ends than Larson's movement. Supporters of the liberal workplace Constitution had long argued that affirmative action *implemented* equal protection. During the 1970s, however, litigants increasingly argued that affirmative action programs *violated* equal protection. New Right activists supported these efforts, as did the

Reagan administration. In 1981, Reagan appointed the New Coalition's president, an affirmative action critic, chairman of the Civil Rights Commission. The next year, he made Fairmont Conference attendee Clarence Thomas chairman of the Equal Employment Opportunity Commission. Thomas immediately sparked controversy by declaring himself "unalterably opposed to programs that force or even cajole people to hire a certain percentage of minorities."[15]

The tangled relationship between affirmative action and the right to work created opportunities for the conservative workplace Constitution and the New Right coalition. At the end of the 1970s, a majority of Supreme Court justices began to treat affirmative action as a form of discrimination as much as, or perhaps even more than, a remedy for it. In 1978, the Supreme Court decided *Regents of the University of California v. Bakke*. The *Bakke* litigants did not ask the Court whether the university was *compelled* by equal protection to implement its affirmative action admissions program, or even whether the university was *allowed* to implement equal protection by adopting this program. Instead, they asked the Court to determine whether the university's affirmative action program, which set a minimum quota for minority admissions, *violated* equal protection. The Court struck down the university's program. Most justices based their conclusion on the Civil Rights Act of 1964, but Justice Powell treated the admissions program the same as the Court would a policy that segregated students by race, applying "strict scrutiny" to the program and finding that it violated equal protection.[16]

Bakke divided the Court over the constitutional status of affirmative action programs. Powell in *Bakke* argued for a new "color-blind" interpretation of the Constitution's equal protection provisions that had gained currency in conservative circles. On this account, any time the government treated people differently based on their race, its actions should be strictly scrutinized and allowed only in limited circumstances. By 1980 three additional justices – Rehnquist, Stewart, and Stevens – joined Powell in subjecting an affirmative action program, this time a minority set-aside for federal contracts, to strict scrutiny. Justices Brennan, Marshall, and Blackmun argued, in contrast, that affirmative action programs were a benign form of discrimination. Therefore they should be examined less searchingly and allowed more frequently than policies that classified by race "on the presumption that one race is inferior to another." By 1986 the Court was evenly split over the color-blind Constitution, with a wavering Justice White in the middle.[17]

The Supreme Court's new direction could scramble the politics of the workplace Constitution. Supporters of the liberal workplace Constitution had stretched the state action doctrine to reach traditionally private workplaces in part to impose affirmative action duties on employers and unions. With the Court tipping toward a color-blind Constitution, broad theories of state action could now threaten these workplaces' affirmative action programs. The Court's 1979 review of an affirmative action plan negotiated by the Steelworkers and Kaiser Aluminum signaled this shift in terrain. The plan set aside at least 50 percent of training slots for African Americans until they were proportionally represented in skilled jobs. Justice Brennan, writing for the majority in *United Steelworkers of America v. Weber*, began by noting that "since the Kaiser-USWA plan does not involve state action, this case does not present an alleged violation of the Equal Protection Clause." As a result, Brennan did not strictly scrutinize the plan, a test it might well have failed. He instead considered whether the plan furthered Title VII's overarching purpose of opening jobs to African Americans, a standard that a majority of the Court found it met. In dissent, Justice Rehnquist accused Brennan of a "Houdini"-like opinion that "eludes clear statutory language [prohibiting racial discrimination], uncontradicted legislative history, and uniform precedent." Private sector affirmative action policies were nonetheless safe, at least so long as they were not evaluated under the equal protection clause.[18]

Affirmative action supporters' safe harbor became the *Beck* plaintiffs' doctrinal hurdle. On appeal to the Fourth Circuit, the CWA's lawyers led with *Weber* and *United Steelworkers of America v. Sadlowski*, a subsequent decision finding that a provision of the Steelworkers' constitution did not involve state action. "Taken together," the union attorneys insisted, *Sadlowski* and *Weber* "make it inconceivable that a private union's negotiation of a union security clause in a collective bargaining agreement with a private employer or such union's decision on how to spend its funds received under the terms of such a clause is state action." *Beck*'s lawyers countered that union security agreements were distinguishable. When Congress amended the NLRA in 1947, it encouraged – not merely allowed – union security agreements "in furtherance of the public interest ... to eliminate free riders," Legal Defense Foundation lawyers argued. This encouragement, they contended, was sufficient to make the fees collected under such agreements the product of state action. The problem with the foundation lawyers' theory, CWA lawyers pointed out, was that *Weber* found that Kaiser's affirmative action program furthered Title VII's overarching purpose, yet still concluded state action was lacking.[19]

Right-to-work advocates' greatest doctrinal challenges were placed before them by the Court's *conservative* justices, however. In a series of decisions in the late 1970s and early 1980s, Chief Justice Burger and Justice Rehnquist led the Court in further contracting the state action doctrine. They narrowly construed when a state "significant[ly] encourage[d]" private action, thereby triggering constitutional protections. Federal regulations that generally encouraged a decision that was nonetheless "made by private parties according to professional standards that are not established by the State" did not suffice. Rehnquist analogized the exclusive representative in *Steele v. Louisville & Nashville Railroad Co.*, which proponents of the workplace Constitution had long described as a state actor, to this private actor taking steps authorized by statute but still not attributable to the state. Rehnquist and Burger also reaffirmed that extensive government regulation did not convert a private actor into an agent of the state; instead there had to be a "sufficiently close nexus between the State and the challenged action of the regulated entity" for the latter to be attributed to the state.[20]

CWA's lawyers relied on these cases when arguing that the agency fees Beck and his coplaintiffs paid did not involve state action. They reasoned that the government merely authorized rather than forced employers and unions to adopt union security agreements, which "does not justify a finding of state action." The CWA lawyers conceded that the NLRA, by granting unions exclusive representation, gave them a monopoly-like status and that labor relations were extensively regulated, but insisted that neither made the union a state actor. CWA also dismissed Legal Defense Foundation arguments that the enforceability of its union security agreements made its agency fees the product of state action. "While ... *Shelley* [*v. Kraemer*] is still good law," the CWA lawyers argued, no one was calling on the courts to enforce the agreement here. "Careful adherence to the 'state action' requirement," the union lawyers maintained, "preserves an area of individual freedom by limiting the reach of federal law and federal judicial power."[21]

Beck's lawyers, in contrast, were forced to abjure Burger's and Rehnquist's state action opinions. They relied on *Lugar v. Edmondson Oil Co., Inc.,* a 1982 decision in which both justices dissented. *Lugar,* foundation lawyers claimed, adopted a simple two-part test for finding state action: first, did the deprivation result from the exercise of a power or right created by the government? And second, did the union receive sufficient aid from the government to make its conduct chargeable to the state? According to Beck's lawyers, the NLRA created a statutory right to adopt agency shop agreements, satisfying the first criterion. The second criterion was met because the NLRA not only encouraged agency shop agreements, Beck's attorneys insisted, but also "impose[d] extraordinary pressure upon employers" to adopt them and provided for their enforcement.[22]

Mainly, however, the Legal Defense Foundation focused on workplace Constitution cases. Foundation lawyers argued that the Court's finding of state action under the Railway Labor Act and the Michigan statute in *Abood* applied equally under the NLRA owing to the laws' similarity. In making this argument, Beck's lawyers bypassed the Court's finding that railroad-union security agreements involved state action because the Railway Labor Act preempted state right-to-work laws, a feature the NLRA lacked. Ignoring decades of Supreme Court decisions denying *Steele*'s constitutional roots, they instead insisted that under *Steele* government action "inheres in the statutory grant to a union of the status of exclusive representative." Any union security agreement the union enters into therefore "partake[s], fully and completely, of … governmental action." This principle would apply equally to unions like Beck's organized under the NLRA. "*Steele,*" Beck's lawyer assured the Fourth Circuit, "solves the state action problem."[23]

The *Beck* plaintiffs and their lawyers could not have asked for a more receptive bench. Judges Robert Chapman and Donald S. Russell were from the early right-to-work state of South Carolina. Russell was its former governor and a Democratic Party insider. President Johnson had nominated him to the bench and, if South Carolina senator and right-to-work champion Strom Thurmond had had his way, President Nixon would have elevated Russell to the Supreme Court. Chapman also owed his seat to Thurmond, who recommended Chapman for the district court in 1971. Chapman, a Goldwater supporter, had been a Republican long before Southern Democrats like Thurmond switched parties. In 1981, President Reagan elevated Chapman to the court of appeals.[24]

In 1985, Chapman and Russell agreed with Beck on all fronts. Legal Defense Foundation attorneys had argued that the court need not reach the state action issue. Instead, it could decide in their favor by interpreting the NLRA to bar the challenged fees, as the Supreme Court had done for the Railway Labor Act in *International Association of Machinists v. Street*, or by finding that the fees violated the union's duty of fair representation. Russell, writing for the court, agreed. Nonetheless, he pointedly and at some length argued that there was sufficient state action to base jurisdiction on the Constitution as well. According to Russell, the fact that the Railway Labor Act preempted state right-to-work laws while the NLRA did not was irrelevant. In Beck's home state of Maryland, which lacked a right-to-work law, Russell reasoned, the two labor laws' union security provisions operated identically. If there was state action under the one, there was state action under the other. He also agreed that, under *Steele*, an exclusive representative "wears the cloak of the government." Finally, Russell concluded that, in practice, various NLRA provisions worked together to compel the adoption of agency shop contracts and the collection of fees thereunder. Beck's case was thus distinguishable from *Weber* and *Sadlowski* and met the Court's recent state-action tests.[25]

In 1986, the *Beck* plaintiffs' luck in landing their particular panel of judges became clear. On rehearing before the entire Fourth Circuit, the panel's judges splintered. The district court judgment survived, but the *Beck* plaintiffs' constitutional claims took a beating: of the seven judges who addressed them, only Russell and Chapman found that Beck's agency fees involved state action. The Legal Defense Foundation proclaimed that the Fourth Circuit's decision at last "clear[ed] the way for the nation's entire industrial work force to seek judicial relief to halt the misuse of compulsory union fees." Whether it would also deliver the right-to-work movement's long-standing goal of getting the Supreme Court to "once and for all declare the Union Shop to be in conflict with the Bill of Rights and therefore un-Constitutional" was another question.[26]

Conservative Constitutional Orthodoxy

When *Beck* was still pending in the district court, a CWA attorney had written to the acting director of the NLRB's regional office in Atlanta. "As you probably know, it is the position of the Right to Work Committee that the National Labor Relations Act is unconstitutional," he began. "We, of course, oppose that stand," the CWA attorney continued. He suspected that the Supreme Court's conservative justices would agree. The Court's 1974 decision in *Jackson v. Metropolitan Edison Co.* "demonstrate[d] that the theory underlying suits like *Beck* has been rejected by the Supreme Court." That opinion, the attorney emphasized, was "written by a conservative," Justice Rehnquist. The CWA lawyer closed by speculating that "when the shoe is on the other foot, ... Right to Work types would be reluctant to extend the reach of the constitution." For Beck's lawyers, however, the speculation had to go the other direction: as the Supreme Court prepared to review his case in 1986, could they convince the conservative justices to extend the reach of state action when the shoe was on the foot of the right-to-work cause?[27]

The Legal Defense Foundation's most immediate task was to win the government's support. Strangely, affirmative action gave right-to-work advocates reason to hope. William Bradford Reynolds, head of the Justice Department's Civil Rights Division, caused an uproar soon after his appointment in 1981 by announcing that he hoped "to get the Supreme Court to rule that it is illegal and unconstitutional to give minorities and women preference in hiring and promotion." Reynolds represented the extreme wing of anti–affirmative action conservatives: he opposed *all* preferences, whether adopted in the public or the private sector and to prevent or remedy inequality. Reynolds gained a powerful ally when Edwin Meese joined the Justice Department in 1985 as attorney general. Meese promptly declared quotas "a new version of the Separate but Equal doctrine" and proclaimed "any policy of Affirmative Action ... unfair." Neither Reynolds nor Meese took particular interest in the right to work, but affirmative action seemed more vulnerable under the Constitution than under Title VII. Affirmative action opponents could use a constitutional victory in *Beck* to attack *Weber*'s finding that private sector collective bargaining agreements involved no state action.[28]

Meese's broader constitutional agenda threatened Beck's claims instead. Meese set the Justice Department on a course of constitutional revolution, using the department as a conservative legal think tank and training ground. Few projects were more controversial or diligently pursued than Meese's efforts to forge a single conservative theory of constitutional interpretation that would provide a coherent alternative to liberal constitutionalism. The Justice Department gave its preferred theory various labels, including "strict construction," "original meaning," and "original intent." Meese is credited with wrestling these varied concepts into what became known as originalism: the principle that judges should interpret the Constitution only as it was understood at the time it was adopted.[29]

Meese made originalism a conservative litmus test. In 1985, he captured headlines in a speech to the American Bar Association titled "Jurisprudence of Original Intent." Justice Brennan, the liberal lion of the Court, issued a public rejoinder, defending his nonoriginalist approach to constitutional interpretation. Meese responded at a meeting of the conservative Federalist Society. Justice Department officials prepared Meese's speech with care, recognizing that he was defining *the* conservative constitutional position to a national audience. The next year, Meese's Justice Department prepared *Original Meaning Jurisprudence: A Sourcebook*, to "educate Department employees, the legal community, and the general public regarding the fundamental principles of original meaning jurisprudence." By 1988, the Justice Department had issued a lengthy document titled *Guidelines on Constitutional Litigation*, which instructed government lawyers to include an "original meaning section" in all briefs on constitutional issues. The Legal Defense Foundation's expansive and dynamic state action theories, which they termed "modern" and recognized were in tension with Reconstruction-era Supreme Court precedent, failed Meese's originalism test miserably.[30]

The "Tenth Justice," Solicitor General Charles Fried, also posed a problem for the *Beck* plaintiffs. Fried was born in Prague and fled the Nazi occupation as a young boy, arriving in New York City at the age of six in 1941. His father had been an executive and a member of the political elite in Prague, but in America Fried followed a well-worn path of immigrant upward mobility, attending public schools in New York and boarding school in New Jersey before earning his bachelor's degree at Princeton, studying jurisprudence at Oxford, and receiving a J.D. from Columbia Law School. In 1960, he clerked for Justice Harlan, whom he revered, then became a professor of jurisprudence at Harvard Law School. On becoming solicitor general in 1985, Fried became an avid warrior in conservatives' constitutional revolution. "In Ronald Reagan's Washington," a reporter observed, "Mr. Fried finds himself in the intellectual vanguard of conservative thought, operating on the legal front."[31]

Fried did not feel bound by Supreme Court precedent and was no fan of organized labor. Fried saw himself as an advocate for the administration's agenda. In one of his first cases as solicitor general, he urged the Court to overturn *Roe v. Wade*. Fried also thought the NLRA was based on an outdated, corporatist, anti–free market model. He was particularly skeptical of the statute's guarantee of exclusive representation, of the free rider problem it purported to solve, and of the restraint it imposed on individual workers' freedom to bargain independently with their employer. In a 1984 article, Fried proposed abandoning the exclusive representation model altogether.[32]

But Fried was a strict constructionist, with strong views about judging in general and constitutional interpretation in particular. He thought the courts in recent decades had "irresponsibly created all sorts of new rights." Like Meese, he believed that "the law should operate as a constraint, not only upon citizens but upon judges." Fried was a more traditional conservative than Meese, however. Fried likened the Constitution to a contract and insisted that judges had no business reading into either the Constitution or contracts provisions that their language did not support. But he never signed on to originalism. "The principal guide for judgment should be the language of the law," Fried urged, not its context or the subjective intent of its drafters.[33]

Fried gave both Legal Defense Foundation and CWA lawyers an opportunity to argue their side. For over an hour, foundation lawyer Hugh Reilly and his colleagues made their case to Fried, the NLRB's general counsel, and other Justice Department officials. The bulk of the time was spent discussing Beck's constitutional claim. Foundation attorneys did not attempt to craft their argument within the tenets of Fried's strict constructionism (an admittedly difficult task). Instead, they relied on *Steele*, a decision that could hardly be more at odds with the strict constructionist creed: in addition to the admittedly "modern" state action theories they attributed to the decision, the cause of action *Steele* recognized had no basis in the text or purpose of the Railway Labor Act.[34]

To say Fried was unconvinced by Reilly would be an understatement. As he later expressed, incredulously, "History did seem to repeat itself, only with Right to Work pressing [NAACP Legal Defense Fund lawyer] Jack Greenberg's line of analysis" from the sit-in cases. Fried's draft brief predictably rejected the Legal Defense Foundation's state action theories. Most surprisingly, Fried also challenged the entire edifice of the right-to-work movement's gains to date. Fried agreed with Beck that the Railway Labor Act's and NLRA's union security provisions were hard to distinguish. Beck used their similarity to argue that unions organized under the NLRA should be subject to the same bar on political use of dues as railroad unions were; Fried, in contrast, used their alikeness to attack the Court's earlier decisions finding that railway union security agreements involved state action. To the extent that these decisions hinged on the Railway Labor Act's unique preemption of state right-to-work laws, Fried thought they were wrongly decided. Nowhere else did federal preemption of state law, he noted, turn action taken under the preemptive federal law into state action. If the Court's prior right-to-work decisions suggested that the associational and speech implications of union security agreements were so grave that the state action bar should be lowered to allow mere state permission to suffice, they were equally misguided. This sanctioning theory of state action, Fried cautioned, "subject[ed] private actors to constitutional restraints that are not designed to restrain them at all."[35]

Fried took an equally strict approach to interpreting the NLRA. He rejected the Legal Defense Foundation lawyers' claim that either the NLRA or the duty of fair representation "precludes an employer and a union from agreeing to require" all employees to pay fees "that the union may use for both collective bargaining and non-collective bargaining purposes." To find otherwise would be to adopt what Justice Rehnquist had called the "Houdini-like interpretive magic" of Justice Brennan's opinions in *Weber* and *Street*, to which Fried had recently objected in a brief to the Court.[36]

Fried had put principle ahead of politics but that did not let him outrun them. Someone at the NLRB leaked the final draft of his brief to the foundation. In Fried's apt assessment, "all hell broke loose." Reed Larson sent outraged letters around Capitol Hill. Calling Fried's brief "scandalous," Larson urged White House chief of staff Howard Baker to bring Fried's position in line with the Republican Party platform, which opposed "using compulsory dues and fees for partisan political purposes." To Attorney General Meese, Larson argued once again the Legal Defense Foundation's position that decades of precedent, starting with *Steele*, had applied "the Constitution to unions as exclusive representatives under the labor laws." The head of Legislative Affairs at the White House reported that Republicans in Congress were furious with Fried.[37]

Larson's agitation touched off a searing debate within the Reagan administration. Fried reported that the foundation's "counterrevolutionary [constitutional arguments] ... had some partisans among the Attorney General's assistants." Others in the Justice Department attacked Fried's statutory analysis. On a Thursday in April 1987, Meese called a meeting to hash out the arguments for and against Fried's brief. Meanwhile, a team of White House and Justice Department lawyers rushed to complete an alternate brief that they hoped Fried would adopt. The day before Fried's brief was due, the right-leaning *Washington Times* broke the story, quoting a Justice Department official who said that Fried's "position is 'not one with which ... Meese ... would feel comfortable.'" Not to be outmaneuvered, Fried filed his brief early, foreclosing efforts to amend it.[38]

President Reagan must not have liked the headlines that greeted him the next day. "Reagan Backs Unions in Court over Use of Fees," the *New York Times* announced. The *Wall Street Journal*'s editors "admit[ted] to being flabbergasted by the administration's apparent turnabout on this issue." Larson's supporters sent "bushels of letters" to Fried and the White House. Fried should either withdraw his brief and submit a new one, Larson urged Howard Baker and Meese, or the White House should file separately "disclaiming administration support for the Solicitor General's brief and setting out the true position of the executive branch." Conservative public interest lawyers filed amicus briefs on Beck's behalf, insisting that his agency fees involved state action. Major Republican Party donors pressed the president for an explanation. Senator Jesse Helms of North Carolina, an ardent right-to-work supporter, had already asked Baker to "urge the Solicitor

General ... to oppose the unconstitutional abuse of forced dues for politics." Now that Fried's brief was filed, he and several congressional allies asked President Reagan to join an amicus brief emphasizing the "constitutional significance of this case to the working men and women of the United States of America."[39]

The White House was unmoved. According to a Legal Defense Foundation staffer, Reagan was "absolutely furious with this [Fried's] decision" but that was not the White House's official position. In a carefully drafted letter, Baker informed Larson that "the decision made by the Justice Department was a difficult one." It had "involv[ed] not only the Administration's support for protections against the use of compulsory dues and fees for partisan political purposes, but also its adherence to strict construction of the Constitution and Federal statutes." As Baker elaborated further in a letter to Senator Helms, this position was complemented by a commitment to "limit[ing] the concept of 'state action' for purposes of constitutional redress." Reagan's devotion to the Republican Party platform "remain[ed] undiminished," but it did not outweigh his allegiance to conservatives' newly obligatory constitutional theory.[40]

Fried may have had the White House's support but he failed to persuade the Supreme Court. There is "some truth to what the union says, but much water under the bridge," Chief Justice Rehnquist mused in January 1988 at the justices' private conference on *Beck*. Justice White agreed: "as a new matter" his position "would be different," but the Court was stuck. "Do we overturn the Railway Labor cases?" White asked. If not, it would be "funny to have different rules" for railroad unions and those governed by the NLRA. Justice Stevens found the case similarly close and also deferred; "History," he concluded, "is important." Only the most liberal justices, Brennan and Marshall, were unequivocal: the Court's prior interpretation of the Railway Labor Act governed. Rehnquist left the conference unsure of his vote. Ultimately, however, he signed on to just the sort of Houdini-like statutory interpretation he had lambasted in *Weber*. History and stability, rather than the foundation's arguments, ensured the *Beck* plaintiffs a majority.[41]

In June 1988, during the twilight of Reagan's presidency, the Supreme Court issued its decision. Justice Brennan wrote for the Court. Like other liberals, owing to *Weber* and the Court's affirmative action decisions, he had a strong incentive to keep the Constitution out of the workplace. Brennan avoided Beck's constitutional claims. Reaching these issues was unnecessary, Brennan argued, because the union security provisions in the federal labor laws were so similar in language, structure, and purpose. As a result, the Court could simply extend Brennan's "entirely reasonable" interpretation of the Railway Labor Act over a quarter century earlier to the NLRA's union security provisions. Henceforth, the NLRA would prohibit unions from using objecting nonmembers' fees for purposes other than collective bargaining, contract administration, and grievance adjustment.[42]

President Reagan's most recent appointee to the Supreme Court, Anthony Kennedy, did not participate in the Court's decision, but two others, Justices Antonin Scalia and Sandra Day O'Connor, joined Justice Blackmun in dissent. Like Solicitor General Fried, they found the majority's interpretation of the NLRA "inconsistent with the congressional purpose clearly expressed in the statutory language and amply documented in the legislative history." In the justices' private conference, all three had also found state action lacking. Justice Scalia even agreed with Fried that the Railway Labor Act cases involved "no state action."[43]

The Reagan administration is generally seen as a triumph for conservatives, particularly for their constitutional agenda. That this agenda created winners and losers among the New Right coalition is less recognized. But the workplace Constitution divided the New Right just as it had split the New Deal coalition in its heyday. The right-to-work movement represented an influential Republican constituency and was an anchor for the party's conservative base. Its constitutional arguments had the support of the public, influential New Right congressmen, and the budding conservative public-interest legal establishment. Reagan's constitutional politics had nonetheless placed them outside the conservative legal mainstream. His Supreme Court appointees had nearly sunk Beck's case and squelched right-to-work advocates' constitutional ambitions. In the end, there were limits to what they could win from the Court through popularizing their view of workers' constitutional rights.[44]

Epilogue

In the twenty-first century, the workplace Constitution has all but vanished. The National Labor Relations Board's antidiscrimination policies are tucked away in an obscure agency manual and rarely put to use. The Supreme Court's desire to "promote equality between government and private employers" has fatefully narrowed the scope of public employees' constitutional rights. Right-to-work advocates have fared somewhat better: despite the general weakening of public employees' constitutional rights, the Supreme Court seems poised to further protect them from having to support unions, fulfilling a goal the movement has pursued since the 1960s. The Court's affirmative action cases have proved the most robust, but at a cost to the liberal workplace Constitution. In the late 1990s, a federal appellate court struck down the Federal Communication Commission's equal employment rules as a violation of equal protection. These precedents also threaten aspects of Title VII of the 1964 Civil Rights Act. Few scholars advocate the workplace Constitution's potential, and no movement rallies around it.[1]

Meanwhile, the workplace has been radically transformed. Union membership has dropped to below 10 percent. The employment relationship is dissolving: temporary, part-time, and contract jobs are on the rise, and new time-management systems allow employers to convert many employees to on-call workers. Even full-time, permanent employees expect to change jobs frequently. Meanwhile, technology has disseminated the workplace into every corner of life.[2]

Workplace rights to speech, association, privacy, and due process may seem irrelevant under these conditions. And yet American workers not only value these rights, they think they have them.[3] This assumption indicates a huge divide between perception and reality. Some legal scholars believe that there is no cause for concern. In the United States, they argue, the threat of unionization and employers' incentives to preserve workplace morale ensure that employers behave as if such protections existed. The fact that most employees believe that they have these rights, the scholars argue, only proves the point. But given the changes in employment, even if employers have adhered to such requirements absent legal mandates in the past, it is far from clear that they will continue to do so. The unofficial workplace Constitution that employers offer to workers in lieu of law or union contracts is precarious at best, deceptive at worst. Both possibilities are disquieting.[4]

This history of the workplace Constitution is instructive today. The midcentury American state depicted in the preceding chapters was remarkably permeable, influenced by, influencing, and pockmarked with social, economic, and political battles. The workplace Constitution was both a weapon in those struggles and a field on which they were fought. The results of engaging with it were unpredictable and it was sometimes difficult to tell victory from defeat. Arguably, constitutional claims channeled workers away from calls for more fundamental change to racial inequality, union governance, or workers' economic security.

But the workplace Constitution united key dimensions of twentieth-century law and politics. It bound together the conservative, labor, and civil rights movements. The Supreme Court's better-known forays into the state action doctrine, which scholars and lawyers have long seen as unrelated, instead were part of a long and searching debate over the private sphere in an era of big government, big business, and big labor. No matter how imperfect, indeterminate, possibly even self-defeating it may be to turn to the Constitution, we are all bound together by law; true disengagement is not an option. From this perspective, the workplace Constitution is everywhere still, although it protects some – reverse discrimination litigants, workers unhappy with their union, and employers fighting unionization – more than others. For those with a different vision for the workplace today, abandoning the Constitution simply cedes it to their opponents.

The history of the workplace Constitution also has more hopeful lessons to offer. Cecil B. DeMille was all but laughed out of court in the 1940s. James Cobb's earlier challenge to unions' racial discrimination was summarily dismissed. Starting from that legal wilderness, both the right-to-work movement and the civil rights movement "change[d] the minds of the city Councils, the legislatures, the governors, and the Congress," as DeMille once promised, ultimately "chang[ing] the mind of the Supreme Court" (or at least a federal agency or two). That success is a reminder of how flexible the Constitution can be, recognizing a right to organize and then a right to refrain from union support; prohibiting discrimination and then its reverse. It is, as the workplace Constitution's fate indicates, the document that we make it.[5]

Perhaps workers ought to rejoin the midcentury fight to extend the state action doctrine to traditionally private workplaces. Today, the state action doctrine is a labyrinth of numerous multipronged and fact-specific tests that give courts a large degree of discretion when they apply it in any particular case. Some scholars contend that this allows judges to hide their judgments about the actual rights being claimed – did the employer violate her employee's free speech rights when she terminated him for attending a protest march? – behind factual determinations about the degree of government involvement in the decision. Relevant to these concerns, in the 1960s, Civil Rights Division lawyers at the Department of Justice argued that it would be better for courts to provide more qualified versions of constitutional rights in the private sector than to deny them altogether. Courts should make it easy to find state action, the argument went, and then focus their analysis on the fundamental question of private actors' competing rights – for instance, whether the employer's right to manage her business outweighed her employee's right to free speech in the example above. If scholars are right that courts' decisions about whether state action is present actually turn on their view of the competing rights at stake, then it would be more forthright and transparent for courts to instead adopt the Civil Rights Division's approach.[6]

But the promise of the workplace Constitution need not be one that workers fulfill in court. This account teaches that expanding state action to reach the workplace could be dangerous as well as empowering, potentially opening a "Pandora's box" as labor law scholar Clyde Summers put it in the 1980s. Federal courts might be plunged into designing rules for private institutions on a host of issues other than workers' rights. Luckily, the Constitution has never been exclusively the courts' domain. Presidents, Congress, and government agencies have translated it into concrete policies. The people themselves have also fought over its meaning. Indeed, this broader, extra-court workplace Constitution mobilized powerful support for change among both proponents and opponents of the New Deal labor regime. Unquestionably, it has unrealized promise for workers today.[7]

This history also reveals that workers have sought collective action in their places of employment more vigorously and variably than previously recognized. This was true not only of union members but also of the black workers who fought to join them on equal terms. It was also true (no doubt for some readers, controversially) of many of the right-to-work litigants: plaintiffs in the major right-to-work cases did not oppose worker solidarity so much as they advanced different versions of what it should look like. Of the hundreds of workers who signed on to the railroad cases in the 1950s, for example, the majority sought a more inclusive alternative to the craft-bound brotherhoods, or a return to their purely voluntary roots. Of the 5 percent of Detroit teachers who joined the right-to-work cases in the 1960s and '70s, many simply favored the union that had lost the election.[8] Even Harry Beck was a union insurgent before he became a union opponent. Collective action is hard, messy, and imperfect. Sometimes it involves forms of oppression. Conflicts have abounded over how and why to join together, yet the bare desire to do so has been profound and persistent. The idea of a workplace Constitution, or at least the knowledge of its current paltry protections, could strengthen this impulse. Whether people today organize around the Constitution or another idea better suited to the time, they may yet bring what A. Philip Randolph called "the breath of democracy" into the twenty-first-century workplace.

Appendix: Figures

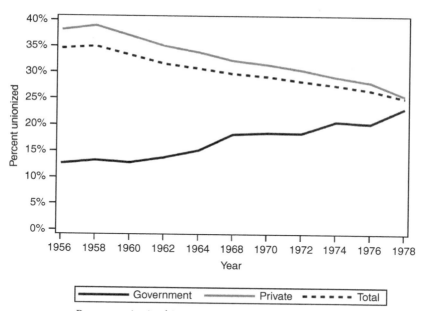

FIGURE A.I. Percent unionized in government and private sectors, 1956–78.
Sources: Table Ba4832–4844 and Table Ba840–848 in *Historical Statistics of the United States*, Millennial Edition Online, ed. Susan B. Carter et al. (New York: Cambridge University Press, 2006).

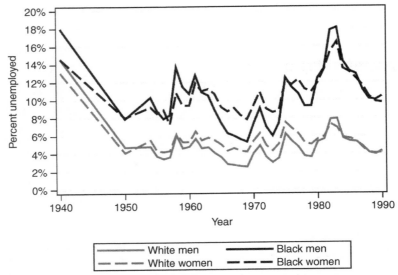

FIGURE A.2. Percent unemployed 1940–90, by race and sex.

Unemployment in 1940 is calculated for the population over age fourteen; for 1950–90 it is calculated for the population age sixteen and older. Prior to 1970, the percentage for blacks includes blacks and other races.

Sources: 1980 Census of Population, Detailed Characteristics, United States Summary Table 86; 1990 Census of Population, Detailed Characteristics, United States Summary Table 44.

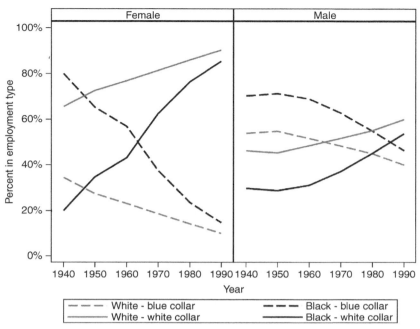

FIGURE A.3. Percent in white-collar and blue-collar employment, 1940–90, by race and sex.

Blue-collar employment is comprised of the following nonfarm occupations: craftsmen, foremen, operatives, domestic-service workers, and all nonfarm laborers (1940–80); precision production, craft, and repair; and operators, fabricators, and laborers (1990). White-collar employment includes the following nonfarm occupations: managerial and professional occupations; technical, sales, and administrative-support occupations; and nondomestic-service occupations (1940–80); managerial and professional occupations; technical, sales, and administrative-support occupations; and service occupations (1990).

Sources: 1940 Census of Population, Detailed Characteristics, United States Summary Table 64; 1950 Census of Population, Detailed Characteristics, United States Summary Table 128; 1960 Census of Population, Detailed Characteristics, United States Summary Table 258; 1980 Census of Population, Detailed Characteristics, United States Summary Table 89; 1990 Census of Population, Detailed Characteristics, United States Summary Table 45.

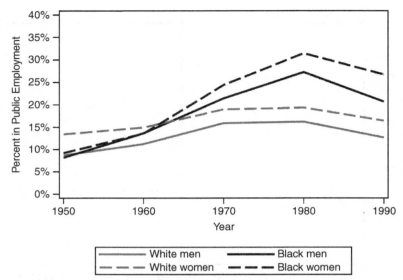

FIGURE A.4. Percent in public employment, 1940–90, by race and sex.

Public workers include all individuals engaged in nonfarm work in federal, state, or local governments. Private workers include all private wage and salary workers, self-employed workers, and family workers.

Sources: 1950 Census of Population, Special Reports 1D, Table 18; 1960 Census of Population, Special Report 7B, Table 25; 1980 Census of Population, Detailed Characteristics, United States Summary Table 90; 1990 Census of Population, Detailed Characteristics, United States Summary Table 47.

Notes

Introduction

1 Michael R. Botson Jr., *Labor, Civil Rights, and the Hughes Tool Company* (College Station: Texas A&M University Press, 2005), 53–54, 113–14; August Meier and Elliot Rudwick, "Attitudes of Negro Leaders toward the American Labor Movement from the Civil War to World War I," in *The Negro and the American Labor Movement*, ed. Julius Jacobson, 27–48 (Garden City, N.Y.: Anchor Books, 1968). International Association of Machinists ritual quoted in Brief of United Steelworkers of America [hereafter USWA], August 16, 1943, "R-5693 Bethlehem Steel Co. San Francisco, Calif. Formal File" Folder, Box 3672, Formal and Informal Unfair Labor Practices and Representation Case Files, 1935–1948 Board, Records of the National Labor Relations Board, RG 25, (National Archives at College Park (NACP), Md.) [hereafter NLRB Papers – CF35-48]. A more nuanced account of unions' racial practices follows. See generally Herbert R. Northrup, *Organized Labor and the Negro* (New York: Harper & Brothers, 1944). Charles S. Johnson, "The Conflict of Caste and Class in an American Industry," *American Journal of Sociology* 42, no. 1 (July 1936): 55–65, 58. Kevin K. Gaines, *Uplifting the Race: Black Leadership, Politics, and Culture in the Twentieth Century* (Chapel Hill: University of North Carolina Press, 1996); Evelyn Brooks Higginbotham, *Righteous Discontent: The Women's Movement in the Black Baptist Church, 1880–1920* (Cambridge, Mass.: Harvard University Press, 1993). Ernest Obadele-Starks, *Black Unionism in the Industrial South* (College Station: Texas A&M University Press, 2000), 26–28.

2 Obadele-Starks, *Black Unionism*, 26–28. For the legal dimension of employer resistance, see especially Andrew Wender Cohen, *The Racketeer's Progress: Chicago and the Struggle for the Modern American Economy, 1900–1940*

(New York: Cambridge University Press, 2004); Daniel R. Ernst, *Lawyers against Labor: From Individual Rights to Corporate Liberalism* (Urbana: University of Illinois Press, 1995); William E. Forbath, *Law and the Shaping of the American Labor Movement* (Cambridge, Mass.: Harvard University Press, 1991). On black strikebreaking, see Sterling D. Spero and Abram L. Harris, *The Black Worker: The Negro and the Labor Movement* (New York: Atheneum, 1968), chap. 7, 254–63; Northrup, *Organized Labor and the Negro*. Botson, *Labor, Civil Rights, and the Hughes Tool Company*, 53–54, 114–15; Tyina Leaneice Steptoe, "Dixie West: Race, Migration, and the Color Lines in Jim Crow Houston," Ph.D. diss., University of Wisconsin–Madison, 2008, 8–9, chap. 1. "Tex. Labor Leader Warns Workers to Be Careful of Both CIO and AFL," *Pittsburgh Courier*, July 17, 1937.

3   I do not mean to suggest that unions, workers, and employers did not invoke the Constitution before the New Deal. See David E. Bernstein, *Rehabilitating Lochner: Defending Individual Rights against Progressive Reform* (Chicago: University of Chicago Press, 2011); Forbath, *Law and the Shaping of the American Labor Movement*. As is discussed further in Part I, many in the labor movement viewed the New Deal labor laws as implementing constitutional rights or as facilitating the enactment by labor and management of privately negotiated "workplace constitutions." The term "workplace Constitution" is capacious enough to encompass them all, but this history of it examines the claims to a workplace Constitution that were made after those laws were in effect.

4   A blocked and randomized study of 200 working-age adults in the United States demonstrated that most of those surveyed thought the Constitution protected employees' freedoms of speech, privacy, and association at work, and that it did so whether they worked for the government or in the private sector. For data and results, contact the author.

5   Tomiko Brown-Nagin, *Courage to Dissent: Atlanta and the Long History of the Civil Rights Movement* (New York: Oxford University Press, 2011); Mark Brilliant, *The Color of America Has Changed: How Racial Diversity Shaped Civil Rights Reform in California, 1941–1978* (New York: Oxford University Press, 2010); Risa L. Goluboff, *The Lost Promise of Civil Rights* (Cambridge, Mass.: Harvard University Press, 2007); Anthony S. Chen, *The Fifth Freedom: Jobs, Politics, and Civil Rights in the United States, 1941–1972* (Princeton, N.J.: Princeton University Press, 2009); Nancy MacLean, *Freedom Is Not Enough: The Opening of the American Workplace* (Cambridge, Mass.: Harvard University Press, 2008); Thomas J. Sugrue, *Sweet Land of Liberty: The Forgotten Struggle for Civil Rights in the North* (New York: Random House, 2009). Some of these scholars include constitutional rights among the civil rights protections they historicize but, with the exceptions of Goluboff and Brown-Nagin, constitutional rights are not their primary focus. In addition, constitutional claims, even in this literature, tend to arise within the context of court

litigation. Civil rights legal histories have traditionally emphasized courts and the Constitution. Even Michael Klarman's magisterial *From Jim Crow to Civil Rights: The Supreme Court and the Struggle for Racial Equality* (New York: Oxford University Press, 2006), which decenters the Supreme Court by arguing that it followed rather than led the civil rights revolution, nonetheless looks only to the Court for constitutional law. Similarly, social movement histories, like Richard Kluger's classic *Simple Justice: The History of Brown v. Board of Education and Black America's Struggle for Equality* (New York: Vintage Books, 1977), focus only on the litigation campaigns that led to seminal Supreme Court cases.

6   Some scholars focus on the diffuse ways that social and political contests over constitutional values influence Supreme Court doctrine. Barry Friedman, *The Will of the People: How Public Opinion Has Influenced the Supreme Court and Shaped the Meaning of the Constitution* (New York: Farrar, Strauss and Giroux, 2009); Jeffrey Rosen, "What's a Liberal Justice Now?" *New York Times Magazine*, May 31, 2009, 50. Others contend that our political system gives noncourt actors – presidents, Congress, and the general public – the power to define the Constitution's meaning differently than the Court. See, for instance, Larry Kramer, *The People Themselves: Popular Constitutionalism and Judicial Review* (New York: Oxford University Press, 2004).

7   On the novelty of this focus, see Sophia Z. Lee, "Race, Sex, and Rulemaking: Administrative Constitutionalism and the Workplace, 1960 to the Present," *Virginia Law Review* 96 (June 2010): 799–881. For growing scholarly interest in administrators' constitutional interpretations, see Gillian E. Metzger, "Administrative Constitutionalism," *Texas Law Review* 91 (June 2013): 1897–1935. For promising work in this area, see Karen M. Tani, "Securing a Right to Welfare: Public Assistance Administration and the Rule of Law, 1935–1965," Ph.D. diss., University of Pennsylvania, 2011.

8   William Novak has described this as the "creation of a modern state in America – a centralized, administrative, regulatory, welfare state – one of the more formidable legal, political, and economic powers in world history." William J. Novak, "The Not-So-Strange Birth of the Modern American State: A Comment on James A. Henretta's 'Charles Evans Hughes and the Strange Death of Liberal America,'" *Law and History Review* 24, no. 1 (Spring 2006): 193–99, 199. Federal administration was not new in the twentieth century, however. Brian Balogh, *A Government Out of Sight: The Mystery of National Authority in Nineteenth-Century America* (New York: Cambridge University Press, 2009); Jerry L. Mashaw, *Creating the Administrative Constitution: The Lost One Hundred Years of American Administrative Law* (New Haven, Conn.: Yale University Press, 2012); William J. Novak, "The Myth of the 'Weak' American State," *American Historical Review* 113, no. 3 (June 2008): 752–72.

268 Notes to pages 4–5

9 Goluboff, *The Lost Promise.* For the broader fusion of civil and labor rights during this period, see Robert R. Korstad, *Civil Rights Unionism: Tobacco Workers and the Struggle for Democracy in the Mid-Twentieth-Century South* (Chapel Hill: University of North Carolina Press, 2003); Patricia Sullivan, *Days of Hope: Race and Democracy in the New Deal Era* (Chapel Hill: University of North Carolina Press, 1996); Glenda Elizabeth Gilmore, *Defying Dixie: The Radical Roots of Civil Rights: 1919–1950* (New York: W. W. Norton, 2008); Martha Biondi, *To Stand and Fight: The Struggle for Civil Rights in Postwar New York City* (Cambridge, Mass.: Harvard University Press, 2006). Chen, *The Fifth Freedom*; Sugrue, *Sweet Land of Liberty*; Brilliant, *The Color of America Has Changed*; MacLean, *Freedom Is Not Enough*; Jennifer Delton, *Racial Integration in Corporate America, 1940–1990* (New York: Cambridge University Press, 2009); Sean Farhang, *The Litigation State: Public Regulation and Private Lawsuits in the United States* (Princeton, N.J.: Princeton University Press, 2010); John David Skrentny, *The Ironies of Affirmative Action: Politics, Culture and Justice in America* (Chicago: University of Chicago Press, 1996). Paul Frymer also examines NLRB approaches to discrimination but argues these were eclipsed by Title VII. Paul Frymer, *Black and Blue: African Americans, the Labor Movement, and the Decline of the Democratic Party* (Princeton, N.J.: Princeton University Press, 2007). Hugh Davis Graham examines the employment discrimination policies of many federal agencies but is focused on civil rights policy more generally. Hugh Davis Graham, *The Civil Rights Era: Origins and Development of National Policy, 1960–1972* (New York: Oxford University Press, 1990).

10 Brilliant, *The Color of America Has Changed*; John D. Skrentny, *The Minority Rights Revolution* (Cambridge, Mass.: Belknap Press of Harvard University Press, 2004).

11 Lisa McGirr, *Suburban Warriors: The Origins of the New American Right.* (Princeton, N.J.: Princeton University Press, 2001); Michelle M. Nickerson, *Mothers of Conservatism: Women and the Postwar Right* (Princeton, N.J.: Princeton University Press, 2012). Darren Dochuk, *From Bible Belt to Sunbelt: Plain-Folk Religion, Grassroots Politics, and the Rise of Evangelical Conservatism* (New York: W. W. Norton, 2011). Kim Phillips-Fein, *Invisible Hands: The Making of the Conservative Movement from the New Deal to Reagan* (New York: W. W. Norton, 2009); Angus Burgin, *The Great Persuasion: Reinventing Free Markets since the Depression* (Cambridge, Mass.: Harvard University Press, 2012); Elizabeth A. Fones-Wolf, *Selling Free Enterprise: The Business Assault on Labor and Liberalism, 1945–60* (Urbana: University of Illinois Press, 1995). Rick Perlstein, *Before the Storm: Barry Goldwater and the Unmaking of the American Consensus* (New York: Hill and Wang, 2001); Elizabeth Tandy Shermer, *Sunbelt Capitalism: Phoenix and the Transformation of American Politics* (Philadelphia: University of Pennsylvania Press, 2013).

12 Dan T. Carter, *The Politics of Rage: George Wallace, the Origins of the New Conservatism, and the Transformation of American Politics* (New York: Simon & Schuster, 1995); Richard Hofstadter, *The Paranoid Style in American Politics and Other Essays* (New York: Alfred A. Knopf, 1965).

13 Joseph Crespino, *In Search of Another Country: Mississippi and the Conservative Counterrevolution* (Princeton, N.J.: Princeton University Press, 2007); Kevin M. Kruse, *White Flight: Atlanta and the Making of Modern Conservatism* (Princeton, N.J.: Princeton University Press, 2007); Matthew D. Lassiter, *The Silent Majority: Suburban Politics in the Sunbelt South* (Princeton, N.J.: Princeton University Press, 2005). They argue, however, that other factors, such as antiunionism, economic booster-ism, religion, and suburbanization, played critical, if not indistinct, roles. But see Ira Katznelson, *When Affirmative Action Was White: An Untold History of Racial Inequality in Twentieth-Century America* (New York: W. W. Norton, 2005).

14 Jonathan Rieder, *Canarsie: The Jews and Italians of Brooklyn against Liberalism* (Cambridge, Mass.: Harvard University Press, 1985); Ronald P. Formisano, *Boston against Busing: Race, Class, and Ethnicity in the 1960s and 1970s* (Chapel Hill: University of North Carolina Press, 1991); MacLean, *Freedom Is Not Enough*; Jefferson Cowie, *Stayin' Alive: The 1970s and the Last Days of the Working Class* (New York: New Press, 2010); Dennis Deslippe, *Protesting Affirmative Action: The Struggle over Equality after the Civil Rights Revolution* (Baltimore: Johns Hopkins University Press, 2012). These scholars emphasize that racial issues often stood in for more amorphous concerns, such as a worker's "control of his life, the fate of his family, and his modest and tenuous place on the social ladder." Cowie, *Stayin' Alive*, 5. Joseph Crespino argues that this regional and class bifurcation – racism for the South and northern working-class whites; economic and cultural issues for the West and northern elites – is false and that postwar conservatism inextricably linked all three issues. Joseph Crespino, *Strom Thurmond's America* (New York: Hill and Wang, 2012).

15 Those pathbreaking legal histories of conservatives that do exist focus on social, not economic, conservatives. Sarah Barringer Gordon, *The Spirit of the Law: Religious Voices and the Constitution in Modern America* (Cambridge, Mass.: Belknap Press of Harvard University Press, 2010). See also Steven Preston Brown, *Trumping Religion: The New Christian Right, the Free Speech Clause, and the Courts* (Tuscaloosa: University of Alabama Press, 2002). Most histories of anti–New Deal conservatives' legal ambitions have focused only on their efforts to pass state right-to-work laws. Gilbert J. Gall, *The Politics of Right to Work: The Labor Federations as Special Interests, 1943–1979* (New York: Greenwood Press, 1988); Fones-Wolf, *Selling Free Enterprise*. To the extent that historians discuss anti–New Deal conservatives' concerted litigation campaigns

or constitutional ambitions, they date them to the 1970s. Phillips-Fein, *Invisible Hands*; Steven M. Teles, *The Rise of the Conservative Legal Movement: The Battle for Control of the Law* (Princeton, N.J.: Princeton University Press, 2008). Other scholars are also filling this gap, although most new work focuses on the 1970s and 1980s. See, for instance, Jefferson Decker, *The Other Rights Revolution: Conservative Lawyers and the Remaking of American Government* (forthcoming).

16   Teles, *The Rise of the Conservative Legal Movement*.

17   Robert O. Self, *All in the Family: The Realignment of American Democracy since the 1960s* (New York: Hill and Wang, 2012).

18   Sugrue, *Sweet Land of Liberty*; Thomas J. Sugrue, *The Origins of the Urban Crisis: Race and Inequality in Postwar Detroit* (Princeton, N.J.: Princeton University Press, 1996). This work can be contrasted with the seminal work by Steve Fraser and Gary Gerstle, *The Rise and Fall of the New Deal Order, 1930–1980* (Princeton. N.J.: Princeton University Press, 1989), and with works attributing the coalition's fracture to Title VII litigation in the 1970s. See, for instance, Judith Stein, *Running Steel, Running America: Race, Economic Policy, and the Decline of Liberalism* (Chapel Hill: University of North Carolina Press, 1998); Nelson Lichtenstein, *State of the Union: A Century of American Labor* (Princeton, N.J.: Princeton University Press, 2002). But see the preface to the second edition of Lichtenstein's *State of the Union* (Princeton, N.J.: Princeton University Press, 2013).

19   Phillips-Fein, *Invisible Hands*; Kim Phillips-Fein, "Business Conservatism on the Shop Floor: Anti-union Campaigns in the 1950s," *Labor* 7, no. 2 (Summer 2010): 9–26; Shermer, *Sunbelt Capitalism*. Historians Jefferson Cowie and Nick Salvatore describe the political coalition the New Deal forged as a "web of internal fractures" and the liberal state it created as "so deeply conflicted in [its] original formation" that it was all but destined to collapse. Jefferson Cowie and Nick Salvatore, "The Long Exception: Rethinking the Place of the New Deal in American History," *International Labor and Working-Class History* 74, no. 1 (Fall 2008): 3–32, 5.

20   For a similar approach, see Reuel Schiller, *Forging Rivals: Race, Class, and the Decline of Postwar Liberalism* (New York: Cambridge University Press, forthcoming).

21   Sean Wilentz, *The Age of Reagan: America from Watergate to the War on Terror* (New York: Harper, 2008); Laura Kalman, *Right Star Rising: A New Politics, 1974–1980* (New York: W. W. Norton, 2010). Welcome exceptions are Donald T. Critchlow, *The Conservative Ascendancy: How the GOP Right Made Political History* (Cambridge, Mass.: Harvard University Press, 2007); Teles, *The Rise of the Conservative Legal Movement*. Jefferson Decker questions the one fault line commonly attributed to the New Right, that between social and economic conservatives. Decker, *The Other Rights Revolution*.

1 Liberals Forge a Workplace Constitution in the Courts

1   Hearing on Proposed Amendments to the National Labor Relations Act
    (NLRA), before the House Committee on Labor, 76th Cong. 1301, 1442
    (1939) [hereafter 1939 Hearing on NLRA Amendments] (statement of
    C. W. Rice, Texas Negro Business and Laboring Men's Association). Railway
    Labor Act of 1934, 48 Stat. 1185; NLRA, Pub. L. No. 74-198, 49 Stat. 449
    (1935). They were preceded by the National Industrial Recovery Act, Pub. L.
    73-90, 48 Stat. 195 (1933), which both as written and as enforced provided a
    much weaker right to organize. Daniel Ernst argues that the New Deal labor
    laws' novelty may be overstated because twenty years prior it was already
    beyond question "that organized labor could lawfully possess great collective
    power." Daniel R. Ernst, *Lawyers against Labor: From Individual Rights to
    Corporate Liberalism* (Urbana: University of Illinois Press, 1995), 8.

2   Christopher Tomlins, *The State and the Unions* (New York: Cambridge
    University Press, 1985), 103–19; Melvyn Dubofsky, *The State and Labor in
    Modern America* (Chapel Hill: University of North Carolina Press, 1994),
    111–19. Robert F. Wagner, "Company Unions: A Vast Industrial Issue,"
    New York Times, March 11, 1934. Labor radicals opposed exclusive rep-
    resentation, rightly worried that it would give more established American
    Federation of Labor unions a lock on worker representation. Laura Weinrib,
    "The Liberal Compromise: Civil Liberties, Labor, and the Limits of State
    Power, 1917–1940," Ph.D. diss., Princeton University, 2011, 283–85, 291–92,
    301–7; Cletus E. Daniel, *The ACLU and the Wagner Act: An Inquiry into the
    Depression-Era Crisis of American Liberalism* (Ithaca, N.Y.: New York State
    School of Industrial and Labor Relations, 1980), 32–44.

3   Patricia Sullivan, *Days of Hope: Race and Democracy in the New Deal Era*
    (Chapel Hill: University of North Carolina Press, 1996), 46-53; Raymond
    Wolters, *Negroes and the Great Depression: The Problem of Economic
    Recovery* (Westport, Ct.: Greenwood Publishing, 1970). 1939 Hearing on
    NLRA Amendments, 1460, 1462.

4   Statement of Evidence, National Federation of Railway Workers (NFRW)
    v. National Mediation Board (NMB), Eq. No. 66833, District Court for the
    District of Columbia (May 24, 1939) in Record on Appeal, NFRW v. NMB,
    Case No. 7422, U.S. Circuit Court of Appeals for the District of Columbia
    (n.d. April 1939 Term), Records of the U.S. Courts of Appeals, District
    of Columbia Circuit, RG 276, Briefs, #7422, Box 870, National Archives
    Building (NAB), Washington, D.C. [hereafter NFRW v. NMB Records].

5   Leon Fink, *Workingmen's Democracy: The Knights of Labor and American
    Politics* (Urbana: University of Illinois Press, 1985); Bruce Laurie, *Artisans
    into Workers: Labor in Nineteenth-Century America* (Urbana: University
    of Illinois Press, 1997), chap. 5. Marc Karson and Ronald Radosh, "The
    American Federation of Labor and the Negro Worker, 1894–1949," in
    The Negro and the American Labor Movement, ed. Julius Jacobson,
    155–87 (New York: Anchor Books, 1968), 158. Less than half of the AFL's

affiliated unions admitted African Americans, and most that did segregated them into separate locals. Sterling D. Spero and Abram L. Harris, *The Black Worker: The Negro and the Labor Movement* (New York: Atheneum, 1968), 103, 117, 120–21, 124–26. On the variability of AFL unions' racial practices and alliances even in the South, see Rick Halpern, "Organized Labor, Black Workers, and the Twentieth Century South: The Emerging Revision," in *Race and Class in the American South since 1890*, ed. Melvyn Stokes and Rick Halpern, 43–76 (Providence: Berg Publishers, 1994). Transcript, Joint Appendix, Oliphant v. Brotherhood of Locomotive Firemen and Enginemen (BLFE), Case No. 13387, U.S. Court of Appeals for the Sixth Circuit, (October 1, 1957), RG 276, National Archives and Records Administration – Great Lakes Region (NARAGLR), Chicago [hereafter Oliphant Transcript] 163a–4a. Eric Arnesen, *Brotherhoods of Color: Black Railroad Workers and the Struggle for Equality* (Cambridge, Mass.: Harvard University Press, 2002); Herbert R. Northrup, *Organized Labor and the Negro* (New York: Harper & Brothers, 1944), chap. 3; Spero and Harris, *The Black Worker*, chap. 13. See generally Paul Michel Taillon, *Good, Reliable, White Men: Railroad Brotherhoods, 1877–1917* (Urbana: University of Illinois Press, 2009). NFRW v. NMB Records (testimony of Robert F. Cole), 79.

6   Compl. NFRW v. NMB Records, pars. 1–2, p. 2. Arnesen, *Brotherhoods of Color*, 204–5; Genna Rae McNeil, *Groundwork: Charles Hamilton Houston and the Struggle for Civil Rights* (Philadelphia: University of Pennsylvania Press, 1984), 158–59; Deborah C. Malamud, "The Story of *Steele v. Louisville & Nashville Railroad*: White Unions, Black Unions, and the Struggle for Racial Justice on the Rails," in *Labor Law Stories*, ed. Laura J. Cooper and Catherine L. Fisk, 55–106 (New York: Foundation Press, 2005). Statement of Evidence, NFRW v. NMB Records (testimony of C. W. Rice), 47.

7   Statement of Evidence, NFRW v. NMB Records (testimony of Ed Carter, C. W. Rice, Frank L. Mulholland), 62, 46, 65–67. Northrup, *Organized Labor and the Negro*, 81. Cobb, Howard, and Hayes, Petition for Writ of Certiorari, NFRW v. NMB, Supreme Court of the United States, No. 842 (October term, 1939), 10.

8   Complaint, NFRW v. NMB Records, 7, 20–21, 23; Statement of Evidence, NFRW v. NMB Records (statement of Associate Justice Daniel W. O'Donoghue), 57.

9   Nancy Joan Weiss, *Farewell to the Party of Lincoln* (Princeton, N.J.: Princeton University Press, 1983), 32–36, 205–8; Leah M. Wright, "The Loneliness of the Black Conservative: Black Republicans and the Grand Ole Party, 1964–1980," Ph.D. diss., Princeton University, 2009, chap. 1. Jonathan Scott Holloway, *Confronting the Veil: Abram Harris Jr., E. Franklin Frazier, and Ralph Bunche, 1919–1941* (Chapel Hill: University of North Carolina Press, 2002); Sullivan, *Days of Hope*. Nelson Lichtenstein, *State of the Union: A Century of American Labor* (Princeton,

N.J.: Princeton University Press, 2002), 40, 66–71; Robert H. Zieger, *The CIO, 1935–1955* (Chapel Hill: University of North Carolina Press, 1997).

10 Michael R. Botson Jr., *Labor, Civil Rights, and the Hughes Tool Company* (College Station: Texas A&M University Press, 2005), 114–15. Zieger, *The CIO*; Steven Rosswurm, *The CIO's Left-Led Unions* (New Brunswick, N.J.: Rutgers University Press, 1992). On the CIO, see also Chapter 2. Rebecca Anne Montes, "Working for American Rights: Black, White, and Mexican American Dockworkers in Texas during the Great Depression," Ph.D. diss. University of Texas at Austin, 2005, 77–78, 239–40.

11 Neil R. McMillen, "Perry W. Howard: Boss of Black-and-Tan Republicanism in Mississippi, 1924–1960," *Journal of Southern History* 48, no. 2 (May 1982): 205–24, 207–8. "Texas GOP Opens Doors to Negroes," *New York Amsterdam News*, June 22, 1940.

12 "Dr. Emmett J. Scott Replies to Dean Kelly Miller on Vital Political Issues," *Chicago Defender*, September 16, 1939, 15. Quintard Taylor, "Scott, Emmett J. (1873–1957)," www.BlackPast.org. See, generally, Wright, "The Loneliness of the Black Conservative." Criticism of the New Deal was not limited to Republicans. African Americans referred sardonically to the National Industrial Recovery Act, which established the National Recovery Administration, or NRA, as the "Negro Removal Act." Harvard Sitkoff, *A New Deal for Blacks: The Emergence of Civil Rights as a National Issue: The Depression Decade* (New York: Oxford University Press, 1981), 52–55; Sullivan, *Days of Hope*, 49–52. Indeed, the NNC's John Davis criticized Roosevelt's record on race. Ibid., 49–57. "Texas GOP Opens Doors to Negroes."

13 McMillen, "Perry W. Howard," 214–22.

14 "Judge Cobb Like Father to Many," *Baltimore Afro-American*, October 18, 1958, 1–2. August Meier and Elliot Rudwick, "Attorneys Black and White: A Case Study of Race Relations within the NAACP," *Journal of American History* 62, no. 4 (March 1976): 913–46, 923, 928–29, 936, 941. On the rarity of African American civil rights lawyering before 1930, see Kenneth W. Mack, *Representing the Race: The Creation of the Civil Rights Lawyer* (Cambridge, Mass.: Harvard University Press, 2012), chap. 2. Nixon v. Herndon, 273 U.S. 536 (1927); Corrigan v. Buckley, 271 U.S. 323 (1926); Fitzhugh Lee Styles, *Negroes and the Law in the Race's Battle for Liberty, Equality and Justice under the Constitution of the United States* (Boston: Christopher Publishing, 1937), 148. Kenneth W. Mack, "Race Uplift, Professional Identity and the Transformation of Civil Rights Lawyering and Politics, 1920–1940," Ph.D. diss., Princeton University, November 2005, 188. Mack, "Law and Mass Politics in the Making of the Civil Rights Lawyer, 1931–1941," *Journal of American History* 93, no. 1 (June 1, 2006): 37–62, 37–42.

15 Statement of Evidence, NFRW v. NMB Records, 75–77, 106; NFRW v. NMB, 110 F.2d 529, 537 (D.C. Ct. App. 1940).

16 The state is arguably involved in every aspect of life, not only through governing – taxing, regulating, adjudicating disputes, policing, and providing – but also through creating the legal rules that carve out spaces in which people generally think of themselves as taking private action: in their homes and the disposition of their property, in their intimate relations and their economic transactions, and, of particular relevance for this history, in their businesses and associational organizations. The state action doctrine, then, determines not whether the state is involved but whether its involvement should trigger constitutional protections. It requires courts to make a value choice more than a descriptive assessment, although the latter is what most state action analysis purports to be. On the deep roots of private-public interdependence, see Brian Balogh, _A Government Out of Sight: The Mystery of National Authority in Nineteenth-Century America_ (New York: Cambridge University Press, 2009); Gail Radford, _The Rise of the Public Authority: Statebuilding and Economic Development in Twentieth-Century America_ (Chicago: University of Chicago Press, 2013); Gautham Rao, "The Creation of the American State: Customhouses, Law, and Commerce in the Age of Revolution," Ph.D. diss., University of Chicago, 2008. For the argument that this interdependence only grew in importance with the rise of the modern administrative state, see William J. Novak, "The Myth of the 'Weak' American State," _American Historical Review_ 113, no. 3 (June 2008): 752–72. For an excellent treatment of the state action doctrine as a normative theory, see Christopher W. Schmidt, "The Sit-Ins and the State Action Doctrine," _William & Mary Bill of Rights Journal_ 18, no. 3 (2010): 767–829. See also Michael J. Klarman, _From Jim Crow to Civil Rights: The Supreme Court and the Struggle for Racial Equality_ (New York: Oxford University Press, 2006), 138–39. Civil Rights Cases, 109 U.S. 3, 19, 23–25 (1883). Congress had enacted the public accommodations statute to enforce the Fourteenth Amendment. For historical treatment, see Pamela Brandwein, _Rethinking the Judicial Settlement of Reconstruction_ (New York: Cambridge University Press, 2011), chap. 6; Barbara Welke, _Recasting American Liberty: Gender, Race, Law, and the Railroad Revolution, 1865–1920_ (New York: Cambridge University Press, 2001), 336–43; William Edward Nelson, _The Fourteenth Amendment: From Political Principle to Judicial Doctrine_ (Cambridge, Mass.: Harvard University Press, 1988), 194–95. Quote in Richard A. Primus, "The Riddle of Hiram Revels," _Harvard Law Review_ 119 (April 2006): 1680–1733, 1728–29.

17 Corrigan v. Buckley, 299 F. 899, 900-01 (D.C. Ct. App. 1924). Buchanan v. Worley, 245 U.S. 60, 82 (1917). Styles, _Negroes and the Law_, 148.

18 Appellants Br., October 15, 1925, Corrigan v. Buckley, 271 U.S. 323 (1926), _The Making of Modern Law: U.S. Supreme Court Records and Briefs, 1832–1978_ (Farmington Hills, Mich.: Gale), available at

http://gdc.gale.com [hereafter *Supreme Court Records and Briefs*], 7–12, 14; *Corrigan*, 271 U.S. at 331–32. Virginia v. Rives, 100 U.S. 313, 318 (1879). Cobb cited only decisions finding that the procedures a court followed during a trial violated the Constitution. But see Gandolfo v. Hartman, 49 Fed. 181, 182 (S.D. Cal. Cir., 1892). *Corrigan*, 271 U.S. at 329–30. Cobb had also argued that the covenant violated the Thirteenth Amendment, which the Supreme Court rejected. *Corrigan*, 271 U.S. at 330. The Court also held that since there was no state action, the covenant did not violate any constitutional rights and that there was no violation of a public policy derived from them. Ibid. James A. Cobb, "The Constitutional Rights of the Negro or Race Distinctions in American Law," in Styles, *Negroes and the Law*, 83. The Supreme Court adopted Cobb's position in Shelley v. Kraemer, 334 U.S. 1 (1948). See Chapter 4, which, in concert with this chapter and Chapter 2, demonstrates that the state action theory adopted in *Shelley* was not novel; indeed it was, if anything, old-fashioned, drawing on Reconstruction- and Redemption- era state action principles.

19 Compl., NFRW v. NMB Records, 7–8; Appellants Br., NFRW v. NMB Records, 9–10; Brief in Support of Pet'n, NFRW v. NMB, Supreme Court of the United States, No. 842 (October term, 1939) [hereafter NFRW SCOTUS Brief], Records of the Supreme Court, NAB, 52, 57. The courts ignored Cobb's contention that the trial and appellate courts' dismissal of the Federation's suit denied his clients their due process and equal protection rights. In his petition for review, Cobb even suggested state action was not required, asserting that "neither organized labor nor organized industry should be able to impose restraint upon freedom of employment which government itself is forbidden by the Constitution to impose." Ibid. at 11. For similar arguments, see Chapter 3.

20 NFRW v. NMB, 110 F.2d 529, 537–38 (D.C. Ct. App. 1940). Court's Oral Opinion, NFRW v. NMB Records, 146–47. Sixty-three of the seventy African American coach cleaners in the unit voted, thirty-five of them for the Federation, leaving twenty-eight votes for the Carmen. Appellant's Br., NFRW v. NMB, Records of the Supreme Court, NAB, 10. NFRW SCOTUS Brief, 50, 73.

21 Rice's suit was not a good vehicle to force the state-action question the Court had dodged in *Corrigan*; in *Corrigan* the lower courts had enforced the covenant, whereas in the Federation's case the Court had dismissed a suit. As is explained in Chapter 3, this was a potentially crucial distinction. Mack, *Representing the Race*. Arnesen, *Brotherhoods of Color*, 1–2.

22 Charles H. Houston to Clark et al., June, 27, 1940, in *Papers of the NAACP, Part 13, Series C: Legal Department Files on Labor*, ed. John H. Bracey and August Meier (Bethesda, Md.: University Publications of

America [UPA], 1991) [hereafter NAACP Papers Part 13C], microfilm, Reel 8, Images 25–30. Arnesen, *Brotherhoods of Color*, 132–36.

23   Mack, *Representing the Race*, 43–45; Kenneth W. Mack, "Rethinking Civil Rights Lawyering and Politics in the Era before Brown," *Yale Law Journal* 115 (2005): 256–354, 320; David E. Bernstein, *Only One Place of Redress: African Americans, Labor Regulations, and the Courts from Reconstruction to the New Deal* (Durham, N.C.: Duke University Press, 2001). See, e.g., Lochner v. New York, 198 U.S. 45 (1905). Bernstein argues that many laws oppressive to African Americans were passed at the behest of discriminatory unions. For more on the history of the constitutional right to work, see Chapter 3.

24   Mack, "Rethinking Civil Rights Lawyering," 308–13; n.a. [Charles H. Houston], "Aim of Course," January 26, 1940, Charles Hamilton Houston Papers, Moorland-Spingarn Research Center, Howard University, Washington, D.C. [hereafter Houston Papers], Box 163-3, Folders 5–11; n.a. [Frank Reeves], "Civil Rights," February 1, 1941, Houston Papers, Box 163-3, Folders 5–11. Names in brackets here and below reflect my best guess of the authors based on the handwriting. Houston engaged Reeves to help him develop the course.

25   Mack, "Law and Mass Politics," 51, 56.

26   Christopher L. Tomlins, *Law, Labor, and Ideology in the Early American Republic* (New York: Cambridge University Press, 1993); Tomlins, *The State and the Unions*; William E. Forbath, *Law and the Shaping of the American Labor Movement* (Cambridge, Mass.: Harvard University Press, 1991); Ernst, *Lawyers against Labor*. Julie Greene, *Pure and Simple Politics: The American Federation of Labor and Political Activism, 1881–1917* (New York: Cambridge University Press, 1998).

27   Nelson Lichtenstein and Howell John Harris, *Industrial Democracy in America: The Ambiguous Promise* (Washington, D.C.: Woodrow Wilson Center Press, 1996); Joseph Anthony McCartin, *Labor's Great War: The Struggle for Industrial Democracy and the Origins of Modern American Labor Relations, 1912–1921* (Chapel Hill: University of North Carolina Press, 1997). For excellent treatments of industrial pluralism see Ernst, *Lawyers against Labor*; Tomlins, *The State and the Unions*; Reuel E. Schiller, "From Group Rights to Individual Liberties: Post-War Labor Law, Liberalism, and the Waning of Union Status," *Berkeley Journal of Labor and Employment Law* 20 (1999): 1–73. For the pluralists' divisions over state intervention within unions, and the quote, see Daniel R. Ernst, "Common Laborers? Industrial Pluralists, Legal Realists, and the Law of Industrial Disputes, 1915–1943," *Law and History Review* 11, no. 1 (Spring 1993): 59–100, 85.

28   Paul Frymer, *Black and Blue: African Americans, the Labor Movement, and the Decline of the Democratic Party* (Princeton, N.J.: Princeton University Press, 2007), 29; Weiss, *Farewell to the Party of Lincoln*, 163-66; Daniel,

The ACLU and the Wagner Act; Weinrib, "The Liberal Compromise,"
283–85, 291–92, 302–5. 1939 Hearing on NLRA Amendments, 1458–59,
1462 (statement of John P. Davis, National Negro Congress). The fact that
antidiscrimination amendments in 1939 could open the NLRA to conservative amendments may have played a role in the NNC's position, but its
consistency with Davis's 1935 views suggests the position was not purely
strategic. "NAACP Delegates Hit WPA Slashes," *Chicago Defender*, July
15, 1939, 5. Mack, "Rethinking Civil Rights Lawyering," 342, 345–46,
348, 350; McNeil, *Groundwork*, 133–36.

29 N.a. [Reeves], "4th Amendment," March 21, 1941, Houston Papers, Box
163-3, Folders 5–11; n.a. [Reeves], "Freedom of Religion: Amendment I,"
January 28, 1940, ibid.; n.a. [Reeves], "Property Rights," n.d., ibid. Mack,
"Rethinking Civil Rights Lawyering," 331–34. N.a., "Memorandum
for Lecture March 3, 1938," n.d. [March 1938], Houston Papers, Box
163-3, Folders 5–11 (discussing Fourteenth Amendment challenges in
Chaires v. City of Atlanta, 164 Ga. 755 (1927)). In theory, the Thirteenth
Amendment provided Houston a way around the state action limit: as
he taught his students, the "13th Amendment covers acts of individuals"
as well as the state. But in Houston's view, it applied only to peonage
and vagrancy. N.a. [Houston], "13th Amendment covers acts of individuals," n.d., ibid. Risa Goluboff notes that this view changed over the next
ten years and in 1947 he argued lawyers should push the Court to find
that occupational segregation was involuntary servitude in violation of
the Thirteenth Amendment. Risa L. Goluboff, *The Lost Promise of Civil
Rights* (Cambridge, Mass.: Harvard University Press, 2007), 215.

30 Lea S. VanderVelde, "The Labor Vision of the Thirteenth Amendment,"
University of Pennsylvania Law Review 138 (December 1989): 437–504;
James Gray Pope, "The Thirteenth Amendment versus the Commerce
Clause: Labor and the Shaping of American Constitutional Law, 1921–
1957," *Columbia Law Review* 102, no. 1 (January 2002): 1–122; Weinrib,
"The Liberal Compromise." Mack, "Rethinking Civil Rights Lawyering,"
320–25.

31 Houston to Clark et al., June, 27, 1940, NAACP Papers Part 13C. On the
mechanical stoker, see International Railway Fuel Association, *Proceedings
of the Annual Convention of the International Railway Fuel Association*,
May 18–24, 1914 (Google eBook), 174–75. Arnesen, *Brotherhoods of
Color*, 204. Charles Houston to Walter White and Thurgood Marshall,
May 15, 1940, NAACP Papers Part 13C, Reel 8, Image 12.

32 Draft Compl., Teague v. BLFE, n.d. [May 15, 1940], NAACP Papers
Part 13C, Reel 8, pars. 3, 7, 9–10.

33 Mark V. Tushnet, *Making Civil Rights Law: Thurgood Marshall and the
Supreme Court, 1956–1961* (New York: Oxford University Press, 1996),
163. Gulf, Mobile & Northern Rwy. Co., Motion to Dismiss, Teague v.
Bro. of Locomotive Firemen et al., June 5, 1940, NAACP Papers Part 13C,

Reel 8. Houston to Clark et al., June 27, 1940, NAACP Papers Part 13C, Reel 8, 4–5.

34 Colloquy, March 15, 1941, in Transcript of Record, Teague v. BLFE, Case No. 8937, 6th Cir. Ct. App. [hereafter Teague Appellate Record], NARAGLR, 43–44. BLFE, Mot. to Dismiss, Oct. 31, 1940, in Teague Appellate Record, 37–41. The brotherhood could so move because Houston had amended his complaint to strengthen his claim to federal-question jurisdiction, by titling it an action "for fraud, breach of contract, breach of trust and violation of the Railway Labor Act," and by referring consistently to the brotherhood as having "statutory" as well as "fiduciary" duties. Amended Compl., October 11, 1940, in Teague Appellate Record, 5; pars. 13–15. Opinion of Court, March 15, 1941, in Teague Appellate Record, 40.

35 Opinion of Court, March 15, 1941, in Teague Appellate Record, 37–41, 40; Houston to Clark et al., June 27, 1940, NAACP Papers Part 13C.

36 Houston to Clark et al., June 27, 1940, NAACP Papers Part 13C, 3–5. Houston's original analogy was in keeping with industrial pluralists' description of the collective-bargaining regime as a private constitutional democracy. Apellant's Brief, Teague v. BLFE, Case No. 8937, 6th Cir. Ct. App., NARAGLR [hereafter Teague Appellant's Brief], 17. Weinrib, "The Liberal Compromise," 314–15. Carter v. Carter Coal Co., 298 U.S. 238, 311 (1936). Charles H. Houston, "Memorandum in re Ed Teague," n.d. [March 1942], Houston Papers, Box 163-21, Folder 18, 1.

37 Teague v. BLFE, 127 F.2d 53, 55–56 (6th Cir. 1942). The court thus found the relevance of the act too speculative to support federal jurisdiction.

38 J. T. Settle to Charles H. Houston, April 14, 1942, Houston Papers, Box 163-21, Folder 18. Petitioner Br., Tunstall v. BLFE, Case No. 37, Supreme Court of the United States, n.d. [1944], on file with author [hereafter Tunstall Petitioner's Brief].

39 Complaint, Tunstall v. BLFE, Case No. 210, District Court for the Eastern District of Virginia (Norfolk Division) [hereafter Tunstall Trial Court Record], August 11, 1942, in appendix to Appellants' Br., Tunstall v. BLFE, Case No. 5125, 4th Cir. Ct. App., September 14, 1943, "Tunstall v. Brotherhood," vol. 840 (1943), RG 276, National Archives at Philadelphia [hereafter Tunstall Appellate Records]. Defendants' Motions to Dismiss, Tunstall Trial Court Record, n.d. [August 1942], in appendix to Apellants' Br., Tunstall Appellate Records. Brief for Appellant, September 14, 1943, Tunstall Appellate Records; Joseph Waddy and Charles H. Houston, "Memorandum on Five United States Supreme Court Cases Decided since the Argument of the Instant Cause on October 15, 1943," n.d. [Jan. 1944], Tunstall Appellate Records. Tunstall v. Brotherhood of Locomotive Firemen and Enginemen, 140 F.2d 35, 36 (1944). Today, lawyers attribute the post–New Deal courts' protection of minority rights to a footnote in the Supreme Court's 1938

United States v. Carolene Products Co. decision, 304 U.S. 144, 152 n. 4 (1938). As Houston's travails indicate, and as historians have shown, little attention was paid to the footnote for many years after *Carolene Products* was decided, and immediately after the decision the Supreme Court's solicitousness toward minority rights was far from clear. Goluboff, *The Lost Promise*, 45. That Houston's constitutional arguments were added for jurisdictional purposes is supported by the fact that his simultaneous complaint filed in the Alabama state courts, where a federal question was unnecessary, made no such claims. Malamud, "The Story of *Steele*," 70–71.

40 For more on World War II and its impact on civil rights activism, see Chapter 2.

41 For more on the CIO and the changing racial politics in the labor movement, see Chapter 2. Historians debate how friendly Roosevelt's Court was to labor, as well as how hostile its predecessors were. For critical treatments, see Karl E. Klare, "Judicial Deradicalization of the Wagner Act and the Origins of Modern Legal Consciousness, 1937–1941," *Minnesota Law Review* 62 (1978): 265–339; Pope, "The Thirteenth Amendment versus the Commerce Clause." For arguments that the Court had accommodated many of labor's demands well before the New Deal, see Ernst, *Lawyers against Labor*. Even if the Roosevelt Court diminished the movement's most transformative aspirations or was not the first to legitimize some aspects of unionization, it was unquestionably more sympathetic to labor than any Court before it. Unknown author to NAACP Board, March 19, 1940, Papers of NAACP, Part II-A [hereafter NAACP Papers-II-A], Box 443, Folder 7, Library of Congress Manuscripts and Archives Division, Washington, D.C. [hereafter LCMD]. Stephen Spingarn to William H. Hastie, March 14, 1940, ibid. Press Service of the NAACP, March 20, 1940, ibid.; Walter White to Committee on Education and Labor, U.S. Senate, March 18, 1940, ibid. AFL unions were increasingly organizing on an industrial rather than a craft basis. Lichtenstein, *State of the Union*, 67. The CIO shift probably resulted from the benefits the amendments would provide its interracial unions when they competed with these AFL unions.

42 West Virginia Board of Education v. Barnette, 319 U.S. 624 (1943); Thornhill v. Alabama, 310 U.S. 88 (1940); Smith v. Allwright, 321 U.S. 649, 663 (1944). Daniel Ernst, "Morgan and the New Dealers," *Journal of Policy History* 20, no. 4 (2008): 447–81; Weinrib, "The Liberal Compromise," chap. 5.

43 Joseph Waddy, Arthur D. Shores, and Charles H. Houston, Petition for Writ of Certiorari, March 29, 1944, Steele v. Louisville and Nashville Ry. Co., 323 U.S. 192 (1944), in *Supreme Court Records and Briefs*, 16–17. Petition for Writ of Certiorari, Tunstall v. BLFE, 323 U.S. 210 (1944) in *Supreme Court Records and Briefs* [hereafter Tunstall Cert. Petition], 21–24, 26. Thurgood Marshall and William H. Hastie, Motion and

Brief for the NAACP as Amicus Curiae, November 20, 1944, Tunstall
v. BLFE, 323 U.S. 210 (1944), in *Supreme Court Records and Briefs*
[hereafter NAACP Tunstall Amicus Brief], 31. Although Houston made
little of his reference to the Thirteenth Amendment, others were pursuing its promise for economic and racial justice. Goluboff, *The Lost
Promise.*

44 Tunstall Cert. Petition, 25–26; Smith v. Allwright, 321 U.S. 649, 663
(1944). NAACP Tunstall Amicus Brief, 33–34 (quoting Nixon v. Condon,
286 U.S. 73, 88–89 (1932)). ACLU, Brief Amicus Curiae, Tunstall v.
BLFE, 323 U.S. 210 (1944) in *Supreme Court Records and Briefs* [here-
after ACLU Tunstall Amicus Brief], 15. For more on the ACLU and the
NAACP, and their changing relationship to the post–New Deal labor–
liberal coalition, see Chapter 2.

45 Teague Appellant's Brief. Tunstall Cert. Petition, 26. NAACP Tunstall
Amicus Brief, 27.

46 Houston to Clark et al., June 27, 1940, NAACP Papers Part 13C, Reel 8.
Tunstall Cert. Petition, 17. Tunstall Petitioner's Brief, 45; ACLU Tunstall
Amicus Brief, 17; NAACP Tunstall Amicus Brief.

47 Steele v. Louisville & Nashville Ry. Co., 323 U.S. 192 (1944); Tunstall
v. Brotherhood of Locomotive Firemen and Enginemen, 323 U.S. 210
(1944). For the justices' deliberations, see Malamud, "The Story of
Steele." Charles Houston to Thurgood Marshall et al., December 20,
1944, NAACP Papers Part 13C, Reel 8, 1.

48 Houston to Marshall et al., December 20, 1944, NAACP Papers Part 13C,
Reel 8, 1, 3. *Steele*, 323 U.S. at 204.

49 Houston to Marshall et al., December 20, 1944, NAACP Papers Part 13C,
Reel 8, 2. N.a. [Houston], Appellants' Draft Brief, Kerr v. Enoch Pratt
Free Library, Case No. 5273, U.S. Circuit Court of Appeals for the Fourth
Circuit, Houston Papers, Box 163-28, Folders 7–9.

50 *Steele*, 323 U.S. at 198, 202. Ibid. at 208–9 (Murphy, J., concurring).

51 Betts v. Easley, 161 Kan. 459, 465, 467–69 (1946). William H. Hastie,
"Appraisal of *Smith v. Allwright*," *Lawyers' Guild Review* 5, no. 2
(March–April 1945): 65–72. E. Merrick Dodd, "The Supreme Court
and Organized Labor, 1941–1945," *Harvard Law Review* 58 (1945):
1018–71. Howard v. Thompson, 72 F. Supp. 695 (E.D. Mo., 1947);
Mitchell v. Gulf, Mobile & Ohio R. Co., 91 F. Supp. 175, 177, 186 (N.D.
Ala., 1950); Rolax v. Atlantic Coast Liner, Co., 91 F. Supp. 585, 591 (E.D.
Va., 1950).

2 Agencies Discover the Liberal Workplace Constitution

1   Stuart Bruce Kaufman, *Challenge and Change: The History of the Tobacco
Workers International Union* (Champaign: University of Illinois Press,

1986), 120. U.S. Bedding Co., 52 N.L.R.B. 382, 388 (1943). Richard Love, "In Defiance of Custom and Tradition: Black Tobacco Workers and Labor Unions in Richmond, Virginia, 1937–1941," *Labor History* 35, no. 1 (1994): 25–47, 27. On CIO organizing at a nearby tobacco plant, see Robert R. Korstad, *Civil Rights Unionism: Tobacco Workers and the Struggle for Democracy in the Mid-Twentieth-Century South* (Chapel Hill: University of North Carolina Press, 2003).

2   Frank Bloom, Report and Recommendations, February 23, 1945 [hereafter Bloom Larus Report], NLRB Papers – CF35–48, Box 3851, "5-R-1413 Larus & Brother Company, Inc., Richmond, Va. Formal File" Folder, 2, 5.

3   "A Guide to the WRVA Radio Collection, 1925–2000," Library of Virginia, available at http://ead.lib.virginia.edu/vivaead/published/lva/vi00565.document. "Larus & Brother Company, Richmond, Virginia Records, 1877–1974: Description and Guide," Virginia Historical Society Department of Manuscripts and Archives, available at http://www.vahistorical.org/arvfind/ larus.htm.

4   Korstad, *Civil Rights Unionism*, 43–44, 71, 96. Love, "In Defiance," 45; Sterling D. Spero and Abram L. Harris, *The Black Worker: The Negro and the Labor Movement* (New York: Atheneum, 1968), 256.

5   Robert H. Zieger, *The CIO, 1935–1955* (Chapel Hill: University of North Carolina Press, 1997); Lizabeth Cohen, *Making a New Deal: Industrial Workers in Chicago, 1919–1939* (New York: Cambridge University Press, 2008); Steve Fraser, *Labor Will Rule: Sidney Hillman and the Rise of American Labor* (Ithaca, N.Y.: Cornell University Press, 1993); Robin D. G. Kelley, *Hammer and Hoe: Alabama Communists during the Great Depression* (Chapel Hill: University of North Carolina Press, 1990); Nelson Lichtenstein, *The Most Dangerous Man in Detroit: Walter Reuther and the Fate of American Labor* (New York: Basic Books, 1995); Glenda Elizabeth Gilmore, *Defying Dixie: The Radical Roots of Civil Rights: 1919–1950* (New York: W. W. Norton, 2008). Love, "In Defiance," 33.

6   Korstad, *Civil Rights Unionism*, 144–45.

7   Kaufman, *Challenge and Change*, 96. Love, "In Defiance," 36. A. J. Marcus to Harry A. Millis, February 24, 1944, NLRB Records – CF35–48, Box 3851, "5-R-1413 Larus & Brother Company, Inc., Richmond, Va. Formal File" Folder. For similar dynamics in Winston-Salem, North Carolina, see Korstad, *Civil Rights Unionism*, 134–35.

8   Daniel Kryder, *Divided Arsenal: Race and the American State during World War II* (New York: Cambridge University Press, 2001), 38–46, 51. Gilmore, *Defying Dixie*, 359–64; Patricia Sullivan, *Days of Hope: Race and Democracy in the New Deal Era* (Chapel Hill: University of North Carolina Press, 1996), 135–36, 157–58; Thomas J. Sugrue, *Sweet Land of*

Liberty: The Forgotten Struggle for Civil Rights in the North (New York: Random House, 2009), 44–49, 54–57.

9   Reuel Schiller, *Forging Rivals: Labor Law, Fair Employment Practices Law, and the Fate of Postwar Liberalism* (New York: Cambridge University Press, forthcoming), chap. 1; Henry N. Marsh, "Memorandum re Complaint of Discrimination in Employment Practices – Shell Oil," July 26, 1955, RG 220, Records of Temporary Committees, Commissions, and Boards, Records of the President's Committee on Government Contracts, 1953–1961, Discrimination Complaint Casefiles, 1951–1961, [hereafter PCGC Papers – DCC], "Case No. 216, Shell Oil Company, Houston, Texas" Folder, NACP. For more on discrimination at the Houston plant, see Chapter 5.

10 "Church Heads Will Discuss Race in War," *Chicago Defender*, April 11, 1942, 3. Love, "In Defiance," 46. Megan Taylor Schockley, *"We, Too, Are Americans": African American Women in Detroit and Richmond, 1940–54* (Urbana: University of Illinois Press, 2004), 80.

11 "Attention Tobacco Workers," n.d. [March 1944], ex. 9, Case No. 5-R-1413, NLRB Transcripts and Exhibits, Records of the National Labor Relations Board, RG 25, NACP [hereafter NLRB Papers – T&E], Box 4004, Folder 6647–48.

12 Love, "In Defiance," 34–35; Richard Love, "The Cigarette Capital of the World: Labor, Race, and Tobacco in Richmond, Virginia, 1880–1980," Ph.D. diss., University of Virginia, 1998, 219. See also Korstad, *Civil Rights Unionism.*

13 Affidavit of Richard Pate and Thomas Johnson, April 24, 1944, ex. 9, Case No. 5-R-1413, NLRB Papers – T&E, Box 4004, Folder 6647–48. Affidavit of A. J. Marcus, July 10, 1944, ex. 16, Case No. 5-R-1413, NLRB Papers – T&E, Box 4004, Folder 6647–48, 3; Affidavit of Isabelle Manigo, May 1, 1944, ex. 9, Case No. 5-R-1413, NLRB Papers – T&E, Box 4004, Folder 6647–48.

14 "Dixie Bloc Hops on Labor Board over Negro Jobs," *Chicago Defender*, July 8, 1944, 11. Malcolm Ross to Harry A. Millis, September 13, 1944, "5-R-1413 Larus & Brother Company, Inc., Richmond, Va. Informal File" Folder, Box 3851, NLRB Papers – CF35–48.

15 Frank Bloom to Walter Wilbur, October 27, 1944, NLRB Papers – CF35–48, Box 4132, "15-R-1232 Carter Manufacturing Co., Memphis, Tenn. Informal File" Folder.

16 James A. Gross, *Reshaping of the National Labor Relations Board* (Albany: State University of New York Press, 1982), 242, 251. David Ashe to Clifford Forster, June 26, 1944, Larus Labor Case, ACLU Records (microfilm), Seeley G. Mudd Manuscript Library, Princeton University, Princeton, N.J., Reel 226, 2.

17 Bethlehem-Alameda Shipyards, 53 N.L.R.B. 999, 1016 (1943). Carter Manufacturing Corp., 59 N.L.R.B. 804 (1944). Gilmore, *Defying Dixie*, 362.

18 Eugene A. Curry to Oscar Smith, October 13, 1944, NLRB Papers – CF35–48, Box 3851, "5-R-1413 Larus & Brother Company, Inc., Richmond, Va. Informal File" Folder, 1–6.

19 Transcript of Hearing, Larus & Brother Co., Case No. 5-R-1413, Jan. 4, 1945, NLRB Papers – T&E, Box 4004, Folder 6648, 375. The organizer was A. J. Marcus. "Rights of Unions Segregating Negroes Challenged," *ACLU Bulletin* 1151, November 6, 1944, ACLU Papers, Series 2, Box 27, Folder 9. George L. Googe to John Houston, June 22, 1944, NLRB Papers – CF35–48, Box 3851, "5-R-1413 Larus & Brother Company, Inc., Richmond, Va. Informal File" Folder. See Chapter 1.

20 Brief for ACLU Am. Cur., Larus & Brother Co., Case Nos. 5-R-1413, 5-R-1437, ex. 18, NLRB Papers – T&E, Box 4004, Folder 6647, 13–14. NAACP to NLRB, September 15, 1943, NLRB Papers – CF35–48, Box 3672, "R-5693 Bethlehem Steel Co. San Francisco, Calif. Formal File" Folder, 5; William R. Ming to H. A. Millis, n.d. [1943], NAACP Papers-II-A, Box 443, Folder 7. William H. Hastie to Harry A. Millis, October 12, 1944, Larus & Brother Co., Case Nos. 5-R-1413, 5-R-1437, ex. 17, NLRB Papers – T&E, Box 4004, Folder 6647; Transcript of Hearing, Larus & Brother Co., Case No. 5-R-1413 [hereafter NLRB Larus Hearing Transcript], June 21, 1945, NLRB Papers – T&E, Box 4004, Folder 6648, 79.

21 NLRB Larus Hearing Transcript, 399, 715–16. Samuel Rosenwein to NLRB, February 2, 1945, NLRB Papers – CF35–48, Box 3851, "5-R-1413 Larus & Brother Company, Inc., Richmond, Va. Formal File" Folder, 10, 13–14.

22 Joseph Jacobs to NLRB, February 13, 1945, NLRB Papers – CF35–48, Box 3851, "5-R-1413 Larus & Brother Company, Inc., Richmond, Va. Formal File" Folder, 5–6, 18–21, 27. Georgia senator Eugene Cox quoted in Gilbert J. Gall, *The Politics of Right to Work: The Labor Federations as Special Interests, 1943–1979* (New York: Greenwood Press, 1988), 33.

23 Bloom's law firm was Sonnenschein, Berkson, Lautmann, Levinson & Morse. American Trust & Safe Deposit Co. v. Eldred, 267 Ill. App. 176 (App. Ct. Ill., 1st Dist. 1932). Louis Stark, "Says NLRB Official Asked C.I.O. Ruling," *New York Times*, April 27, 1940, 1. Special House Committee to Investigate the National Labor Relations Board, September 11, 13, 1940 (testimony of Frank Bloom), Papers of James Gross [hereafter Gross Papers], Kheel Center for Labor-Management Documentation and Archives, Cornell University, Ithaca, N.Y. [hereafter Kheel], Box 10, Folder 12.

24 Bloom Larus Report, 14–15.

25 Bloom Larus Report, 14–15.

26 Marjorie McKenzie, "Significant Battle Won by Trial Examiner for NLRB," *Pittsburgh Courier*, March 24, 1945. "Labor Board Bans Jim Crow Unions," *Atlanta Daily World*, March 4, 1945, 1; "Outlaws

Separate Locals for Workers," *Pittsburgh Courier*, March 3, 1945, 4.
George L. Googe to NLRB, April 6, 1945, NLRB Papers – CF35–48,
Box 3851, "5-R-1413 Larus & Brother Company, Inc., Richmond, Va.
Informal File" Folder, 2, 4.

27 Reuel E. Schiller, "Free Speech and Expertise: Administrative Censorship
and the Birth of the Modern First Amendment," *Virginia Law Review*
86 (February 2000): 1–101. Bi-Metallic Investment Co. v. State Board of
Equalization, 239 U.S. 441 (1915); Morgan v. United States, 298 U.S. 468
(1936); Daniel Ernst, "Morgan and the New Dealers," *Journal of Policy
History* 20, no. 4 (2008): 447–81. Ford Motor Co. v. NLRB, 305 U.S.
364 (1939); Laura Weinrib, "The Liberal Compromise: Civil Liberties,
Labor, and the Limits of State Power, 1917–1940," Ph.D. diss., Princeton
University, 2011, chap. 6. In the Matter of Tennessee Copper Company,
59 N.L.R.B. 1079, 1081 n.3 (1944); Famous-Barr Co., 59 N.L.R.B. 976,
1063–64 (1944).

28 Bloom Larus Report, February 23, 1945, NLRB Papers – CF35–48, Box
3851, "5-R-1413 Larus & Brother Company, Inc., Richmond, Va. Formal
File" Folder, 14–15. Steele v. Louisville and Nashville Ry. Co., 323 U.S.
192, 204 (1944).

29 See Chapter 1. Smith v. Allwright, 321 U.S. 649, 663 (1944).

30 The statute reached actions committed "under color of" the law, a
rough equivalent of the state action requirement. Senator quoted in
Francis Biddle, "Civil Rights and Federal Law," in Carl L. Becker et al.,
Safeguarding Civil Liberty Today (Ithaca, N.Y.: Cornell University Press,
1945), 124. Pamela Brandwein, *Rethinking the Judicial Settlement of
Reconstruction* (New York: Cambridge University Press, 2011), chaps.
2, 6. Victor W. Rotnem, "Clarifications of the Civil Rights Statutes," *Bill
of Rights Review* 2 (1942): 252–61, 260. Risa L. Goluboff, *The Lost
Promise of Civil Rights* (Cambridge, Mass.: Harvard University Press,
2007), 138. Shelley v. Kraemer, 334 U.S. 1 (1948).

31 NLRB Larus Hearing Transcript, 84–85, 88. R. Alton Lee, "John M.
Houston: Congressman and Labor Mediator," *Kansas History* (Autumn
2002): 200–13, 207–9. On Millis and industrial pluralism, see Christopher
Tomlins, *The State and the Unions* (New York: Cambridge University
Press, 1985), chap. 6; Daniel R. Ernst, "Common Laborers? Industrial
Pluralists, Legal Realists, and the Law of Industrial Disputes, 1915–
1943," *Law and History Review* 11, no. 1 (Spring 1993): 59–100; Reuel
E. Schiller, "From Group Rights to Individual Liberties: Post-War Labor
Law, Liberalism, and the Waning of Union Strength," *Berkeley Journal of
Employment and Labor Law* 20 (1999): 1–73.

32 NLRB Larus Hearing Transcript, 19–20, 52, 62–63, 76, 79.

33 William Sentner to NLRB, April 27, 1945, NLRB Papers – CF35–48,
Box 4220, "14-R-1163 General Motors Corporation (Chevrolet
Shell Division, St. Louis, Missouri), Informal File" Folder, 2 n. 1, 4.
"Memorandum Argument on Behalf of Atlanta Oak Flooring Co.," May

7, 1945, NLRB Papers – CF35–48, Box 4089, "10-R-1464: Atlanta Oak Flooring Company" Folder, 2–5.

34 NLRB Larus Hearing Transcript, 29.

35 General Motors Corp., 62 N.L.R.B. 427, 431 (1945). Atlanta Oak Flooring Co., 62 N.L.R.B. 973, 975 (1945).

36 On labor pluralism and the NLRA, see Chapter 1. *Steele*, 323 U.S. at 204. Larus & Brother Co., 62 N.L.R.B. 1075, 1081–1085 (1945).

37 "NLRB Again Tackles Biased Union Issue," *Pittsburgh Courier*, October 6, 1945, 14.

38 Irene G. Osborn to NLRB, September 24, 1945, NLRB Papers – CF35–48, Box 3851, "5-R-1413 Larus & Brother Company, Inc., Richmond, Va. Informal File" Folder; Mrs. R. P. Milburn to NLRB, October 30, 1945, ibid.

39 Julia Cooley Altrocchi to NLRB, September 26, 1945, NLRB Papers – CF35–48, Box 3851, "5-R-1413 Larus & Brother Company, Inc., Richmond, Va. Informal File" Folder; Milburn to NLRB, October 30, 1945, ibid.; C. L. Dellums to NLRB, September 27, 1945, ibid.

40 NLRB, Order, October 16, 1945, NLRB Papers – CF35–48, Box 4296, "5-R-2035 Larus & Brother Company, Inc., Richmond, Va., Informal File" Folder. See, e.g., Oscar S. Smith to Mrs. R. P. Milburn, November 7, 1945, NLRB Papers – CF35–48, Box 3851, "5-R-1413 Larus & Brother Company, Inc., Richmond, Va. Informal File" Folder.

41 Clarence Mitchell to Boris Shishkin, July 2, 1947, RG 9 -001, Series 1, Department of Civil Rights Records [hereafter DCR Papers], 1943–1967, Box 2, Folder 19, George Meany Memorial Archives, Silver Spring, Md. [hereafter GMMA]. On Republican and southern Democrats' resistance to the NLRB, see Chapter 3. Gross, *Reshaping of the National Labor Relations Board*, 45–46, 252–53. Taft–Hartley Act, 61 Stat. 136 (1947). Clarence Mitchell, "NAACP Statement before Senate Committee on Labor and Public Welfare," February 18, 1947, CIO Secretary-Treasurer's Office Collection [hereafter CIOSO Papers], Box 149, "NAACP, 1946–47" Folder, Archive of Labor and Urban Affairs, Walter P. Reuther Library, Wayne State University, Detroit [hereafter ALUA], 2, 4–6.

42 Taft-Hartley Act, secs. 8, 8(b)(1)(A), 8(b)(2). Testimony of Senator Howard Taft, 93 Cong. Rec. 4193 (April 29, 1947); House Conf. Rept. No. 510 on H.R. 3020, Labor-Management Relations Act, 80th Cong., 1st Sess. (June 3, 1947), 41. Mitchell to Shishkin, July 2, 1947, DCR Papers.

43 Marian Wynn Perry to NLRB, January 30, 1948, NAACP Papers Part 13C, Reel 7, 1–3. On the Teamsters, see William B. Gould, *Black Workers in White Unions: Job Discrimination in the United States* (Ithaca, N.Y.: Cornell University Press, 1977), 365–71. Christopher Dixie to NLRB, December 19, 1947, NLRB Papers – CF35–48, Box 5601, "16-R-2223 Texas Pacific Motor Transport Co., Dallas, Texas Formal File" Folder, 15, 18–20.

44 Gross, *Reshaping of the National Labor Relations Board*, 248. Plywood-
    Plastics Corp., 85 N.L.R.B. 265, 265 (1949). See also Mine Safety
    Appliances Co., 85 N.L.R.B. 290, n. 13 (1949); Veneer Products, Inc.,
    81 N.L.R.B. 492 (1949); Norfolk Southern Bus Corp., 76 N.L.R.B. 488,
    489 (1948); Texas & Pacific Motor Transport Corp., 77 N.L.R.B. 87, 89
    (1948).

45 Quoted in "NAACP Urges Safeguards in Taft-Hartley Act against Abuse,"
    Chicago Defender, March 26, 1949, 4. Clarence Mitchell, July 14, 1949,
    in Randolph Boehm and August Meier, eds., *Papers of the NAACP, Part 1:
    Meetings of the Board of Directors, Records of Annual Conferences,
    Major Speeches, and Special Reports, 1909–1950* (Bethesda, Md.: UPA,
    1982), microfilm, Reel 12.

46 *NLRB Tenth Annual Report* (Washington, D.C.: Government Printing
    Office, 1946), 17–18.

47 Williams v. International Brotherhood of Boilermakers, 165 P.2d 903
    (Cal. 1946); James v. Marinship Corp. 155 P.2d 329 (1945); Goluboff,
    The Lost Promise, 195, 205–6, 212.

3 Conservatives Create a Workplace Constitution in the Courts

1 Cecil B. DeMille to Neil S. McCarthy, August 16, 1944, Folder 7, Box
    1134, MSS 1400, Cecil B. DeMille Papers [hereafter DeMille Papers], L.
    Tom Perry Special Collections, Harold B. Lee Library, Brigham Young
    University, Provo, Utah. Scott Eyman, *Empire of Dreams: The Epic Life
    of Cecil B. DeMille* (New York: Simon & Schuster, 2010), 373, 393.

2 "Dollar Assessments May Keep AFRA Members Off Air," *Billboard*,
    November 18, 1944, 6. Joseph Tanenhaus, "Organized Labor's Political
    Spending: The Law and Its Consequences," *Journal of Politics* 16,
    no. 3 (August 1954): 441–71, 449; Warner v. Screen Office Employees
    Guild, Case No. 497025, Los Angeles Superior Court, County of Los
    Angeles (1944). "Lux Theater May Be DeMille-less Any Day," *Billboard*,
    December 9, 1944, 7. Cecil B. DeMille, press release, December 5, 1944,
    DeMille Papers, Box 1209, Folder 9.

3 Daniel R. Ernst, *Lawyers against Labor: From Individual Rights to
    Corporate Liberalism* (Urbana: University of Illinois Press, 1995).
    David Witwer, *Shadow of the Racketeer: Scandal in Organized Labor*
    (Urbana: University of Illinois Press, 2009), 7. Nelson Lichtenstein, *State
    of the Union: A Century of American Labor* (Princeton, N.J.: Princeton
    University Press, 2002), 68. Nelson Lichtenstein, *Labor's War at Home:
    The CIO in World War II* (New York: Cambridge University Press, 1991),
    22–24, 67–69, 78–81. Edward S. Cowdrick, "Must Workers Swallow the
    Closed Shop?" *Nation's Business*, October 1941, 25.

4 Howell John Harris, *The Right to Manage: Industrial Relations Policies
    of American Business in the 1940s* (Madison: University of Wisconsin

Press, 1982), 23; Kim Phillips-Fein, *Invisible Hands: The Making of the Conservative Movement from the New Deal to Reagan* (New York: W. W. Norton, 2009), 10. Jennifer Delton, *Racial Integration in Corporate America, 1940–1990* (New York: Cambridge University Press, 2009), 196; Gilbert J. Gall, *The Politics of Right to Work: The Labor Federations as Special Interests, 1943–1979* (New York: Greenwood Press, 1988), 14. George Wolfskill, *The Revolt of the Conservatives: A History of the American Liberty League, 1934–1940* (Boston: Houghton Mifflin, 1962); Frederick Rudolph, "The American Liberty League, 1934–1940," *American Historical Review* 56 (October 1950): 19–33. Witwer, *Shadow of the Racketeer*, 179.

5   Ibid., 5, 32; quote at 5.
6   Elizabeth A. Fones-Wolf, *Selling Free Enterprise: The Business Assault on Labor and Liberalism, 1945–60* (Urbana: University of Illinois Press, 1995), 25. Gall, *The Politics of Right to Work*, 14; Harris, *The Right to Manage*, 24. Sean Farhang and Ira Katznelson, "The Southern Imposition: Congress and Labor in the New Deal and Fair Deal," *Studies in American Political Development* 19, no. 1 (2005): 1–30, 23.
7   Witwer, *Shadow of the Racketeer*, 197, 200. Lichtenstein, *Labor's War at Home*, 78–81; Harris, *The Right to Manage*, 106.
8   David E. Bernstein, *Rehabilitating Lochner: Defending Individual Rights against Progressive Reform* (Chicago: University Of Chicago Press, 2011), 18–20. Ray Stannard Baker, "The Right to Work," *McClure's Magazine*, January 1903, 323. Compare "New U.S. Secretary of Labor Criticized for Alleged Opposition to Negro Labor," *New York Amsterdam News*, December 24, 1930, 5 with "Closed-Shop Contracts," *Los Angeles Times*, May 12, 1930, A4. Carolyn Dixon, "FEPC Given Funds to Continue Investigation," *New York Amsterdam Star-News*, December 5, 1942, 2; letter quoted in Witwer, *Shadow of the Racketeer*, 177. See also Risa L. Goluboff, *The Lost Promise of Civil Rights* (Cambridge, Mass.: Harvard University Press, 2007).
9   E. Merrick Dodd, "State Legislatures Go to War – On Unions," *Iowa Law Review* 29 (1943): 148–74, 148–50. Cheryl Hall, "DMN Writer Coined Term 'Right to Work,' Opposed Forced Union Membership," *Dallas Morning News*, July 12, 2010, available at http://www.dallasnews.com. Marc Dixon, "Limiting Labor: Business Political Mobilization and Union Setback in the States," *Journal of Policy History* 19, no. 03 (2007): 313–44, 321; George Norris Green, *The Establishment in Texas Politics: The Primitive Years, 1938–57* (Westport, Conn.: Greenwood Press, 1979), 61–63; William Canak and Berkeley Miller, "Gumbo Politics: Unions, Business, and Louisiana Right-to-Work Legislation," *Industrial and Labor Relations Review* 43, no. 2 (January 1, 1990): 258–71, 260. Elizabeth Tandy Shermer, "Counter-Organizing the Sunbelt: Right-to-Work Campaigns and Anti-Union Conservatism, 1943–1958," *Pacific*

Historical Review 78, no. 1 (February 2009): 81–118, 93–94. "Major Studio Strike Feared as 200 Quit," *Los Angeles Times*, October 6, 1944 1; Phil A. Koury, *Yes, Mr. DeMille* (New York: G. P. Putnam's Sons, 1959), 292.

10   Sumiko Higashi, *Cecil B. DeMille: A Guide to References and Resources* (Boston: G. K. Hall, 1985), 12. Michael Denning, *The Cultural Front: The Laboring of American Culture in the Twentieth Century* (New York: Verso, 1997). Eyman, *Empire of Dreams*, 350, 397.

11   Cecil B. DeMille, press release, December 5, 1944, DeMille Papers, Box 1209, Folder 9. Quoted in Koury, *Yes, Mr. DeMille*, 294. For more on the right-to-work movement's gender dynamics, see Chapter 12.

12   DeMille to McCarthy, August 16, 1944. Clayton R. Koppes and Gregory D. Black, *Hollywood Goes to War: How Politics, Profits, and Propaganda Shaped World War II Movies* (Berkeley: University of California Press, 1990), 111. Walter White quoted in Thomas Cripps, *Making Movies Black: The Hollywood Message Movie from World War II to the Civil Rights Era* (New York: Oxford University Press, 1993), 45. Maury Klein, *Union Pacific: The Rebirth 1894–1969* (New York: Doubleday, 1989). Koury, *Yes, Mr. DeMille*, 292–93.

13   Eyman, *Empire of Dreams*, 92, 164. Neil S. McCarthy, "History of Labor Suit," n.d. [1947], DeMille Papers, Box 1134, Folder 6, 1–2.

14   Pl. Mem. Pts. Auth. Opp. Defs.' Mot. Dismiss, DeMille v. American Federation of Radio Artists [AFRA], No. 498033, Los Angeles Superior Court, County of Los Angeles, n.d. [December 1944–January 1945], DeMille Papers, Box 1134, Folder 3, 11–14, 20–23.

15   Bernstein, *Rehabilitating Lochner*, 18–20. The Slaughterhouse Cases, 111 U.S. 746, 762, 764–65 (1884) (Bradley concurring); Allgeyer v. State of Louisiana, 165 U.S. 578, 589–92 (1897); Lochner v. New York, 198 U.S. 45 (1905); Truax v. Raich, 239 U.S. 33, 41 (1915). "Freedom of contract" is also known anachronistically as substantive due process. Scholars debate how strong a limit freedom of contract ever was on such regulation and how robust it remained by the time of the New Deal. See, generally, Laura Kalman, "Law, Politics, and the New Deal(s)," *Yale Law Journal* 108, no. 8 (June 1999): 2165–213. Blanchard v. Golden Age Brewing Co., 188 Wash. 396, 421–22 (1936). Cameron v. Internat'l Alliance of Theatrical Stage Employees, 118 N.J. Eq. 11, 27 (1935). Pl. Mem. Opp. Defs.' Mot. Dismiss, DeMille v. AFRA, No. 498033, Superior Court of the State of California, County of Los Angeles, n.d. [December 1944–January 1945], DeMille Papers, Box 1134, Folder 3, 8.

16   Bernstein, *Rehabilitating Lochner*, 102–3, 108. NAM speech described in E. M. Voorhees to Gladys Rosson, February 18, 1947, DeMille Papers, Box 1199, Folder 38. West Virginia Board of Education v. Barnette, 319 U.S. 624 (1943); Thornhill v. Alabama, 310 U.S. 88 (1940). Goluboff, *The Lost Promise*, 206.

17 T. Richard Witmer, "Civil Liberties and the Trade Union," *The Yale Law Journal* 50, no. 4 (1941): 621–35, 627. Brief for Complainants, Hill v. Intern'l Bro. of Boilermakers, No. 17760, Superior Court of Providence, R.I., n.d., NAACP Papers Part 13C, Reel 1, Images 1109–15, 5–11. Risa L. Goluboff, *The Lost Promise*. Pauli Murray, "The Right to Equal Opportunity in Employment," *California Law Review* 33 (1945): 388–433, 425.

18 Swank v. Patterson, 139 F.2d 145, 146 (9th Cir. 1943); Mason v. Hitchcock, 108 F.2d 134, 135 (1st Cir. 1939); Nat'l Fed. Rwy Workers v. Nat'l Med. Bd., 110 F.2d 529, 537–38 (D.C. Cir. 1940). James v. Marinship, 54 F.Supp. 94 (N.D. Cal. 1944); Reuel Schiller, *Forging Rivals: Race, Class, and the Decline of Postwar Liberalism* (New York: Cambridge University Press, forthcoming), chap. 2. The Thirteenth Amendment has no state action requirement.

19 Defs. Mem. Pts. Auths. Supp. Mot. Dismiss, DeMille v. AFRA, No. 498033, Los Angeles Sup. Ct., n.d. [December 1944–January 1945], DeMille Papers, Box 1134, Folder 6, 11–12.

20 DeMille v. AFRA, No. 498033, Los Angeles Superior Ct., January 24, 1945, DeMille Papers, Box 1134, Folder 6, 4–6.

21 Cecil B. DeMille, press release, January 25, 1945, DeMille Papers, Box 1209, Folder 9.

22 Cecil B. DeMille, speech at Union Pacific Railroad St. Patrick's Day luncheon, Omaha, March 17, 1945 [hereafter DeMille St. Patrick's Day speech], DeMille Papers, Box 1209, Folder 9.

23 Lichtenstein, *Labor's War at Home*, 207–8. W. M. Jeffers to E. F. Hutton, March 30, 1945, DeMille Papers, Box 1143, Folder 2.

24 Fones-Wolf, *Selling Free Enterprise*, 27–28, 35; Harris, *The Right to Manage*, 111–13. DeMille St. Patrick's Day speech, 2. Canak and Miller, "Gumbo Politics." Phillips-Fein, *Invisible Hands*.

25 "Notes from Luncheon," June 18, 1945, DeMille Papers, Box 1147, Folder 17, 2. Cecil B. DeMille to E. F. Hutton, dictated notes, April 30, 1945, DeMille Papers, Box 1143, Folder 2, 1–3.

26 "Notes on Wm. Jeffers Luncheon," May 28, 1945, DeMille Papers, Box 1147, Folder 17. "Frank Doherty Rites Slated," *Los Angeles Times*, July 26, 1974, A26. "Notes from Luncheon," June 18, 1945, DeMille Papers, Box 1147, Folder 17.

27 E. F. Hutton to Cecil B. DeMille, April 23, 1945, DeMille Papers, Box 1143, Folder 2. Cecil B. DeMille to E. F. Hutton, draft, n.d. [April 1945], ibid., 2.

28 Donald Hayne, notes, April 17, 1946, DeMille Papers, Box 1147, Folder 17. DeMille to Hutton, draft, n.d. [April 1945].

29 Hayne, notes, April 17, 1946. Cecil B. DeMille, "Labor's Right to Be Free," speech to Los Angeles Realty Board, Ambassador Hotel, Los Angeles, February 8, 1946, DeMille Papers, Box 1209, Folder 9.

30 DeMille v. AFRA, 175 P.2d 851, 854 (Cal. Ct. App. 1946).

31 Cecil B. DeMille, "Two Roads for America," speech to Southern California Republican Women, Biltmore Hotel, Los Angeles, May 10, 1945, DeMille Papers, Box 1209, Folder 9. Cecil B. DeMille, "Stand Up and Be Counted," speech for National Bill of Rights Day, Federal Hall, New York, September 25, 1945, ibid.; "DeMille Decries Union Tyranny," *New York Times*, September 26, 1945, 5. "Copies of Editorials from the Below List," March 13, 1945, Box 112, Folder 7; "DeMille Dollar," *Newsweek*, February 5, 1945, 41; "AFRA and Mr. DeMille," *New Republic* 112, no. 6 (February 5, 1945), 164–65; "The $1 Issue," *Time*, February 5, 1945, 53; "Yes, Cecil de Mille Can Still Vote," *Saturday Evening Post*, February 24, 1945, 104. Eyman, *Empire of Dreams*, 399. Allen Thomas, report, December 31, [1945], DeMille Papers, Box 1134, Folder 2; Mr. Mounts to Mr. DeMille, December 30, 1946, ibid.; "Activity Report for Fiscal Year (October 1946 to October 1947) and October, November, December, 1947," December 1947, ibid.; [John W. Miner], Activity Report, May 6, 1947, ibid. Phillips-Fein, *Invisible Hands*, 10. DeMille, St. Patrick's Day speech.

32 Cecil B. DeMille to Neil S. McCarthy, August 16, 1944, DeMille Papers, Box 1134, Folder 7. DeMille, St. Patrick's Day speech, 5. By early 1947, Florida, Arkansas, South Dakota, Nebraska, and Arizona had passed right-to-work laws. Texas and Louisiana, like California, were home to vigorous if ultimately unsuccessful right-to-work campaigns. Cecil B. DeMille, Statement before the Senate Committee on Labor and Public Welfare, February 14, 1947 [hereafter DeMille Senate Statement], DeMille Papers, Box 1209, Folder 9, 4, 8.

33 Cecil B. DeMille, "Majority Rights – And Wrongs," speech to Town Hall Committee, Wichita, Kans., June 29, 1945, DeMille Papers, Box 1209, Folder 9, 4, 6; Cecil B. DeMille, speech to Junior Chamber of Commerce, Huntington Hotel, Pasadena, Calif., June 6, 1945, ibid., 7; DeMille "Stand Up and Be Counted"; Cecil B. DeMille, radio address, *March of Time* program, February 1, 1945, DeMille Papers, Box 1209, Folder 9. DeMille Senate Statement, 12–13 (emphasis added).

34 DeMille, St. Patrick's Day speech, 5. DeMille, "Majority Rights," 3–4.

35 DeMille Senate Statement, 15–17. Pet. Hr'g, DeMille v. AFRA, No. 5132, Cal. Sup. Ct., February 7, 1947, RG 267, Records of the Supreme Court, Case File 679 October Term 1947, Box 5288 [hereafter DeMille SCOTUS Records], NAB, 26–27. It is possible McCarthy made a similar argument in his brief to the California Court of Appeals but I have been unable to locate a copy of that brief in DeMille's papers, the California Supreme Court archives, or the archives of the Supreme Court of the United States.

36 Cecil B. DeMille, "A House United: Equal Opportunity for All," *Vital Speeches of the Day* 13, no. 5 (December 15, 1946): 151–53, 151. DeMille Senate Statement, 18. DeMille, "Stand Up and Be Counted," 50.

37   Farhang and Katznelson, "The Southern Imposition," 27. Donald R. Richberg, statement before the Committee on Education and Labor, House of Representatives, on H. Res. 111, 80th Cong., May 11–12, 1948, 41.

38   Cecil B. DeMille to Messrs. Adams and Duque, March 15, 1947, DeMille Papers, Box 1135, Folder 6. Donald Hayne to Fred Hartley, draft, July 20, 1948, DeMille Papers, Box 1141, Folder 7. Cecil B. DeMille to J. P. McEvoy, Aug. 31, 1950, DeMille Papers, Box 1145, Folder 4.

39   DeMille, "Majority Rights," 4. DeMille Senate Statement, 7–8, 14, 17. DeMille, Junior Chamber of Commerce speech, 7. Pet'n Hr'g, DeMille v. AFRA, February 7, 1947, DeMille SCOTUS Records. Cecil B. DeMille, Statement before the Committee on Education and Labor, House of Representatives, on H. Res. 111, 80th Cong., May 11–12, 1948.

40   Taft-Hartley Act, Pub. L. 80-101, 61 Stat. 136, sec. 8(b)(2) (1947). "Notes on interview with Harlan Logan," April 4, 1948, DeMille Papers, Box 932, Folder 4.

41   DeMille v. AFRA, 31 Cal. 2d 139, 149 (1947).

42   James v. Marinship, 25 Cal. 2d 721 (1945); Bautista v. Jones, 25 Cal. 2d 746, 749 (1945). Cecil B. DeMille, press release, December 16, 1947, DeMille Papers, Box 1134, Folder 7.

43   See Chapters 1 and 2. Clyde W. Summers, "The Right to Join a Union," *Columbia Law Review* 47 (1947): 33–74, 56–57.

44   On Cobb, see Chapter 1, and for Bloom, see Chapter 2. Pet. Writ Cert., March 16, 1948, DeMille SCOTUS Records, 13–14.

45   Br. Resp. Opp. Pet. Writ Cert., April 3, 1948, DeMille SCOTUS Records, 19–20. DeMille v. AFRA, 333 U.S. 876 (1948); Shelley v. Kraemer 334 U.S. 1 (1948).

46   Meeting minutes, October 14, 1948, DeMille Papers, Box 1134, Folder 8.

47   "Notes on interview with Harlan Logan," April 4, 1948, DeMille Papers, Box 932, Folder 4, 2.

4 Liberals Test the Workplace Constitution in the Courts

1   Carl Flowers, "To the Colored Firemen and Outside Hostler Helpers Employed on the Central of Georgia Railway," May 11, 1953, appended to Pls.' Req. for Admission, Oliphant v. Brotherhood of Locomotive Firemen and Enginemen, July 25, 1955, Case No. 31464, U.S. District Court for the Northern District of Ohio [hereafter Oliphant DC Records], NARAGLR. For more on the brotherhood's campaigns, see Chapter 1.

2   Houston to Marshall et al., December 20, 1944, NAACP Papers Part 13C, Reel 8, Image 90, 1, 3. Eric Arnesen, *Brotherhoods of Color: Black Railroad Workers and the Struggle for Equality* (Cambridge, Mass.: Harvard University Press, 2002), 210. Litigation by black unions provides

an intriguing alternative to the dominant model of civil rights lawyering in which lawyers' interests may have been quite distinct from their clients'. Risa L. Goluboff, *The Lost Promise of Civil Rights* (Cambridge, Mass.: Harvard University Press, 2007); Tomiko Brown-Nagin, *Courage to Dissent: Atlanta and the Long History of the Civil Rights Movement* (New York: Oxford University Press, 2011).

3   Mark D. Rosen, "Was *Shelley v. Kraemer* Incorrectly Decided? Some New Answers," *California Law Review* 95 (2007): 451–512. William O. Douglas, conference notes, February 1, 1948, William O. Douglas Papers [hereafter Douglas Papers], Box 161, "Nos. 50–74 Argued: Certiorari, Conference & Misc. Memos, O.T. 1947" Folder, LCMD. Mark V. Tushnet, *Making Civil Rights Law: Thurgood Marshall and the Supreme Court, 1956–1961* (New York: Oxford University Press, 1996), 94–95.

4   Although there are extensive studies of the Supreme Court's and the individual justices' civil rights and labor jurisprudence during the 1950s, little attention has been paid to the Court's state action decisions during this decade, let alone its union discrimination decisions. Exceptions include Deborah C. Malamud, "The Story of *Steele v. Louisville & Nashville Railroad*: White Unions, Black Unions, and the Struggle for Racial Justice on the Rails," in *Labor Law Stories*, ed. Laura J. Cooper and Catherine L. Fisk, 55–106 (New York: Foundation Press, 2005); Reuel E. Schiller, "From Group Rights to Individual Liberties: Post-War Labor Law, Liberalism, and the Waning of Union Strength," *Berkeley Journal of Employment and Labor Law* 20 (1999): 1–73; Michael J. Klarman, "An Interpretive History of Modern Equal Protection," *Michigan Law Review* 90, no. 2 (November 1991): 213–318. Even less studied is *Brown*'s influence on challenges to discrimination in the workplace, not only in public accommodations. For a recent treatment of the latter challenges, see Victoria W. Wolcott, *Race, Riots, and Roller Coasters: The Struggle over Segregated Recreation in America* (Philadelphia: University of Pennsylvania Press, 2012).

5   Testimony of Theodore E. Brown before the House Committee on Interstate and Foreign Commerce, June 7, 1950, 81st Cong., 2d Sess., 278, 282. Testimony of Joseph Waddy before the Senate Subcommittee of the Committee on Labor and Public Welfare, May 18, 1950, 81st Cong., 2d Sess., S. 3295, 301.

6   Kevin M. Schultz, "The FEPC and the Legacy of the Labor-Based Civil Rights Movement of the 1940s," *Labor History* 49, no. 1 (February 2008): 71–92. Ira Katznelson, Kim Geiger, and Daniel Kryder, "Limiting Liberalism: The Southern Veto in Congress, 1933–1950," *Political Science Quarterly* 108, no. 2 (Summer 1993): 283–306. James C. Cobb, *Redefining Southern Culture: Mind and Identity in the Modern South* (Athens: University of Georgia Press, 1999), 18. National Council for a Permanent FEPC, Policy Committee Meeting, January 16, 1947, DCR Papers, Box 1, Folder 26; Herbert Hill to Roy Wilkins, October 10, 1949, in John H. Bracey and

August Meier, eds., *Papers of the NAACP, Part 13, Series A: Subject Files on Labor Conditions and Employment Discrimination* (Bethesda: UPA, 1991), microfilm [hereafter NAACP Papers Part 13A], Reel 20. Lewis G. Hines, notes, September 30, 1949, DCR Papers, Box 1, Folder 17. On the devastating effects the CIO's leftist expulsions had on African American labor, see Gerald Horne, *Red Seas: Ferdinand Smith and Radical Black Sailors in the United States and Jamaica* (New York: New York University Press, 2009); Robert R. Korstad, *Civil Rights Unionism: Tobacco Workers and the Struggle for Democracy in the Mid-Twentieth-Century South* (Chapel Hill: University of North Carolina Press, 2003). Robert H. Zieger, *The CIO, 1935–1955* (Chapel Hill: University of North Carolina Press, 1997), 253. For a counterargument, see Eric Arnesen, "Civil Rights and the Cold War at Home: Postwar Activism, Anticommunism, and the Decline of the Left," *American Communist History* 11, no. 1 (2012): 5–44. On the Cold War as leverage for civil rights, see Mary L. Dudziak, *Cold War Civil Rights: Race and the Image of American Democracy* (Princeton, N.J.: Princeton University Press, 2002); Brenda Gayle Plummer, *Rising Wind: Black Americans and U.S. Foreign Affairs, 1935–1960* (Chapel Hill: University of North Carolina Press, 1996); John David Skrentny, "The Effect of the Cold War on African-American Civil Rights: America and the World Audience, 1945–1968," *Theory and Society* 27, no. 2 (April 1998): 237–285. Walter White, "Address to the Tenth Constitutional Convention of the CIO in Portland, OR," November 22–26, 1948, UAW Fair Practices Department Collection [hereafter UAWFPD Papers], Box 27, Folder 18, ALUA, 3.

7   See Schultz, "The FEPC," 81–83. On the importance of agency enforcement, see Anthony S. Chen, *The Fifth Freedom: Jobs, Politics, and Civil Rights in the United States, 1941–1972* (Princeton, N.J.: Princeton University Press, 2009); David F. Engstrom, "The Lost Origins of American Fair Employment Law: Regulatory Choice and the Making of Modern Civil Rights, 1943–1972," *Stanford Law Review* 63 (May 2011): 1071–144. Statement of A. Philip Randolph on H.R. 4453, House Committee of Education and Labor, 81st Congress, May 17, 1949, DCR Papers, Box 1, Folder 17. Patricia Sullivan, *Lift Every Voice: The NAACP and the Making of the Civil Rights Movement* (New York: New Press, 2010), 367. Walter White to The Branches, July 16, 1948, CIOSO Papers, Box 154, "White, Walter, 1948" Folder. On federal fair employment legislation during the 1950s, see Paul D. Moreno, *From Direct Action to Affirmative Action: Fair Employment Law and Policy in America, 1933–1972* (Baton Rouge: Louisiana State University Press, 1999), 162–77; Chen, *The Fifth Freedom*, 47–87. "NAACP Urges Congress to Bar Jim Crow Closed Shop," *Atlanta Daily World*, February 15, 1949, 6. Paul Sifton to Roy L. Reuther, April 9, 1953, CIOSO Papers, Box 160, "Leadership Conference on Civil Rights" Folder (2 of 5); "Taft-Hartley Revision," *Wall Street*

Journal, May 4, 1954, 2; "Labor Anti-Bias Clause Stirs Filibuster Threat," *Chicago Defender*, May 15, 1954, 1. Walter White, "White Says There Should Be Checkup on Who Gets Credit for What in Politics," *Chicago Defender*, May 15, 1954, 11. Leadership Conference on Civil Rights [hereafter LCCR] Executive Committee, minutes, March 3, 1955, DCR Papers, Box 1, Folder 10. Statements of Theodore Brown, Clarence Mitchell, and Joseph Waddy, Hearings before the Sub-Committee of the Committee on Labor and Welfare on S.3296, 81st Cong., 2d Sess., May 18, 1950, 237, 302. 96 Cong. Rec. 16378, Jan. 1, 1951, 81st Cong., 2d Sess., vol. 96, pt. 12. Harry Read to James B. Carey, March 23, 1953, CIOSO Papers, Box 80, "Committee to Abolish Discrimination, 1953–55" Folder.

8 A. Philip Randolph to Joseph L. Rauh, December 15, 1955, Joseph L. Rauh Papers [hereafter Rauh Papers], Part I, Box 57, "Brotherhood of Sleeping Car Porters" [hereafter BSCP] Folder 1, LCMD. Oliphant Transcript (testimony of B. F. McLaurin), 156a. Arnesen, *Brotherhoods of Color*, 89, 91–92, 108, 110; Michael E. Parrish, *Citizen Rauh: An American Liberal's Life in Law and Politics* (Ann Arbor: University of Michigan Press, 2010), 131–32.

9 Arnesen, *Brotherhoods of Color*, 111, 147–48, 210, 214. Oliphant Transcript (testimony of B. F. McLaurin), 158a–159a.

10 Arnesen, *Brotherhoods of Color*, 214. Joseph L. Rauh to A. Philip Randolph, February 9, 1954, Rauh Papers, Part I, Box 57, "BSCP" Folder 2. Brown v. Board of Education, 347 U.S. 483 (1954); Bolling v. Sharpe, 347 U.S. 497 (1954). Reva B. Siegel, "Equality Talk: Antisubordination and Anticlassification Values in Constitutional Struggles over *Brown*," *Harvard Law Review* 117, no. 5 (March 2004): 1470–1547, 1482–83. See, for instance, Paul G. Kauper, "Segregation in Public Education: The Decline of *Plessy v. Ferguson*," *Michigan Law Review*, 52 (1954): 1137–58; Edmund Cahn, "Jurisprudence," *New York University Law Review*, 30 (1955): 150–70. Muir v. Louisville Park Theatrical Ass'n, 347 U.S. 971 (1954). "Memorandum of Discussion between Messrs. McLaurin and Rauh," January 28, 1955, Rauh Papers, Part I, Box 57, "BSCP" Folder 1.

11 Parrish, *Citizen Rauh*, 83–85, 123, 130–31. B. F. McLaurin to Joseph L. Rauh, September 24, 1954, Rauh Papers, Part I, Box 57, "BSCP" Folder 2.

12 Joseph L. Rauh to B. F. McLaurin (Mac), October 5, 1954, Rauh Papers, Part I, Box 57, "BSCP" Folder 2. Joseph Goldstein, "Report on Negro Firemen," ibid. Complaint, November 16, 1954, Oliphant DC Records, pars. 29–45.

13 "Begin U.S. Test of Race Clauses by Rail Unions," *Daily Defender*, June 4, 1957, 8 (contains "time has come" quote). "The Labor Drive on Bias," *New York Times*, August 27, 1957, 26. George Meany (speech to National Urban League Convention, Milwaukee, September 6, 1955), RG 1–0027, Series 6, AFL-CIO Office of the President, George Meany,

1952–1960, National and International Union Correspondence [hereafter Meany Papers – NIUC], Box 59, Folder 69, GMMA, 5–6. Boris Shishkin to Charles Heymanns, April 26, 1957, DCR Papers, Box 3, Folder 21. Shishkin took a similarly antilitigation position during his FEPC tenure, when he tried to postpone government action to make inevitably futile efforts to persuade some of the AFL's most notoriously racially exclusive unions to change their practices. Merl Elwyn Reed, *Seedtime for the Modern Civil Rights Movement: The President's Committee on Fair Employment Practice, 1941–1946* (Baton Rouge: Louisiana State University Press, 1991), 150. This may explain why Randolph did not want to ask the AFL-CIO to join the suit as amicus. Joseph L. Rauh to A. Philip Randolph, November 5, 1956, Rauh Papers, Part I, Box 57, "BSCP" Folder 1. A. Philip Randolph to Joseph L. Rauh, December 15, 1955, ibid.

14 Pls.' Br. in Support of Power of This Equity Ct. to Order the Admission of Pls. to Def. Union, July 12, 1957, Oliphant DC Records, 1–3; Tr. of Evidence, June 3, 1957, Oliphant DC Records, 5–14, 19–20, 70. Rauh's partner argued the case at trial.

15 Oliphant v. Brotherhood of Locomotive Firemen and Enginemen, 156 F. Supp. 89, 90–93 (N.D. Ohio 1957).

16 Pet'n for Writ of Cert., Oliphant v. B'hood of Locomotive Firemen and Enginemen, Case No. 536 (Supreme Court of the United States, October 8, 1957), 6, 8–9.

17 Anthony Lewis, "Girard College Poses Problem," *New York Times*, September 16, 1957, 19. Barrows v. Jackson, 346 U.S. 249 (1953). An evenly divided Supreme Court affirmed a state court decision the next year that found *Shelley* did not bar courts from allowing restrictive covenants to be used as a defense, but since it did so without explanation, there is no way to know the nature of the Court's disagreement or how likely it was a full Court would come to the same conclusion. Rice v. Sioux City Memorial Park Cemetery, 348 U.S. 880 (1954), *vacated and dismissed as improvidently granted*, 349 U.S. 70 (1955). There was no question that the existing board of trustees was a state agency. Pennsylvania v. Bd. of Dir. of City Trusts, 353 U.S. 230, 231 (1957).

18 Liberals would soon critique *Brown* itself, but in 1957, those debates were still in the future. Herbert Wechsler, "Toward Neutral Principles of Constitutional Law," *Harvard Law Review* 73, no. 1 (November 1, 1959): 1–35; Siegel, "Equality Talk"; Anders Walker, "Neutral Principles: Rethinking the Legal History of Civil Rights, 1934–1964," *Loyola University Chicago Law Journal* 40 (2009): 385–436. Holmes v. Atlanta, 350 U.S. 879 (1955); Baltimore City v. Dawson, 350 U.S. 877 (1955). Lewis, "Girard College Poses Problem," 19. Cahn, "Jurisprudence," 156. Elias Clark, "Charitable Trusts, the Fourteenth Amendment, and the Will of Stephen Girard," *Yale Law Journal* 66 (1957): 979–1015, 1009.

19 Additional civil rights and civil liberties cases include Sweatt v. Painter, 339 U.S. 629 (1950); Thomas v. Collins, 323 U.S. 516 (1945); Burstyn v. Wilson, 343 U.S. 495 (1952). Broad state action cases include Derrington v. Plummer, 240 F.2d 922, 926 (5th Cir., 1957); Valle v. Stengel, 176 F.2d 697 (Ct. App. 3rd Cir., 1949). Cf. Whiteside v. Southern Bus Lines, Inc., 177 F.2d 949, 953 (6th Cir., 1949). Other courts explored the equation from the opposite direction, determining how much privatization was sufficient to remove state actor status and thus constitutional constraints. See, e.g., Lawrence v. Hancock, 76 F. Supp. 1004, 1008 (S.D.W. Va., 1948); Culver v. City of Warren, 83 N.E.2d 82, 87 (Ohio, 1948). But see Clifton v. Puente, 218 S.W.2d 272 (Tex. Civ. App., 1948); Norris v. Mayor & City Council of Baltimore, 78 F. Supp. 451 (D.C. Md., 1948); Dorsey v. Stuyvesant Town Corp., 299 N.Y. 512 (N.Y., 1949), *cert. denied*, 339 U.S. 981 (1950).

20 Brotherhood of R.R. Trainmen v. Howard, 343 U.S. 768, 773–74 (1952) (using the signal "cf." to indicate that *Shelley* asserted a rule that was different from yet analogous to *Howard*'s). A three-justice dissent to *Howard* recognized the majority's reliance on the Constitution, arguing that there was no basis to strike down the disputed contract because government-certified unions were not state actors. *Howard*, 343 U.S. at 778 (Minton, J., dissenting). American Communications Ass'n v. Douds, 339 U.S. 382, 401–2 (1950).

21 Syres v. Oil Workers International Union, 350 U.S. 892 (1956) (per curiam). *Howard*, 343 U.S. at 773. Note, "Labor Union as a Governmental Agent," *Stanford Law Review* 5 (1952): 135–39. See also Chapter 5.

22 Public Utilities Commission of District of Columbia v. Pollak, 343 U.S. 451, 462–63, 466–67 (1952). Railway Employees' Department v. Hanson, 351 U.S. 225, 231 (1956) (using the signal "cf." to analogize its current holding to those in *Steele, Howard, Pollak*, and Smith v. Allwright, 321 U.S. 649 (1944)).

23 Compl., Conley v. Gibson, Case No. 8443, U.S. District Court for the Southern District of Texas, Houston Division, August 21, 1954, National Archives at Fort Worth, Texas. Conley v. Gibson, 138 F. Supp. 60, 62–63 (D.C. S.D. Tex. 1955), *aff'd*, 229 F.2d 436 (5th Cir. 1956) (per curiam). The trial court's approach was not uncommon. Hayes v. Union Pac. R. Co., 88 F. Supp. 108, 110 (N.D. Ca., 1950), *aff'd*, 184 F.2d 337, 338 (9th Cir., 1950); Syres v. Oil Workers Intern. Union, Local No. 23, 223 F.2d 739 (5th Cir., 1955). But see Dillard v. Chesapeake & O. Ry. Co., 199 F.2d 948 (4th Cir., 1952). William O. Douglas, conference notes, October 28, 1957, Douglas Papers, Box 1185, "Nos. 1–24 Argued Cases, O.T. 1957" Folder. Affirming the appellate court would require only four votes, as there were only eight justices seated at the time. Frankfurter had cultivated influence with at least three of them (in addition to Harlan). Kim Isaac Eisler, *A Justice for All: William J. Brennan, Jr., and the Decisions*

That Transformed America (New York: Simon & Schuster, 1993), 88, 100, 102, 105–6. Justices Burton and Whittaker hesitated in other workplace Constitution cases. William O. Douglas, conference notes, April 26, 1952, Douglas Papers, Box 211, "Nos. 450–499 Argued Cases Memos, O.T. 1951" Folder; Harold H. Burton to Hugo L. Black, June 3, 1952, Papers of Hugo Lafayette Black [hereafter Black Papers], Box 311, "B'hood of Trainmen v. Howard Folder," LCMD; C.E.W. to William J. Brennan, January 30, 1961, William J. Brennan Papers [hereafter Brennan Papers], Part I, Box 45, Folder 4, LCMD.

24 Conley v. Gibson, 355 U.S. 41, 45–46 (1957). Black v. Cutter Laboratories, 351 U.S. 292, 302 n. (1956) (Douglas, J., dissenting). Anonymously authored [Hugo Black], Conley v. Gibson draft opinion, n.d. [November 1957], Black Papers, Box 332, "Conley v. Gibson, October Term 1957" Folder, 2. The Court recognized that it needed only to resolve the procedural issues but at its discretion went beyond them. Even in post-*Steele* cases like *Conley* that the Court heard only on procedural matters, it used the occasion to support the merits of plaintiffs' claims. Graham v. BLFE, 338 U.S. 232, 234 (1949).

25 According to Justice Douglas's clerk, Rauh's motion to postpone argument in *Conley* "was not called to the Court's attention in time." Memo, n.d. [November–December 1957], Douglas Papers, Box 1187, "Memoranda" Folder. Oliphant v. Brotherhood of Locomotive Firemen and Enginemen, 355 U.S. 893 (1957). McLaurin to Rauh, December 6, 1957, Rauh Papers, Part I, Box 57, "BSCP" Folder 1. Oliphant v. Brotherhood of Locomotive Firemen and Enginemen, 262 F.2d 359, 360, 362–63 (6th Cir. 1958).

26 Pet'n for a Writ of Cert., Oliphant v. Brotherhood of Locomotive Firemen and Enginemen, Case No. 560 (Supreme Court of the United States, December 1958), 9, 19 n. 17.

27 A. A. Berle, *Economic Power and the Free Society* (New York: Fund for the Republic, 1957), 15, 17–18. See, for instance, Robert L. Hale, "Force and the State: A Comparison of Political and Economic Compulsion," *Columbia Law Review* 35 (February 1935): 149–201, 199–200. Barbara H. Fried, *The Progressive Assault on Laissez Faire: Robert Hale and the First Law and Economics Movement* (Cambridge, Mass.: Harvard University Press, 2001). Greeley H. Ellis Jr., "Notes: Constitutional Right to Membership in a Labor Union – 5th and 14th Amendments," *Journal of Public Law* 8 (1959): 580–95, 582. Series 8, Subseries 3, "Study of the Corporation (The Individual and the Corporation), 1956–1962," Fund for the Republic Records, Public Policy Papers, Department of Rare Books and Special Collections, Princeton University Library, Princeton, N.J.; Series 8, Subseries 4, "Study of the Trade Union (The Individual and the Trade Union), 1956–1962," ibid. For union democracy debates, see Clyde W. Summers, "The Right to Join a Union," *Columbia Law Review* 47 (1947): 33–74; Clyde W. Summers, "Union Power and Workers' Rights,"

Michigan Law Review 49 (1951): 805–37, 811; Homer H. Hewitt III, "Right to Membership in a Labor Union," *University of Pennsylvania Law Review* 99 (1951): 919–48, 939–42; Archibald Cox, "Uses and Abuses of Union Power," *Notre Dame Lawyer* 35, no. 5 (1960): 624–39; Archibald Cox, "The Duty of Fair Representation," *Villanova Law Review* 2, no. 2 (January 1957): 151–77; Harry H. Wellington, "Union Democracy and Fair Representation: Federal Responsibility in a Federal System," *Yale Law Journal* 67 (1958): 1327–62. Liberals' shift was driven by the growing influence of those industrial pluralists concerned with individual rights (see Chapter 1) and liberals' increasing emphasis on racial and ethnic rather than class pluralism. See generally Gary Gerstle, "The Protean Character of American Liberalism," *American Historical Review* 99, no. 4 (October 1, 1994): 1043–73. On constitutional limits on business and labor, see additionally Robert L. Hale, *Freedom through Law: Public Control of Private Governing Power* (New York: Columbia University Press, 1952); William R. Ming Jr., "Racial Restrictions and the Fourteenth Amendment: The Restrictive Covenant Cases," *University of Chicago Law Review* 16, no. 2 (Winter 1949): 203–38, 229–38; Adolph A. Berle, "Constitutional Limitations on Corporate Activity – Protection of Personal Rights from Invasion through Economic Power," *University of Pennsylvania Law Review* 100, no. 7 (May 1952): 933–55; Arthur S. Miller, "The Constitutional Law of the 'Security State,'" *Stanford Law Review* 10 (1958): 620–73, 655–56. Cf. Clay Malick, "Toward a New Constitutional Status for Labor Unions: A Proposal," *Rocky Mountain Law Review* 21 (1949): 260–78; Wolfgang G. Friedmann, "Corporate Power, Government by Public Groups, and the Law," *Columbia Law Review* 57, no. 2 (February 1957): 155–86. The Labor-Management Reporting and Disclosure Act of 1959, Pub. L. 86-257, September 14, 1959, 73 Stat. 519–46. See also Chapter 6.

28 Pet'n for a Writ of Cert., Oliphant v. Brotherhood of Locomotive Firemen and Enginemen, Case No. 560 (Supreme Court of the United States, December 1958), 2–3, 9–10, 13 n. 12, 14, 18–19, 21. See also Reply Br., Oliphant v. Brotherhood of Locomotive Firemen and Enginemen, Case No. 560 (Supreme Court of the United States, January 12, 1959).

29 William O. Douglas, docket book, March 9, 1959, Douglas Papers, LCMD, Box 1199, Administrative Docket Book # 401–600, O.T. 1958 Folder. The justices had already stated their position on Rauh's petition. Stewart was elevated before the Sixth Circuit handed down its decision. Eisler, *A Justice for All*, 120–25. If Stewart also recused himself from review on the merits, which would have been likely, four votes would have been sufficient to affirm the appellate court without establishing binding precedent on the membership issue. The result would have been no different than denying certiorari in the first instance. It thus seems unlikely that Black refrained from voting to review the case in order to avoid that outcome.

30 *Graham*, 338 U.S. 232 (1949); *Douds*, 339 U.S. 382 (1950); *Howard*, 343 U.S. 768 (1952); *Cutter Laboratories*, 351 U.S. 292 (1956); *Conley*, 355 U.S. 41 (1957). Hugo L. Black Jr. to Hugo L. Black, March 26, 1950, Black Papers, Box 3, "Black, Hugo Jr. (1949–1952) (son)" Folder, 4. Hugo L. Black to Hugo L. Black Jr., March 29, 1950, ibid. See, e.g., William O. Douglas, docket book, January 15, 1951, Douglas Papers, Box 199, "Administrative Docket Book #470–#783, O.T. 1950" Folder (Hayes v. Pacific RR, no. 495); William O. Douglas, docket book, 1952, Douglas Papers, Box 210, "Administrative Docket Book, #301–499, O.T. 1951" Folder (Howard, No. 458); William O. Douglas, docket book, April 27, 1953, Douglas Papers, Box 1146, "Administrative Docket Book, 751–815, Miscellaneous Docket #1–637, O.T. 1953" Folder (Dargan v. Yellow Cab, No. 4); William O. Douglas, docket book, October 8, 1956, Douglas Papers, Box 1184, "Administrative Docket Book #1–199, O.T. 1957" Folder (No. 7, Conley v. Gibson).

31 Siegel, "Equality Talk," 1481–85. Naim v. Naim, 350 U.S. 891, 891 (1955) (per curiam) (vacating and remanding); 350 U.S. 985 (1956) (mem.) (denying motion to recall mandate). The justices' reluctance was driven partly by a desire to limit resistance to *Brown*. Klarman, *From Jim Crow to Civil Rights*, 321–23. Answer, January 13, 1955, Oliphant DC Records, 9–10; Theodore E. Brown to Boris Shishkin, January 3, 1957, AFL-CIO Department of Civil Rights Discrimination Case Files, 1947–1984, Series 1, RG 9–002 [hereafter DCR-DCF Papers], Box 12, Folder 90, GMMA. Pete Daniel, *Lost Revolutions: The South in the 1950s* (Chapel Hill: University of North Carolina Press, 2000), 255–57. Resp. Opp'n to Cert., Oliphant v. Brotherhood of Locomotive Firemen and Enginemen, Case No. 560 (Supreme Court of the United States, January 2, 1959), 12. These social-equality concerns may have dovetailed with respect for unions' freedom of association. NAACP v. Patterson, 357 U.S. 449 (1958). But Kotch v. Bd. of River Port Pilot Com'rs, 330 U.S. 552, 563 (1947), provides further evidence that interracial intimacy affected the justices. In *Kotch*, a case with racial undertones, the Court found that nepotism in the selection of pilots did not violate equal protection, in part due to "the close association in which pilots must work and live in their pilot communities and on the water."

32 Dawley v. Norfolk, 359 U.S. 935 (1959). Tobias Barrington Wolff, "Civil Rights Reform and the Body," *Harvard Law & Policy Review* 6 (2012): 201–31. Which civil rights challenges trenched too much on social equality was a matter of social construction, not logic, since integrating public schools and parks, which the Supreme Court did, arguably also raised the specter of intimate interracial contact. Richard L. Lyons, "Court Refuses Race Bar Upset," *Washington Post*, March 10, 1959, A2. William O. Douglas to Conference, February 20, 1959, Douglas Papers, Box 1200,

"Memoranda by Court, O.T. 1958 Folder." Potter Stewart to William O. Douglas, February 20, 1959, ibid. Tom C. Clark to Conference, March 3, 1959, ibid. John M. Harlan to William O. Douglas, February 20, 1959, ibid. John M. Harlan to Conference, March 4, 1959, Brennan Papers, Box 27, Folder 15; Oliphant v. Brotherhood of Locomotive Firemen and Enginemen, 359 U.S. 935 (1959). Pet. for Reh'g, Oliphant v. Brotherhood of Locomotive Firemen and Enginemen, Case No. 560 (Supreme Court of the United States, March 9, 1959) [hereafter Oliphant SCOTUS Records], 17.

33 Pet. for Reh'g, March 9, 1959, Oliphant SCOTUS Records, 3–4. Oliphant v. Brotherhood of Locomotive Firemen and Enginemen, 359 U.S. 962 (1959). Michael Klarman argues that the justices may have been leery of further desegregation decisions that term because the Court "already faced withering assaults from several directions." Klarman, *From Jim Crow to Civil Rights*, 334.

34 "Court Won't Hear Two Racial Cases," *New York Times*, March 10, 1959, 18.

35 Report on Subcommittee on Compliance, May 20, 1958, DCR-DCF Papers, Box 1, Folder 64. For a particularly sad case in which the AFL-CIO Civil Rights Department convinced Provisional Committee members to forgo the courts in favor of union law, only to do nothing to remedy their complaint (to the growing desperation of Brown), see Theodore Brown to Boris Shishkin, March 8, 1957, DCR-DCF Papers, Box 3, Folder 40; Theodore Brown to Boris Shishkin, July 30, 1957, DCR-DCF Papers, Box 1, Folder 64; Theodore Brown to Boris Shishkin, March 20, 1959, DCR-DCF Papers, Box 3, Folder 40; Theodore Brown to Boris Shishkin, April 28, 1960, DCR-DCF Papers, Box 3, Folder 78; Theodore Brown to Boris Shishkin, July 29, 1960, DCR-DCF Papers, Box 8, Folder 81. Boris Shishkin to George Meany, December 4, 1958, DCR-DCF Papers, Box 12, Folder 90. Theodore Brown to Boris Shishkin, July 20, 1959, ibid. Theodore Brown to Boris Shishkin, August 18, 1959, ibid. Randolph quoted in "Sleeping Car Porters Told to Start Merger," *New York Amsterdam News*, September 19, 1959, 6. African American unionists were divided on separate versus interracial unionization. See Arnesen, *Brotherhoods of Color*; Bruce Nelson, *Divided We Stand* (Princeton, N.J.: Princeton University Press, 2001). This issue often put all–black locals in conflict with integrationist national labor and civil rights leadership. See NAACP, "Executive Office Reports," September 9, 1957, John H. Bracey Jr. and August Meier, eds., *Papers of the NAACP, Supplement to Part 1, 1956–1960* (Bethesda, Md.: UPA, 1991), microfilm [hereafter NAACP Papers Part 1, 1956–1960], Reel 1. Nadine Brown, "Who the H... Named You Negroes Guardian? Meany Asks Randolph," *Pittsburgh Courier*, October 3, 1959, 1; "Split with Negro Denied by Meany," *New York Times*, October 6, 1959, 33.

5 Agencies Consider the Liberal Workplace Constitution

1 Louisiana's oil output increased from 131 million barrels in 1945 to 400 million barrels in 1960. Adam Fairclough, *Race & Democracy: The Civil Rights Struggle in Louisiana, 1915–1972* (Atlanta: University of Georgia Press, 1995), 149. "Main Office Building, Baton Rouge Refinery, Esso Standard Oil Company," postcard, n.d. [1950s] (in author's possession); "Baton Rouge Esso Refinery," photograph, 1945 (in author's possession). In the mid-1950s, a survey of Texas and Louisiana oil refineries found that African Americans were overrepresented in production work, as they constituted only 12% of refinery workers but 15% of production workers. Only ten African Americans, or 2% of the workers, were in white-collar jobs. Carol B. King and Howard W. Risher Jr., *The Negro in the Petroleum Industry* (Philadelphia: University of Pennsylvania Industrial Research Unit, 1968), 35–36, cited in Fairclough, *Race & Democracy*, 149. President's Committee on Government Contracts, "Compliance Report: Gulf Oil, Port Arthur, TX," June 12, 1958, RG220, Records of Temporary Committees, Commissions, and Boards, President's Committee on Government Contracts Records [hereafter PCGC Papers], Box 16, "Gulf Oil Corporation, Port Arthur, Texas, DD #163" Folder, NACP.

2 Michael Urquhart, "The Employment Shift to Services: Where Did It Come From?" *Monthly Labor Review* (April 1984): 15–22, 16. Note that "white-collar" is meant here as a contrast to blue-collar and agricultural labor, not to signal the professions; it includes service and clerical workers. For these trends, see Appendix, Figure A.3. Thomas J. Sugrue, *The Origins of the Urban Crisis: Race and Inequality in Postwar Detroit* (Princeton, N.J.: Princeton University Press, 1996); Jefferson Cowie, *Capital Moves: RCA's Seventy-Year Quest for Cheap Labor* (Ithaca, N.Y.: Cornell University Press, 1999).

3 Thomas Davis, interviewed by C. L. Gilbert, Baton Rouge, La., August 28, 1957, RG 220, Records of Temporary Committees, Commissions, and Boards, Records of the President's Committee on Government Contracts, 1953–1961, Discrimination Complaint Casefiles, 1951–1961 [hereafter PCGC Papers – DCC], Box 30, "Case No. 122, Esso Standard Oil Co." Folder (1 of 2). Fairclough, *Race & Democracy*, 159–62; Dean Sinclair, "Equal in All Places: The Civil Rights Struggle in Baton Rouge, 1953–1963," *Louisiana History: The Journal of the Louisiana Historical Association* 39, no. 3 (Summer 1998): 347–66. James Wilson, interviewed by C. L. Gilbert, Baton Rouge, La., August 28, 1957, PCGC Papers – DCC, Box 30, "Case No. 122, Esso Standard Oil Co." Folder (1 of 2). Theodore Smith, interviewed by C. L. Gilbert, Baton Rouge, La., August 27, 1957, ibid.; Calvin Joseph Black, George T. Guthrie, and Vincent C. Byrd Sr., interviewed by C. L. Gilbert, August 28, 1957, ibid. On the role of the Masons among African Americans in Louisiana, see Fairclough,

Race & Democracy. For the deep roots of Free Masonry and black politics, see Stephen Kantrowitz, "'Intended for the Better Government of Man': The Political History of African American Freemasonry in the Era of Emancipation," *Journal of American History* 96, no. 4 (March 2010): 1001–26.

4   DeCarlous Y. Spearman, "Roberson Lloyd King, 1922–1996: Professor, Attorney, Civil Rights Activist," unpublished manuscript, August 24, 2010. Syres v. Oil Workers International Union, Local No. 23, 350 U.S. 892 (1955); Conley v. Gibson, 355 U.S. 41 (1957); Whitfield v. United Steelworkers of America, Local No. 2708, 360 U.S. 902 (1959). Doris M. Toll, "Professor Roberson L. King," *Law School News* 5 (May 1964). Thank you to DeCarlous Y. Spearman for sharing this source.

5   Complaint, Holt v. Oil Workers International Union, No. 430-707, District Court, Harris County, Tex. (January 12, 1954), 4; Complaint, Syres v. Oil Workers International Union, No. 2638, United States District Court for the Eastern District of Texas, May 25, 1954, NAACP Papers Part 13C, Roll 4. Risa Goluboff has noted that substantive due process claims like King's persisted long after the New Deal supposedly interred them. Risa L. Goluboff, *The Lost Promise of Civil Rights* (Cambridge, Mass.: Harvard University Press, 2007), 24, 206, 207, 266–67; Risa L. Goluboff, "Deaths Greatly Exaggerated," *Law and History Review* 24, no. 1 (Spring 2006): 201–8.

6   "Weaver, George L.P.," n.d. [1960], RG 174, Records of the Department of Labor [hereafter DOL Records], Secretary of Labor Arthur J. Goldberg, 1961–1962, Box 81, "PE-4-2: Weaver, George L.P. (Special Assistant to the Secy.) 1961" Folder, NACP; "Weaver, George Leon-Paul," n.d., CIOSO Papers, Box 154, "Weaver, George L-P: Biographical Sketches" Folder; George L. P. Weaver, "Investigation Data Request," April 8, 1953, ibid. On the redcap union, see Eric Arnesen, *Brotherhoods of Color: Black Railroad Workers and the Struggle for Equality* (Cambridge, Mass.: Harvard University Press, 2002), 114, 164–66. Robert L. Carter, *A Matter of Law: A Memoir of Struggle in the Cause of Equal Rights* (New York: New Press, 2005). George L. P. Weaver to Robert L. Carter, March 5, 1954, NAACP Papers Part 13C, Reel 4.

7   Robert L. Carter to Jack Greenberg et al., June 23, 1954, CIOSO Papers, Box 161, "NAACP Convention, 1954" Folder; George L. P. Weaver to Robert L. Carter, August 23, 1954, NAACP Papers, Part III-J, Box 9, "PCGC, Complaint to, 1954–55" Folder. Elizabeth to Herbert Hill, June 25, 1954, NAACP Papers Part 13A, Reel 20. Herbert Hill to Leonard P. Avery, July 13, 1954, NAACP Papers, Part II-A, Box 345, "Labor Cases: Oil Industries, 1945–55" Folder; see also Herbert Hill to U. Simpson Tate, July 12, 1954, NAACP Papers Part 13A, Reel 13. Thomas Davis, Alvin M. Scott, Louis T. Betz, and Tom Bell interviewed by C. L. Gilbert, Baton Rouge, La., August 28, 1957, PCGC Papers – DCC, Box 30, "Case No.

122, Esso Standard Oil Co." Folder (1 of 2). Theodore Smith, interviewed by C. L. Gilbert, Baton Rouge, La., August 27, 1957, ibid. B. T. Johnson, Dennis Scott, and Benjamin Hunter interviewed by C. L. Gilbert, Texas City, Tex., August 21, 1957, PCGC Papers – DCC, Box 31, "Case No. 124, Carbide & Chemical Co., Texas City, Texas" Folder (1 of 2). U. Simpson Tate, "Report on Meeting with Employees of Carbide-Carbon Company," September 7, 1954, NAACP Papers, Part III-J, Box 9, "PCGC, Complaint to, 1954–55" Folder; Herbert Hill to Mr. E. O. Eelback, January 7, 1955, NAACP Papers Part 13A, Reel 13.

8 Herbert Hill to Walter White, September 3, 1954, NAACP Papers Part 13A, Reel 13; Herbert Hill to Roy Wilkins, September 14, 1954, ibid., Reel 20; Herbert Hill to Lawrence H. Conley, October 19, 1954, ibid., Reel 13; Herbert Hill to Robert L. Carter, November 17, 1954, ibid.; Executive Office Reports, December 13, 1954, Randolph Boehm, August Meier, and John H. Bracey Jr., eds., *Papers of the NAACP, Supplement to Part 1, 1951–1955* (Bethesda, Md.: UPA, 1987), microfilm [hereafter NAACP Papers Part 1, 1951–55], Reel 2; Herbert Hill to Henry L. Moon, February 1, 1955, NAACP Papers Part 13A, Reel 20; Herbert Hill to Roy Wilkins et al., March 2, 1955, ibid., Reel 13; Executive Office Reports, April 11, 1955, NAACP Papers Part 1, 1951–55, Reel 2.

9 Legal Department Report, February–March 1953, NAACP Papers Part 1, 1951–55, Reel 2; Legal Department Report, May 1953, ibid.; Legal Department Report, June 1–15, 1953, ibid.; Thurgood Marshall and Robert L. Carter to Lawyers' Conference Participants, June 12, 1953, ibid., Reel 7; "We are here to discuss … ," n.d. [1954–55], NAACP Papers, Part III-J, Box 8, "Oil Workers Background Information, 1954, n.d." Folder; "Introduction," n.d. [1954–55], ibid. Risa Goluboff notes that the NAACP and its LDF increased their organizational separation in 1952, a move she argues further contributed to LDF's and the NAACP's abandonment of workplace litigation and the NAACP's relegation of economic inequality to political advocacy only. Goluboff, *The Lost Promise*, 226, 237. This chapter's evidence suggests the LDF's separation from the NAACP did not end its interest in workplace claims or rend the NAACP's political and legal pursuits.

10 Because government employers were clearly state actors, the NAACP lawyers already knew a sure way to challenge their discriminatory practices. We are here to discuss … ," n.d. [1954–55], NAACP Papers. Report of the Committee on Discrimination in Employment, n.d. [1953], NAACP Papers, Part III-J, Box 8, "Oil Workers Background Information, 1954, n.d." Folder.

11 Report of the Committee on Discrimination in Employment, n.d. [1953], NAACP Papers. NAACP lawyers reconsidered this position after Ford Motor Co. v. Huffman, 345 U.S. 330 (1953), which stated that the NLRA

imposed a duty of fair representation, but they still first brought their
actions before the Board, assumedly because Carter wanted to establish the NLRB's ability to issue unfair labor practice orders for racial
discrimination. "We are here to discuss … ," n.d. [1954–55], NAACP
Papers.

12 Civil rights advocates had been challenging discrimination in government
contract work since at least the early 1930s. See Chapter 1. Robert L.
Carter and Thurgood Marshall, n.d. [1955], complaint, NAACP Papers,
Part III-J, Box 9, "PCGC, Complaint to, 1954–55" Folder; E.O. 10479,
18 Fed. Reg. 4899 (August 18, 1953).

13 "Introduction," n.d. [1954–55], NAACP Papers. Report of the Committee
on Discrimination in Employment, n.d. [1953], NAACP Papers, 10–11;
"We are here to discuss … ," n.d. [1954–55], NAACP Papers, 4, 6–8;
NLRA secs. 8(a)(1), 8(b)(1). They also suggested that a union that
negotiated discriminatory contracts failed to "bargain collectively with
an employer," another basis for an unfair labor practice order. We are
here to discuss … ," n.d. [1954–55], NAACP Papers; NLRA sec. 8(b)
(3). Finally, NAACP lawyers reasoned that employers and unions that
adopted more favorable contract terms for the members of racially exclusive unions than for African American nonmembers discriminated on the
basis of union membership, also grounds for unfair labor practice orders.
"We are here to discuss …," n.d. [1954–55], NAACP Papers; Report of
the Committee on Discrimination in Employment, n.d. [1953], NAACP
Papers; NLRA secs. 8(a)(3), 8(b)(2). U. Simpson Tate to All Attorneys –
Southwest Region NAACP, CIOSO Papers, 1, 5–6.

14 Arthur Christopher, "Application for Federal Employment," September 15,
1945, Papers of Arthur Christopher, 1913–1967 [hereafter Christopher
Papers], Box 15-6, Folder 88, Moorland-Spingarn Research Center,
Howard University, Washington, D.C. J. Clay Smith Jr., *Emancipation:
The Making of the Black Lawyer, 1844–1944* (Philadelphia: University of
Pennsylvania Press, 1999). Arthur Christopher Jr., Affidavit, August 19,
1964, Christopher Papers, Box 15-5, "Lahne, Herbert J." Folder 75.

15 See Chapter 2. "Controlling Board Principles," n.d. [January or February
1955], Christopher Papers, Box 15-2, "NLRB Policies Respecting
Discrimination Practices of Labor Unions" Folder 163, 11. I cannot be
certain that Christopher was the author of the draft report I found in
his papers; however, the draft took constitutional positions that only
Christopher endorsed in his separate concurrence to the final committee
report. W. R. Consadine, Arthur Christopher Jr., and Herbert Lahne to
NLRB, July 18, 1955 [hereafter NLRB Memo], RG 25, NLRB, Committee
Management Files, 1934–1974: Former Chairman Miller, 1953–1973,
1973 [hereafter NLRB Papers – CMFMiller], Box 8, "Chairman's Files
Policy and Procedure – Race Discrimination Matters" Folder, NACP, 6;
Hurd v. Hodge, 334 U.S. 24 (1948). Note that this is not an entirely

accurate assessment of *Hurd*'s holding. The Court does not rely directly on the Fifth Amendment, instead using the Constitution as a source of the public policy that would be violated if federal courts were able to enforce covenants that the Fourteenth Amendment barred state courts from enforcing. *Hurd*, 334 U.S. at 34–35. NRLB Memo, 6, 7 (discussing NLRB v. Pacific Maritime Shipowners Ass'n, 218 F.2d 913, 917 (9th Cir., 1955) (Pope, J., separate opinion); Betts v. Easley, 169 P.2d 831, 839 (Kan. 1946)).

16 See Chapter 2. NLRB Memo, 6, 9, 12–13. Brown v. Board of Education, 347 U.S. 483 (1954); Bolling v. Sharpe, 347 U.S. 497 (1954). Christopher and one other committee member wrote strong concurrences; the committee report came to the same conclusion, albeit with more hedging and qualifications.

17 Guy Farmer, "'New' NLRB in Middle of Same Old Controversies," *Washington Post*, January 3, 1954, F10. James A. Gross, *Broken Promise: The Subversion of U.S. Labor Relations Policy, 1947–1994* (Philadelphia: Temple University Press, 2003), 98, 125–26. Clayton Knowles, "6 Democrats Seek New Beeson Study," *New York Times*, February 2, 1954, 12. Pittsburgh Plate Glass, 111 N.L.R.B. No. 194 (1955); Gulf Coast Piping Contractors (1955). Neither NLRB decision mentioned race. For their racial underpinnings, see NLRB Memo; Arthur Leff, Gulf Coast Piping Contractor Assoc., Case No. 39-RC-572, September 30, 1955, Christopher Papers, Box 15-12, "NLRB Policies Respecting Discrimination Practices of Labor Unions" Folder, 164.

18 Mary L. Dudziak, *Cold War Civil Rights: Race and the Image of American Democracy* (Princeton, N.J.: Princeton University Press, 2002). "Broad State Rule over Labor Urged," *New York Times*, May 4, 1954. S. 1831, 83rd Cong., 1st Sess., May 5, 1953. On Goldwater's antiunionism see Elizabeth Tandy Shermer, "Origins of the Conservative Ascendancy: Barry Goldwater's Early Senate Career and the De-legitimization of Organized Labor," *The Journal of American History* 95, no. 3 (December 2008): 678–709. On the split in the Republican Party between liberals and anti–New Deal conservatives and the way it created space for anti–New Deal and anti-FEPC conservatives to support fair employment policies in order to fester divisions in the Democratic Party, see Anthony S. Chen, *The Fifth Freedom: Jobs, Politics, and Civil Rights in the United States, 1941–1972* (Princeton, N.J.: Princeton University Press, 2009), 70–71. Jennifer Delton, *Racial Integration in Corporate America, 1940–1990* (New York: Cambridge University Press, 2009); Chen, *The Fifth Freedom*; Timothy M. Thurber, "Forgotten Architects of the Second Reconstruction: Republicans and Civil Rights, 1945–1972," in *Making Sense of American Liberalism*, ed. Jonathan Bell and Timothy Stanley, 181–201 (Chicago: University of Illinois Press, 2012), 184–85; Anthony S. Chen, "The Party of Lincoln and the Politics of State Fair Employment Practices Legislation

in the North, 1945–1964," *American Journal of Sociology* 112, no. 6 (May 1, 2007): 1713–74. See Chapter 2.

19 Board members nonetheless disagreed about whether they were empowered to determine the constitutionality of the NLRA or had to assume the statute was constitutional. See In the Matter of United Brotherhood of Carpenters and Joiners of America, 81 N.L.R.B. 802 (1949). For more on these debates, see Chapter 7. Joanna Grisinger, *The Unwieldy American State: Administrative Politics since the New Deal* (New York: Cambridge University Press, 2012), 154–55. Compare Wong Yang Sung v. McGrath, 339 U.S. 33 (1950) and Marcello v. Bonds, 349 U.S. 302 (1955).

20 Gross, *Broken Promise*, chap. 6. On Eisenhower's desire not to alienate the labor vote, see Gilbert J. Gall, *The Politics of Right to Work: The Labor Federations as Special Interests, 1943–1979* (New York: Greenwood Press, 1988), 61–67. See, generally, Anne Joseph O'Connell, "Political Cycles of Rulemaking: An Empirical Portrait of the Modern Administrative State," *Virginia Law Review* 94 (2008): 889–986.

21 Grisinger, *The Unwieldy American State*, 86–89; Gross, *Broken Promise*, 18–19; Harry A. Millis and Emily C. Brown, *From the Wagner Act to Taft-Hartley: A Study of National Labor Policy and Labor Relations* (Chicago: University of Chicago Press, 1950). Memorandum for the National Labor Relations Board in Ford Motor Co. v. Huffman, Case Nos. 193–94, Supreme Court of the United States, October 1952, 15–19. "NLRB Counsel Quits Post," *Sarasota Journal*, December 20, 1954; "2 Gain Approval to NLRB Posts," *New York Times*, February 26, 1955, 6.

22 Daniel Byrd to Robert L. Carter, August 17, 1955, NAACP Papers, Part III-J, Box 9, "PCGC, Complaint to, 1954–55" Folder. John F. LeBus to Robert Carter and Thurgood Marshal, October 31, 1955, PCGC Papers – DCC, Box 30, "Case No. 122, Esso Standard Oil Co." Folder (1 of 2). Kenneth C. McGuiness to Robert Carter and Thurgood Marshall, November 17, 1955, ibid.; Kenneth C. McGuiness to Robert Carter and Thurgood Marshall, March 13, 1956, ibid.

23 Yevette Richards, *Maida Springer: Pan-Africanist and International Labor Leader* (Pittsburgh: University of Pittsburgh Press, 2004).

24 E.O. 10479, August 13, 1953, 18 Fed. Reg. 4899 (1953), secs. 4–5.

25 John D. Morris, "Nixon Urges Ban by U.S. on Poll Tax," *New York Times*, October 3, 1952, 14. See Chen, *The Fifth Freedom*, 71–72, 76. For the argument that voluntary approaches were more successful than has been recognized, see Delton, *Racial Integration*, 164–74. For examples of Republican state and federal FEPC proposals that included sanctions but empowered courts, not administrative agencies, to impose them, see David F. Engstrom, "The Lost Origins of American Fair Employment Law: Regulatory Choice and the Making of Modern Civil Rights, 1943–1972," *Stanford Law Review* 63 (May 2011): 1071–144, 1080–81. Ted Wood, "Nixon Won't Go Beyond Voluntary FEPC Law," *Chicago Defender*, August 16, 1952, 3.

26 See Chapter 1; Joel William Friedman, *Champion of Civil Rights: Judge John Minor Wisdom* (Baton Rouge: Louisiana State University Press, 2009), 14–15, 40, 42, 79. Richard M. Nixon to Jacob Seidenberg, May 17, 1955, RG 220; Records of Temporary Committees, Commissions, and Boards; Records of the President's Committee on Government Contracts, 1953–1961; General Subject Files, 1953–61: Subcommittees [hereafter PCGC Papers – GSFS], Box 30, "Subcommittees: 6–7a Subcommittee on Oil Industry" Folder, NACP. Assistant Secretary of Defense Thomas Pike and Deputy Attorney General William P. Rogers rounded out the committee. Richard Nixon to James P. Mitchell, June 29, 1955, ibid.

27 Jacob Seidenberg to file, July 22, 1955, PCGC Papers – DCC, Box 54, "Oil Refining Industry" Folder. Roberson King, "Complaint," February 18, 1955 (received), PCGC Papers – DCC, "Case No. 113, Shell Oil Co. & Refinery, Shell Chemical Corp., Houston, Texas" Folder; Roberson King, "Amended Complaint," n.d. [May 1955], ibid. "Report on Complaint of Discrimination Against Shell, Houston, Texas," n.d. [May, 1955], ibid. [hereafter Shell Investigation], 2, 3, 5. "Case No. 113," October 20, 1955, ibid., 2. (PCGC files are sometimes delivered in unnumbered dummy boxes but should be locatable by case name in the collection's card index.) On large corporations' growing willingness to undertake voluntary fair employment reforms in the 1950s, see Delton, *Racial Integration*.

28 George Meany to Jacob Seidenberg, October 6, 1955, PCGC Papers, Discrimination Complaint Casefiles, 1951–1961: Pending Jurisdiction – X Ref Cards [hereafter PCGC Papers – DCC:PJ], Box 54, "Oil Refining Industry" Folder. George L. P. Weaver to Walter P. Reuther, June 2, 1955, CIOSO Papers, Box 182, "(Office of the) President, 1955" Folder; Richard P. Nixon, "Minutes of PCGC Meeting (Confidential)," October 25, 1955, DCR Papers, Box 4, Folder 4. Lindsay P. Walden to All Officers et al., June 22, 1954, CIOSO Papers, Box 57, "Oil Workers, 1951–55" Folder. Oil Workers International Union, motion and brief, January 13, 1955, NAACP Papers, Part V, Box 2337, "Syres v. Oil Workers Int'l Union, Local 23, 1955" Folder. Executive Office Reports, May 14, 1956, NAACP Papers Part 1, 1956–60, Reel 1. Shell Investigation, PCGC Papers – DCC, 5.

29 Shell Investigation, PCGC Papers – DCC, 5. "Memorandum," June 23, 1955, PCGC Papers – DCC, "Case No. 113, Shell Oil Co. & Refinery, Shell Chemical Corp., Houston, Texas" Folder; William E. Rentfro to George L. P. Weaver, June 28, 1955, UAWFPD Papers, Box 25, Folder 31. "Summary Report on Complaint and Investigation," January 31, 1957, PCGC Papers – DCC, "Case No. 216, Shell Oil Company, Houston, Texas" Folder. Lt. Col. Norman P. Herr, "Report re Complaint of Discrimination," September 27, 1956, PCGC Papers – DCC, "Case No. 216, Shell Oil Company, Houston, Texas" Folder. Esso, "Management Information Bulletin No. 87," October 14, 1955, PCGC Papers – DCC, Box 30, "Case No. 122, Esso Standard Oil Co." Folder (1 of 2). Herbert

Hill to Warner Brown, March 12, 1956, in John H. Bracey Jr. and August
Meier, eds., *Papers of the NAACP, Supplement to Part 13: The NAACP and
Labor* (Bethesda, Md.: UPA, 1997), microfilm [hereafter NAACP Papers
Part 13S], Reel 12; Herbert Hill to E. D. Sprott, March 21, 1956, ibid.;
Herbert Hill to Florence Irving, June 12, 1956, ibid.; Muriel S. Outlaw to
Henry L. Moon, April 9, 1956, ibid.; Executive Office Reports, May 14,
1956, NAACP Papers Part 1, 1956–60, Reel 1. The Oil Workers' name had
recently changed to the Oil, Chemical and Atomic Workers International
Union. I continue to use "Oil Workers" for simplicity's sake.

30 PCGC Minutes, August 10, 1955, PCGC Papers – GSFS, Box 30,
"Subcommittees: 6–7a Subcommittee on Oil Industry" Folder; Jacob
Seidenberg to James Mitchell, August 11, 1955, PCGC Papers – DCC,
Box 30, "Case No. 122, Esso Standard Oil Co." Folder (2 of 2). On
southern liberals and moderates see Joseph Crespino, *In Search of
Another Country: Mississippi and the Conservative Counterrevolution*
(Princeton, N.J.: Princeton University Press, 2007), chap. 1; Glenda
Elizabeth Gilmore, *Defying Dixie: The Radical Roots of Civil Rights:
1919–1950* (New York: W. W. Norton, 2008); Patricia Sullivan, *Days
of Hope: Race and Democracy in the New Deal Era* (Chapel Hill:
University of North Carolina Press, 1996); Anders Walker, *The Ghost
of Jim Crow: How Southern Moderates Used* Brown v. Board of
Education *to Stall Civil Rights* (New York: Oxford University Press,
2009); Jason Morgan Ward, *Defending White Democracy: The Making
of a Segregationist Movement and the Remaking of Racial Politics,
1936–1965* (Chapel Hill: University of North Carolina Press, 2011).
Seidenberg, PCGC Executive Director's Report, August 17, 1955, DCR
Papers, Box 4, Folder 2, 2. For the mixed success of the oil workers' litigation see Ray F. Marshall, "Some Factors Influencing the Upgrading of
Negroes in the Southern Petroleum Refining Industry," *Social Forces* 42,
no. 2 (December 1963): 186–95.

31 Michael J. Klarman, *From Jim Crow to Civil Rights: The Supreme Court
and the Struggle for Racial Equality* (New York: Oxford University Press,
2006); Pete Daniel, *Lost Revolutions: The South in the 1950s* (Chapel
Hill: The University of North Carolina Press, 2000); Dan T. Carter, *The
Politics of Rage: George Wallace, the Origins of the New Conservatism,
and the Transformation of American Politics* (New York: Simon &
Schuster, 1995). Jason Ward's *Defending White Democracy* challenges the
backlash thesis. Mark V. Tushnet, *Making Civil Rights Law: Thurgood
Marshall and the Supreme Court, 1956–1961* (New York: Oxford
University Press, 1996), chap. 19–20. William H. Oliver to George L.P.
Weaver, February 10, 1956, UAWFPD, Box 24, Folder 25; Lester Graham
to Boris Shishkin, April 9, 1956, Series 8, Subject Files, 1955–1970, 1981,
Organizing Department Records, 1955–1975 [hereafter AFL-CIO ODR
Papers], Box 47, Folder 9.

32 C. L. Gilbert, "Interview with Management," August 22, 1957, PCGC Papers – DCC, Box 31, "Case No. 124, Carbide & Chemicals Co., Texas City, Texas" Folder (1 of 2). Summarized and quoted in C. L. Gilbert to Chief of Naval Material, October 2, 1957, PCGC Papers – DCC, Box 30, "Case No. 122, Esso Standard Oil Co." Folder (1 of 2), 4.

33 Louisiana repealed its right-to-work law in 1956. William Rentfro to George L. P. Weaver, February 15, 1956, CIOSO Papers, Box 178, "(International Union of) Oil, Chemical and Atomic Workers" Folder. On the AFL–CIO merger and the CIO's negotiation of an antidiscrimination guarantee, see Arthur J. Goldberg, *AFL-CIO: Labor United* (New York: McGraw-Hill, 1956); Robert H. Zieger, *The CIO, 1935–1955* (Chapel Hill: University of North Carolina Press, 1997), 360–64. George L. P. Weaver to Boris Shishkin, May 2, 1956, CRD Papers, Box 16, Folder 113. This judgment may seem harsh but, having reviewed every race discrimination complaint in the department's records during its first years of operation, I believe it is accurate. Compare, for instance, DCR-DCF Papers, Box 3, Folder 21 with DCR-DCF Papers, Box 8, Folder 81. The pleas of the department's own field staff in the latter case are particularly damning. C. L. Gilbert interview of G. J. Le Unes, August 22, 1957, PCGC Papers – DCC, Box 31, "Case No. 124, Carbide & Chemical Co., Texas City, Texas" Folder (1 of 2).

34 George L. P. Weaver, March 1, 1957, CIOSO Papers, Box 178, "(International Union of) Oil, Chemical and Atomic Workers" Folder. Herbert Hill to A. Maceo Smith, February 2, 1953, NAACP Papers Part 13A, Reel 20.

35 George L. P. Weaver to Francis Shane, July 14, 1954, CIOSO Papers, Box 190, "Shane, Francis (Steel)" Folder (2 of 2); William H. Oliver to All Regional Directors, July 28, 1954, UAWFPD Papers, Box 19, Folder 49.

36 Steve Fraser, *Labor Will Rule: Sidney Hillman and the Rise of American Labor* (Ithaca, N.Y.: Cornell University Press, 1993). David Stebenne, *Arthur J. Goldberg: New Deal Liberal* (New York: Oxford University Press, 1996), 1–10. Gilbert J. Gall, *Pursuing Justice: Lee Pressman, the New Deal, and the CIO* (Albany: State University of New York Press, 1999).

37 On industrial pluralism, see Chapter 1; on labor pluralism, see Christopher Tomlins, *The State and the Unions* (New York: Cambridge University Press, 1985); Daniel R. Ernst, "Common Laborers? Industrial Pluralists, Legal Realists, and the Law of Industrial Disputes, 1915–1943," *Law and History Review* 11, no. 1 (Spring 1993): 59–100; Karl E. Klare, "Judicial Deradicalization of the Wagner Act and the Origins of Modern Legal Consciousness, 1937–1941," *Minnesota Law Review* 62 (1978): 265–339; Reuel E. Schiller, "From Group Rights to Individual Liberties: Post-War Labor Law, Liberalism, and the Waning of Union Strength," *Berkeley Journal of Employment and Labor Law* 20 (1999): 1–73; Katherine Van

Wezel Stone, "The Post-War Paradigm in American Labor Law," *Yale Law Journal* 90, no. 7 (1981): 1509–80. Arthur J. Goldberg, "Labor in the Free Society: A Trade Union Point of View," May 3, 1958, Meany Papers – NIUC, Box 29, Folder 23, 12–13, 16–20. Arthur J. Goldberg, "Civil Rights in Labor-Management Relations: A Labor Viewpoint," *Annals of the American Academy of Political and Social Science* 275 (May 1951): 148–54, 149, 151.

38   Goldberg, "Labor in the Free Society," 15.
39   David J. McDonald, I. W. Abel, and James G. Thimmes to All USA District Directors, Staff Representatives, and Local Union Recording Secretaries, August 31, 1954, UAWFPD Papers, Box 25, Folder 31. Although the memo is not signed by Goldberg, it states that it is presenting his legal interpretation. G. L. Patterson, open letter, January 11, 1955, CIOSO Papers, Box 80, "Committee to Abolish Discrimination, 1953–55" Folder.
40   Herbert Hill to Boris Shishkin, December 4, 1958, NAACP Papers Part 13S, Roll 1.
41   Herbert Hill to Roy Wilkins and Robert L. Carter, April 20, 1956, CIOSO Papers, Box 178, "(International Union of) Oil, Chemical and Atomic Workers" Folder; O. P. Lattu to Chief of Naval Material, June 1, 1959, PCGC Papers – DCC, Box 30, "Case No. 122, Esso Standard Oil Co." Folder (2 of 2). J. H. Carmical, "Optimism Shown by U.S. Oil Men," *New York Times*, September 28, 1958, F1; Marshall, "Some Factors." Jesse Johnson to Jacob Seidenberg, September 4, 1959, PCGC Papers – DCC, Box 30, "Case No. 122, Esso Standard Oil Co." Folder (1 of 2). Summary Report on Investigation and Complaint, February 23, 1960, ibid. Thomas Davis interviewed by C. L. Gilbert, August 28, 1957, ibid.
42   Syres v. Oil Workers International Union, 223 F.2d 739, 745–47 (5th Cir. 1955) (Rives, J., dissenting).

6   Conservatives Pursue the Workplace Constitution in the Courts

1   W. T. Harrison to Hon. Frank W. Boykin, December 26, 1950, reproduced in 96 Cong. Rec. A7936, January 1, 1951. On the fusion of anti–civil rights and anticommunist politics in the South and Southwest during the early postwar period, see Joseph Crespino, *Strom Thurmond's America* (New York: Hill and Wang, 2012); Karl Campbell, *Senator Sam Ervin, Last of the Founding Fathers* (Chapel Hill: University of North Carolina Press, 2007); Michelle M. Nickerson, *Mothers of Conservatism: Women and the Postwar Right* (Princeton, N.J.: Princeton University Press, 2012); Jeff Woods, *Black Struggle, Red Scare: Segregation and Anti-Communism in the South, 1948–1968* (Baton Rouge: Louisiana State University Press, 2003).
2   "Unfair to Independent Railway Clerks," *Chicago Daily Tribune*, May 5, 1951, 12. Mrs. E. S., "Job Liberty Threat Feared," *Los Angeles Times*, September 4, 1951, A4.

3 Note, "The New Union Shop Provision in the Railway Labor Act," *Indiana Law Journal* 31 (1955): 148–59, 149, 152, 156; George Rose, "The Railway Labor Act: The Union Shop and Impartial Tribunals," *American Bar Association Journal* 42 (January 1956): 35–38, 36.
4 George R. Horton and H. Ellsworth Steele, "The Unity Issue among Railroad Engineers and Firemen," *Industrial and Labor Relations Review* 10 (1956): 48–69, 67. *Seventeenth Annual Report of the National Mediation Board* (Washington, D.C.: Government Printing Office, 1952), 17; *Eighteenth Annual Report of the National Mediation Board* (Washington, D.C.: Government Printing Office, 1953), 10–11; *Nineteenth Annual Report of the National Mediation Board* (Washington, D.C.: Government Printing Office, 1954), 9–10. "Group of Union Rail Workers Rips Union Shop," *Chicago Daily Tribune*, July 27, 1952, 12; "Rail Unionists Join for Fight on Union Shop," *Chicago Daily Tribune*, August 6, 1952, B9.
5 National Committee for Union Shop Abolition, "Its Background, Origin and Plan of Action," n.d. [1952–54], National Right to Work Committee Papers [hereafter NRWC Papers], Box 1, Hoover Institution Archives, Stanford, Calif.; William T. Harrison to J. H. Wynn, December 22, 1953, DeMille Papers, Box 1197, Folder 15. Horton and Steele, "The Unity Issue," 67–68; Rose, "Impartial Tribunals," 35–36.
6 Horton and Steele, "The Unity Issue," 67. Sidney Roger, *A Liberal Journalist on the Air and on the Waterfront: Labor and Political Issues, 1932–1990*, an oral history conducted in 1989 and 1990 by Julie Shearer, Regional Oral History Office, Bancroft Library, University of California, Berkeley, 1998, chap. 16, 441.
7 On the centrality of Hayek and Mises to 1950s conservatism, see Kim Phillips-Fein, *Invisible Hands: The Making of the Conservative Movement from the New Deal to Reagan* (New York: W. W. Norton, 2009), 36–39; Donald T. Critchlow, *The Conservative Ascendancy: How the GOP Right Made Political History* (Cambridge, Mass.: Harvard University Press, 2007), 6; Gregory L. Schneider, *The Conservative Century: From Reaction to Revolution* (Lanham, Md.: Rowman & Littlefield, 2008), 40–48; Angus Burgin, *The Great Persuasion: Reinventing Free Markets since the Depression* (Cambridge, Mass.: Harvard University Press, 2012). These historians see their intellectual work as a critical building block of the Right's postwar rise.
8 Phillips-Fein, *Invisible Hands*, 70–77, 82–85; Nickerson, *Mothers of Conservatism*, 35–36; Darren Dochuk, *From Bible Belt to Sunbelt: Plain-Folk Religion, Grassroots Politics, and the Rise of Evangelical Conservatism* (New York: W. W. Norton, 2011), 117; Rick Perlstein, *Before the Storm: Barry Goldwater and the Unmaking of the American Consensus* (New York: Hill and Wang, 2001), 7–12. Craig R. Prentiss, *Debating God's Economy: Social Justice in America on the Eve of Vatican II* (University Park: Pennsylvania State University Press, 2008). See, e.g., the extended

debate on right-to-work laws in articles published in the journal *Catholic Lawyer*, vol. 2 (1956). Donald Hayne to Rev. Edward A. Keller, February 9, 1955, DeMille Papers, Box 1193, Folder 15. Robert Wuthnow, *The Restructuring of American Religion: Society and Faith since World War II* (Princeton, N.J.: Princeton University Press, 1988).

9 Nickerson, *Mothers of Conservatism*, xvii, xxii; Crespino, *Strom Thurmond's America*; Phillips-Fein, *Invisible Hands*, 58, 60; Critchlow, *The Conservative Ascendancy*, 1, 6, 32–37; Schneider, *The Conservative Century*, 59.

10 W. T. Harrison to Donald MacLean, November 3, 1951, DeMille Papers, Box 1207, Folder 5; Donald MacLean to Cecil B. DeMille, n.d. [1954], DeMille Papers, Box 1145, Folder 5. Harrison to Wynn, December 22, 1953, DeMille Papers. Maurice R. Franks, "The Basic Rule of Industrial Relations: The Master Key," *Vital Speeches of the Day* 15, no. 17 (June 15, 1949): 527–29, 527, 529; "Forescript: Rebellion on the Rails," *Partners* 6, no. 6 (August 1952): 2–3, 3. Maurice R. Franks, "Labor and Education: Industrial Strife Due to the NLRA," *Vital Speeches of the Day* 10, no. 11 (March 15, 1944): 346–49, 347–48. For a subtle treatment of women's exclusion from the post–Civil War concept of free labor, see Amy Dru Stanley, *From Bondage to Contract: Wage Labor, Marriage, and the Market in the Age of Slave Emancipation* (New York: Cambridge University Press, 1998). For midcentury gender politics in the labor movement, see Dennis Deslippe, *Rights, Not Roses: Unions and the Rise of Working-Class Feminism, 1945–80* (Urbana: University of Illinois Press, 2000); Dorothy Sue Cobble, *The Other Women's Movement: Workplace Justice and Social Rights in Modern America* (Princeton, N.J.: Princeton University Press, 2004). Maurice R. Franks, "Facing the Facts of Industrial Relations: As Ye Sow, So Shall Ye Reap," *Vital Speeches of the Day* 16 (June 15, 1948): 525–27, 526.

11 "Alfred Haake, 76, Consultant to G.M.," *New York Times*, November 3, 1961, 36. Alfred P. Haake, "Unshackled, It Can Assure the Future," *Rotarian* 62, no. 5 (November 1943): 27–28, 28; William Shinnick, "Blast New Deal in 7th District," *Chicago Daily Tribune*, April 9, 1944, NW1. William Shinnick, "Battles Seen in Congress Races: G.O.P. Girding for Win in Big 7th District," *Chicago Daily Tribune*, March 5, 1944, W1; "Spiritual Mobilization Begins Preaching Crusade," *Pittsburgh Courier*, August 30, 1947, 12; "Warns on Communism: General Motors Aide Cites Need for Safety in Moral Force," *New York Times*, March 21, 1947, 23. Alfred P. Haake, *Faith and Fact: A Guide to Economics through Christian Understanding* (Pittsburgh, Pa.: Stackpole, 1952). Rev. Edward A. Keller to Donald Hayne, February 14, 1955, DeMille Papers, Box 1143, Folder 13. See, generally, Prentiss, *Debating God's Economy*, 164–71.

12 J. C. Gibson to Donald Hayne, July 7, 1955, DeMille Papers, Box 1193, Folder 13. Some news reports put the number of cases as high as fourteen.

Complaint, May 18, 1953 [Santa Fe Date Stamp], Bugg v. Seaboard Air Line Railroad Co., Court of Law and Chancery of the City of Norfolk, Va., DeMille Papers, Box 1209, Folder 4. Harrison to Wynn, December 22, 1953, DeMille Papers; J. C. Gibson to Donald Hayne, July 7, 1955, DeMille Papers, Box 1193, Folder 13. "Court Test of the Right to Work," August 18, 1953, DeMille Papers, Box 1136, Folder 13.

13 Merle Armitage, *Operations Santa Fe* (New York: Duell, Sloan & Pearce, 1948), 17, 49; James Marshall, *Santa Fe: The Railroad That Built an Empire* (New York: Random House, 1945), 238, 285, 328–29; Keith L. Bryant Jr., ed., *History of Atchison, Topeka and Santa Fe Railway* (New York: Macmillan, 1974), 274, 283–87. F. G. Gurley, "Unalienable Rights vs. Union Shop" (speech to the Academy of Political Science, Hotel Astor, New York, April 21, 1954), DeMille Papers, Box 1200, Folder 2.

14 Phillips-Fein, *Invisible Hands*, chap. 3, 56, 65, 70–80, 100–102; Perlstein, *Before the Storm*, 5; Elizabeth A. Fones-Wolf, *Selling Free Enterprise: The Business Assault on Labor and Liberalism, 1945–60* (Urbana: University of Illinois Press, 1995). Harold Walsh, "March of Finance: Economic Education Project Here Arouses Wide Interest," *Los Angeles Times*, July 24, 1952, A10.

15 Historians generally overlook anti–New Deal conservatives' investments in law during the 1950s. For a welcome exception see Kim Phillips-Fein, "Business Conservatism on the Shop Floor: Anti-Union Campaigns in the 1950s," *Labor* 7, no. 2 (Summer 2010): 9–26. "I.C.C. Member Resigns," *Wall Street Journal*, November 12, 1930, 14; "Jonathan C. Gibson Gets Santa Fe Railway Post," *Washington Post*, March 20, 1934, 10; "Fall and Winter Affairs Slated at Country Club," *Washington Post*, September 20, 1936, S7; "People and Events," *Chicago Daily Tribune*, February 1, 1946, 25; "People and Events," *Chicago Daily Tribune*, December 22, 1947, 55.

16 "Jury Rules for Workers Fighting Union Shop," *Los Angeles Times*, January 30, 1954, 8; "Opinion That May Make History," *Los Angeles Times*, February 20, 1954, A4 (includes Nelson quotes). Gibson also threw in Ninth and Thirteenth Amendment violations. Armitage, *Operations Santa Fe*, 230. "Foremost authority" quoted in "Right-to-Work Law Advocates to Meet Today in Kansas City," *Wall Street Journal*, June 8, 1959, 26. Jonathan C. Gibson et al., "State Right to Work Laws: Pros and Cons," *Management Record* 31 (July 1955): 271–80, 271–74; "Sunday," *Chicago Daily Tribune*, November 16, 1957, C10. J. C. Gibson, "The Legal and Moral Basis of Right to Work Laws" (speech to the American Bar Association Section on Labor Relations Law, Philadelphia, n.d. [1955]), NRWC Papers, Box 1. Donald MacLean to Cecil B. DeMille, June 25, 1957, DeMille Papers, Box 1145, Folder 5, 2.

17 International Ass'n of Machinists v. Sandsberry, 277 S.W.2d 776, 780 (Tx. Ct. Civ. App. 1954). The state action argument occupied about twenty pages

toward the end of a more-than-200-page brief to the appeals court and occupied about the first third (though not many more pages) of the Texas Supreme Court brief. Appellees' Br., International Ass'n of Machinists v. Sandsberry, Case No. 6437, Court of Civil Appeals for the Seventh Supreme Judicial District of Texas, September 3, 1954 [hereafter Gibson Sandsberry Appellate Court Brief], 180–98; Appellants' Application for Writ of Error, Sandsberry v. International Ass'n of Machinists, Case No. A-5061, Supreme Court of Texas, January 17, 1955 [hereafter Gibson Sandsberry Texas Supreme Court Brief], 8–31.

18 Gibson Sandsberry Appellate Court Brief, 180–82, 184–85, 189; Gibson Sandsberry Texas Supreme Court Brief, 12–13, 21–23. For two other arguments that pertained specifically to the Railway Labor Act's union shop provisions, see Gibson Sandsberry Appellate Court Brief, 191–98; Gibson Sandsberry Texas Supreme Court Brief, 5, 13–17. So far as I have been able to ascertain, Gibson was the first to make at least one of these arguments, which raises the possibility that advocates of a liberal workplace Constitution borrowed them from him. See Chapter 4 for discussion of *Pollak*, 343 U.S. 451 (1952) and *Douds*, 339 U.S. 382 (1950). See Chapter 1 for *Steele*, 323 U.S. 192 (1944) and *Betts*, 161 Kan. 159 (Kan. S. Ct. 1946). Jonathan C. Gibson, "State Authority and Labor Relations," *Vital Speeches of the Day* 22, no. 10 (March 1, 1956): 309–12, 309.

19 160 Neb. 669, 696–700 (1955). "Is the Right to Work Written into the Constitution of the United States?" *DeMille Foundation Bulletin* 10, no. 1 (February, 1956), DeMille Papers, Box 1136, Folder 9.

20 Cecil B. DeMille to Arthur C. Nielsen, March 19, 1957, DeMille Papers, Box 1193, Folder 11. Donald MacLean to Louie E. Weiss, July 29, 1957, DeMille Papers, Box 1194, Folder 4; Donald MacLean to Joseph C. Fagan, October 13, 1954, DeMille Papers, Box 1198, Folder 1.

21 Donald MacLean to J. C. Gibson, December 7, 1955, DeMille Papers, Box 1193, Folder 13; Barbara L. Malm to Virginia McDowell, March 23, 1956, ibid.; J. C. Gibson to Virginia McDowell, April 23, 1957, ibid. Donald MacLean to Jonathan C. Gibson, January 25, 1956, ibid. Donald MacLean to Cecil B. DeMille, June 25, 1957, DeMille Papers, Box 1145, Folder 5.

22 Fred A. Hartley to Cecil B. DeMille, July 28, 1954, DeMille Papers, Box 1197, Folder 12. Donald MacLean to Cecil B. DeMille, June 25, 1957, DeMille Papers, Box 1145, Folder 5. Robert C. Albright, "Fight within GOP Highlights N.J. Race," *Washington Post*, October 4, 1954, 6. W. T. Harrison to Donald MacLean, July 12, 1956, DeMille Papers, Box 1197, Folder 15. Gibson et al., "State Right to Work Laws: Pros and Cons," 271–80, 271; Karin Chenoweth, "Disguising Bosses as Workers," *AFL-CIO News*, June 14, 1986, 2. William T. Harrison, "Forced Union Membership Steals Your Freedom," National Right to Work Committee, n.d. [1956].

23 W. T. Harrison to Edwin S. Dillard, January 28, 1956, DeMille Papers, Box 1197, Folder 15. Characterizing the numbers of workers litigating or supporting the right to work is a matter of perspective. On the one hand, 500 to 600 out of the hundreds of thousands of railroad workers nation-wide is a paltry proportion. On the other hand, it is inaccurate to depict the right to work as attracting no more than a few prominently displayed disaffected workers. A 1957 Gallup Poll cited in right-to-work literature found that 73% of the general public and 52% of union members agreed with the statement "No American should be required to join any private organization, like a labor union, against his will," but that 63% of the general public and 33% of union members said they would vote for a right-to-work law "that say[s] each worker has the right to hold his job in a company, no matter whether he joins the labor union or not." In each case, 9–10% of the general public and 6–7% of union members had no opinion, while all others polled were opposed. Quoted in William T. Harrison, *The Truth about Right-to-Work Laws: The Union Arguments, the People's Case* (National Right to Work Committee, 1959).

24 They relied on *Steele, Betts v. Easley*, as well as *Marsh v. Alabama*, 326 U.S. 501 (1946), and the white-primary cases. Br. Amicus Curiae for American Farm Bureau Federation, April 12, 1956, Railway Employes' Dept. v. Hanson, Case No. 451, Supreme Court of the United States, [hereafter Hanson Supreme Court Records], 3–4; Brief of Amicus Curiae of United States Chamber of Commerce, April 18, 1956, Hanson Supreme Court Records, 7–9; Brief of Amicus Curiae of State of Utah, April 16, 1956, Hanson Supreme Court Records, 29–31; Brief of Amicus Curiae for States, April 16, 1956, Hanson Supreme Court Records, 11–12; Brief of Amicus Curiae of J. Lindsay Almond Jr., Attorney General of Virginia, April 13, 1956 [hereafter Virginia Amicus Brief], Hanson Supreme Court Records, 12–13; Respondents' Br., April 18, 1956 [hereafter Hanson Respondents' Brief], Hanson Supreme Court Records, 100; Brief of Amicus Curiae of Sandsberry Petitioners, April 18, 1956 [hereafter Sandsberry Amicus Brief], Hanson Supreme Court Records, 6, 36–38, 46–47; Brief of Amicus Curiae of the Southern States Industrial Council, April 18, 1956 [hereafter SSIC Amicus Brief], Hanson Supreme Court Records, 4–5; Brief of Amicus Curiae of National Right to Work Committee [hereafter NRWC Amicus Brief], April 18, 1956, Hanson Supreme Court Records, 6–8. Gibson went further, arguing that railroad companies and their unions were affected with a public interest and were thus quasi-governmental actors subject to constitutional restraints. Sandsberry Amicus Brief, 6, 45–47. Permission standard examples include Sandsberry Amicus Brief, 29–33; NRWC Amicus Brief, 2–7; Hanson Respondents' Brief 37–52, esp. 45–51. Generally, the briefs cited *Pollak, Douds*, the white-primary cases, and *Steele* for this principle. The segregationist Southern States Industrial Council and the Virginia attorney general also attributed this

principle to *Brown v. Board of Education* (the unconstitutional Kansas statute, they noted, had merely permitted districts to racially segregate students). SSIC Amicus Brief, 7.

25 On conservatives' use of human rights, see Samuel Moyn, "The Secret History of Constitutional Dignity," in *Understanding Human Dignity*, ed. Christopher McCrudden (New York: Oxford University Press, 2013), 95–112. NRWC Amicus Brief, compare 22–23 with 10–12, 18–24. Virginia Amicus Brief, 10; Brief of Amicus Curiae of Charles L. Bradford et al., April 16, 1956, Hanson Supreme Court Records, 8–9. "Forced Followers" in NRWC Amicus Brief, 15–16; Sandsberry Amicus Brief, 65.

26 Railway Employes' Department v. Hanson, 352 U.S. 225 (1956); Sandsberry v. International Association of Machinists, 295 S.W.2d 412 (Tex. S. Ct. 1956). Raymond Moley, "The Court and Labor," *Los Angeles Times*, May 29, 1956, A5. Donald MacLean and Cecil B. DeMille, phone call minutes, May 22, 1956, DeMille Papers, Box 1145, Folder 5. "'Right-to-Work' Returns Watched in Six States," *Washington Post*, November 5, 1958, A8. On the 1958 elections, see Kim Phillips-Fein, "'As Great an Issue as Slavery or Abolition': Economic Populism, the Conservative Movement, and the Right-to-Work Campaigns of 1958," *Journal of Policy History* 23, no. 4 (2011): 491–512; Reuel E. Schiller, "Singing 'The Right-to-Work Blues': The Politics of Race in the Campaign for 'Voluntary Unionism' in Postwar California," in *The Right and Labor in America: Politics, Ideology, and Imagination*, ed. Nelson Lichtenstein and Elizabeth Tandy Shermer, 139–59 (Philadelphia: University of Pennsylvania Press, 2012). "1945–1959," *DeMille Foundation Bulletin* 13, no. 1 (February 11, 1959), DeMille Papers, Box 1136, Folder 13. "Right-to-Work Law Advocates," 26.

27 "Right to Work Laws," *Chicago Daily Tribune*, May 23, 1956, 18. Barsky v. Board of Regents, 347 U.S. 442, 472 (1954) (Douglas, J., dissenting). E. C. Krauss, "A Justice on a Limb," *Los Angeles Times*, June 10, 1954, A5.

28 William O. Douglas, conference notes, May 4, 1956, Douglas Papers, Box 1171, "No. 451 Railway Employees Dept v. Hanson, O.T. 1955" Folder. *Hanson*, 352 U.S. at 232. Justice Douglas probably intended at least the ambiguity, if not the broader meaning. In a dissent joined by Justice Black and Chief Justice Warren, Douglas cited *Hanson*, along with the Court's fair representation cases, for the proposition that government-sanctioned unions "may not make discriminations that the Government may not make." Black v. Cutter Laboratories, 351 U.S. 292, 302 n.* (1956) (Douglas, J. dissenting). In this sense, the intellectual and legal turn from collective to individual rights that Reuel Schiller has richly depicted was not only a diachronic shift but also a long-standing synchronic tension within postwar liberalism, one that dates back at least to Charles Houston's divergent results under different district court judges

in *Teague* and which appears more evident on the Supreme Court if one looks at the justices' internal deliberations and opinions outside the labor context. Reuel E. Schiller, "From Group Rights to Individual Liberties: Post-War Labor Law, Liberalism, and the Waning of Union Strength," *Berkeley Journal of Employment and Labor Law* 20 (1999): 1–73, esp. 45–48. Appellants' Br., March —, 1956 [date stamp faded], Hanson Supreme Court Records, 14–16; Amicus Br. of Railway Labor Executives' Assoc'n, March 14, 1956, Hanson Supreme Court Records, 16. But see Br. of AFL-CIO, March 1—, 1956 [date stamp faded], Hanson Supreme Court Records, 5 (arguing the Railway Labor Act was state action but not with any unconstitutional effects). *Hanson*, 351 U.S. at 235, 238. Cecil B. DeMille to E. F. Hutton, dictation, April 30, 1945, DeMille Papers, Box 1143, Folder 2, 3.

29 Raymond Moley, "The Santa Fe Formula for Political Freedom," *Los Angeles Times*, September 9, 1957, B4. Raymond Moley, "On the Union Shop," *Los Angeles Times*, December 2, 1958, B5.

30 Labor-Management Reporting and Disclosure Act of 1959 (Landrum-Griffin Act), Pub. L. No. 86-257, 73 Stat. 519 (1959). Labor historians see the law as a watershed for labor, one that reflected a deep erosion of the union idea. Nelson Lichtenstein, *State of the Union: A Century of American Labor* (Princeton, N.J.: Princeton University Press, 2002), 163; Schiller, "From Group Rights to Individual Liberties," 58–62. Moley, "Santa Fe Formula," B4. International Ass'n of Machinists v. Street, 215 Ga. 27 (1959). "Political Captives," *Chicago Daily Tribune*, November 30, 1958, 20. "Reuther Social Democrats" refers to United Auto Workers president Walter Reuther.

31 Complaint, Ward v. Seaboard Air Lines Railroad Co., June 6, 1953, Hustings Court of the City of Richmond, Va., DeMille Papers, Box 1209, Folder 4, par. 7. Race is not mentioned in the extant records of the case but is inferable from the fact that the plaintiffs were BSCP members and lived, according to the 1940 census, on blocks in Richmond's highly segregated black neighborhoods.

32 Cecil B. DeMille, "Who Owns Your Right to Work," *U.S.A.: The Magazine of American Affairs* (January 1953), DeMille Papers, Box 1195, Folder 19; Gurley, "Unalienable Rights vs. Union Shop," April 21, 1954, DeMille Papers, 7; Jonathan C. Gibson, "The Challenge to Compulsory Union Membership," (Washington, D.C.: U.S. Chamber of Commerce, 1959), 31; National Right to Work Committee, Constitution & By-laws, June 21, 1958, NRWC Papers, Box 1. See Chapter 5 for Goldwater's 1952 NLRA amendment. Barry Goldwater to Donald MacLean, August 30, 1956, DeMille Papers, Box 1197, Folder 11. Goldwater, along with other Republicans, frequently used antidiscrimination measures as poison pills for disfavored legislation. Timothy N. Thurber, *Republicans and Race: The GOP's Frayed Relationship with African Americans, 1945–1974*

(Lawrence: University Press of Kansas, 2013), 97, 123. On the strong overlap between Goldwater's voting record on civil rights and that of southern Democrats during the 1950s, see ibid., 122–23. For a doctrinal analogue arguing that the *Hanson* plaintiffs' rights were as deserving of protection as those of the African American schoolchildren in *Brown*, see J. A. McClain Jr., "The Union Shop Amendment: Compulsory 'Freedom' to Join a Union," *American Bar Association Journal* 3, reprint (August 1956), NRWC Papers, Box 5, 5. See Perlstein, *Before the Storm*, 20, 22, 27–34.

33 Roger, *A Liberal Journalist*, chap. 16, 424–27. Crespino, *Strom Thurmond's America*, 79–80, 94–97, 103, 118–23; Campbell, *Senator Sam Ervin*, 75. See generally James C. Cobb, *The Selling of the South: The Southern Crusade for Industrial Development, 1936–1990* (Urbana: University of Illinois Press, 1993); Bruce J. Schulman, *From Cotton Belt to Sunbelt: Federal Policy, Economic Development, and the Transformation of the South, 1938–1980* (New York: Oxford University Press, 1991); Tami J. Friedman, "Exploiting the North-South Differential: Corporate Power, Southern Politics, and the Decline of Organized Labor after World War II," *Journal of American History* 95, no. 2 (September 2008): 323–48. William Oliver to George L-P Weaver, February 10, 1956, UAWFPD Papers, Box 24, Folder 25; Lester Graham to Boris Shishkin, April 9, 1956, RG 28–002, Series 8, Subject Files, 1955–1970, 1981, Organizing Department Records, 1955–1975 [hereafter AFL-CIO ODR Papers], Box 47, Folder 9, GMMA.

34 Nickerson, *Mothers of Conservatism*, xxi. Fifield quoted in Phillips-Fein, *Invisible Hands*, 73. Crespino, *Strom Thurmond's America*, 66. Donald R. Richberg, statement before the Committee on Education and Labor, House of Representatives, on H. Res. 111, 80th Cong., May 11–12, 1948, 41.

35 Right-to-work measures appeared on ballots in California, Idaho, Ohio, and Washington in the mid- to late 1950s. Charles W. Baird, "Right to Work Before and After 14(b)," *Journal of Labor Research* 19 (1998): 471–93, 490. Donald MacLean to Cecil B. DeMille, December 1956, DeMille Papers, Box 1145, Folder 5. "Victory in Indiana," *DeMille Foundation Bulletin* 11, no. 1 (March 1957), DeMille Papers, Box 1136, Folder 9.

36 In 1958, the black vote was pivotal to the defeat of right-to-work laws in Ohio and Oklahoma. Gilbert J. Gall, "Thoughts on Defeating Right-to-Work: Reflections on Two Referendum Campaigns," *Organized Labor and American Politics, 1894–1994: The Labor-Liberal Alliance*, ed. Kevin Boyle, 195–216 (Albany: State University of New York Press, 1998). William J. Grede, "NAM Speaks Out for Equal Opportunity" (speech to Lincoln University, Jefferson City, Mo., April 30, 1953), Papers of the National Association of Manufacturers, Series 7, Box 135,

Folder 1, Manuscripts and Archive Department, Hagley Museum and
Library, Wilmington, Del., 3. Californians for Yes on 18, "Proposition 18
Campaign Speakers Manual," n.d. [ca. November 1958], DeMille Papers,
Box 192, Folder 20. On race in the California campaign, see Schiller,
"Singing 'The Right to Work Blues.'"

37 John Jurkanin to George Meany, October 18, 1956, DCR-DCF Papers,
Box 6, Folder 9; see also "Gordon Freeman, Joe Keenan, Community
Relations Board," anonymous handwritten meeting minutes, April 19,
1957, ibid. Clayton R. Williams to George Meany, July 21, 1958, DCR-
DCF Papers, Box 11, Folder 93. "Labor Can't Have It Both Ways,"
Milwaukee Journal, December 3, 1956, 20. Donald MacLean to Reed
Larson, October 6, 1958, DeMille Papers, Box 1194, Folder 5. 103 Cong.
Rec. 966 (January 25, 1957).

38 Hugo L. Black to Earl Warren et al., June 9, 1960, Black Papers, Box 348,
"International Machinists v. Street II, Oct. Term 1960" Folder, 1, 8–9.

39 William O. Douglas, docket book, n.d., Douglas Papers, Box 1232,
"Administrative Docket Book No. 1–199, O.T. 1960" Folder. Brief for the
United States, November 19, 1960, International Ass'n of Machinists v.
Street, No. 534, Supreme Court of the United States, 35–40, 49–53. [Earl
Warren] to [William J. Brennan], February 6, 1961, Brennan Papers, Part
I, Box 45, Folder 4.

40 Hugo L. Black to William J. Brennan, May 23, 1961, Black Papers,
Box 348, "International Machinists v. Street I, Oct. Term 1960" Folder;
William O. Douglas to Conference, January 23, 1961, Douglas Papers,
Box 1234, "Memoranda by Douglas, J., O.T. 1960" Folder; C[harles] E.
W[hittaker] to William J. Brennan, January 30, 1961, Brennan Papers,
Part I, Box 45, Folder 4. William J. Brennan to Conference, June 13, 1961,
Black Papers, Box 348, "International Machinists v. Street I, Oct. Term
1960" Folder.

41 International Ass'n of Machinists v. Street, 367 U.S. 740, 764, 768 (1961).
Ibid. at 775–97 (Justice Douglas titled his a concurrence, and Black called
his argument to the same effect a dissent).

42 "Supreme Court Will Review Georgia Court's Ruling Which Would
Curtail Political Power of Unions," *Wall Street Journal*, October 13,
1959, 3. *Street*, 367 U.S. at 771, 774–75 (1961). In yet another of the per-
colating railroad cases, the Court subsequently clarified that all protesting
members had a right to opt out of the portion of their dues or fees that
the union spent on objected-to political activities. Railway Clerks v. Allen,
373 U.S. 113, 120–22 (1963); see also Chapter 12. Harrison quoted in
"High Court Curbs Use of Union Dues for Political Aims," *Wall Street
Journal*, June 20, 1961, 2.

43 Barnard D. Nossiter, "High Court's Ruling Leaves Labor Calm,"
Washington Post, June 22, 1961, A8.

44 "Alfred Haake, 76, Consultant to G.M.," 36.

7 Agencies Recognize the Liberal Workplace Constitution in the New Frontier

1   IMWU Local 2, "Joint Meeting with Independent Metal Workers Union Locals 1 & 2," January 24, 1962, NAACP Papers, Part V, Box 2308, Folder 12 (emphasis added). For the history of race and labor at Hughes Tool, see Michael R. Botson Jr., *Labor, Civil Rights, and the Hughes Tool Company* (College Station: Texas A & M University Press, 2005). Quotes in C. B. Marshall, February 27, 1962, RG 25, National Labor Relations Board, Selected Taft-Hartley Case Files [hereafter NLRB Papers – STHF], Box 1976, "23-CB-429 Independent Metal Workers Union, Local No. 1, Houston, Texas" Folder; C.B. Marshall, "Memorandum," February 21, 1962, ibid.

2   William H. Chafe, *Civilities and Civil Rights: Greensboro, North Carolina, and the Black Struggle for Freedom* (New York.: Oxford University Press, 1980); Clayborne Carson, *In Struggle: SNCC and the Black Awakening of the 1960s* (Cambridge, Mass.: Harvard University Press, 1982), 9. David Halberstam, *The Children* (New York: Random House, 1998); Charles M. Payne, *I've Got the Light of Freedom: The Organizing Tradition and the Mississippi Freedom Struggle* (Berkeley: University of California Press, 1995); Taylor Branch, *Parting the Waters: America in the King Years, 1954–63* (New York: Simon and Schuster, 1988). Thomas Sugrue, "Affirmative Action from Below: Civil Rights, the Building Trades, and the Politics of Racial Equality in the North, 1945–1969," *Journal of American History* (June 2004): 145. See generally Thomas J. Sugrue, *Sweet Land of Liberty: The Forgotten Struggle for Civil Rights in the North* (New York: Random House, 2009), 301–2, 313, 362. Sugrue is among historians who have begun to reinsert the workplace into the history of the civil-rights 1960s. Jacquelyn Dowd Hall, "The Long Civil Rights Movement and the Political Uses of the Past," *Journal of American History* 91, no. 4 (March 2005): 1233–63; Nancy MacLean, *Freedom Is Not Enough: The Opening of the American Workplace* (Cambridge, Mass.: Harvard University Press, 2008); Thomas F. Jackson, *From Civil Rights to Human Rights: Martin Luther King, Jr., and the Struggle for Economic Justice* (Philadelphia: University of Pennsylvania Press, 2007); William P. Jones, *The March on Washington: Jobs, Freedom, and the Forgotten History of Civil Rights* (New York: W. W. Norton, 2013); Robert O. Self, *American Babylon: Race and the Struggle for Postwar Oakland* (Princeton, N.J.: Princeton University Press, 2003). "NAACP in Legal Attack," October 16, 1962, NAACP Papers Part 13S, Reel 11; "Racial Cases," n.d. [April–June 1964], Papers of Frank McCulloch [hereafter McCulloch Papers], Box 12, Folder 21, Kheel Center for Labor-Management Documentation and Archives, Cornell University, Ithaca, N.Y. [hereafter Kheel]; F. H. B. [likely Frank Boornstein], "Racial Discrimination Cases Handled by

Advice Branch," March 18, 1965, McCulloch Papers, Box 12, Folder
21. Even histories that address early 1960s challenges to workplace dis-
crimination generally do not include NLRB petitions or the workplace
Constitution. Sophia Z. Lee, "Hotspots in a Cold War: The NAACP's
Postwar Workplace Constitutionalism, 1948–1964," *Law and History
Review* 26, no. 2 (Summer 2008): 327–78.

3　Historians have brilliantly addressed the sit-ins and sit-in cases' significance for the civil rights movement. See, for example, Carson, *In
Struggle*; Chafe, *Civilities and Civil Rights*; Halberstam, *The Children*;
Payne, *I've Got the Light of Freedom*; Barbara Ransby, *Ella Baker and
the Black Freedom Movement: A Radical Democratic Vision* (Chapel
Hill: University of North Carolina Press, 2003). Legal historians gen-
erally treat the protestors' broad state-action arguments as civil rights
attorneys' expedient effort to fit the protests within a viable legal claim.
Jack Greenberg, *Crusaders in the Courts: Legal Battles of the Civil
Rights Movement, Anniversary Edition* (New York: Basic Books, 1994),
chaps. 22–23; Michael J. Klarman, *From Jim Crow to Civil Rights: The
Supreme Court and the Struggle for Racial Equality* (New York: Oxford
University Press, 2006), 378–79; Mark V. Tushnet, *Making Civil Rights
Law: Thurgood Marshall and the Supreme Court, 1956–1961* (New
York: Oxford University Press, 1996), 310. But see Christopher W.
Schmidt, "The Sit-Ins and the State Action Doctrine," *William & Mary
Bill of Rights Journal* 18, no. 3 (2010): 767–829, pt. I. Meanwhile, the
Court, in its opinions, is described as having striven to reach the right
result, supporting the sit-in protesters, above all, without stretching the
state-action doctrine. Michal R. Belknap, *The Supreme Court under
Earl Warren, 1953–1969* (Columbia: University of South Carolina
Press, 2005), 160; Lucas A. Powe Jr., *The Warren Court and American
Politics* (Cambridge, Mass.: Belknap Press of Harvard University Press,
2002), 171–75, 227–29; Michael J. Klarman, "An Interpretive History of
Modern Equal Protection," *Michigan Law Review* 90, no. 2 (November
1991): 213–318, 272–79. Within the Department of Justice, these cases
are known mostly for highlighting the differing approaches, and resulting conflicts, between Solicitor General Archibald Cox and his attorney
general, Robert F. Kennedy. Ken Gormley, *Archibald Cox: Conscience
of a Nation* (Reading, Mass.: Addison-Wesley, 1997), 155–60; Victor S.
Navasky, *Kennedy Justice* (New York: Atheneum, 1971), 289–94. Their
consequences for the workplace Constitution, however, are unexplored.

4　Robert S. Breaux to Clifford Potter, July 6, 1962, NLRB Papers – STHF,
Box 1976, "23-CB-429 Independent Metal Workers Union, Local No. 1,
Houston, Texas" Folder. Clifford Potter to Stuart Rothman and George
McInerny, July 6, 1962, ibid. [hereafter Potter Memo]. See Chapter 5.

5　Clyde W. Summers, "The Right to Join a Union," *Columbia Law
Review* 47 (1947): 33–75; Clay Malick, "Toward a New Constitutional

Status for Labor Unions: A Proposal," *Rocky Mountain Law Review* 21 (1949): 260–78. For a working definition of union democracy, see Harry H. Wellington, "Union Democracy and Fair Representation: Federal Responsibility in a Federal System," *Yale Law Journal* 67, no. 8 (July 1958): 1327–62, 1329. See Chapter 4. See also Earl Latham, "The Commonwealth of the Corporation," *Northwestern University Law Review* 55 (1960): 25–38, 35–38.

6 Ford Motor Co. v. Huffman, 345 U.S. 330 (1953); Labor-Management Reporting and Disclosure Act of 1959, Pub. L. 86-257, September 14, 1959, 73 Stat. 519–546. Archibald Cox, "The Duty of Fair Representation," *Villanova Law Review* 2, no. 2 (January 1957): 151–77, 173–74; Wellington, "Union Democracy," 1339, 1360; Harry H. Wellington, "The Constitution, the Labor Union, and 'Governmental Action,'" *Yale Law Journal* 70, no. 3 (January 1961): 345–75, 361–66. Compare Michael I. Sovern, "The National Labor Relations Act and Racial Discrimination," *Columbia Law Review* 62, no. 4 (April 1962): 563–632, with Leo Weiss, "Federal Remedies for Racial Discrimination by Labor Unions," *Georgetown Law Journal* 50, no. 3 (Spring 1962): 457–77.

7 "Laboring Labor Expert: Stuart Rothman," *New York Times*, March 27, 1959, 15. Norman Walker, "Ike Names Rothman to NLRB Post," *Washington Post*, March 27, 1959, A11; "President Names NLRB Counsel," *New York Times*, March 27, 1959, 15. Philip Warden, "NLRB Promises Quicker Action against Goons," *Chicago Daily Tribune*, May 31, 1960, 19. "NLRB Orders Its Field Offices to Aid in Prosecution of Labor Racketeers," *Washington Post*, December 31, 1959, A7. "U.S. Speeds Labor Cases," *New York Times*, January 7, 1960, 16. "New Picketing Curb Is Used First Time," *New York Times*, November 20, 1959, 20. Potter Memo.

8 Potter Memo. "NLRB General Counsel Authorizes Unfair Labor Practice Complaint," August 20, 1962, NAACP Papers, Part V, Box 2309, Folder 1. Gerald Brissman to Clifford Potter, August 20, 1962, NLRB Papers – STHF, Box 1976, "23-CB-429 Independent Metal Workers Union, Local No. 1, Houston, Texas" Folder.

9 "NAACP in Legal Attack," October 16, 1962, NAACP Papers Part 13S, Reel 11.

10 Roy Wilkins to George Meany, May 25, 1960, NAACP Papers Part 13S, Reel 1; George Meany to Roy Wilkins, May 27, 1960, ibid.; "NAACP Prods Meany on No Bias Vow," *New York Times*, May 25, 1960, C10. Herbert Hill, "Racism within Organized Labor: A Report of Five Years of the AFL-CIO, 1955–1960," January 3, 1961, NAACP Papers Part 13S, Reel 7. On the International Ladies' Garment Workers' Union (ILGWU) and civil rights, see Robert D. Parmet, *The Master of Seventh Avenue: David Dubinsky and the American Labor Movement* (New York: New York University Press, 2005); Yevette Richards, *Maida Springer: Pan-*

Africanist and International Labor Leader (Pittsburgh, Pa.: University of Pittsburgh Press, 2004). For the ILGWU's early history, see Steve Fraser, *Labor Will Rule: Sidney Hillman and the Rise of American Labor* (Ithaca, N.Y.: Cornell University Press, 1993).

11 Described in Clifford Potter to Arthur Safos, October 23, 1962, NLRB Papers – STHF, Box 1976, "23-CB-429 Independent Metal Workers Union, Local No. 1, Houston, Texas" Folder. Arthur Safos to Clifford Potter and James Webster, January 14, 1963, ibid.

12 "Labor Seen Leading Fight against Bias," *UAW Solidarity*, October, 1961, UAW President's Office: Walter Reuther Papers [hereafter Reuther Papers], Box 504, Folder 1, ALUA. AFL-CIO Civil Rights Committee, Minutes, March 19, 1963, DCR Papers, Box 6, Folder 10, 3. Walter Davis to Boris Shishkin, August 22, 1962, DCR Papers, Box 6, Folder 7, 3. Harry Fleischman to Frank W. McCulloch, February 1, 1963, NAACP Papers Part 13S, Reel 11. Enclosed in Harry Fleischman to Roy Wilkins, December 27, 1962, ibid.

13 Robert S. Breaux to Clifford Potter, July 6, 1962, NLRB Papers – STHF, Box 1976, "23-CB-429 Independent Metal Workers Union, Local No. 1, Houston, Texas" Folder. Robert Carter to Tom M. Davis, November 9, 1962, NAACP Papers, Part V, Box 2309, Folder 2. T. B. Everitt to L. A. Ashley, November 19, 1962, ibid. The union refused to make this offer the subject of a Board order, however, a condition on which Carter insisted, so no settlement was reached. Robert L. Carter and Maria Marcus to NLRB, February 8, 1963, NLRB Papers – STHF, Box 1977, "23-CB-429 Independent Metal Workers Locals # 1 & 2 (Hughes Tool Co.) #1" Folder, 7.

14 Terry Francois et al., "Petition for Revocation of Certification," James C. Dixon v. Seafarers International Union, October 1962, NAACP Papers Part 13C, Reel 11. George Meany (speech, Negro American Labor Council, New York, N.Y., November 9, 1962), reprinted in "News from the AFL-CIO," November 9, 1962, RG 1–0038, Series 6, AFL-CIO Office of the President, George Meany Files 1940–1980, Speeches 1961–1979 [hereafter Meany Papers – Speeches], Box 80, Folder 55, GMMA; Walter Davis to Boris Shishkin, May 15, 1963, DCR Papers, Box 6, Folder 11. "Moves to Ban Apprentice Racial Curbs," *Chicago Tribune*, December 18, 1963, B9; "Federal Job Rules Bar Racial Quotas," *New York Times*, October 20, 1963, 1.

15 Hughes Tool Company, NLRB Case Nos. 23–RC–1758, October 24, 1962, NAACP Papers Part 13C, Reel 11. Brief of the Charging Party, Case Nos. 23-CB-429 and 23-RC-1758, February 8, 1963, John H. Bracey and August Meier, eds., *Papers of the NAACP, Part 23, Legal Department Case Files, 1956–1965, Series A: The South* (Bethesda, Md.: UPA, 1997), microfilm [hereafter NAACP Papers Part 23A], Reel 41, 20–22 (citing Burton v. Wilmington Parking Authority, 365 U.S.

715 (1961); NAACP v. Alabama, 357 U.S. 449 (1958); Bowman v. Birmingham Transit Company, 280 F.2d 531 (5th Cir., 1960); Baldwin v. Morgan, 287 F.2d 750 (5th Cir., 1961); Guillory v. Administrators of Tulane University of Louisiana, 203 F. Supp. 855, 859 (ED La., 1962)). Labor and liberal critics had long argued this standard would obliterate the public-private divide.

16 Cox, "The Duty of Fair Representation," 151–53.

17 For more on these cases, see Chapters 4 and 6, respectively. Wellington, "The Constitution," 360, 366–72, 374.

18 DOJ to Bill Moyers, February 27, 1961, Department of Justice, Civil Rights Division, Employment, Micro-copy No. NK-2 [hereafter Micro-copy NK-2-E], Reel 91, John F. Kennedy Presidential Library and Museum, Boston [hereafter JFKPLM]. This microfilm is held by JFKPLM, but NACP has a copy that James Mathis helpfully made available to me. Most likely the filmed documents came from the files of Nicholas deB. Katzenbach (NK). Harris L. Wofford Jr. (speech, Annual Conference of National Civil Liberties Clearing House, March 23, 1961), Papers of President Kennedy, Subjects, President's Office Files [hereafter Kennedy Papers – POF], Box 96, "Civil Rights: General, 1961" Folder, JFKPLM. Historians are generally critical of Kennedy's civil rights record. Carl M. Brauer, *John F. Kennedy and the Second Reconstruction* (New York: Columbia University Press, 1979); Nick Bryant, *The Bystander: John F. Kennedy and the Struggle for Black Equality* (New York: Basic Books, 2006). For the work of the Civil Rights Division, see the division's "Monday and Wednesday Reports" in Papers of Burke Marshall [hereafter Burke Marshall Papers], JFKPLM. Office of the White House Press Secretary, "The White House Special Message on Civil Rights," February 28, 1963, Congresslink: The Dirksen Congressional Center, www.congresslink.org/civil/cr1.html. Robert E. Baker, "Kennedy's Rights Proposals Seen Facing Slim Prospects," *Washington Post*, March 3, 1963, A8; Carroll Kilpatrick, "Legislation on Rights Is Asked by President," *Washington Post*, March 1, 1963, A1.

19 The examiner's already completed decision was held for release until the day of the president's speech. Miranda Fuel, 140 N.L.R.B. 181 (1962). Hughes Tool, 147 N.L.R.B. 1573, 1600–02, 1604 (1964). The general counsel brought 8(b)(1)(a) charges for restraining or coercing Davis in the exercise of his Section 7 rights to representation. The examiner also recommended 8(b)(2) unfair labor practice charges for discriminating on the basis of union membership and 8(b)(3) charges for failing to bargain collectively with the employer. "N.L.R.B. Aide Urges Ouster of Hughes' Unions for Racism," *New York Times*, March 1, 1963, 5.

20 Howard A. Glickstein to Burke Marshall, Harold H. Greene, March 22, 1963, Department of Justice, Civil Rights Division, Employment, Micro-copy No. NK-2 [hereafter Micro-Copy NK-2-E], Reel 91, JFKLPM/

NACP, 2, 4, 7–9. The Civil Rights Division used to be expert in labor and civil rights. Goluboff, *The Lost Promise*, 111–12.

21 Charles A. Horsky to Burke Marshall, March 5, 1963, Department of Justice, Civil Rights Division, Employment, NLRB Case, Micro-copy No. NK-2 [hereafter Micro-copy NK-2-E-NC], Reel 91, JFKPLM/NACP; Charles A. Horsky to Burke Marshall, March 20, 1963, ibid. Charles A. Horsky to Burke Marshall, March 12, 1963, ibid. Burke Marshall to Stuart Rothman, March 27, 1963, ibid.

22 IMWU Local 1 to NLRB, April 4, 1963, NLRB Papers – STHF, Box 1977, "23-CB-429 Independent Metal Workers Lo. # 1 & 2 (Hughes Tool Co.) #2" Folder, 3, 4–12; IMWU Local 1 to NLRB, Exceptions, April 4, 1963, ibid., par. 11. Quoted in Department of Justice, "For Immediate Release," May 15, 1963, McCulloch Papers, Box 12, Folder 23.

23 Howard A. Glickstein to [Burke Marshall], n.d. [Summer 1963], "The Solicitor General's Office: Two Years of Obstructing Civil Rights Progress," n.d. [Summer 1963], Howard A. Glickstein Papers [hereafter Glickstein Papers], MGLI 20.2539, University of Notre Dame Archives, Notre Dame, Ind., 7–8. Howard Glickstein to Harold H. Greene, April 13, 1961, Glickstein Papers, MGLI 15.2491.

24 Burton v. Wilmington Parking Authority, 365 U.S. 715, 724–725 (1961).

25 Although Marshall had played a behind-the-scenes role in drafting civil rights legislation, he was picked for the job in part because he was not publicly associated with the civil rights movement. Michal R. Belknap, "The Vindication of Burke Marshall: The Southern Legal System and the Anti–Civil-Rights Violence of the 1960's," *Emory Law Journal* 33 (1984): 93–134, 94–95. During the 1950s, Marshall participated in the Fund for the Republic's Seminar on the Corporation. See Chapter 4. See also Ross and Harris Wofford Jr., "Some Remarks on Corporations and Constitutions (Marshall)," n.d., Burke Marshall Papers, Box 13, "Some Remarks on Corporations and Constitutions, undated" Folder, 6–7. Memorandum of the United States, May 14, 1962, Simkins v. Moses H. Cone Memorial Hospital, No. C-57-G-62, U.S. District Court for the Middle District of North Carolina, Greensboro Division, National Archives at Atlanta, 24, 26–27. For a similar use of *Steele*, see "Proposed Civil Rights Act of 1964, H.R. 7152," RG 60, Department of Justice, Civil Rights Division, 1961–1965, Records of Burke Marshall, Attorney [hereafter DOJ Papers – BM], Box 3, "Proposed Civil Rights Act-1964" Folder, 27–28, NACP. Burke Marshall to Archibald Cox, June 15, 1961, DOJ Papers – BM, Box 3, "July 1962 Sit-in Cases: Avent et al. v. North Carolina (2 of 2)" Folder, 6–22, 25–26.

26 Ralph S. Spritzer to Nicholas deB. Katzenbach, August 8, 1961, Department of Justice, Civil Rights Division, Micro-copy NK-2, Employment, Executive Orders, microfilm [hereafter Micro-Copy NK-2-E-EO], Reel 91, JFKPLM/NACP; Ralph S. Spritzer to SG [J. Lee Rankin], April 6,

1960, RG 60, Department of Justice Records, Civil Rights Division, Class 144 Litigation Case Files [hereafter DOJ Papers – CRD-C144], Box 1685, Folder 144-79-188. Bruce Terris to Archibald Cox, June 27, 1962, Glickstein Papers, MGLI 16.2501, 25–27.

27 Howard A. Glickstein and Alan G. Marer to Harold H. Greene, n.d. [July, 1962], DOJ Papers – BM, Box 3, "July 1962 Sit-in Cases: Avent et al. v. North Carolina (2 of 2)" Folder. Archibald Cox to Terris, Claiborne, and Heymann, June 7, 1963, Glickstein Papers, MGLI 16.2501, 6. Archibald Cox to Burke Marshall, August 3, 1962, DOJ Papers – BM, Box 3, "July 1962 Sit-in Cases: Avent et al. v. North Carolina (1 of 2)" Folder, 3. Lincoln Caplan, *The Tenth Justice: The Solicitor General and the Rule of Law* (New York: Knopf, 1987). The division of labor between the Civil Rights Division attorneys and the Solicitor General's Office was more compli-cated than the prosecutor-versus-defense-attorney analogy captures, but that is the gist of their respective roles. Phil Elman to Archibald Cox, December 29, 1960, Papers of Archibald Cox [hereafter Cox Papers], Box 36, Folder 9, Harvard Law School Library, Historical and Special Collections, Cambridge, Mass.

28 Brief of the United States as Amicus Curiae, Boynton v. Virginia, Case No. 7, Supreme Court of the United States, September, 1960, Glickstein Papers, MGLI 8.2174, 1–3, 5, 17, 19–20, 22, 24–25. Brief of the United States as Amicus Curiae, Burton v. Wilmington Parking Authority, Case No. 164, Supreme Court of the United States, January, 1961, Glickstein Papers, MGLI 8.2047, 2–4. A lawyer on Rankin's staff later described Rankin as "instinctively" adopting his broad view of state action. Navasky, *Kennedy Justice*, 289–90. The justices might have also adopted his rea-soning in *Boynton* but found that the facts justifying state action were not in the record. Todd C. Peppers and Artemus Ward, eds., *In Chambers: Stories of Supreme Court Law Clerks and Their Justices* (Charlottesville: University of Virginia Press, 2013), 276–77. Archibald Cox to Frank Donner, October 31, 1946, Cox Papers, Box 36, Folder 8; Archibald Cox to Ruth Weyand, June 9, 1947, Cox Papers, Box 42, Folder 12; Archibald Cox to E. Merrick Dodd, January 19, 1948, Cox Papers, Box 38, Folder 5; Cox, "The Duty of Fair Representation." Archibald Cox to Philips Ketchum, May 13, 1949, Cox Papers, Box 39, Folder 20. Archibald Cox, "Government Regulation of the Negotiation and Terms of Collective Agreement: An Address," *University of Pennsylvania Law Review* 101 (1952): 1137–53, 1153; Archibald Cox, "Role of Law in Labor Disputes," *Cornell Law Quarterly* 39 (1953): 592–610, especially, 604–5; Archibald Cox, "Uses and Abuses of Union Power," *Notre Dame Lawyer* 35 (1959): 624–39, especially 632, 638. Cox internalized tensions between New Deal liberals. Daniel R. Ernst, "Common Laborers? Industrial Pluralists, Legal Realists, and the Law of Industrial Disputes, 1915–1943," *Law and History Review* 11, no. 1 (Spring 1993): 59–100. Archibald Cox, "The

Role of Law in Preserving Union Democracy," *Harvard Law Review* 72, no. 4 (February 1959): 609–43, 620. Archibald Cox, "Racial Equality and the Law" (speech, Biennial Religious Conference of Princeton University, Princeton, N.J., April 28, 1962), Burke Marshall Papers, Box 35, "CL-CO" Folder, 5. Archibald Cox, "The Nature of Supreme Court Litigation" (speech, Annual Banquet of the Federal Bar Association, Washington, D.C., September 8, 1962), Box 109, Folder 17, 3–4. See also Cox to Terris, Claiborne, and Heymann, June 7, 1963, Glickstein Papers, 29–32, 34.

29 Cox to Terris, Claiborne, and Heymann, June 7, 1963, Glickstein Papers. Ken Gormley's biography of Cox mentions the dialogue, but he does not provide a citation and seems to have been told about the document, not to have read it. Gormley, *Archibald Cox: Conscience of a Nation*, 157. He does, however, address Cox's agony over the sit-in cases. Ibid., 155–60. Brief for the United States as Amicus Curiae, Garner v. Louisiana et al., Case Nos. 26–28, Supreme Court of the United States, September 1961, Glickstein Papers, MGLI 8.2191; Archibald Cox, "Law and the People" (speech, Multnomah County Bar Association, Portland, Ore., May 1, 1962), Burke Marshall Papers, Box 35, "CL-CO" Folder, 5; Brief for the United States as Amicus Curiae, Avent v. North Carolina, Lombard v. Louisiana, Gober v. City of Birmingham, Shuttlesworth v. City of Birmingham, Peterson v. City of Greenville, October, 1962, DOJ Papers – CRD-C144, Section 1, Box 1299, Folder 144-62; Archibald Cox to John F. Davis, October 10, 1962, ibid. Brief for the United States as Amicus Curiae, Griffin v. Maryland et al., Case Nos. 6, 9, 10, 12, and 60, Supreme Court of the United States, August 1963, Glickstein Papers, MGLI 16.2501.

30 Cox argued in 1957 that the Board had the authority to issue unfair labor practice orders for duty of fair representation violations under section 8(b)(3) of the National Labor Relations Act. Cox, "The Duty of Fair Representation." The government's brief argued that the Board could issue them under all three possible provisions. Burke Marshall et al., DOJ Br. Nos. 23-CB-429 & 23-RC-1758, June 24, 1963, NAACP Papers, Part 23A, Reel 41, 12–28, 37 (emphasis added). It also argued, much to Cox's chagrin, that even if the Board began issuing the urged unfair labor practice orders, the courts would still retain jurisdiction over duty of fair representation claims. Archibald Cox to Harold H. Greene, June 25, 1963, Micro-copy NK-2-E-NC, Reel 91.

31 [First name illegible] A. Larey, "NLRB Eyeing Bias Charge at Hughes," *Houston Chronicle*, September 12, 1963.

32 Marid Connor, Shelly Kopek, and Patricia Greenfield, Interview with Frank McCulloch, December 7, 1984, Cornell University, Ithaca, N.Y., Collection 5740, Box 1, Folder "McCulloch, F.," Kheel [hereafter McCulloch Interview 12-7-84], 4–7.

33 Frank W. McCulloch and Robert P. Weintraub to Board, n.d. [after August 1963], McCulloch Papers, Box 12, Folder 25, 14, 20–39. McCulloch also did not think the NLRB could consider Carter's broader allegations. Ibid., 21, 41. Senator Taft had promised that the provision preserving unions' power to set their membership policies protected their color bars. Miranda Fuel, 140 N.L.R.B. 181, 200–02 (1962).

34 Pioneer Bus Co. v. Transport Workers Union of America, 140 N.L.R.B. 54, 55 n. 3 (1962) (citing *Brown*; Bailey v. Patterson, 369 U.S. 31 (1962); Boynton v. Virginia, 364 U.S. 454 (1960); and *Burton*). William Feldesman, "Contract Bar to Representation Elections," *George Washington Law Review* 29, no. 2 (1960): 450–65, 450–51. Bernie to Chairman, transmittal slip, August 30 [1963], McCulloch Papers, Box 12, Folder 24.

35 Barbara Stoyle Mulhallen interview of Howard Jenkins Jr., August 9, 1988, at his home in Kensington, Md., Collection 5843, Box 1, Folder 1155, Kheel [hereafter Jenkins Interview], 1. "Equality Is Their Right," *New York Times*, August 29, 1963, 23; untitled, *New York Times*, August 30, 1963, 12; NLRB, "Howard Jenkins Sworn in as Member of NLRB," August 29, 1963, Howard Jenkins Jr. Collection [hereafter Jenkins Papers], Box 1, Folder 16, Penrose Library, University of Denver, Denver, Colo.

36 Harry M. Leet to Chief Counsels Leff, Ruskin, Beisinger, and Vinkleff, November 5, 1963, NLRB Papers – STHF, Box 1977, "23-CB-429 Independent Metal Workers Un. Locals # 1 & 2 (Hughes Tool Co.)" Folder, 1–2.

37 Leet to Leff et al., November 5, 1963, NLRB Papers – STHF, 1–2 (describing Jenkins's position). Jenkins's argument bore traces of Joseph Rauh's amicus arguments in *Hughes Tool* and *Miranda Fuel* on behalf of the United Auto Workers. Rauh and Silard, "Brief of the United Automobile, Aerospace, and Agricultural Implement Workers," October 11, 1963, NAACP Papers Part 23A, Reel 41.

38 John F. Kennedy, "Address on Civil Rights," June 11, 1963, available at http://millercenter.org/president/speeches/detail/3375. For unemployment and white-collar work rates by race and sex, see Appendix, Figures A.2 and A.3.

39 James Lee, "NLRB Is Poised to Plunge into Race Bias Swim," *Daily News Record*, February 5, 1964, McCulloch Papers, Box 12, Folder 25. Burke Marshall to Harold H. Greene, January 3, 1964, Micro-copy NK-2-E-NC, Reel 91; Burke Marshall to Howard A. Glickstein, December 17, 1963, ibid. Testimony of Senator Spessard Holland, 110 Cong. Rec. 6800, 91st Cong., April 6, 1964; Testimony of Senator Allen Ellender, 110 Cong. Rec. 7041, 91st Cong., April 8, 1964. This testimony was in McCulloch's papers. McCulloch Interview 12–7–84, 31; Barbara Stoyle Mulhallen, Interview with Frank McCulloch, Sept 5, 1989, Charlottesville, Va., Collection 5843, Box 1, Folder 1159, Kheel [hereafter McCulloch Interview 9–5–89], 89.

40   Described in SPP to William J. Brennan, n.d. [September 1964], Brennan
     Papers, Box 127, Folder 5. Hearing on H.R. 7152, Before the H. Comm. on
     the Judiciary, 88th Cong. 2656, 2698–700 (1963) (statement of Robert F.
     Kennedy); Hearing on S. 1731, Before the S. Judiciary Comm., 88th Cong. 5
     (1963) (statement of Robert F. Kennedy), Glickstein Papers, MGLI 13.2479.
     The law defined businesses' discrimination or segregation that "is supported
     by State action" to include only discrimination required by the state, taken
     under color of law, or taken under color of an officially enforced custom.
     Civil Rights Act of 1964, 42 U.S.C. sec. 2000a(b), (d) (2006).
41   Reported in William O. Douglas, memo re. Salter v. City of Jackson, June
     18, 1963, Douglas Papers, Box 1281, "Memoranda by Douglas, J., O.T.
     62" Folder. Reported in William O. Douglas, memo re Ford v. Tennessee,
     June 18, 1963, ibid. Christopher Schmidt argues that the justices' discom-
     fort with the sit-in protesters' civil disobedience played an overlooked role
     in how they decided the sit-in cases. Schmidt, "The Sit-Ins and the State
     Action Doctrine." Garner v. Louisiana, 368 U.S. 157 (1961); Lombard
     v. Louisiana, 373 U.S. 267 (1963); Peterson v. Greenville, 373 U.S. 245
     (1963); Garner 373 U.S. at 185 (1963) (Harlan, J., concurring and dissent-
     ing). For the justices' internal divisions, see William O. Douglas, confer-
     ence notes, March 17, 1961, Douglas Papers, Box 1269, "Nos. 26, 27, 28
     (c), Garner v. Louisiana, Misc. Memos, Certs, O.T. 1961" Folder; William
     O. Douglas, conference notes, November 9, 1962, Douglas Papers, Box
     1281, "Argued Memos 1–25, O.T. 62" Folder. William J. Brennan, Avent
     v. North Carolina, Case No. 11, conference notes, n.d. [November 9,
     1962], Brennan Papers, Box 76, Folder 1.
42   William O. Douglas, conference notes, October 23, 1963, Douglas Papers,
     Box 1301, "Argued Cases Nos. 6–11, O.T. 1963" Folder. William J. Brennan,
     Avent v. North Carolina, Case No. 11, conference notes, n.d. [November 9,
     1962], Brennan Papers, Box 76, Folder 1 (abbreviations in notes expanded
     in text). Garner v. Louisiana, 368 U.S. 157, 178–79 (1961) (Douglas, J.,
     concurring) (relying on the Civil Rights Cases, 109 U.S. 3 (1883); Baldwin
     v. Morgan, 287 F.2d 750 (5th Cir., 1961)); Lombard v. Louisiana, 373 U.S.
     267, 274–75 (1963) (Douglas, J., concurring). Douglas's reasoning about
     the true privacy of the home presages his penumbral reasoning the next
     year in Griswold v. Connecticut, 381 U.S. 479 (1935). Drew Days notes the
     doctrinal connection between the two cases in Drew S. Days III, "Justice
     William O. Douglas and Civil Rights," in *"He Shall Not Pass This Way
     Again": The Legacy of Justice William O. Douglas*, ed. Stephen L. Wasby,
     109–17 (Pittsburgh, PA: University of Pittsburgh Press, 1990), 110–11. The
     connection between cultural and legal concerns about racial privacy and
     the emergence of sexual privacy doctrines has yet to be explored.
43   Hugo L. Black, Bell v. Maryland, No. 12, draft opinion, March 5, 1964,
     Black Papers, Box 377, "Bell v. Maryland I, Oct. Term 1963" Folder, 6,
     8–9, 11–13. On White's years in the Justice Department, see Dennis J.

Hutchinson, *The Man Who Once Was Whizzer White: A Portrait of Justice Byron R. White* (New York: Free Press, 1998), chap. 12. On the prevalence of the free-enterprise trope during the mid-twentieth century, see Elizabeth A. Fones-Wolf, *Selling Free Enterprise: The Business Assault on Labor and Liberalism, 1945–60* (Urbana: University of Illinois Press, 1995); Kim Phillips-Fein, *Invisible Hands: The Making of the Conservative Movement from the New Deal to Reagan* (New York: W. W. Norton, 2009). Reported in A. E. Dick Howard and John G. Kester, "The Deliberations of the Justices in Deciding the Sit-in Cases of June 22, 1964," manuscript, n.d. [1964], Black Papers, Box 376, "Sit-in Cases, October Term 1963" Folder.

44   The justices had the hardest time deciding the cases from Maryland on narrow grounds. Maryland had recently passed a statute banning discrimination in public accommodations, which Brennan argued provided a basis to avoid the constitutional issues. William J. Brennan, Barr v. City of Columbia draft opinion, May 5, 1964, Douglas Papers, Box 1301, "No. 9 Barr v. City of Columbia; No. 10 Bouie and Neal v. City of Columbia; No. 12, Bell et al. v. Maryland, O.T. 1963" Folder. William J. Brennan, Barr v. City of Columbia, No. 9, draft dissent, May 13, 1964, ibid. Howard and Kester, "The Deliberations of the Justices," Black Papers. McKenzie Webster argues that Clark was swayed by the Civil Rights Act's rising prospect of passage. Webster, "Note: The Warren Court's Struggle with the Sit-in Cases and the Constitutionality of Segregation in Places of Public Accommodation," *Journal of Law and Politics* 17 (2001): 373–407, 400–401. Brennan's biographers argue that the liberal justices wanted to delay decision regardless of its basis, for similar reasons. Seth Stern and Steven Wermiel, *Justice Brennan: Liberal Champion* (New York: Houghton Mifflin Harcourt, 2010), 218–19.

45   Howard and Kester, "The Deliberations of the Justices," Black Papers. William O. Douglas to Arthur J. Goldberg, May 8, 1964, Douglas Papers, Box 1300, "Memoranda by Douglas, J., O.T. 1963" Folder. William O. Douglas, Bell v. Maryland, draft dissent, April 23, 1964, Brennan Papers, Box 98, Folder 7. William O. Douglas to Conference, May 27, 1964, Douglas Papers, Box 1315, "No. 12 Bell v. Maryland, Misc. Memos, Cert Memos, O.T. 1963" Folder.

46   Tom Clark, draft opinion, June 11, 1964, Bell v. Maryland, No. 12, Douglas Papers, Box 1312, "No. 12, Bell v. Maryland, folder 4, O.T. 1963" Folder. Earl Warren to Conference, June 11, 1964, Douglas Papers, Box 1315, "No. 12 Bell v. Maryland, Misc. Memos, Cert Memos, O.T. 1963" Folder. Howard and Kester, "The Deliberations of the Justices," Black Papers. William O. Douglas to Files, June 20, 1964, Douglas Papers, Box 1315, "No. 12 Bell v. Maryland, Misc. Memos, Cert Memos, O.T. 1963" Folder. Michael Belknap argues that Clark drafted his broad state action opinion in an effort to scare Potter Stewart into joining (and moderating) the majority in favor of overturning the protesters' convictions. Belknap, *The*

Supreme Court, 165. Twenty years later, Brennan attributed his avoidance strategy to his desire not to thwart the Civil Rights Act's passage. Howard Ball and Phillip J. Cooper, *Of Power and Right: Hugo Black, William O. Douglas, and America's Constitutional Revolution* (New York: Oxford University Press, 1992), 168.

47 Bell v. Maryland, 378 U.S. 226 (1964).

48 For excellent treatments of the Civil Rights Act's long journey into law that emphasize Title VII and the intersection of labor and civil rights, see Anthony S. Chen, *The Fifth Freedom: Jobs, Politics, and Civil Rights in the United States, 1941–1972* (Princeton, N.J.: Princeton University Press, 2009); MacLean, *Freedom Is Not Enough*. Hughes Tool, 137 N.L.R.B. at 1574, 1577–78 (citing *Brown*; Bolling v. Sharpe, 347 U.S. 497 (1954); Shelley v. Kraemer, 334 U.S. 1 (1948); Hurd v. Hodge, 334 U.S. 24 (1948)).

49 John D. Pomfret, "Union Race Discrimination Is Ruled an Unfair Practice," *New York Times*, July 3, 1964, 1; "In the Name of Equality," *Wall Street Journal*, May 27, 1963, 20. Title VII's eventual dominance of workplace discrimination litigation has obscured its initial status as one skeptically viewed option among several. This and the following chapters insert contingency into that story.

50 Howard Jenkins Jr., "Collective Action, Individual Liberty and the National Labor Relations Board" (speech, Labor Law Section, Texas Bar Association, Houston TX, July 3, 1964), Jenkins Papers, Box 1, Folder 22. Robert Carter to Branch Presidents, August 13, 1964, NAACP Papers Part 13S, Reel 11; NAACP, Board of Directors Meeting, September 14, 1964, John H. Bracey Jr. and August Meier, *Papers of the NAACP: Supplement to Part 1, 1961–1965* (Bethesda, Md.: UPA, 1995), Reel 1; NAACP, Annual Meeting, January 4, 1965, ibid., Reel 2. The NAACP's enthusiasm for the NLRB actions may also have resulted from the fact that the now separate NAACP Legal Defense Fund had dedicated itself to shaping Title VII doctrine. Greenberg, *Crusaders in the Courts*; Joseph L. Mosnier, "Crafting Law in the Second Reconstruction: Julius Chambers, the NAACP Legal Defense Fund, and Title VII," Ph.D. diss., University of North Carolina, 2005, 302–5.

8 The Liberal Workplace Constitution on the Air and over the Wires

1 "New Challenges from Every Side," *Broadcasting*, September 8, 1969, 25–27. On white suburbanization, see Matthew D. Lassiter, *The Silent Majority: Suburban Politics in the Sunbelt South* (Princeton, N.J.: Princeton University Press, 2005); Joseph Crespino, *In Search of Another Country: Mississippi and the Conservative Counterrevolution* (Princeton, N.J.: Princeton University Press, 2007).

2   "Color and Television," *Washington Post*, June 21, 1970, B6. Reuel E.
    Schiller, "From Group Rights to Individual Liberties: Post-War Labor Law,
    Liberalism, and the Waning of Union Status," *Berkeley Journal of Labor
    and Employment Law* 20 (1999): 1–73. Historians attribute the rise of
    identity-group policies to a quest for bureaucratic efficiency and interest-
    group opportunism. Hugh Davis Graham, *The Civil Rights Era: Origins
    and Development of National Policy, 1960–1972* (New York: Oxford
    University Press, 1990); John David Skrentny, *The Ironies of Affirmative
    Action: Politics, Culture, and Justice in America* (Chicago: University of
    Chicago Press, 1996); John D. Skrentny, *The Minority Rights Revolution*
    (Cambridge, Mass.: Belknap Press of Harvard University Press, 2004).
    They may undercount the level of popular faith in identity-group plural-
    ism, of which the *Post* editorial is an example. Identity-group pluralism
    seemed to resolve a weakness of older models of interest-group plural-
    ism: the perception that the groups were constructed rather than organic.
    On these concerns, see Daniel R. Ernst, "Common Laborers? Industrial
    Pluralists, Legal Realists, and the Law of Industrial Disputes, 1915–1943,"
    Law and History Review 11, no. 1 (Spring 1993): 59–100. The novelty of
    such pluralism in the 1960s can be overstated, however. Mark Brilliant,
    *The Color of America Has Changed: How Racial Diversity Shaped Civil
    Rights Reform in California, 1941–1978* (New York: Oxford University
    Press, 2010).
3   On urban uprisings, see Thomas J. Sugrue, *The Origins of the Urban
    Crisis: Race and Inequality in Postwar Detroit* (Princeton, N.J.: Princeton
    University Press, 1996); Heather Ann Thompson, *Whose Detroit: Politics,
    Labor, and Race in a Modern American City* (Ithaca, N.Y.: Cornell
    University Press, 2002); Robert O. Self, *American Babylon: Race and the
    Struggle for Postwar Oakland* (Princeton, N.J.: Princeton University Press,
    2003); Thomas J. Sugrue, *Sweet Land of Liberty: The Forgotten Struggle
    for Civil Rights in the North* (Random House Trade Paperbacks, 2009).
    On the Black Panther Party and the black power movement more generally,
    see Jakobi Williams, *From the Bullet to the Ballot: The Illinois Chapter of
    the Black Panther Party and Racial Coalition Politics in Chicago* (Chapel
    Hill: University of North Carolina Press, 2013); Joshua Bloom and Waldo
    E. Martin, *Black against Empire: The History and Politics of the Black
    Panther Party* (Berkeley: University of California Press, 2012); Sugrue,
    Sweet Land of Liberty.
4   *Report of the National Advisory Commission on Civil Disorders*
    (Washington, D.C.: Government Printing Office, 1968) [hereafter Kerner
    Commission Report], 92, 139, 210–11. "The FCC Creates Some Static,"
    Newsweek, March 17, 1969, 80. Michael J. Klarman, *From Jim Crow
    to Civil Rights: The Supreme Court and the Struggle for Racial Equality*
    (New York: Oxford University Press, 2006), 429.
5   Kerner Commission Report, 212–13.

6 On the rise of consumer activism, see Lizabeth Cohen, *A Consumers' Republic: The Politics of Mass Consumption in Postwar America* (New York: Knopf, 2003). Kay Mills, *Changing Channels: The Civil Rights Case That Transformed Television* (Jackson: University Press of Mississippi, 2004), 20, 26, 65–66. Office of Communication for the UCC v. Federal Communications Commission (FCC), 359 F.2d 994, 998–99, 1006 (D.C. Cir., 1966). There is more work needed to understand how advocates made use of this new standing and how it changed administration. For a brief discussion, see Graham, *The Civil Rights Era*, 470. "$160,000 Grant to Aid Church Fight for Negro in TV-Radio," *New Pittsburgh Courier*, March 9, 1968, 5. "Another Guide to Lifting Licenses," *Broadcasting*, October 6, 1969, 36. "Employment Rules Rapped," *Broadcasting*, October 6, 1969, 10, MSS 142, Rosel Hyde Papers [hereafter Hyde Papers], Box 58, Folder 4, L. Tom Perry Special Collections, Harold B. Lee Library, Brigham Young University, Provo, Utah. "New Challenges," 25–27; Bruce Galphin, "Atlanta Blacks Win TV-Radio Involvement," *Washington Post*, March 31, 1970, A6. See also case descriptions that follow.

7 Kerner Commission Report, 203, 211–12.

8 Jerry L. Mashaw, "The Story of Motor Vehicle Manufacturers Association of the U.S. v. State Farm Mutual Automobile Insurance Co.: Law, Science and Politics in the Administrative State," in *Administrative Law Stories*, ed. Peter L. Strauss, 334–97 (New York: Foundation Press, 2006), 339–42; Reuel E. Schiller, "Rulemaking's Promise: Administrative Law and Legal Culture in the 1960s and 1970s," *Administrative Law Review* 53 (2001): 1139–88, 1140. See also Graham, *The Civil Rights Era*, 465–66. Orrin G. Judd and Earle K. Moore to FCC, April 24, 1967, RG 173, Federal Communications Commission, Hearing Docket Files, Docket No. 18244 [hereafter FCC Papers – Docket 18244], FRC Box 2, Folder 1, NACP, pars. 1–2.

9 "FCC Appointments – A Paradox," *Washington Star*, June 21, 1966, Hyde Papers, Box 51, Folder 4. "33 Years Old – And Growing," *Television Age*, March 27, 1967, 43, 45. Lawrence Laurent, "Heat's Off Broadcasters," *Washington Post*, July 21, 1966, A30. "The Quiet Man," *Broadcasting*, March 15, 1965, Hyde Papers, Box 51, Folder 4.

10 "33 Years Old – And Growing," 120; "Inside the FCC," *Television Age*, March 25, 1968, Hyde Papers, Box 52, Folder 1. "How to Become FCC Chairman: Five Who Should Know Tell Their Story," *Television Age*, May 19, 1969, 23. "F.C.C. Head Bids TV Men Reform 'Vast Wasteland,'" *New York Times*, May 9, 1961, 1. "The FCC Creates Some Static," 80. "Mr. Johnson and Mr. Hyde of the Federal Idiot Box Regulatory Agency," *Washingtonian*, December 1968, 53.

11 In re Application of Lamar Life Insurance Co., 14 F.C.C. 2d 495, 549 (1967). In re Application of Lamar Life Broadcasting Co., 14 F.C.C. 2d 431, 444, 448 (1968).

12 Nondiscrimination in Employment Practices of Broadcast Licensees, 33
    Fed. Reg. 9960, pars. 2, 4, 7–9 (1968).
13 See, e.g., Senator Abraham Ribicoff to FCC, June 16, 1967, FCC Papers –
    Docket 18244, FRC Box 2, Folder 1; Representative Samuel N. Friedel to
    Rosel H. Hyde, August 23, 1968, ibid.; Representative John Conyers, Jr.,
    to FCC, July 13, 1967, ibid. "The Chairman: A Three-Word Solution,"
    Television Age, March 27, 1967, 51. "Rivals in Partnership," ibid., 48;
    "The Commission, Congress and the Executive," ibid., March 24, 1969,
    64. Stephen J. Pollak to Rosel H. Hyde, May 21, 1968, 33 Fed. Reg. 9960,
    9964 (1968).
14 Nondiscrimination in Employment Practices of Broadcast Licensees, 33
    Fed. Reg. 9960, par. 3 (1968).
15 Howard A. Glickstein to Rosel H. Hyde, September 9, 1968, FCC Papers –
    Docket 18244, FRC Box 2, Folder 1, 3.
16 Pollak to Hyde, May 21, 1968, 33 Fed. Reg. at 9964. Ward McCreedy
    to FCC, November 12, 1968, FCC Papers – Docket 18244, FRC Box 2,
    Folder 2, 1–2. FCC, "Background Staff Legal Memorandum," n.d. [Spring
    1963] [hereafter FCC 1963 Memo], enclosed in N. Thompson Powers to
    Norbert A. Schlei, July 8, 1963, Micro-copy NK-2-E-EO, Reel 91, 3.
17 FCC 1963 Memo, 2–3. Pollak to Hyde, May 21, 1968, 33 Fed. Reg. at
    9964; Robert L. Carter and Barbara A. Morris to FCC, June 9, 1967,
    NAACP Papers, Part V, Box 315, Folder 15; Robert L. Carter to FCC,
    September 6, 1968, FCC Papers – Docket 18244, FRC Box 2, Folder 1.
    Glickstein to Hyde, September 9, 1968, FCC Papers – Docket 18244,
    A-7. Earle K. Moore and Edward A. Bernstein to FCC, October 7,
    1968, FCC Papers – Docket 18244, FRC Box 2, Folder 1 (citing Burton
    v. Wilmington Parking Authority and Public Utilities Commission of
    District of Columbia v. Pollak).
18 FCC 1963 Memo; Pollak to Hyde, May 21, 1968, 33 Fed. Reg. at 9964
    (citing *Burton*, the Court's broadest sit-in case). Earle K. Moore and
    Orrin G. Judd, July 19, 1967, FCC Papers – Docket 18244, FRC Box 2,
    Folder 1. *Burton*, 365 U.S. 715, 722 (1961) (emphasis added). Glickstein
    to Hyde, September 9, 1968, FCC Papers – Docket 18244, A-2-A-4
    (emphasis added). Glickstein's sufficiency-of-contacts argument was simi-
    lar to those the NAACP and the Oil Workers made during the 1950s. See
    Chapter 5.
19 McCreedy to Hyde, November 12, 1968, FCC Papers – Docket 18244,
    1–2. Glickstein to Hyde, September 9, 1968, ibid., 6, App. B.
20 Graham, *The Civil Rights Era*; Skrentny, *Ironies of Affirmative Action*;
    Bruce Ackerman, *We the People*, vol. 3: *The Civil Rights Revolution*
    (Cambridge, Mass.: Harvard University Press, 2014). "Wirtz Says No to
    Race Quotas," *Washington Post*, June 27, 1968, 71.
21 "1967 Broadcasting Yearbook," *Broadcasting*, January, 1967, A-170.
    Even after Congress expanded Title VII in 1972 to cover smaller

employers, 76% of AM radio stations, 86% of FM stations, and 12% of TV broadcasters still fell outside the law's reach. Ibid. Alan Reitman to FCC, October 7, 1968, FCC Papers – Docket 18244, FRC Box 2, Folder 2. Glickstein to Hyde, September 9, 1968, ibid., 3–4, 8 n. 9.

22 "The FCC Creates Some Static," 80. "Mr. Johnson and Mr. Hyde of the Federal Idiot Box Regulatory Agency," 53. LeGrand Baker interview of Rosel H. Hyde, October 1983, Hyde Papers, Box 64, Folder 3. Technically, the FCC's common carrier policies affected licensees and permittees; for simplicity's sake, I use "licensee" to refer to the broadcasters and common carriers affected by the FCC's rules.

23 John Herbers, "Decline of Rights Issue," *New York Times*, January 19, 1968, 19; John W. Finney, "Congress: A Mood of Weariness and Frustration," *New York Times*, May 26, 1968, E8.

24 Part 73 – Radio Broadcast Services: Nondiscrimination in Employment Practices, 34 Fed. Reg. 9284, 9284–86 (June 12, 1969). Nondiscrimination in Employment Practices of Broadcast Licensees, 35 Fed. Reg. 8825, 8826–28 (June 6, 1970). Nondiscrimination in Employment Practices of Communication Common Carriers, 35 Fed. Reg. 12892, 12894 (August 14, 1970). The FCC's requirements applied to broadcasters with five or more full-time employees and common carriers with sixteen or more.

25 FCC 1963 Memo, 3. Part 73 – Radio Broadcast Services: Nondiscrimination in Employment Practices, 34 Fed. Reg. at 9284 (June 12, 1969). Communications Common Carriers: Nondiscrimination in Employment Practices, 34 Fed. Reg. 19200, 19201 (December 4, 1969). Richard K. Berg to Nicholas deB. Katzenbach, October 10, 1961, Micro-copy NK-2-E-EO, Reel 91; "Effect of Monopoly-Type Licenses," n.d. [1963], DOJ Papers – BM, Box 2, "1964 Sit-in Cases" Folder.

26 Part 73 – Radio Broadcast Services: Nondiscrimination in Employment Practices, 34 Fed. Reg. 9284 (June 12, 1969) (Comm'r Bartley not participating; Comm'r Robert E. Lee concurring and dissenting in part). See also Communications Common Carriers: Nondiscrimination in Employment Practices, 34 Fed. Reg. 19200 (December 4, 1969) (Comm'r Bartley dissenting; Comm'r Robert E. Lee concurring; Chairman Burch and Comm'r Wells not participating). No Republicans other than Lee participated in the latter decision. "Nixon Ready to Move on FCC," *Broadcasting*, September 1, 1969, 22; "New Chief for the FCC," *Time*, September 5, 1969, 75. "Senate OK Appears Set for Burch, Wells," *Broadcasting*, October 20, 1969, 60. Nondiscrimination in Employment Practices of Broadcast Licensees, 35 Fed. Reg. 8825 (June 6, 1970); Nondiscrimination in Employment Practices of Communications Common Carriers, 35 Fed. Reg. 12892 (August 14, 1970). All but Bartley signed on to amending the broadcast rules to protect against sex discrimination. Part 73 – Radio Broadcast Services: Equal Employment Opportunities, 36 Fed. Reg. 25012 (December 28, 1971).

27 "New Chief for the FCC," 76; "Strange New Man at the FCC," *Forbes*, November 15, 1969, 27. Nancy MacLean, *Freedom Is Not Enough: The Opening of the American Workplace* (Cambridge, Mass.: Harvard University Press, 2008), 70–71; Anthony S. Chen, *The Fifth Freedom: Jobs, Politics, and Civil Rights in the United States, 1941–1972* (Princeton, N.J.: Princeton University Press, 2009), 182–90; Ackerman, *We the People*, vol. 3. For Nixon's campaign pledge, see ibid., 77–78. On the Philadelphia Plan, see Graham, *The Civil Rights Era*, chap. 13; MacLean, *Freedom Is Not Enough*, 95–100; Skrentny, *Ironies of Affirmative Action*, 193–209; Sugrue, *Sweet Land of Liberty*, 363–64. The DOL claimed the Fifth Amendment authorized these policies. Graham, *The Civil Rights Era*, 330–31. Don Irwin, "Burch Faces Question of Politics vs. FCC," *Los Angeles Times*, September 20, 1970, G4. "Senate OK Appears Set for Burch, Wells," 60.

28 Leah M. Wright, "The Loneliness of the Black Conservative: Black Republicans and the Grand Ole Party, 1964–1980," Ph.D. diss., Princeton University, 2009. "Senate OK Appears Set for Burch, Wells," 62. Barry Goldwater, "Civil Rights," 110 Cong. Rec. 14318, 14318–19 (1964). "Fair Employment Milestone – Statement by Senator Goldwater," *Congressional Record*, July 9, 1964, Jenkins Papers, Box 1, Folder 20. "Terry," n.d. [ca. 1970], Personal and Political Papers of Senator Barry M. Goldwater, Manuscript 1 [hereafter Goldwater Papers], "Goldwater: Media, 85th Congress; Speeches, Statements, Remarks – 'The Labor Bosses – America's Third Party,' June 16, 1958" Folder, Arizona Historical Society, Phoenix. Barry M. Goldwater, "Individual Views of Mr. Goldwater," n.d. [ca. Jan.–June 1964], Goldwater Papers, "Goldwater: 1964 Presidential Campaign Speeches – Labor, 1961–1964" Folder, 7. See Chapters 4, 6, and 12. See also Sophia Z. Lee, "Whose Rights? Litigating the Right to Work, 1940–1980," in *The Right and Labor in America: Politics, Ideology, and Imagination*, ed. Nelson Lichtenstein and Elizabeth Tandy Shermer, 160–80 (Philadelphia: University of Pennsylvania Press, 2012).

29 "Strange New Man at the FCC," 26; "New Chief for the FCC," 75–76. Elizabeth Tandy Shermer, *Sunbelt Capitalism: Phoenix and the Transformation of American Politics* (Philadelphia: University of Pennsylvania Press, 2013). Bayard Rustin, "The Blacks and the Unions," *Harper's Magazine*, May 1971, Glickstein Papers, MGLI 29.2657, 78–79. On the complicated politics of Nixon's Philadelphia Plan, compare Dean J. Kotlowski, *Nixon's Civil Rights: Politics, Principle, and Policy* (Cambridge, Mass.: Harvard University Press, 2002), 97–114; Jefferson Cowie, *Stayin' Alive: The 1970s and the Last Days of the Working Class* (New York: New Press, 2010), 150–51; Graham, *The Civil Rights Era*, 325. Nondiscrimination in Employment Practices of Broadcast Licensees, 35 Fed. Reg. at 8826–27; Nondiscrimination in Employment Practices of

Communications Common Carriers, 35 Fed. Reg. at 12894. For more on Republican attacks on union discrimination, see Chapter 9.

30 NAACP, "NAACP Urges No Rate Increase for AT&T Because of Job Bias," January 30, 1971, NAACP Papers, Part VI-A, Box 38, Folder 1.

31 "New Challenges," 25–27. "$160,000 Grant to Aid Church Fight for Negro in TV-Radio," 5; "How United Church Stirs Up the Cats," *Broadcasting*, October 6, 1969, 37; "United Church of Christ, NAACP Plan Fair Employment Drive in Radio, TV," *Philadelphia Tribune*, March 17, 1970, 20. "Senate OK Appears Set for Burch, Wells," 62. "Suit by Mexican-Americans to Charge TV Discrimination," *Washington Post*, July 22, 1969, A8. WGN of Colorado, Inc., 31 F.C.C.2d 413 (1971). NOW, NY Chapter v. FCC, 555 F.2d 1002 (D.C. Cir. 1977); In re Applications of 1972 License Renewal Applications for 17 Broadcast Facilities Licensed to the Richmond, Va. Area, 54 F.C.C.2d 953 (1975); In re Application of 1972 License Renewal Applications for 28 Broadcast Facilities Licensed to the Philadelphia, Pa. Area, 53 F.C.C.2d 104 (1975); In re Inquiry into the Employment Policies and Practices of Certain Broadcast Stations Located in Florida, 44 F.C.C.2d 735 (1974); Galphin, "Atlanta Blacks Win TV-Radio Involvement."

32 Hearing before Subcommittee on Communications of the Senate Commerce Committee, November 11, 1975 (Statement of Richard A. Wiley, Chairman, FCC), Leadership Conference on Civil Rights Records [hereafter LCCR Papers], Part I, Box 101, "FCC Guidelines, 1975–77" Folder, LCMD, 13–14; see, e.g., 1972 License Renewal Applications for 17 Broadcast Facilities Licensed to the Richmond, Va. Area, 54 F.C.C.2d at 958–59. In re Application of Evening Star Broadcasting Co., 27 F.C.C.2d 316, 327 (1971) (increasing from 16 to 23 full-time-equivalent positions); Columbus Broadcasting Coalition v. F.C.C., 505 F.2d 320, 329 (1974). CBS, Inc., 51 F.C.C.2d 273, 275 (1975). In the Matter of Letter to Everett C. Parker, 44 F.C.C.2d 647, 655–56 (1974); 1972 License Renewal Applications for 17 Broadcast Facilities Licensed to the Richmond, Va. Area, 54 F.C.C.2d at 959. In re Application of Time-Life Broadcast, Inc., 33 F.C.C.2d 1050, 1058–59 (1972).

33 1972 License Renewal Applications for 17 Broadcast Facilities Licensed to the Richmond, Va. Area, 54 F.C.C.2d at 959. In re Applications of Rust Communications Group, Inc., 53 F.C.C.2d 355, 363 (1975). Columbus Broadcasting Coalition v. F.C.C., 505 F.2d at 329 (internal quotations omitted); CBS, Inc., 51 F.C.C.2d at 274–75. Larger stations may have worried about Title VII complaints as well, and in a few instances simultaneous complaints were filed, but since the FCC generally deferred action once the EEOC was involved, most employers described here were under immediate scrutiny from the FCC only. Also note that in many of these cases, change began before employers generally started to perceive Title VII as a serious threat.

34   A. A. Berle, *Economic Power and the Free Society* (New York: Fund for the Republic, 1957), 15; Sanford L. Jacobs, "Women Employes Call Bell System Duties Boring, Oppressive," *Wall Street Journal*, May 12, 1972, 24. AT&T had two dozen subsidiary operating companies, referred to collectively as the Bell System. Phyllis A. Wallace, "Introduction," in *Equal Employment Opportunity and the AT&T Case*, ed. Phyllis A. Wallace, 1–8 (Cambridge, Mass.: MIT Press, 1976), 1.

35   Aaron Porter, "Norris, Schmidt, Green, Harris, Higginbotham & Associates: The Sociological Import of Philadelphia Cause Lawyers," in *Cause Lawyering: Political Commitments and Professional Responsibilities*, ed. Austin Sarat and Stuart A. Scheingold, 151–80 (New York: Oxford University Press, 1998), 151–52. Petitions Opposing Proposed AT&T System Increased Tariff Schedules and for Other Relief, January 6, 1971, RG 173, FCC, Hearing Docket Files, Docket 19129, FRC Box 1, Binder 1, NACP; Stanley P. Hebert and David A. Copus to FCC, Memorandum in Support of EEOC Petition to Intervene, December 10, 1970, NAACP Papers, Part V, Box 353, Folder 1, 1–2. For a detailed account of the EEOC petition's origins, see Marjorie A. Stockford, *The Bellwomen: The Story of the Landmark AT&T Sex Discrimination Case* (New Brunswick, N.J.: Rutgers University Press, 2004), 21–30. For the EEOC's constitutional arguments, see Sophia Z. Lee, "Race, Sex, and Rulemaking: Administrative Constitutionalism and the Workplace, 1960 to the Present," *Virginia Law Review* 96 (June 2010): 799–881. David Cashdan for California Rural Legal Assistance and Mexican American Legal Defense Fund to FCC, January 18, 1971, NAACP Papers, Part V, Box 352, Folder 8; David Cashdan for American Civil Liberties Union to FCC, January 18, 1971, NAACP Papers, Part V, Box 352, Folder 8; David Cashdan for Nathaniel Jones to FCC, January 18, 1971, NAACP Papers, Part V, Box 353, Folder 1. Phyllis A. Wallace and Jack E. Nelson, "Legal Processes and Strategies of Intervention," in *Equal Employment Opportunity and the AT&T Case*, ed. Phyllis A. Wallace, 243–52 (Cambridge, Mass.: MIT Press, 1976), 244 n. 4. Christopher Lydon, "Job Bias at Bell Charged by Panel: 20,000-Page Report Finds Women Are Oppressed – Policy on Blacks Scored," *New York Times*, December 2, 1971, 1, 30. On how computers facilitated statistical measures of discrimination, see Ackerman, *We the People*, vol. 3, chap. 8. For a summary of AT&T's defense, see "Bias Charges in Hiring: AT&T Fights Back," *U.S. News & World Report*, August 14, 1972, 66–68. Grace Lichtenstein, "AT&T Assailed as Racist Monopoly," *New York Times*, May 9, 1972, 33. On the daily drama of the hearings, see Stockford, *The Bellwomen*, 114–32. See also Benton Williams, "AT&T and the Private-Sector Origins of Private-Sector Affirmative Action," *Journal of Policy History* 20, no. 4 (2008): 542–68, 550–52. Jacobs, "Women Employes Call Bell System Duties Boring, Oppressive."

36 Jo Anne Levine, "Landmark Bias Case Settlement," *Washington Post*, September 9, 1973. Griggs v. Duke Power Co., 401 U.S. 424 (1971). For disagreement about the settlement's effectiveness, compare Stockford, *The Bellwomen*, 212–13, and Lois Kathryn Herr, *Women, Power and AT&T: Winning Rights in the Workplace* (Boston: Northeastern University Press, 2003), 156–63, who emphasize the settlement's positive effect, particularly on women's opportunities, with Venus Green, *Race on the Line: Gender, Labor, and Technology in the Bell System, 1880–1980* (Durham, N.C.: Duke University Press, 2001), 237–42, who argues that racism and sexism in the telecommunications industry changed little.

37 William Chapman, "AT&T Agrees to Pay Victims of Alleged Discrimination," *Washington Post,* January 19, 1973, 1; Shapiro, "Women on the Line," 90; Douglas W. Cray, "Job Discrimination Charges Grow: Federal Agency's Efforts Broaden," *New York Times*, March 4, 1973, 170. Equal Employment Opportunity Act of 1972, sec. 5, Pub. L. 92-261, 86 Stat. 103 (March 24, 1972). Jo Anne Levine, "Landmark Bias Case Settlement," *Washington Post*, September 9, 1973, G1.

38 Dorothy Sue Cobble, *The Other Women's Movement: Workplace Justice and Social Rights in Modern America* (Princeton, N.J.: Princeton University Press, 2004); Serena Mayeri, *Reasoning from Race: Feminism, Law, and the Civil Rights Revolution* (Cambridge, Mass.: Harvard University Press, 2011); Kenneth W. Mack, *Representing the Race: The Creation of the Civil Rights Lawyer* (Cambridge, Mass.: Harvard University Press, 2012), chap. 9; MacLean, *Freedom Is Not Enough*. Robert C. Post and Reva B. Siegel, "Legislative Constitutionalism and Section Five Power: Policentric Interpretation of the Family and Medical Leave Act," *Yale Law Journal* 112 (2003): 1943–2059, 1988–93. For a history of the feminist movement's constitutional strategy, see Mayeri, *Reasoning from Race*; Cary A. Franklin, "The Anti-Stereotyping Principle in Constitutional Sex Discrimination Law," *New York University Law Review* 85, no. 1 (2010): 83–173.

39 NOW, NY Chapter v. FCC, 555 F.2d 1002 (D.C. Cir. 1977); National Broadcasting Co., 58 F.C.C.2d 419 (1976). Herbert and Copus to FCC, December 10, 1970, NAACP Papers, 33–35, 47. The Supreme Court first considered the status of sex discrimination under its post-*Brown* equal protection doctrine in the fall of 1971. Reed v. Reed, 404 U.S. 71, 72–73, 77 (1971). Maclean, *Freedom Is Not Enough*; Mayeri, *Reasoning from Race*; Skrentny, *The Minority Rights Revolution*; William N. Eskridge and John Ferejohn, *A Republic of Statutes: The New American Constitution* (New Haven, Conn.: Yale University Press, 2010); Deborah Dinner, "The Costs of Reproduction: History and the Legal Construction of Sex Equality," *Harvard Civil Rights–Civil Liberties Law Review* 46 (2011): 415–95; Franklin, "The Anti-Stereotyping Principle."

40 Executive Order No. 10925, 26 Fed. Reg. 1977 (March 8, 1961). Report
    of the White House Conference on Equal Employment Opportunity, n.d.
    [ca. September 1965], NLRB Papers – CMF Miller, Box 8, "Chairman's
    Files, Government Agencies and Organizations, Equal Employment
    Opportunity Comm." Folder, 8–9, 20–23. In re Application of Evening
    Star Broadcasting Co., 27 F.C.C.2d at 327. See also In re Application of
    Universal Communications Corp., 27 F.C.C.2d 1022, 1028 (March 3,
    1971); In re Application of Time-Life Broadcast, Inc., 33 F.C.C.2d at 1059.
    1972 License Renewal Applications for 17 Broadcast Facilities Licensed
    to the Richmond, Va. Area, 54 F.C.C.2d at 956–57; In re Applications of
    Rust Communications Group, Inc., 53 F.C.C.2d at 363; In the Matter of
    Nondiscrimination in the Employment Policies and Practices of Broad.
    Licensees, 60 F.C.C.2d 226, par. 44 (1976). Also see this order for policy
    detail and nuance; see as well Patricia Eileen Naktenis, "Use of Petitions
    by Minority Groups to Deny Broadcast License Renewals," *Duke Law
    Journal* 1978, no. 1 (March 1978): 271–301.
41 William E. Pollard, "Ending Job Discrimination: The Union Role,"
    (speech, Twenty-Fifth Annual Meeting of the Industrial Relations Research
    Association, 1972), Glickstein Papers, MGLI 29.2657, 374–78. Report
    of the White House Conference, NLRB Papers – CMF Miller, 8–9. For
    a nuanced account of labor's position on affirmative action, see Dennis
    Deslippe, *Protesting Affirmative Action: The Struggle over Equality after
    the Civil Rights Revolution* (Baltimore: Johns Hopkins University Press,
    2012).
42 Irving Spiegel, "Two Jewish Leaders Score Minority Job Quotas,'" *New
    York Times,* June 30, 1972, 11. Philip E. Hoffman to President Nixon
    and Senator McGovern, August 4, 1972, LCCR Papers, Part I, Box 114,
    "Quota Hiring: Affirmative Action, 1972" Folder. Samuel Rabinove,
    Letter to the Editor, "Crow Jimism," *New York Times*, March 27, 1972,
    34. For excellent treatments of the complicated politics of affirmative
    action and its opponents, see Deslippe, *Protesting Affirmative Action*;
    Cowie, *Stayin' Alive*, 240–43; MacLean, *Freedom Is Not Enough*; Reva
    B. Siegel, "Equality Talk: Antisubordination and Anticlassification Values
    in Constitutional Struggles over Brown," *Harvard Law Review* 117, no. 5
    (March 2004):1470–1547, 1473. Kenyon C. Burke to David A. Shulte,
    July 13, 1972, LCCR Papers, Part I, Box 114, "Quota Hiring: Affirmative
    Action, 1972" Folder. Vernon Jordan, "Quotas Designed to Split Labor-
    Civil Rights Alliance," September 19, 1972, ibid., 2. For unemployment
    rates, see Appendix, Figure A.2. Note, however, that white unemployment
    rates in the 1970s at their worst were only slightly higher than African
    American unemployment rates at their best.
43 Robert E. Hampton to Heads of Departments and Agencies, May 11,
    1971, LCCR Papers, Part I, Box 114, "Quota Hiring: Affirmative Action,
    1972" Folder. American Jewish Committee, "Statement on Affirmative

Action," December 3, 1972, ibid. For more thorough treatments of liberal Jewish groups' disagreements over and critiques of quotas, see Deslippe, *Protesting Affirmative Action*; Laura Kalman, *Right Star Rising: A New Politics, 1974–1980* (New York: W. W. Norton, 2010), 183–84, 191–94; MacLean, *Freedom Is Not Enough*, 185–224.

44 Daniel Seligman, "How 'Equal Opportunity' Turned into Employment Quotas," *Fortune*, March 1973, 160, 165, 168. This book's front cover is based on the artwork that accompanied Seligman's article. On cultural manifestations of the kind of white anxiety depicted in the article, see Eric Porter, "Affirming and Disaffirming Actions," in *America in the Seventies*, ed. Beth L. Bailey and Dave Farber, 50–74 (Lawrence: University Press of Kansas, 2004), 67–70.

45 For why this issue turned liberal unions from affirmative action supporters to opponents, see Deslippe, *Protesting Affirmative Action*. On employers' adoption of affirmative action policies, see MacLean, *Freedom Is Not Enough*, chaps. 7, 9; Jennifer Delton, *Racial Integration in Corporate America, 1940–1990* (New York: Cambridge University Press, 2009), pt. 2. Equal Employment Opportunity Commission v. Amer. Tel. & Telegraph, 419 F. Supp. 1022, 1044 (E.D. Pa. 1976). For the history of debates over the relationship between pregnancy discrimination and sex discrimination under Title VII and the Constitution's equal protection provisions, see Mayeri, *Reasoning from Race*; Dinner, "The Costs of Reproduction."

46 EEOC v. AT&T, 419 F. Supp. at 1044–45. EEOC v. AT&T, 556 F.2d 167, 179–80 (3rd Cir. 1977) (internal quotations omitted). The Supreme Court denied review. Communications Workers of America v. Equal Employment Opportunity Commission, 438 U.S. 915 (1978); Telephone Coordinating Council, IBEW v. Equal Employment Opportunity Commission, 438 U.S. 915 (1978); Alliance of Independent Telephone Unions v. Equal Employment Opportunity Commission, 438 U.S. 915 (1978).

47 In the Matter of Nondiscrimination in the Employment Policies and Practices of Broad. Licensees, 60 F.C.C.2d 226, par. 10 (1976). Labor Press Service, "Landmark Employment Discrimination Decision Confirms $150 Million Settlement for Workers," May 30, 1977, RG 98–002, Series 1, Artificial Collections: George Meany Memorial Archives, Vertical Files, 1881–1999 [hereafter GMMA-VF Papers], Box 10, Folder 12. EEOC v. AT&T, 556 F.2d at 180. On complaint-by-complaint Title VII litigation in the textile industry, see MacLean, *Freedom Is Not Enough*, chap. 3. For the steel-industry consent decree, see Judith Stein, *Running Steel, Running America: Race, Economic Policy, and the Decline of Liberalism* (Chapel Hill: University of North Carolina Press, 1998), 170–76.

48 Labor Press Service, "Landmark Employment Discrimination Decision," May 30, 1977, GMMA-VF Papers. EEOC v. AT&T, 556 F.2d at 180.

9 The NLRB Expands the Liberal Workplace Constitution

1   See Chapter 7 for more on the NLRB's decision. Howard Jenkins Jr. to
     Mother, July 31, 1968, Jenkins Papers, Box 1, Folder 32. Howard Jenkins,
     interviewed by Barbara Stoyle Mulhallen, Kensington, Md., August 9,
     1988, Jenkins Papers, Box 2, Folder 25, 7, 35–36.
2   Examples include Robert L. Molinar, "The National Labor Relations Act
     and Racial Discrimination," *Boston College Industrial and Commercial
     Law Review* 7 (1965): 601–16, 602; Herbert Hill, "The Role of Law
     in Securing Equal Employment Opportunity: Legal Powers and Social
     Change," *Boston College Industrial and Commercial Law Review*
     7 (1965): 625–52, 648; and Sanford Jay Rosen, "The Law and Racial
     Discrimination in Employment," *California Law Review* 53 (1965):
     729–99, 795. Sam Barone, "The Impact of Recent Developments in Civil
     Rights on Employers and Unions," *Labor Law Journal* (July 1966): 413–40,
     Goldwater Papers, "Goldwater: Legislative Health, Education & Welfare;
     Racial Discrimination in Unions, 1966–1970" Folder. William B. Gould,
     "The Negro Revolution and the Law of Collective Bargaining," *Fordham
     Law Review* 34 (December 1965): 207–68, 246–49. Murray Seeger,
     "NLRB May Be Forced to Rule on Bias Cases," *Los Angeles Times*, March
     16, 1969, 14. Louis M. Kohlmeier, "NLRB's Role in Job Bias Disputes
     Is Enhanced by the Supreme Court," *Wall Street Journal*, November 11,
     1969, 3. "Hail Court's Bias Case Ruling as Legal Landmark for Labor,"
     Chicago Defender, December 6, 1969, 36. Recent scholarship declares
     Title VII an unexpected and unparalleled success as a remedy for work-
     place discrimination. Paul Frymer, *Black and Blue: African Americans, the
     Labor Movement, and the Decline of the Democratic Party* (Princeton,
     N.J.: Princeton University Press, 2007); Nancy MacLean, *Freedom Is Not
     Enough: The Opening of the American Workplace* (Cambridge, Mass.:
     Harvard University Press, 2008). I do not question these scholars' assess-
     ment of Title VII. I do, however, wish to insert some contingency into
     their narratives by demonstrating that it was not until years after the Civil
     Rights Act's passage that Title VII's efficacy became clear and it became
     civil rights advocates' nearly exclusive means for redressing workplace
     discrimination.
3   "Nixon Plans to Name Chicago Labor Lawyer for NLRB Chairman,"
     Wall Street Journal, February 19, 1970, 23. E. B. Miller, "How to Create
     Business for Labor Lawyers," *Business Lawyer*, January 1970, McCulloch
     Papers, Box 5, Folder 21. Christopher Lydon, "Business Lawyer Named
     to N.L.R.B.," *New York Times*, February 19, 1970, 1. "Labor Board
     Nominee," *New York Times*, February 21, 1970, 64. Charles Culhane,
     "NLRB, Busy Defusing Disputes, Draws Little Notice until Appointment
     Time," *CPR National Journal*, December 19, 1970, 2757, Jenkins Papers,
     Box 1, Folder 36. Al Prince, "How to Create Business for Labor Lawyers,"

Houston Post, April 26, 1970, 2, McCulloch Papers, Box 5, Folder 21; Mainest Connor, Patricia Greenfield, and Shelley Coppock interview with Edward B. Miller, ILR Conference Room, Cornell University, Ithaca, N.Y., October 23, 1984, Collection 5740, Box 1, "Miller" Folder, Kheel, 3.

4   Donald MacLean to Jay Hall, July 31, 1958, DeMille Papers, Box 1195, Folder 4. Gilbert J. Gall, *The Politics of Right to Work: The Labor Federations as Special Interests, 1943–1979* (New York: Greenwood Press, 1988), 97–98. See Chapter 6. Rick Perlstein, *Before the Storm: Barry Goldwater and the Unmaking of the American Consensus* (New York: Hill and Wang, 2001), 24; Richard J. H. Johnston, "Drive to Socialism Charged by Taft," *New York Times*, March 1, 1952, 7; "Illinois Senator Urges Election of Knowland," *Los Angeles Times*, October 15, 1958, 24. On Dirksen's role in civil rights legislation, see Bruce Ackerman, *We the People*: vol. 3: *The Civil Rights Revolution* (Cambridge, Mass.: Harvard University Press, 2014); Sean Farhang, *The Litigation State: Public Regulation and Private Lawsuits in the United States* (Princeton, N.J.: Princeton University Press, 2010); MacLean, *Freedom Is Not Enough*; Anthony S. Chen, *The Fifth Freedom: Jobs, Politics, and Civil Rights in the United States, 1941–1972* (Princeton, N.J.: Princeton University Press, 2009). Griffin switched from the House to the Senate in 1966. For his moderate voting record, see http://www.govtrack.us/congress/members/robert_griffin/404810. Republican Party Platform of 1968, August 5, 1968, available at http://www.presidency.ucsb.edu/ws/ index.php?pid=25841; Orville Freeman to Frank W. McCulloch, confidential memo, September 9, 1968, McCulloch Papers, Box 12, Folder 10 [hereafter Freeman Memo]; Richard Levine, "NLRB under Fire," *Wall Street Journal*, March 29, 1968, 1.

5   Dorothy A. McRae to Peter Dominick, August 30, 1965, Senator Peter H. Dominick Papers [hereafter Dominick Papers], Box 80, Folder 2, University of Denver Penrose Library Special Collections, Denver; James P. Rigg to Peter Dominick, February 7, 1966, Dominick Papers, Box 81, Folder 5; *Congressional Record* 116, no. 104, June 23, 1970 (91st Congress, 2d Sess.), Dominick Papers, Box 134, Folder 106; Peter H. Dominick to J. Nicholas Shriver Jr., September 22, 1970, Dominick Papers, Box 144, Folder 9; Senator Peter H. Dominick to Senator Barry M. Goldwater, May 27, 1970, Goldwater Papers, "Goldwater: Legislative, Labor & Public Welfare, Labor Unions, 1969–1970" Folder. "Labor Law Writers Criticize the N.L.R.B," *New York Times*, March 27, 1965, 34; Charles Bartlett, "Right-to-work Donnybrook Looms," *Los Angeles Times*, May 25, 1965, A5. Statement by Representative John J. Rhodes, Chairman, Republican Policy Committee, on H.R. 77, June 24, 1965, Dominick Papers, Box 80, Folder 39. Thomas J. Foley, "Kuchel Opposes 'Right-to-Work,'" *Los Angeles Times*, January 15, 1965, 2; Editors, "Mr. Powell's Quick Draw," *Pittsburgh Courier*, January 23, 1965, 8; "Adams Holds Out for Job Rights," *Chicago Defender*, January 21, 1965, 4.

Walter Davis to Don Slaiman, January 5, 1965, DCR Papers, Box 6, Folder 21. "New Powell Plan on Union Bias Due," *New York Times,* May 27, 1965, 25; "Powell Snags Right to Work Laws' Repeal," *Chicago Tribune,* June 1, 1965, B23; "Rep. Powell's Price," *Wall Street Journal,* August 2, 1965, 10. Charles V. Hamilton, *Adam Clayton Powell, Jr.: The Political Biography of an American Dilemma* (New York: Atheneum, 1991).

6   Jennifer Delton recognizes but does not explore in depth the antiunion uses to which employers put their antidiscrimination efforts. Jennifer Delton, *Racial Integration in Corporate America, 1940–1990* (New York: Cambridge University Press, 2009). This preceded and to an extent presaged employer support for reverse discrimination claims in the 1970s. See MacLean, *Freedom Is Not Enough,* chap. 7. Republican Party Platform of 1960, July 25, 1960; Republican Party Platform of 1964, July 13, 1964; Republican Party Platform of 1968, August 5, 1968, all available at http://www.presidency.ucsb.edu/platforms.php. C. B. Powell, "Rockefeller Didn't Pull Any Punches," *New York Amsterdam News,* July 30, 1960, 1; Dean J. Kotlowski, *Nixon's Civil Rights: Politics, Principle, and Policy* (Cambridge, Mass.: Harvard University Press, 2002), 106–7; "Transcript of the Second Nixon-Kennedy Debate on Nation-Wide Television," *New York Times,* October 8, 1960, 10. Under the 1960 platform, employers would be subject only to a permanent version of Eisenhower's Government Contract Committee. Statement by John J. Rhodes, June 24, 1965, Dominick Papers. Freeman Memo. Thomas O'Hanlon, "The Case against the Unions," *Fortune,* January 1968, McCulloch Papers, Box 12, Folder 27; "Job Bias Article Branded Dishonest," *AFL-CIO News,* January 13, 1968, ibid. For similar Republican arguments, see Chapter 8.

7   Freeman Memo; quoted in Christopher Lydon, "Business Lawyer Named to NLRB," reprinted in *Daily Labor News,* February 19, 1970, McCulloch Papers, Box 5, Folder 21. Harry Bernstein, "Negro Reported Nixon Choice to Head NLRB," *Los Angeles Times,* March 2, 1969, A9. Carl L. Shipley to Peter Flanigan, November 23, 1968, Jenkins Papers, Box 1, Folder 35. "Delay in Naming NLRB Chairman," n.a., n.d., McCulloch Papers, Box 5, Folder 22; Levine, "NLRB under Fire."

8   On Wallace, see Dan T. Carter, *The Politics of Rage: George Wallace, the Origins of the New Conservatism, and the Transformation of American Politics* (New York: Simon & Schuster, 1995). Kevin P. Phillips, *The Emerging Republican Majority* (New Rochelle, N.Y.: Arlington House, 1969). See, generally, Jefferson Cowie, *Stayin' Alive: The 1970s and the Last Days of the Working Class* (New York: New Press, 2010), chap. 3. Nixon's Silent Majority and rhetoric quotes in ibid., pages 126 and 127, respectively. Republican Party Platform of 1972, August 21, 1972 available at http://www.presidency.ucsb.edu/platforms.php.

For instance, Nixon had a muted response to the 1970 postal workers strike, a hot-button issue for right-to-work advocates. Cowie, *Stayin' Alive*, 140.

9   Edward B. Miller, "A View from the National Labor Relations Board" (speech, Kansas City Bar Association Seminar, Kansas City, Mo., April 11, 1974), UAW Washington Office: Steve Schlossberg Collection [hereafter Schlossberg Papers], Box 23, Folder 6, ALUA, 5, 10–11, 19.

10 Howard Jenkins Jr. (speech, Colorado and Denver Bar Associations' Institute on Civil Rights, December 12, 1964), Jenkins Papers, Box 1, Folder 22. Miller, "A View," Schlossberg Papers, 2, 6, 12. Bekins Moving & Storage Co. of Florida, Inc., 211 N.L.R.B. 138, 143–45 (1974) (Kennedy, Member, concurring). Howard Jenkins Jr., "Duty of Fair Representation" (speech, American Bar Association, Washington, D.C., March 29, 1969), Jenkins Papers, Box 1, Folder 37, 10. Bekins Moving & Storage, 211 N.L.R.B. at 145–46, 148 n. 50 (Fanning and Penello, Members, dissenting).

11 Miller, "A View," Schlossberg Papers, 19.

12 John C. Miller to Board, February 14, 1973, RG 25, National Labor Relations Board, Program Correspondence Files, 1934–79: Group II Former Chairmen, 1935–74 [hereafter NLRB Papers – GFC], Box 5, "Rules Revision: Revocation of Certification and/or Withholding of Certification" Folder, NACP, 1, 3. NLRB, "Special Board Agenda," March 9, 1973, RG 25, National Labor Relations Board, Board Agenda Records [hereafter NLRB Papers – BAR], FRC Box, unlabeled folder, NACP. Quote is from Edward B. Miller to Board, June 11, 1973, NLRB Papers – GFC, Box 5, "Rules Revision: Revocation of Certification and/or Withholding of Certification" Folder. Also see Charles W. Schneider to Rules Revision Committee, May 23, 1973, ibid. John C. Miller to Board, March 5, 1973, ibid.

13 Ed Townsend, "NLRB Watched for Policy Shift," *Christian Science Monitor*, June 20, 1970, 2, McCulloch Papers, Box 5, Folder 21. A plurality of the Supreme Court had recently upbraided the Board for announcing prospective policy in an adjudication rather than through rulemaking. National Labor Relations Board v. Wyman-Gordon Co., 394 U.S. 759 (1969). John C. Miller to Board, February 14, 1973, NLRB Papers – GFC. NLRB, "Board Agenda," minutes, November 14, 1973, NLRB Papers – BAR, FRC Box, unlabeled folder.

14 Granville M. Alley Jr. to NLRB, May 29, 1973, RG 25, National Labor Relations Board, Description of Records [hereafter NLRB Papers – DR], Box 61, "Employer's Exhibits, May 29 & 30, 1973," 12-RC-4352 Bekins Moving & Storage Co. of Florida, Inc. (loose), NACP. Granville M. Alley Jr. to Travis H. Dumas, May 29, 1973, ibid.

15 NLRB, "Board Agenda," minutes, November 14, 1973, NLRB Papers – BAR, FRC Box, unlabeled folder. Bekins Moving & Storage, 211

N.L.R.B. at 138–40, 145–46, 148 n. 50 (Fanning and Penello, Members, dissenting).

16 Bekins Moving & Storage, 211 N.L.R.B. at 138–39. Ibid. at 144–45 (Kennedy, Member, concurring), citing Kahn v. Shevin, 416 U.S. 351 (1974).

17 Ibid. at 147–48 (Fanning and Penello, Members, dissenting). The NLRA said that the Board "shall" provide a preelection hearing and that if the Board "finds upon the record of such hearing that such a question of representation exists, it *shall* direct an election by secret ballot and *shall* certify the results thereof." NLRA sec. 9(c)(1) (emphasis added). The dissenters' approach would assumedly let the Board use its discrimination finding to determine that no question of representation existed, thus avoiding a direct clash between its statutory and constitutional mandates.

18 Bekins Moving & Storage, 211 N.L.R.B. at 138–41, 143–44, 148. Ibid. at 143–45 (1974) (Kennedy, Member, concurring). Jenkins took a similar position in Houston Maritime Ass'n, Inc., 168 N.L.R.B. 615, 617 n. 16 (1967).

19 Mortimer Riemer to Lovic A. Brooks Jr. and Arthur M. Schiller, July 3, 1973, NLRB Papers – GFC, Box 5, "Rules Revision: Revocation of Certification and/or Withholding of Certification" Folder. Arthur M. Schiller and Lovic A. Brooks Jr. to Edward B. Miller, July 16, 1973, ibid. Edward B. Miller to NLRB, August 6, 1973, ibid. Edward B. Miller to Lovic A. Brooks Jr., August 21, 1973, ibid.; Edward B. Miller to Arthur M. Schiller, July 20, 1973, ibid.

20 Farhang, *The Litigation State*; MacLean, *Freedom Is Not Enough*; Delton, *Racial Integration*, 214–16.

21 118 Cong. Rec. 3959, 3960–61. Miller, "A View," Schlossberg Papers, 8, 12, 20. Jubilee Manufacturing Co., 202 N.L.R.B. 272, 275–76, 278 (1973) (Jenkins, Member, dissenting). See, e.g., Safety Cabs, Inc., 173 N.L.R.B. 17 (1968).

22 Jubilee Manufacturing Co., 202 N.L.R.B. at 275–76, 278 (Jenkins, Member, dissenting). Edward B. Miller, "A View," Schlossberg Papers, 16. Historically inclined political scientists and policy historians have demonstrated that the state is an independent variable in historical analysis rather than a neutral field on which interest groups and social movements engage in battle. A foundational text in this literature is Peter B. Evans, Dietrich Rueschemeyer, and Theda Skocpol, *Bringing the State Back In* (New York: Cambridge University Press, 1985). Exemplary texts include Brian Balogh, *Chain Reaction: Expert Debate and Public Participation in American Commercial Nuclear Power 1945–1975* (New York: Cambridge University Press, 1991); Daniel P. Carpenter, *The Forging of Bureaucratic Autonomy: Reputations, Networks, and Policy Innovation in Executive Agencies, 1862–1928.* (Princeton, N.J.: Princeton University Press, 2001); Martha Derthick, *Agency under Stress: The Social Security Administration*

in American Government (Washington, D.C.: Brookings Institution Press, 1990); Frymer, *Black and Blue*; Stephen Skowronek, *Building a New American State: The Expansion of National Administrative Capacities* (New York: Cambridge University Press, 1982). As many of these scholars have demonstrated, agency officials are often motivated as much by the desire to defend their policy turf and establish independence from political actors as by political ideology. See, e.g., Balogh, *Chain Reaction*; Carpenter, *The Forging of Bureaucratic Autonomy*. This can often lead to unexpected policy outcomes. Frymer, *Black and Blue*.

23 Farmers' Cooperative Compress, 169 N.L.R.B. 290, 296 (1968). United Packinghouse, Food, & Allied Workers International, 416 F.2d at 1130, 1135; NLRA secs. 7, 8(a)(1). "Hail Court's Bias Case Ruling as Legal Landmark for Labor," *Chicago Defender*, December 6, 1969, 36.

24 Farmers Cooperative Compress, 194 N.L.R.B. 85, 86–87, 89–90 (1971). United Packinghouse, Food, & Allied Workers Intern. Union, AFL-CIO, 416 F.2d 1126, 1130, 1135 (1969). Jubilee Manufacturing Co., 202 N.L.R.B. at 272–73. Ibid. at 275–76, 278 (Jenkins, Member, dissenting). See also "Farmers Cooperative," notes, n.d. [1969] McCulloch Papers, Box 12, Folder 30.

25 Griggs v. Duke Power Co., 401 U.S. 424 (1971). On *Griggs*, see Frymer, *Black and Blue*, 87–88; Hugh Davis Graham, *The Civil Rights Era: Origins and Development of National Policy, 1960–1972* (New York: Oxford University Press, 1990), 383–90; MacLean, *Freedom Is Not Enough*, 108–10; Joseph L. Mosnier, "Crafting Law in the Second Reconstruction: Julius Chambers, the NAACP Legal Defense Fund, and Title VII," Ph.D. diss., University of North Carolina, 2005. Mansion House Center Mgt. Corp., 190 N.L.R.B. 437, 437 n. 3 (1971). NLRB v. Mansion House Center Mgt. Corp., 473 F.2d 471, 475–77 (8th Cir. 1973). See Davis v. Washington, 512 F.2d 956, 958 n. 2 (D.C. Cir. 1975) (collecting cases); Armstead v. Starkville Municipal Separate School District, 461 F.2d 276, 281 n. 1 (5th Cir. 1972) (Rives, J., concurring in part and dissenting in part). Serena Mayeri, *Reasoning from Race: Feminism, Law, and the Civil Rights Revolution* (Cambridge, Mass.: Harvard University Press, 2011). Miller came to allow statistical evidence where it was accompanied by evidence that the union controlled hiring. Grants Furniture Plaza, Inc., 213 N.L.R.B. 410, 410–11 (1974). Even Jenkins was persuaded by this reasoning.

26 Farmers' Cooperative Compress, 194 N.L.R.B. at 86–87, 89.

27 Ibid. at 91 (Jenkins, Member, dissenting).

28 Herbert Hill, NAACP Labor Manual, 1968, NAACP Papers, Part V, Box 2693, "Labor: NAACP Publications, 1962–74" Folder; Robert L. Carter and Maria Marcus, "Trade Union Racial Practices and the Law," in *The Negro and the American Labor Movement*, ed. Julius Jacobson, 380–400 (Garden City, N.Y.: Doubleday, 1968), 392–93. Local Union No. 2, 152

N.L.R.B. 1093 (1965). Leonard H. Carter, West Coast Regional Office Annual Report, December 21, 1967, NAACP Papers, Part V, Box 2551, Folder 6. See charges enclosed with Robert Carter to Sidney Gibson, May 25, 1968, NAACP Papers, Part V, Box 2693, Folder 4.

29 James Gross argues that Miller emphasized worker choice and minimized government oversight instead of fostering collective bargaining, a record he argues makes Miller a more conservative and antiunion chairman than Miller's evenhanded reputation indicated. His positions on the Board's race policies defy as well as fit this description. James A. Gross, *Broken Promise: The Subversion of U.S. Labor Relations Policy, 1947–1994* (Philadelphia: Temple University Press, 2003), 220–31. Alan Kistler, "NLRB Nomination," *Washington Post*, October 3, 1970, McCulloch Papers, Box 6, Folder 31.

30 Stanley S. Scott to Alexander M. Haig and Jerry Jones, August 23, 1973, Jenkins Papers, Box 1, Folder 40. Peter H. Dominick to Elaine Jenkins, January 27, 1969, Jenkins Papers, Box 1, Folder 35. Harry Bernstein, "Plan for Negro to Head Labor Board Dropped," *Los Angeles Times*, April 26, 1969, A9. Simeon Booker, "Jenkins: NLRB Black Chairman," n.d. [ca. March 1969], Jenkins Papers, Box 1, Folder 33; Levine, "NLRB under Fire." "Delay in Naming NLRB Chairman," n.d., McCulloch Papers, Box 5, Folder 22. Howard Jenkins Jr. (speech, West Coast Regional NAACP Conference, September 23, 1967), Jenkins Papers, Box 1, Folder 25, 2, 3. Howard Jenkins Jr., "Social Action in the World of Work" (speech, Urban League of Kansas City Annual Meeting to Observe Equal Opportunity Day, Kansas City, Mo., November 18, 1963), Jenkins Papers, Box 1, Folder 21, 10. Howard Jenkins Jr. (speech, Urban League of the Pikes Peak Region, Colorado Springs, Colo., August 16, 1967), Jenkins Papers, Box 1, Folder 25. Thomas J. Sugrue, *Sweet Land of Liberty: The Forgotten Struggle for Civil Rights in the North* (New York: Random House, 2009), 325–34. Howard Jenkins Jr., "Duty of Fair Representation" (speech, American Bar Association, Washington, D.C., March 29, 1969), Jenkins Papers, Box 1, Folder 3, 13. NLRB, "Howard Jenkins Sworn in for Second Term on NLRB," August 1, 1968, NLRB Papers – CMFMiller, Box 16, "Board Member: Howard Jenkins" Folder.

31 Kim Phillips-Fein, *Invisible Hands: The Making of the Conservative Movement from the New Deal to Reagan* (New York: W. W. Norton, 2009); Cowie, *Stayin' Alive*, 226–32; Sean Wilentz, *The Age of Reagan: America from Watergate to the War on Terror* (New York: Harper, 2008), 90–92; Kim McQuaid, *Uneasy Partners: Big Business in American Politics, 1945–1990* (Baltimore: Johns Hopkins University Press, 1993). The difference in employers' opposition to unionization before and after the mid-1970s may have been more one of salience and success than of effort. See Chapter 6. For earlier examples of employer resistance, see Kim Phillips-Fein, "Business Conservatism

on the Shop Floor: Anti-Union Campaigns in the 1950s," *Labor* 7, no. 2 (Summer 2010): 9–26. On employers' early post–New Deal anti-union campaigns, see Elizabeth A. Fones-Wolf, *Selling Free Enterprise: The Business Assault on Labor and Liberalism, 1945–60* (Urbana: University of Illinois Press, 1995); Howell John Harris, *The Right to Manage: Industrial Relations Policies of American Business in the 1940s* (Madison: University of Wisconsin Press, 1982); Sanford M. Jacoby, *Modern Manors* (Princeton, N.J.: Princeton University Press, 1997); Stephen H. Norwood, *Strikebreaking and Intimidation: Mercenaries and Masculinity in Twentieth-Century America* (Chapel Hill: University of North Carolina Press, 2002), epilogue; Robert Michael Smith, *From Blackjacks to Briefcases: A History of Commercialized Strikebreaking and Unionbusting in the United States* (Athens: Ohio University Press, 2003), chap. 4; David Witwer, *Shadow of the Racketeer: Scandal in Organized Labor* (Urbana: University of Illinois Press, 2009). NRWC, Meeting Minutes, January 15, 1964, Ernest L. Wilkinson Papers [hereafter Wilkinson Papers], Box 219, Folder 26, L. Tom Perry Special Collections, Harold B. Lee Library, Brigham Young University, Provo, Utah. "Truly vast" quote in Freeman Memo, 2. Neil Ulman, "Keeping Unions Out," *Wall Street Journal*, January 19, 1966, 1. For examples of employer resistance, see Ruth Weyand, "Present Status of Individual Employee Rights," in *Proceeding of New York University Twenty-Second Annual Conference on Labor* (New York: Matthew Bender, 1970), 171–216. "How to Keep the Unions Out of the Plant," *Business Week*, April 18, 1970, 4, McCulloch Papers, Box 6, Folder 31.

32 Alex V. Barbour to Joseph E. De Sio, July 11, 1973, NLRB Papers – GFC, Box 5, "Rules Revision: Revocation of Certification and/or Withholding of Certification" Folder. Norman A. Cole to Harold A. Boire, July 11, 1973, ibid. Joseph V. Moran to Harold A. Boire, July 10, 1973, ibid. Milo V. Price to Joseph E. De Sio, July 11, 1973, ibid. Walter C. Philips to Thomas W. Kennedy, July 12, 1973, ibid. Arthur M. Schiller and Lovic A. Brooks Jr. to Edward B. Miller, July 16, 1973, ibid. Mortimer Riemer to Lovic A. Brooks Jr. and Arthur M. Schiller, July 3, 1973, ibid. Plato E. Papps to Edward B. Miller, August 6, 1973, ibid.

33 Richard Bader, "Note: The Impact of De Facto Discrimination by Unions on the Availability of NLRB Bargaining Orders," *Southern California Law Review* 47 (1974): 1353–92, 1353, 1377; Bernard D. Meltzer, "The National Labor Relations Act and Racial Discrimination: The More Remedies, the Better?" *University of Chicago Law Review* 42 (1974): 1–46, 3, 9–10. See also "Questions of Race and Sex Bias Aired at Atlanta Labor Conference," *Daily Labor Reporter*, November 18, 1974, Jenkins Papers, Box 2, Folder 3.

34 "Cases Involving Racial Discrimination since Hughes Tool Co.," October 15, 1969, McCulloch Papers, Box 12, Folder 21.

10 Conservatives Reject the Liberal Workplace Constitution

1   William L. Taylor, "Problems in Developing and Enforcing Fair Employment Law in the United States" (speech to the Villa Sebelloni Conference at Lake Como, Italy, October 2–6, 1972), Glickstein Papers, MGLI 26.2609, 18–19.

2   William L. Taylor, *The Passion of My Times: An Advocate's Fifty-Year Journey in the Civil Rights Movement* (New York: Carroll & Graf Publishers, 2004), 15, 29–30, 35–36, 44–48, 96–97. William L. Taylor (speech, Vanderbilt Bar Association, Vanderbilt University, Nashville, Tenn., February 5, 1964), Glickstein Papers, MGLI 20.2536; Wofford, (speech, Annual Conference of National Civil Liberties Clearing House, March 23, 1961), Kennedy Papers – POF. William L. Taylor, "Executive Implementation of Federal Civil Rights Laws," December 3, 1968, LCCR Papers, Part II, Box 11, "Compliance & Enforcement Committee: Miscellaneous Reports, 1968–77, n.d." Folder. Taylor, "Problems in Developing," Glickstein Papers, 19.

3   Nathan Lewin to Thurgood Marshall, January 9, 1967, RG 60, Department of Justice Records, Civil Rights Division, Class 171 Litigation Case Files [hereafter DOJ Papers – CRD-C171], Box 2, "171–12C-1" Folder, NACP. See generally Thomas J. Sugrue, *Sweet Land of Liberty: The Forgotten Struggle for Civil Rights in the North* (New York: Random House, 2009); Robert O. Self, *American Babylon: Race and the Struggle for Postwar Oakland* (Princeton, N.J.: Princeton University Press, 2003). Mulkey v. Reitman, 64 Cal. 2d 529, 541–542 (Cal., 1966).

4   Bell v. Maryland, 378 U.S. 226, 333 (1964); Lewin to Marshall, January 9, 1967, DOJ Papers – CRD-C171. Shelley v. Kraemer held in 1948 that the courts could not enforce homeowners' racially restrictive covenants. In sit-in cases other than *Bell*, all but Justice Harlan had found sufficient state action where state or local laws required segregation in public accommodations. See, e.g., Peterson v. City of Greenville, 373 U.S. 244 (1963). Evans v. Newton, 382 U.S. 296, 305–07 (1966) (White, J., concurring). John Doar to Thurgood Marshall, December 28, 1966, DOJ Papers – CRD-C171, Box 2, "171–12C-1" Folder; John Doar to Thurgood Marshall, February 28, 1967, Papers of Thurgood Marshall [hereafter Thurgood Marshall Papers], Box 28, Folder 1, LCMD. Justice Department lawyers could reasonably count on the votes of Chief Justice Warren and Justice Douglas, who concurred in *Bell* on broad state action grounds, as well as the vote of Justice Goldberg's liberal replacement, Abe Fortas. Beyond that, they probably hoped for Justice Brennan's vote but would still need either Justice White or Clark for a majority. Save White's recent concurrence, both justices' support seemed unlikely.

5   Ralph S. Spritzer to SG, January 25, 1967, DOJ Papers – CRD-C171, Box 2, "171–12C-1" Folder; Alan G. Marer to Louis F. Claiborne March 3, 1967, DOJ Papers – CRD-C171, Box 2, "171–12C-1" Folder.

6 Thurgood Marshall et al., Amicus Brief for U.S. Government, Reitman v. Mulkey, No. 483, March 1967, Thurgood Marshall Papers, Box 28, Folder 1, 15–20. On Marshall and Cox, see Chapters 5 and 7, respectively.

7 William O. Douglas, conference notes, March 24, 1967, Douglas Papers, Box 1379, "Argued Cases No.477–650, O.T. 1966" Folder.

8 Ibid. Reitman v. Mulkey, 387 U.S. 369, 375–77 (1967). Charles L. Black Jr., "Foreword: 'State Action,' Equal Protection, and California's Proposition 14," *Harvard Law Review* 81 (1967): 69–109, 97–98.

9 *Reitman*, 387 U.S. at 391, 394; ibid. at 395 (Harlan, J., dissenting).

10 "A Highly Critical View of Progress on Rights," *New York Times*, October 18, 1970, E3. U.S. Commission on Civil Rights, *Federal Civil Rights Enforcement Effort: A Report of the United States Commission on Civil Rights* (Washington, D.C.: Government Printing Office, 1970) [hereafter Civil Rights Enforcement], 813–45.

11 Civil Rights Enforcement, 844, 1095–115, esp. 1095–96, 1101–4, 1107 (emphasis added). In support, the Civil Rights Commission quoted broad language in *Burton* that said the state, "by its inaction[,] ... made itself a party" to its tenant's discrimination and ignored the Court's indication in *Reitman* that something more than inaction was required. Ibid. at 1107 (quoting Burton v. Wilmington Parking Auth., 365 U.S. 715, 725 (1961)). For a discussion of *Burton*, see Chapter 7.

12 Howard A. Glickstein to Martin E. Sloane and James D. Williams, October 16, 1970, Glickstein Papers, MGLI 23.2578; Howard A. Glickstein to Martin E. Sloane, November 10, 1970, Glickstein Papers, MGLI 23.2577. Howard A. Glickstein to Martin A. Sloane, November 20, 1970, ibid. Taylor proposal described in Howard A. Glickstein to John H. Powell Jr., November 10, 1970, Glickstein Papers, MGLI 23.2577; Howard A. Glickstein to Commissioners, November 10, 1970, ibid.

13 Robert J. Samuelson, "Discrimination Is Charged against Trucking Industry," *Washington Post*, March 12, 1971, D10. Equal Opportunity in Surface Transportation, 36 Fed. Reg. 10471 (June 2, 1971). Jack Greenberg et al. to Interstate Commerce Commission (ICC), Petition for Rulemaking, In the Matter of Ex Parte No. 278 Equal Opportunity in Surface Transportation, October 25, 1971, NAACP Papers, Part V, Box 303, Folder 5, 30, 49–54; Joseph Rauh and Frank Pohlhaus, LCCR, William L. Taylor, Center for National Policy Review (CNPR) to ICC, Initial Statement, In the Matter of Ex Parte No. 278 Equal Opportunity in Surface Transportation, December 28, 1971, ibid., Folder 9; Jack Greenberg et al. to ICC, Proposed Rule, In the Matter of Ex Parte No. 278 Equal Opportunity in Surface Transportation, October 25, 1971, ibid., Folder 5, 5–7. John A. Buggs to ICC, Initial Statement, In the Matter of Ex Parte No. 278 Equal Opportunity in Surface Transportation, November 30, 1971, ibid., Folder 6; William H. Brown III et al. to ICC, Initial Statement, In the Matter of Ex Parte No. 278 Equal Opportunity

in Surface Transportation, December 1, 1971, ibid., Folder 8, 101–7. J. Thomas Tidd to ICC, Initial Statement, In the Matter of Ex Parte No. 278 Equal Opportunity in Surface Transportation, December 1, 1971, ibid., Folder 7, 3. David L. Norman to ICC, Initial Statement, In the Matter of Ex Parte No. 278 Equal Opportunity in Surface Transportation, December 1, 1971, ibid.; John L. Wilks to ICC, Initial Statement, In the Matter of Ex Parte No. 278 Equal Opportunity in Surface Transportation, December 1, 1971, ibid.; Clarence H. Featherson to ICC, Initial Statement, In the Matter of Ex Parte No. 278 Equal Opportunity in Surface Transportation, November 29, 1971, NAACP Papers, Part V, Box 303, Folder 6. Paul Delaney, "Rights Panel Again Assails Efforts by U.S. Agencies," *New York Times*, November 17, 1971, 1.

14   Dean J. Kotlowski, *Nixon's Civil Rights: Politics, Principle, and Policy* (Cambridge, Mass.: Harvard University Press, 2002), 166–76, esp. 175. Howard A. Glickstein to Theodore Hesburgh, October 30, 1970, Glickstein Papers, MGLI 23.2578.

15   Petition described in National Resources Defense Council v. Securities Exchange Commission, 389 F. Supp. 689, 694 (1974). Civil Aeronautics Board, Discrimination in Airline Employment: Advanced Notice of Proposed Rule Making, 37 Fed. Reg. 15518 (1972). See Chapter 8 for the FCC's AT&T action. William L. Taylor et al. to FPC, June 22, 1972, Equal Employment Opportunity in the Electric and Gas Utility Industry, RG 138, FPC, Docket Files, Docket No. RM-447 [hereafter FPC Papers – Docket RM-447], FRC Box 55, Folder 1. Taylor's clients for his FPC petition included the NAACP, the National Urban League, the Mexican American Legal Defense and Education Fund, the National Organization for Women, the Women's Equity Action League, League of United Latin American Citizens, the Association for the Betterment of Black Edison Employees, United Church, the Center for Community Change, the American G.I. Forum, the Mexican American Political Association, and United Native Americans, Inc.

16   Pacific Gas & Elec. Co., 42 F.P.C. 243, 243–44 (1969). Robert Sherrill, "Nassikas Sets Your Gas Bill," *Nation*, January 17, 1972, 73–79, 76–78. Thomas K. McCraw, *Prophets of Regulation: Charles Francis Adams, Louis D. Brandeis, James M. Landis, Alfred E. Kahn* (Cambridge, Mass.: Harvard University Press, 1984), 234.

17   Jefferson Cowie, *Stayin' Alive: The 1970s and the Last Days of the Working Class* (New York: New Press, 2010), 235. Lizabeth Cohen, *A Consumers' Republic: The Politics of Mass Consumption in Postwar America* (New York: Knopf, 2003); Thomas J. Sugrue, *The Origins of the Urban Crisis: Race and Inequality in Postwar Detroit* (Princeton, N.J.: Princeton University Press, 1996). William H. Brown III, Opening Statement, November 15, 1971, LCCR Papers, Part I, Box 99, "EEOC, 1971" Folder.

18 "EEOC Probes Find Job Bias Still Rampant," *Chicago Daily Defender*, August 10, 1968, 38. "EEOC Schedules Public Utilities Hearings," November 7, 1971, LCCR Papers, Box 99, "EEOC, 1971" Folder, 2–3.

19 Richard K. Berg, July 18, 1961, Micro-copy NK-2-E-EO, Reel 91, 7. Joseph L. Mosnier, "Crafting Law in the Second Reconstruction: Julius Chambers, the NAACP Legal Defense Fund, and Title VII," Ph.D. diss., University of North Carolina, 2005, chap. 5.

20 Enclosed in Hobart Taylor Jr., to Nicholas deB. Katzenbach, October 4, 1961, Micro-copy NK-2-E-EO, Reel 91, 6, 9–10 (citing *Pollak*, the Washington, D.C., streetcar case, duty of fair representation decisions such as *Howard* and *Steele*, and *Marsh v. Alabama*, 326 U.S. 501 (1946), which involved religious freedom rather than race). In *Marsh*, the Court reasoned that where a private entity (in this instance, a company town) was the functional equivalent of a public entity (in this case, a municipal government) it became a state actor bound by the Fourteenth Amendment. For a historical account of why the Kennedy committee's description of utilities was apt, see Gail Radford, "From Municipal Socialism to Public Authorities: Institutional Factors in the Shaping of American Public Enterprise," *Journal of American History* 90, no. 3 (December 2003): 863–90. David J. Bardin to Lee C. White, in Hearings on Responsibilities of the Federal Power Commission in the Area of Civil Rights, before the Subcommittee on Civil Rights Oversight of the House Committee on the Judiciary, 92d Cong. (1972) [hereafter Responsibilities], 90. See, e.g., 16 U.S.C. secs. 797, 824, 824d (2006). Robert A. Jablon to David J. Bardin, April 17, 1969, in Responsibilities, 99–109, 104 n. 10, 106, 109.

21 Quoted in Sherrill, "Nassikas Sets Your Gas Bill," 73–79, 73–75. "John Nassikas, 81, Who Led Deregulation of Natural Gas," *New York Times*, June 13, 1998, A10; "John N. Nassikas Dies, Player in Energy Battles," *New Hampshire Union Leader*, June 10, 1998, n.p.

22 Gordon Gooch to David L. Norman, September 29, 1971, in Responsibilities, 68. Pacific Gas & Elec. Co., 44 F.P.C. 1365, 1366 (1970). Hearing on Fed. Power Commission Oversight, before the Subcomm. on Energy, Natural Resources, and the Environment of the S. Comm. on Commerce, 91st Cong. 35–36 (1970) (statement of John Nassikas).

23 Pacific Gas & Elec. Co., 44 F.P.C. at 1366–68. If the petitioners argued that the FPC had a constitutional obligation to regulate licensees' employment practices, the FPC did not acknowledge it. Unfortunately, the National Archives do not have the records for this license petition, and I have been unable to find the petitioners' arguments in other archives.

24 Sherrill, "Nassikas Sets Your Gas Bill," 78. Under the Federal Regulation and Development of Power Act, 16 U.S.C. 12, Subch. I, sec. 793, and Reorganization Plan No. 9 of 1950, 15 Fed. Reg. 3175, May 24, 1950, sec. 1, the general counsel was appointed by the chairman, subject to the commission's approval. Ed Cray, *Chief Justice: A Biography of Earl*

Warren (New York: Simon & Schuster, 2008), 395–96. "Alumni to Know," *Alcalde*, January 1970, 35. Gooch to Norman, September 29, 1971, in Responsibilities, 68. Gordon Gooch to Fed. Power Comm'n, February 17, 1972, ibid. at 61–65.

25 Taylor et al. to FPC, June 22, 1972, FPC Papers – Docket RM-447, 35. Edward Cowan, "A Fair-Jobs Role Barred by F.P.C.: Agency Says It Cannot Deal with Hiring by Utilities," *New York Times*, July 12, 1972, 11. NAACP et al., 48 F.P.C. 40, 41–42 (1972). William L. Taylor and Robert B. Marcin to FPC, August 8, 1972, FPC Papers – Docket RM-447, FRC Box 55, Folder 1. William H. Brown III to John N. Nassikas, July 13, 1972, ibid. NAACP et al., 48 F.P.C. 371 (1972).

26 Warren Burger to Harry Blackmun, February 15, 1973, Papers of Harry A. Blackmun [hereafter Blackmun Papers], Box 157, Folder 6, LCMD. Louis M. Kohlmeier, "Nixon Picks Warren E. Burger to Be Chief Justice," *Wall Street Journal*, May 22, 1969, 3; Sidney E. Zion, "Nixon's Nominee for the Post of Chief Justice: Warren Earl Burger," *New York Times*, May 22, 1969, 36; "Chief Justice Choice – and Why," *Los Angeles Times*, May 25, 1969, F4. Charles M. Lamb, "Chief Justice Warren E. Burger: A Conservative Chief for Conservative Times," in *The Burger Court: Political and Judicial Profiles*, ed. Charles M. Lamb and Stephen C. Halpern, 129–62 (Urbana: University of Illinois Press, 1991), 130. Roe v. Wade, 410 U.S. 113 (1973). Vincent Blasi, *Burger Court: The Counter-Revolution That Wasn't* (New Haven, Conn.: Yale University Press, 1983); Barry Friedman, *The Will of the People: How Public Opinion Has Influenced the Supreme Court and Shaped the Meaning of the Constitution* (New York: Farrar, Straus and Giroux, 2009), 283–85. For an array of views on the Burger Court's impact, see Bernard Schwartz, ed., *The Burger Court: Counter-Revolution or Confirmation?* (New York: Oxford University Press, 1998). Terri Peretti, "Constructing the State Action Doctrine, 1940–1990," *Law and Social Inquiry* 35, no. 2 (Spring 2010): 273–310.

27 Richard West, "Rehnquist Backed by Liberals in Hometown," *Los Angeles Times*, October 30, 1971, 16. John H. Averill, "Rehnquist Gentle but Staunch Conservative," *Los Angeles Times*, October 22, 1971, A15; William V. Shannon, "'No' to Rehnquist," *New York Times*, November 22, 1971, 39. John A. Jenkins, *The Partisan: The Life of William Rehnquist* (New York: PublicAffairs, 2012), 37–39, 70–73. Elizabeth Tandy Shermer, *Sunbelt Capitalism: Phoenix and the Transformation of American Politics* (Philadelphia: University of Pennsylvania Press, 2013), 293–94; David E. Rosenbaum, "William Hubbs Rehnquist," *New York Times*, October 22, 1971, 25.

28 Even Rehnquist's analysis of the *quantitative* differences between *Moose Lodge* and *Burton* were as much about quality. Moose Lodge v. Irvis, 407 U.S. 163, 173–76 (1972). Essentially, Rehnquist applied the limits from decisions such as *Reitman*, which determined what involvement the *state* could permissibly have with private acts of discrimination, to determine

when a private actor became a state actor. *Moose Lodge* did enjoin the state from enforcing a regulation that required licensed clubs to follow their own constitutions and bylaws insofar as those were racially discriminatory. Ibid. at 179.

29 Business Executives' Move for Vietnam Peace v. FCC, 450 F.2d 642, 651–52, 655 (D.C. Cir. 1971). Columbia Broadcasting System (CBS) v. Democratic National Committee (DNC), 412 U.S. 94, 119–20 (1973). The Court also held that there was no statutory basis for requiring broadcasters to allow the ads.

30 William Brennan, conference notes, n.d. [October 20, 1972], Brennan Papers, Part I, Box 280, Folder 6. *CBS*, 412 U.S. at 150–51 (Douglas, J., concurring); ibid. at 174–75, 177–80 (Brennan, J., dissenting).

31 CBS v. DNC, 412 U.S. 94, 115 (1973) (emphasis added). Justice White declined to join Burger's finding of no state action because he thought the facts met the *Moose Lodge* standard, a position with which Blackmun agreed. Byron R. White to Warren E. Burger, February 9, 1973, Blackmun Papers, Box 157, Folder 6; Harry A. Blackmun to Warren E. Burger, February 12, 1973, ibid. Justice Powell thought *Pollak*, the 1950s streetcar case discussed in Chapter 4, rendered the state action question uncertain. Lewis F. Powell to Warren E. Burger and Harry A. Blackmun, April 19, 1973, ibid. Burger distinguished *Pollak* the same way that Gooch had: Congress had denied the FCC the authority to micromanage broadcasters' content decisions, Burger argued, thus "the Commission has not fostered the licensee policy challenged here; it has simply declined to command particular action because it fell" outside its regulatory authority to do so. *CBS*, 412 U.S. at 120. Ibid. at 177 (Brennan, J. dissenting).

32 See, e.g. [Warren E.] Burger to [Thurgood] Marshall, [Harry] Blackmun, and [Lewis] Powell, March 29, 1973, Blackmun Papers, Box 157, Folder 6. Blackmun nicknames quoted in Stephen L. Wasby, "Justice Harry A. Blackmun: Transformation from 'Minnesota Twin' to Independent Voice," in *The Burger Court: Political and Judicial Profiles*, ed. Charles M. Lamb and Stephen C. Halpern, 63–99 (Urbana: University of Illinois Press, 1991), 64. Linda Greenhouse, *Becoming Justice Blackmun: Harry Blackmun's Supreme Court Journey* (New York: Henry Holt, 2005). Warren Burger to Harry Blackmun, February 15, 1973, Blackmun Papers, Box 157, Folder 6.

33 William O. Douglas, n.d. [ca. February 1974], docket book entry for Jackson v. Metropolitan Edison Co., Douglas Papers, Box 1623, "Administrative Docket Book IFP Cases 73–5001 to 73–6480, O.T. 1973" Folder. Byron R. White, February 14, 1974, draft dissent, Jackson v. Metropolitan Edison Co., Thurgood Marshall Papers, Box 154, Folder 4. William O. Douglas to Byron R. White, February 14, 1974, Blackmun Papers, Box 205, Folder 7; Thurgood Marshall to Byron R. White, February 14, 1974, ibid. W[illiam]H[.]R[ehnquist], "Jackson v. Metropolitan Edison Co. Discussion," October 18, 1974, William H. Rehnquist Papers, Box 82,

Folder 73–5845, Hoover Institution Archives, Stanford, Calif. William J. Brennan, n.d. [ca. October 1974], conference notes, Brennan Papers, Box 340, Folder 6.

34 Jackson v. Metropolitan Edison Co., 419 U.S. 345, 351 (1974). Compare Douglas L. Leslie, "Governmental Action and Standing: NLRB Certification of Discriminatory Unions," *Arizona State Law Journal* 1974, no. 1 (1974): 35–73 with Jonathan G. Axelrod and Howard J. Kaufman, "*Mansion House – Bekins – Handy Andy*: The National Labor Relations Board's Role in Racial Discrimination Cases," *George Washington Law Review* 45 (1977): 675–711, 692–93.

35 NAACP v. Fed. Power Comm'n, 520 F.2d 432, 445–47 (D.C. Cir. 1975).

36 Ibid., 437, 443–44, 446. CNPR, *Annual Report*, August 1975, NAACP Papers, Part V, Box 2588, Folder 10.

37 Petition for a Writ of Certiorari, June 20, 1975, NAACP v. Fed. Power Comm'n, No. 74–1619, Supreme Court of the United States; NAACP Board of Directors, minutes, January 10, 1976, NAACP Papers, Part VIII, Box 62, Folder 26.

38 Wayne E. Green, "Tipping the Scales: Supreme Court Shows a Pro-Business Tilt in Series of Rulings," *Wall Street Journal*, July 1, 1975, 1 (quotes in the article).

39 McCraw, *Prophets of Regulation*, 228–29, 237, chap. 7; Cowie, *Stayin' Alive*, 163; Sean Wilentz, *The Age of Reagan: America from Watergate to the War on Terror* (New York: Harper, 2008), 23, 35–36, 41; Daniel T. Rodgers, *Age of Fracture* (Cambridge, Mass.: Belknap Press of Harvard University Press, 2011). See Chapter 6 for free-market thought. For pro-deregulation liberals see, e.g., Stephen G. Breyer and Paul W. Macavoy, *Energy Regulation by the Federal Power Commission* (Washington, D.C.: Brookings Institution Press, 1974). For unemployment rates see Appendix, Figure A.2.

40 Ralph Nader and Mark J. Green, eds., *Corporate Power in America* (New York: Grossman Publishers, 1973), 133, 231; Mark J. Green, ed., *The Monopoly Makers: Ralph Nader's Study Group Report on Regulation and Competition* (New York: Grossman Publishers, 1973). Nader popularized, but did not invent, the New Left critique of regulation. For its academic counterpart, see Theodore J. Lowi, *The End of Liberalism: Ideology, Policy, and the Crisis of Public Authority* (New York: W. W. Norton, 1969). Cohen, *A Consumers' Republic*. On the rise of antigovernment sentiment more generally, see David Farber, "The Torch Had Fallen," in *America in the 70s*, ed. Beth Bailey and David Farber, 9–28 (Lawrence: University of Kansas Press, 2004), 21–22; Laura Kalman, *Right Star Rising: A New Politics, 1974–1980* (New York: W. W. Norton, 2010), 240–41; Cowie, *Stayin' Alive*, 226–28; Kim Phillips-Fein, *Invisible Hands: The Making of the Conservative Movement from the New Deal to*

Reagan (New York: W. W. Norton, 2009), 194–205. "Plan to Deregulate Airlines May Reach Congress This Week," *Wall Street Journal*, September 8, 1975, 4; Frank G. Zarb, "The Need to Deregulate Natural Gas," *Los Angeles Times*, November 18, 1975, B7. Government in the Sunshine Act, Pub. L. No. 94–409, sec. 3(a) (September 13, 1976). See McCraw, *Prophets of Regulation*, 259. "Washington and Business: Debate on Deregulation," *New York Times*, October 28, 1976, 77. On the deregulatory turn, see Cowie, *Stayin' Alive*, 226; Wilentz, *The Age of Reagan*, 23.

41 Sean Farhang, *The Litigation State: Public Regulation and Private Lawsuits in the United States* (Princeton, N.J.: Princeton University Press, 2010), 137–42, 150–55 (includes quotes). The Civil Rights Attorney's Fees Award Act of 1976, Pub. L. 94–559 sec. 2, 90 Stat. 2641, codified at 42 U.S.C. sec. 1988.

42 William J. Brennan, docket sheet for NAACP v. FPC, n.d. [1976], Brennan Papers, Part I, Box 369, Folder 1; Harry A. Blackmun, docket sheet for NAACP v. FPC, n.d. [1976], Box 674, Folder 4. W[illiam]H[.]B[rennan] to Harry A. Blackmun, February 17, 1976, Blackmun Papers, Box 225, Folder 5 (emphasis added). Louis H. Pollak to William L. Taylor, November 25, 1975, Center for National Policy Review Records [hereafter CNPR Papers], Box 125, Folder 5, LCMD.

43 Quotes in "Today's Summary and Analysis," *Daily Labor Reporter*, no. 39, February 26, 1976, CNPR Papers, Box 126, Folder 1, 2, A-9-A-12. William J. Brennan, conference notes, n.d. [February 27, 1976], Brennan Papers, Part I, Box 369, Folder 1.

44 William L. Taylor to Ronald Brown, March 4, 1976, CNPR Papers, Box 126, Folder 1. NAACP v. FPC, 425 U.S. 662, 665 n. 2, 668 (1976).

45 Ibid. at 669, 670 n. 7. The Court did not address the fact that this rationale did not apply to the FCC's common-carrier rules.

46 John P. MacKenzie, "Court Backs FPC Role on Job Bias," *Washington Post*, May 20, 1976, A1; Linda Mathews, "Agencies Needn't Curb Industry Job Bias, Court Says," *Los Angeles Times*, May 20, 1976, 1. Compare "F.P.C. Rights Role Is Found Limited: Supreme Court Says Agency Cannot Order Job Equality," *New York Times*, May 20, 1976, 31, with "High Court Clears FPC to Consider Bias in Jobs in Passing on Utility Rate Boosts," *Wall Street Journal*, May 20, 1976, 4. Accounting for Fed. Power Commission, Order on Completion of Judicial Review of Commission Opinion No. 623, Docket No. R-447, July 15, 1976, NAACP Papers, Part V, Box 353, Folder 6. Richard L. Dunham to Chief Executive Officers of Each Natural Gas Company, Licensee and Public Utility, n.d., CNPR Papers, Box 126, Folder 1. Robert J. Samuelson, "Discrimination Is Charged against Trucking Industry," *Washington Post*, March 12, 1971, D10. Discrimination of Airline Employment, Notice Terminating Proceeding, Civil Aeronautics Board, Docket No. 24636, August 13,

1976, NAACP Papers, Part V, Box 353, Folder 6; Equal Opportunity in Surface Transportation, 353 I.C.C. 425 (1977).

47 William L. Taylor to Petitioners and Other Interested Parties, June 11, 1976, CNPR Papers, Box 126, Folder 1. William L. Taylor to Howard A. Glickstein et al., July 19, 1976, ibid. William L. Taylor to Thomas Mitchell, July 12, 1976, ibid. Clark Arrington to Richard L. Dunham, May 12, 1977, ibid. Charles E. Hill and Craig Iscoe to William L. Taylor, January 31, 1979, ibid.

11 Liberals Rethink the Workplace Constitution

1 "NLRB to Hear Race and Sex Arguments," January 29, 1976, NLRB (on file with author). Nancy Hicks, "A Woman for N.L.R.B.," *New York Times*, January 9, 1975, 14. Carol Kleiman, "Tough Lawyer Lives Life Her Way," *Chicago Tribune*, May 26, 1975, B6. "New NLRB Chief Takes Oath Tuesday," *Chicago Tribune*, February 18, 1975, B14. Bell & Howell, 230 N.L.R.B. 420, 423 n. 22 (1977); "Biography," August 14, 1974, RG 6891, WHCF Name Files, Box 2268, "Murphy, Betty Southard" Folder, Gerald R. Ford Library and Archive, Ann Arbor, Mich. On *Bekins*, see Chapter 9.

2 Hughes and De Maria quoted in James C. Hyatt, "Firms Learn Art of Keeping Unions Out," *Wall Street Journal*, April 21, 1977, 3, McCulloch Papers, Box 6, Folder 30. On the shift in the 1970s to a service economy, see Jefferson Cowie, *Stayin' Alive: The 1970s and the Last Days of the Working Class* (New York: New Press, 2010), 216; Judith Stein, *Pivotal Decade: How the United States Traded Factories for Finance in the Seventies* (New Haven, Conn.: Yale University Press, 2010). A description of typical attendees is in Dick Wilson, "Employers Bone Up on ABCs of Slick Union-Busting Tactics," *AFL-CIO News*, October 8, 1977, 5, McCulloch Papers, Box 6, Folder 29. Dedra Hauser, "The Union-Busting Hustle," *New Republic*, August 25, 1979, 16, McCulloch Papers, Box 6, Folder 29, 18.

3 "Embattled Unions Strike Back at Management," *Business Week*, December 4, 1978, 54, McCulloch Papers, Box 6, Folder 29. "NAM Forms a Council Meant to Help Employers Keep Out Labor Unions," *New York Times*, December 19, 1977, McCulloch Papers, Box 6, Folder 29.

4 Orville Freeman to Frank W. McCulloch, September 9, 1968, McCulloch Papers, Box 12, Folder 10, 2, 4 n. 2; James Gross, *Broken Promise: The Subversion of U.S. Labor Relations Policy* (Philadelphia: Temple University Press, 2003), 234–35; Cowie, *Stayin' Alive*, 232. Cowie treats the Roundtable as a break from older organizations, such as the Chamber of Commerce and the Right to Work Committee. The secrecy of its predecessor organizations made the Roundtable appear newer than it was.

On the Business Roundtable, see Kim McQuaid, *Uneasy Partners: Big Business in American Politics, 1945–1990* (Baltimore: Johns Hopkins University Press, 1993); Kim Phillips-Fein, *Invisible Hands: The Making of the Conservative Movement from the New Deal to Reagan* (New York: W. W. Norton, 2009). For the 1960s movement, see Chapter 9. Wilson, "Employers Bone Up"; Hyatt, "Firms Learn Art," April 21, 1977, McCulloch Papers; Hauser, "The Union-Busting Hustle." "Embattled Unions Strike Back," December 4, 1978, McCulloch Papers; Hyatt, "Firms Learn Art," April 21, 1977, McCulloch Papers.

5 "Embattled Unions Strike Back," December 4, 1978, McCulloch Papers, 55–56; Hyatt, "Firms Learn Art," April 21, 1977, McCulloch Papers. Cowie, *Stayin' Alive*, 234, 289. Historians agree that employer resistance played an important role in unions' decline. For a useful summary, see the preface to Nelson Lichtenstein, *State of the Union: A Century of American Labor*, 2nd ed. (Princeton, N.J.: Princeton University Press, 2013). For unionization rates see Appendix, Figure A.1.

6 NRWC, "Board of Directors," January 31, 1964, Wilkinson Papers, Box 219, Folder 26. Granville M. Alley Jr. to NLRB, May 29, 1973, NLRB Papers – DR, Box 61, "Employer's Exhibits, May 29 & 30, 1973," 12-RC-4352 Bekins Moving & Storage Co. of Florida, Inc. (loose), NACP [hereafter Bekins Records]. Alden Press Inc., 212 N.L.R.B. 580, 580, 581 n. 6 (1974). Granville M. Alley Jr. to Travis H. Dumas, May 29, 1973, subpoenas, Bekins Records. S. H. Kress & Co., 212 N.L.R.B. 132, 132 (1974). Cases where employers sought to disqualify a union petitioning for certification include Grants Furniture Plaza, 213 N.L.R.B. 410 (1974); Bell & Howell Co., 213 N.L.R.B. 407 (1974); Lee Office Equipment, 226 N.L.R.B. 826 (1976); Trumbull Asphalt Co., 240 N.L.R.B. 646, 646–47 (1977). See also Handy Andy, Inc., 228 N.L.R.B. 447 (1977), where the certification followed a decertification election.

7 NLRB v. Mansion House Center Mgt. Corp., 473 F.2d 471, 475–77 (8th Cir. 1973). Wilson, "Employers Bone Up." Murcel Manufacturing Co., 231 N.L.R.B. 623, 623 (1977); NLRB v. Sumter Plywood, 535 F.2d 917 (5th Cir. 1976).

8 NLRB, "Official Report of Proceedings," Murcel Manufacturing Co., Docket No. 10-CA-10122 et al., February 2, 1976 [hereafter 1976 Board Hearing Transcript], RG 25, Selected Taft-Hartley Cases, 1978 [hereafter NLRB Papers – STHC-78], FRC Boxes 54–55, NACP, 44, 53, 55, 63–78, 110–12.

9 Remarks of Nathaniel Jones, NAACP West Coast Regional Conference Lawyers' Conference, April 3, 1970, Las Vegas, Nevada, NAACP Papers, Part V, Box 2551, Folder 7. The NAACP's labor secretary, Herbert Hill, occasionally brought NLRB charges in the early 1970s. Grover Smith Jr. to NLRB, November 30, 1970, NAACP Papers, Part V, Box 2693, Folder 4; Grover Smith Jr. to Herbert Hill, December 20, 1972, ibid., Folder 3;

Grover Smith Jr. to NLRB, November 1, 1973, ibid., Folder 4; Herbert Hill, "Black Workers & Unemployment: Court Orders Must Be Policed," *Vital Speeches of the Day*, August 15, 1971, GMMA-VF Papers, Box 10, Folder 13. See Chapter 10 for the NAACP's FPC action. The Library of Congress's collection of the NAACP's papers includes a large number of FCC cases. Interview with Benjamin Hooks, *Retail Clerks Advocate*, April 27, 1977, GMMA-VF, Box 39, Folder 12. On the NAACP's decline, see Thomas J. Sugrue, *Sweet Land of Liberty: The Forgotten Struggle for Civil Rights in the North* (New York: Random House), 494–500. On divisions between civil rights and labor over affirmative action, see Dennis Deslippe, *Protesting Affirmative Action: The Struggle over Equality after the Civil Rights Revolution* (Baltimore: Johns Hopkins University Press, 2012), chaps. 1, 5; Cowie, *Stayin' Alive*, 236–47.

10   Brief for the AFL-CIO as Amicus Curiae, Trumbull et al., NLRB, February 13, 1976 [hereafter 1976 Board Hearing Brief – AFL-CIO], NLRB Papers – STHC-78, FRC Boxes 54–55, pp. 24–25. 1976 Board Hearing Transcript, 14, 44, 48, 85, 120, 130, 134.

11   Robert T. Thompson, "Public Employee Unionization," *Vital Speeches of the Day* 43, no. 5 (December 15, 1976): 143–145. Warren Weaver Jr., "The Chamber's Public Interest Law Firm," *New York Times*, March 31, 1977, 75; Harry Bernstein and Larry Pryor, "Brown Urged to Veto Retirement Legislation," *Los Angeles Times*, September 10, 1977, OC12A. 1976 Board Hearing Transcript, 18.

12   Brief on Behalf of the Chamber of Commerce of the United States of America as Amicus Curiae, Trumbull Asphalt Co. et al., NLRB, n.d. [January 29, 1976], Murcel Manufacturing Co., NLRB Papers – STHC-78, FRC Boxes 54–55, 1, 6–7. Note that Thompson assumed exclusive representatives were state actors. Ibid., 9–10. Thompson's "fiat" argument was in keeping with right-to-work activists' and anti–New Deal conservatives' long-standing critique that the NLRB was constitutionally unsound and should be replaced by a specialized labor court or, like the EEOC, enforce its statute in the federal courts. James Gross, *Reshaping of the National Labor Relations Board* (Albany: State University of New York Press, 1982). Hauser, "The Union-Busting Hustle." "Region 15 Monthly Round-up Report for January 1969," February 16, 1969, AFL-CIO ODR Papers, Box 56, Folder 11. Wilson, "Employers Bone Up." The decertification strategy appeared effective. John J. Lawler, "The Influence of Management Consultants on the Outcome of Union Certification Elections," *Industrial and Labor Relations Review* 38, no. 1 (October 1984): 38–51.

13   1976 Board Hearing Transcript, 35, 42, 110. The Board's general counsel, John Irving, did not appear at the hearing but subsequently filed a statement. Irving had helped design the *Bekins* and *Mansion House* policies as a deputy general counsel during Edward Miller's chairmanship. He was

the only nonemployer to defend them, and the state action theories on which they rested, to the Board. John S. Irving et al., "General Counsel's Statement of Position," February 17, 1976, NLRB (on file with author); Standau E. Weinbrecht to Rules Revision Committee, May 18, 1973, NLRB Papers – GFC, Box 5, "Rules Revision: Revocation of Certification and/or Withholding of Certification" Folder.

14 1976 Board Hearing Brief – AFL-CIO, 4; 1976 Board Hearing Transcript, 16. NAACP v. FPC, 425 U.S. 662, 673 (1976) (Burger, C.J., concurring), citing Murray L. Weidenbaum, "The New Wave of Government Regulation of Business," *Business and Society Review* (Fall 1975): 81–86. The "fences" quote is in "Today's Summary and Analysis," *Daily Labor Reporter*, no. 39 (February 26, 1976), CNPR Papers, Box 126, Folder 1, A-9-A-12.

15 Alexander v. Gardner-Denver Co., 415 U.S. 36, 51 (1974). Reuel E. Schiller, "The Emporium Capwell Case: Race, Labor Law, and the Crisis of Post-War Liberalism," *Berkeley Journal of Employment and Labor Law* 25 (2004): 129–65, 157. Robert M. Cassel, "The Emporium Case: Title VII Rights and the Collective Bargaining Process," *Hastings Law Journal* 26 (1975): 1347–75, 1350. See also Vaca v. Sipes, 386 U.S. 171, 183 (1967), calling "tardy" the Board's foray into granting unfair labor practice orders for violations of the duty of fair representation.

16 Emporium Capwell v. Western Addition Community Organization, 420 U.S. 50, 66, 69, 71–72 (1975). Harry A. Blackmun, October 25, 1974, Blackmun Papers, Box 195, Folder 8.

17 Washington v. Davis, 426 U.S. 229, 239, 243–45 (1976). Congress's 1972 amendments extended Title VII to state and municipal employees. Harry A. Blackmun, March 5, 1976, Blackmun Papers, Box 224, Folder 5. The dissenters instead defended against what they saw as a threat to the robustness of Title VII's bar on disparate impact and specifically stated that they did not "intend to address the constitutional questions considered by the" majority. *Davis*, 426 U.S. at 257 (Brennan, J., dissenting).

18 William J. Brennan, *Emporium Capwell* conference notes, n.d. [October 25, 1974], Brennan Papers, Part I, Box 338, Folder 1. For several justices' subsequent efforts to preserve disparate impact under Title VII from its fate under equal protection, see Serena Mayeri, *Reasoning from Race: Feminism, Law, and the Civil Rights Revolution* (Cambridge, Mass.: Harvard University Press, 2011), 113–14.

19 Handy Andy, Inc., 228 N.L.R.B. 447, 452–53, 456 (1977). The other decisions were Bell & Howell, 230 N.L.R.B. 420 (1977); Murcel Manufacturing Co., 231 N.L.R.B. 623 (1977); and Trumbull Asphalt Co., 240 N.L.R.B. 646 (1977). Bell & Howell, 230 N.L.R.B. at 421–23 (1977). James Gross, in his illuminating history of the NLRB, generally treats the NLRA's worker-choice emphasis as being in tension with its goal of fostering collective bargaining and describes Republicans' emphasis on

the former goal as a betrayal of the latter. Gross, *Broken Promise*. The decisions overturning *Bekins* and the *Mansion House* rule demonstrate that these two statutory purposes can align and that Republicans' respect for the former goal sometimes facilitated the latter.

20 Bell & Howell, 230 N.L.R.B. at 421, 423. Handy Andy, Inc., 228 N.L.R.B. at 448–51, 454–56.
21 Handy Andy, Inc, 228 N.L.R.B. at 448, 452, quoting Johnson, Administrator of Veterans' Affairs v. Robison, 415 U.S. 361, 368 (1974).
22 Ibid., 454, 459–60 (Jenkins, Member, dissenting).
23 Bell & Howell, 230 N.L.R.B. at 421–23. Handy Andy, Inc, 228 N.L.R.B. at 451.
24 Handy Andy, Inc, 228 N.L.R.B. at 459–60 (Jenkins, Member, dissenting).
25 Bell & Howell Co. v. NLRB, 598 F.2d 136, 146, 149 (1979). The other members of the panel were Carl E. McGowan, also a liberal, and Roger Robb, a Goldwater Republican with a reputation for leaving his politics outside the courthouse door. Paul Friedman, "Civility, Judicial Independence, and the Role of the Bar," *Washington Lawyer* (December 2002), available at www.dcbar.org. *NAACP v. FPC* is discussed earlier in this chapter and in Chapter 10.
26 1976 Board Hearing Transcript, 130.

12 Conservatives Unite the Workplace Constitutions

1 Ernest C. Smith, "Why an All Black Party," *Illustrated News* 4, no. 1 (January 13, 1964): 5–6. Detroit Teachers Opposed to Compulsory Unionism (DTOCU), press release, August 22, 1969, Ernest C. Smith Papers [hereafter Smith Papers], Box 2, Folder 21, ALUA. See Chapter 2 for the Cannery Workers. "Freedom Now Party Formed by Negroes," *New York Amsterdam News*, November 30, 1963, 23; James H. Meriwether, *Proudly We Can Be Africans: Black Americans and Africa, 1935–1961* (Chapel Hill: University of North Carolina Press, 2002). On another of the party's founders, see H. Timothy Lovelace, "Race around the World: William Worthy, Black Internationalism, and the Universal Declaration of Human Rights," unpublished manuscript, 2013.
2 On a better-known example of blacks' response to this predicament, see Charles M. Payne, *I've Got the Light of Freedom: The Organizing Tradition and the Mississippi Freedom Struggle* (Berkeley: University of California Press, 1995); Nelson Lichtenstein, *The Most Dangerous Man in Detroit: Walter Reuther and the Fate of American Labor* (New York: Basic Books, 1995), 392–95.
3 Glenn Engle, "Michigan Negro Party Studies Poor Showing," *Washington Post*, November 26, 1964, A44. Black nationalist politics continued to

thrive in Detroit even after the party's demise. Heather Ann Thompson, *Whose Detroit? Politics, Labor, and Race in a Modern American City* (Ithaca, N.Y.: Cornell University Press, 2002). On the Black Panther Party and the black power movement more generally, see Chapter 8.

4   Inner City Organization, "News Release," September 9, 1967, Smith Papers, Box 3, Folder 1.

5   Tomiko Brown-Nagin, *Courage to Dissent: Atlanta and the Long History of the Civil Rights Movement* (New York: Oxford University Press, 2011), 86–87. Nelson Lichtenstein, *State of the Union: A Century of American Labor* (Princeton, N.J.: Princeton University Press, 2002), 181–82. For employment patterns, see *Historical Statistics of the United States: Millennial Edition Online*, Series Ba1117–1130 and Ba1089–1102 (New York: Cambridge University Press), and Appendix, Figures A.3 and A.4.

6   Brown-Nagin, *Courage to Dissent*, 107–9.

7   Ernest C. Smith, "Detroit Public Schools Department of Personnel Claim," June 12, 1962, Smith Papers, Box 1, Folder 15. Marjorie Murphy, *Blackboard Unions: The AFT and the NEA, 1900–1980* (Ithaca, N.Y.: Cornell University Press, 1990), chap. 12, esp. 236; Brown-Nagin, *Courage to Dissent*, chaps. 11–12.

8   The comparison of the NEA and AFT in this and the following paragraph draws heavily from Murphy, *Blackboard Unions*; quotations on 223.

9   On Brooklyn's Oceanville-Brownsville strike, see ibid., chap. 12; Joshua B. Freeman, *Working-Class New York: Life and Labor since World War II* (New York: New Press, 2000).

10 Lichtenstein, *State of the Union*, 181–83; Joseph A. McCartin, *Collision Course: Ronald Reagan, the Air Traffic Controllers, and the Strike That Changed America* (New York: Oxford University Press, 2011), 31–32, 123–26. Murphy, *Blackboard Unions*, 214, 219. Nationally, during the early 1960s, the NEA won more elections but the AFT represented more workers because it won in the larger urban school districts. Ibid., 224–28.

11 "'Agency Shop' for Steel," *New York Times*, January 27, 1960, 24. William Grant, "Teachers Fighting Compulsory Dues," *Detroit Free Press*, August 1969, Smith Papers, Box 2, Folder 17.

12 Jerry Norton, "A Fighter for Freedom," *Conservative Digest*, November 1975, Schlossberg Papers, Box 29, Folder 14; Gilbert J. Gall, *The Politics of Right to Work: The Labor Federations as Special Interests, 1943–1979* (New York: Greenwood Press, 1988), 115–17, 144. Donald MacLean to Reed Larson, January 6, 1955, DeMille Papers, Box 1194, Folder 5. Donald MacLean to Reed Larson, August 15, 1956, ibid.

13 Reed Larson report enclosed in National Right to Work Committee (NRWC), "Minutes of Meeting," January 16, 1964 [hereafter Larson 1964 Report], Wilkinson Papers, Box 219, Folder 26. Republican Party

Platform of 1964, July 13, 1964, available at http://www.presidency.ucsb.
edu/ws/index.php?pid=25840.

14 Karin Chenoweth, "Disguising Bosses as Workers," *AFL-CIO News*,
June 14, 1986, 2. Larson 1964 Report, 2. Brotherhood of Railway and
Steamship Clerks v. Allen, 373 U.S. 113 (1963). Ibid. at 129–31 (Harlan,
J., concurring and dissenting).

15 An example of Larson's involvement in the Railway Labor Act cases is
Reed Larson to Hon. John Patterson, February 8, 1956, DeMille Papers,
Box 1194, Folder 5. NRWC, "Area of Increase in 1962 Program," n.d.
[1962], NRWC Papers, Box 1. An example of an article publicizing the
committee's cases is "29 Workers File Suit against Douglas IAM in Legal
Challenge to Compulsory Unionism," *Free Choice* 3, no. 10 (October
1967), NRWC Papers, Box 3.

16 On the right-to-work movement's legislative fortunes, see Chapters 9
and 11. NRWC, "Bitter Congressional Fight Slated on Postal Workers'
Right to Work," April 17, 1970, RG 1–0038, Series 3, AFL-CIO Office
of the President, George Meany Files, 1940–1980, Miscellaneous
Correspondence and Subject Files, 1949–1979 [hereafter Meany Papers –
MCSF], Box 50, Folder 22, GMMA; Postal Reorganization Act, 39
U.S.C. 1209(c) (1970). Everett McKinley Dirksen, "Individual Freedom
versus Compulsory Unionism: A Constitutional Problem," *De Paul Law
Review* 15, no. 2 (1966): 259–75. John Kilcullen, "Background on Legal
Challenges of Compulsory Unionism," October 1, 1967, NRWC Papers,
Box 2. On the growth of individual rights during this period and their
adverse potential for labor, see Reuel E. Schiller, "From Group Rights to
Individual Liberties: Post-War Labor Law, Liberalism, and the Waning
of Union Strength," *Berkeley Journal of Employment and Labor Law* 20
(1999): 1–73.

17 "Stoking Up a Drive for Right-to-Work," *Business Week*, March 14,
1970, Smith Papers, Box 2, Folder 17. "With Honesty and Courage:
Defending America's Working Men and Women," enclosed in Ray Bowie
to Reed Larson et al., October 17, 1979, John A. Davenport Papers [here-
after Davenport Papers], Box 25, Folder 1, Hoover Institution Archives,
Stanford University, Stanford, Calif.; "Foundation Fights Union Shop,"
Detroit Free Press, December 29, 1969, McCulloch Papers, Box 6, Folder
31. National Right to Work Legal Defense Foundation (NRWLDF), "1976:
a year of VICTORY," 1976, Wilkinson Papers, Box 87, Folder 3, 3.

18 Reed Larson, "Compulsory Unionism … A Major Obstacle to Full
Employment Opportunities," February 17, 1967, NRWC Papers, Box 1.
Reed Larson to Donald MacLean, September 23, 1958, DeMille Papers,
Box 1194, Folder 5.

19 "Free Choice: Another Area of Civil Rights That Jim Nixon Deeply
Believes In," *Free Choice*, May–June 1972, NRWC Papers, Box 3. For
a more extensive treatment of this transition, see Sophia Z. Lee, "Whose

Rights? Litigating the Right to Work, 1940–1980," in *The Right and Labor in America: Politics, Ideology, and Imagination*, ed. Nelson Lichtenstein and Elizabeth Tandy Shermer, 160–80 (Philadelphia: University of Pennsylvania Press, 2012).

20 "New Missouri Board Member Tough Battler for Voluntarism," *Free Choice*, May 1969, NRWC Papers, Box 3. "CORE Chapter Votes to Endorse Right to Work," *Free Choice*, January 1969, NRWC Papers, Box 3. The UAW was shaken at the time by splinter unions influenced by leftist student radicalism, anti-imperialism, and the Black Power movement. Kevin Boyle, *The UAW and the Heyday of American Liberalism, 1945–1968* (Ithaca, N.Y.: Cornell University Press, 1998), 251–54; Dan Georgakas and Marvin Surkin, *Detroit: I Do Mind Dying: A Study in Urban Revolution* (Cambridge, Mass.: South End Press, 1999); Lichtenstein, *The Most Dangerous Man in Detroit*, 433–34; Thompson, *Whose Detroit?*, chap. 3.

21 Cecil B. DeMille, "America Still Needs Pioneers," (speech, Broadcast Pioneers Dinner, Statler Hilton Hotel, Los Angeles, California, April 29, 1958), Wilkinson Papers, Box 168, Folder 9. NRWC, "Use of Union Dues for Political Purposes Is Admitted in Court by Officials of 15 Unions," pamphlet, May 1, 1966, NRWC Papers, Box 5. "Right-to-Work Battle Shifts to Grassroots," *Human Events*, August 13, 1966, NRWC Papers, Box 1. The film *... And Women Must Weep* was copyrighted in 1962 but may have been produced in 1958; it is available from the Library of Congress Motion Picture and Television Reading Room or at www.nrtwc. org. Anna McCarthy, *The Citizen Machine: Governing by Television in 1950s America* (New York: New Press, 2010), 237–38. The Right to Work Committee's strategy presaged the better-known mobilization of conservative women around social issues in the 1970s and 1980s. See Introduction.

22 Jefferson Cowie, *Stayin' Alive: The 1970s and the Last Days of the Working Class* (New York: New Press, 2010), chap. 1. Reed Larson, "Is Monopoly in the American Tradition?" *Vital Speeches of the Day* 39, no. 17 (June 15, 1973): 527–30, 527. NRWLDF, "1976: A year of VICTORY!" Wilkinson Papers.

23 Reed Larson to Ernest Smith, April 9, 1970, Smith Papers, Box 3, Folder 16.

24 Leonard A. Keller to John L. Kilcullen, November 5, 1969, Smith Papers, Box 3, Folder 15. "Leonard Keller: Lawyer, Professor," *Detroit Free Press*, September 19, 1970, ibid., Box 2, Folder 17. George P. McDonnell to Wayne Bonney, October 13, 1969, ibid., Box 3, Folder 15. Hillsdale Community Schools v. Michigan Labor Mediation Bd., 24 Mich. App. 36 (1970); School Dist. for City of Holland, Ottowa and Allegan Counties v. Holland Ed. Ass'n, 380 Mich. 314 (1968). Both local organizations' letterhead bore the Right to Work Committee's trademark image of the Liberty

Bell emblazoned with "RIGHT TO WORK." Michigan Citizens for Right to Work, meeting minutes, May 12, 1970, Smith Papers, Box 3, Folder 2. On Vigeurie, see Laura Kalman, *Right Star Rising: A New Politics, 1974–1980* (New York: W. W. Norton, 2010), 25–27. James Nixon to Friend, August 19, 1969, Smith Papers, Box 3, Folder 5.

25   Grant, "Teachers Fighting Compulsory Dues"; Harry Salsinger, "New Teacher Group Hits Agency Shop," *Detroit News*, August 23, 1969, Smith Papers, Box 2, Folder 17. Ernest C. Smith to Fellow Teacher, March 20, 1970, ibid., Folder 18; Teachers Opposed, "Press Release," ibid., Box 3, Folder 16. Abood v. Detroit Board of Education, 431 U.S. 209, 211 (1977).

26   Ruth Weyand, "Present Status of Individual Employee Rights," in *Proceedings of New York University Twenty-Second Annual Conference on Labor* (New York: Matthew Bender, 1970), 171–216, 177. NLRB v. Century Broadcasting Corp., 419 F.2d 771, 778 (8th Cir. 1970). McAuliffe v. New Bedford, 155 Mass. 216 (1892); United Public Workers of America v. Mitchell, 330 U.S. 75, 99 (1947). Courts' favorable response to NAACP lawsuits challenging the constitutionality of southern pay differentials between black and white teachers are an important exception. Brown-Nagin, *Courage to Dissent*, 88–90; Mark V. Tushnet, *Making Civil Rights Law: Thurgood Marshall and the Supreme Court, 1956–1961* (New York: Oxford University Press, 1996), 21–26. Jerome J. Shestack, "The Public Employee and His Government: Conditions and Disabilities of Public Employment," *Vanderbilt Law Review* 8 (1955): 816–37. Wieman v. Updegraff, 344 U.S. 183 (1952); Beilan v. Board of Public Education, 357 U.S. 399 (1958). James E. Leahy, "The Public Employee and the First Amendment: Must He Sacrifice His Civil Rights to Be a Civil Servant?" *California Western Law Review* 4 (1968): 1–18. Keyishian v. Board of Regents, 385 U.S. 589, 624–25 (1967) (Clark, J., dissenting). Pickering v. Board of Education, 391 U.S. 563 (1968); Perry v. Sindermann, 408 U.S. 593 (1972).

27   This paragraph draws heavily from Joseph A. McCartin, "'A Wagner Act for Public Employees': Labor's Deferred Dream and the Rise of Conservatism, 1970–1976," *Journal of American History* 95, no. 1 (June 2008): 123–48, 123, 140–42. See also Joseph A. McCartin and Jean-Christian Vinel, "'Compulsory Unionism': Sylvester Petro and the Career of an Anti-Union Idea, 1957–1987," in *The Right and Labor in America: Politics, Ideology, and Imagination*, ed. Nelson Lichtenstein and Elizabeth Tandy Shermer, 226–51 (Philadelphia: University of Pennsylvania Press, 2012). Quote is in "A Place to Turn," *Right to Work News Service*, June 14, 1973, NRWC Papers, Box 1.

28   Brief in Support of Claim of Appeal, Warczak v. Board of Education, Mich. Ct. App., Case Nos. 19523, 19465, April 11, 1974, 13, 17–19, 35–45.

29 Raymond LaJeunesse Jr. to Plaintiff, August 22, 1975, Smith Papers, Box 3, Folder 9. Abood v. Detroit Board of Education, 230 N.W.2d 322, 326–27 (Mich. Ct. App. 1975) (per curiam) ("benefits of its work" quote from *Hanson*, 351 U.S. at 238). The Michigan court departed from the Railway Labor Act cases in one respect: it required workers to object to specific expenditures rather than to the union's political spending generally.

30 Lewis F. Powell to Potter Stewart, January 18, 1977, Thurgood Marshall Papers, Box 185, Folder 4. McCartin, "A Wagner Act for Public Employees," 144–45. National League of Cities v. Usery, 426 U.S. 833 (1976). McCartin and Vinel, "'Compulsory Unionism,'" 248.

31 This paragraph draws on McCartin and Vinel, "'Compulsory Unionism.'" Sylvester Petro, "Sovereignty and Compulsory Public-Sector Bargaining," *Wake Forest Law Review* 10 (March 1974): 25–165. Petro wage and hour brief quoted in McCartin and Vinel, "'Compulsory Unionism,'" 247. Brief for Appellants, Abood v. Board of Education, Supreme Court of the United States, Case No. 75–1153, July 9, 1976, pt. I.B.3., 63. Petro also tried to distinguish *Hanson* with a new unconstitutional-conditions argument, which the justices ignored.

32 Potter Stewart to Lewis F. Powell, January 14, 1977, Thurgood Marshall Papers, Box 185, Folder 4.

33 Abood v. Detroit Board of Education, 431 U.S. 209 (1977). Elrod v. Burns, 427 U.S. 347 (1976) (plurality). Powell quotes and biographic details are in Kim Phillips-Fein, *Invisible Hands: The Making of the Conservative Movement from the New Deal to Reagan* (New York: W. W. Norton, 2009), 156–60.

34 Raymond LaJeunesse Jr. to Detroit Teacher, May 27, 1977, Wilkinson Papers, Box 87, Folder 2. *Abood*, 431 U.S. at 255, 250–54, 257–58, 261–64 (Powell, J., concurring). Stewart disagreed not with the characterization of collective bargaining as political but with its relevance: the First Amendment protected all kinds of speech, he countered; the dispositive question thus was not whether public sector unions' activities were political, but whether the government was justified in compelling participation in them. Ibid. at 230–32. In a novel twist, Powell also argued that differences in the type of state action – compulsion, in the case of the teachers' agency shop contract; permission, in the case of workers organized under the Railway Labor Act – affected the robustness of the workers' substantive rights. Ibid. at 259–60 (Powell, J., concurring); Lewis F. Powell to Potter Stewart, January 13, 1977, Thurgood Marshall Papers, Box 185, Folder 4. Stewart objected that "*Hanson* nowhere suggested that [its] constitutional scrutiny … was watered down because the governmental action operated less directly than" in *Abood*. *Abood*, 431 U.S. at 226 n. 23 (1977).

35 "Burger Sails into All Windy Lawyers," *Detroit News*, November 10, 1976, Smith Papers, Box 2, Folder 17; Warren E. Burger to Conference, March 14, 1977, Thurgood Marshall Papers, Box 185, Folder 4.

36 Raymond LaJeunesse Jr. to Detroit Teacher, May 27, 1977, Wilkinson Papers, Box 87, Folder 2. *Abood*, 431 U.S. at 234–35. "Freedom of millions" quote in NRWLDF, press release, June 2, 1977, Wilkinson Papers, Box 87, Folder 2. For DeMille's earlier claim, see Chapter 3.

37 "Bias in the Classroom," March 6, 1977, Wilkinson Papers, Box 87, Folder 6. Concerned Educators against Forced Unionism, "Recaps," October–November 1978, RG 98–002, Artificial Collections: George Meany Memorial Archives, Vertical Files, 1881–1999, Series 1, Box 39, Folder 25, GMMA, 3. NRWC, "Catalogue of Educational Materials," August 1977, NRWC Papers, Box 1; Reed Larson, interviewed by Stan Evans, January 15, 1976, transcript (1 of 2), NRWC Papers, Box 2, 26–28. NRWC Executive Committee, meeting minutes, February 24, 1977, Wilkinson Papers, Box 87, Folder 1. "Nineteen Wage-Earners Honored for Right to Work Leadership," *Free Choice*, June 14, 1973, NRWC Papers, Box 3; "Minority Union Favors Right to Work, Opposes Big Labor," *Free Choice*, December 20, 1977, ibid.; W. Earl Douglas, "Unions Like 'Massah,'" *Charleston Post*, November 1, 1976, reprinted in *Free Choice*, December 13, 1976, ibid.

38 Jerry Flint, "Reed Larson vs. The Union Shop," *New York Times Magazine*, December 4, 1977, 1; Walter Mossberg, "20-Year Fight: Right to Work Drive: A Friend to Workers or a Menace to Them?" *Wall Street Journal*, April 22, 1975, 1.

39 William H. Rehnquist, "Notion of a Living Constitution," *Texas Law Review* 54, no. 4 (May 1976): 693–706, 699. *Abood*, 431 U.S. at 243–44, 255 (1977) (Rehnquist, J., concurring).

13 The Conservative Workplace Constitution Divides the New Right Coalition

1 "Beck Rights 2001: Are Workers Being Heard?" Hearing before the Subcommittee on Workforce Protections of the House Committee on Education and the Workforce, Serial No. 107–15, May 10, 2001 (testimony and written statement of Harry Beck) (Washington, D.C.: Government Printing Office, 2002), 16, 110–11. On working-class politics in the 1970s, see Jefferson Cowie, *Stayin' Alive: The 1970s and the Last Days of the Working Class* (New York: New Press, 2010). But see Lawrence Richards, *Union-Free America: Workers and Antiunion Culture* (Urbana: University of Illinois Press, 2010). On the particular complexity of these politics, see Jefferson Cowie, "'Vigorously Left, Right, and Center': The Crosscurrents of Working-Class America in the 1970s," in *America in the Seventies*, ed. Beth L. Bailey and Dave Farber, 75–106 (Lawrence: University Press of Kansas, 2004).

2 Cecil B. DeMille, dictation, April 30, 1945, DeMille Papers, Box 1143, Folder 2.

3 Thomas R. Brooks, *Communication Workers of America* (New York: Mason/Charter, 1977), 232, 234–35, 243.
4 "Spotlight on Steve and Sue Havas," included in Godfrey Schmidt, "The Constitutionality of the 'Agency Shop,'" transcription, May 11, 1973, NRWC Papers, Box 1. "Harry Beck: Telephone Worker Fights Compulsory Union Dues Politicking," *Free Choice*, September–October 1980, NRWC Papers, Box 3, 9–10. Like the teachers' cases in Chapter 12, these workers' campaigns provide a conservative counternarrative to the better-known, often left-leaning worker insurgencies against "stale bureaucratic union leadership" in unions such as the UAW, Steelworkers, and Mine Workers. Cowie, *Stayin' Alive*, 7–8 and chap. 1.
5 *National Right to Work Newsletter*, May 25, 1973, NRWC Papers. The plaintiffs also made fiduciary duty, contract breach, duty of fair representation, and campaign finance law claims. Beck Compl., June 4, 1976, Communications Workers of America Papers, WAG 124 [hereafter CWA Papers], Box 217, Folder 28, Wagner Archives, Tamiment Library, New York University, 8, 10–11, 20–21.
6 "The Right-to-Work Issue: Sleeping but Not Dead," *Industry Week*, June 16, 1975, Schlossberg Papers, Box 25, Folder 5; NRWLDF, "1976: A year of VICTORY!" 1976, Wilkinson Papers, Box 87, Folder 3, 3, 15–17; "Stoking Up a Drive for Right-to-Work," *Business Week*, March 14, 1970, Smith Papers, Box 2, Folder 17.
7 Walter Mossberg, "20-Year Fight: Right to Work Drive: A Friend to Workers or a Menace to Them?" *Wall Street Journal*, April 22, 1975, 1; Jerry Flint, "Reed Larson vs. the Union Shop," *New York Times Magazine*, December 4, 1977, 1. NRWC, "The Nation's Press and Compulsory Unionism," Spring 1977, Wilkinson Papers, Box 87, Folder 6. Herb Berkowitz, "Despite Big Labor's Claims, Right to Work State Voters Responsible for Carter Victory," *Free Choice*, December 13, 1976, Wilkinson Papers, Box 87, Folder 1, 1; Republican Party Platform of 1976, August 18, 1976, available at http://www.presidency.ucsb.edu/ws/index.php?pid=25843. Cowie, *Stayin' Alive*, 295; Laura Kalman, *Right Star Rising: A New Politics, 1974–1980* (New York: W. W. Norton, 2010), 162. Richardson v. Communications Workers of America, 443 F.2d 974 (8th Cir. 1971). The court found that Richardson's termination for nonmembership violated the governing collective bargaining agreement. See also Linscott v. Millers Falls Co., 440 F.2d 14 (1st Cir. 1971); Evans v. American Federation of Television and Radio Artists, 354 F. Supp. 823 (S.D.N.Y. 1973); Seay v. McDonnell Douglas Corp., 427 F.2d 996 (9th Cir. 1970); Seay v. McDonnell Douglas Corp., 533 F.2d 1126 (9th Cir. 1976).
8 Sean Wilentz, *The Age of Reagan: America from Watergate to the War on Terror* (New York: Harper, 2008), 76, 91–92; Kalman, *Right Star Rising*, 162–63. Phillips quoted in ibid., 29.

9   Kalman, *Right Star Rising*, 29–30. According to Kalman, the New Right activists "exaggerated their differences with the old right." Ibid. This is true not only of the New Right's focus on social, cultural, and religious issues, but also of its efforts to woo working-class support. "Hugh Lawrence Reilly," *Boston Globe*, available at http://www. legacy.com/obituaries/bostonglobe/obituary.aspx?n=hugh-lawrence-reilly&pid=101503580&eid=sp_shareobit; "Remembering Hugh Reilly, Right to Work Litigator," *Foundation Action*, March/April 2008, 7. NRWLDF, "Job Announcement," January 1978, Wilkinson Papers, Box 87, Folder 5. See, for instance, Hugh L. Reilly to Matthew A. Kane, June 15, 1977, CWA Papers, Box 217, Folder 29; Hugh L. Reilly to Michael T. Leibig, April 22, 1981, ibid., Folder 2; J[ames]B[.]C[opess], "Note to file, Beck v. CWA," August 14, 1981, ibid.

10   Abood v. Detroit Board of Education, 431 U.S. 209, 218 n. 12 (1977). [Plaintiffs'] Opposition to Defendant CWA's Motion to Dismiss or for Stay, and Request for Hearing Thereon, August 26, 1977, Beck v. CWA, No. B-76-839, U.S. District Court for the District of Maryland [hereafter Beck District Court Case], CWA Papers, Box 218, Folder 1, 11; Reply [of] CWA Defendants to Plaintiffs' Opposition to CWA's Motion to Dismiss or for Stay, August 31, 1977, Beck District Court Case, ibid.

11   Beck v. CWA, 468 F. Supp. 93, 96, 97 (D. Md. 1979). "No More Free Ride ... For Union Officials," *Washington Post*, July 29, 1979, D4 (advertisement).

12   "Harry Beck, Hero," *National Review* 32, no. 23 (November 14, 1980): 1417. Lykins v. Aluminum Workers of America, 510 F. Supp. 21, 25–26 (E.D. Pa. 1980). Havas v. CWA, 509 F. Supp. 144, 148–49 (N.D.N.Y. 1981). John Chamberlain, "Agency Shop: Is It Illegal?" *St. Petersburg Independent*, July 11, 1973, 15-A; "Spotlight on Steve and Sue Havas," May 11, 1973, NRWC Papers; "New York Telephone Co. Employees Begin Right to Work Newsletter," *Free Choice*, September 9, 1973, NRWC Papers, Box 3. Kolinske v. Lubbers, 516 F. Supp. 1171, 1179 (D.D.C. 1981). Demonstrating the conservative workplace Constitution's effect on its liberal alternative, Joseph Rauh, longtime advocate of the liberal workplace Constitution, had argued against a finding of state action in *Kolinske*.

13   Edwin Meese III (speech to New Coalition for Economic and Social Change [NCESC], September 13, 1982), Edwin Meese Papers [hereafter Meese Papers], Box 7, "New Coalition for Economic & Social Change" Folder, Hoover Institution Archives, Stanford University, Stanford, Calif. Clarence M. Pendleton Jr. to Edwin Meese III, July 29, 1982, ibid. On Weyrich and Coors, see Kim Phillips-Fein, *Invisible Hands: The Making of the Conservative Movement from the New Deal to Reagan* (New York: W. W. Norton, 2009), 171–72; Kalman, *Right Star Rising*, 26–27. [NCESC], "Statement of Purpose," September 13, 1982, Meese Papers, Box 7, "New

Coalition for Economic & Social Change" Folder. Arch Parsons, "Black Conservatives Grow More Visible, But No More Organized," *Baltimore Sun*, July 11, 1991, 1A. For Nixon's earlier cultivation of black conservatives, see Dean J. Kotlowski, *Nixon's Civil Rights: Politics, Principle, and Policy* (Cambridge, Mass.: Harvard University Press, 2002), 176–78.

14 Not all historians agree that Reagan came into office antiunion. Joseph A. McCartin, *Collision Course: Ronald Reagan, the Air Traffic Controllers, and the Strike That Changed America* (New York: Oxford University Press, 2011). Ronald Reagan, "Nomination of Donald L. Dotson to Be an Assistant Secretary of Labor," April 17, 1981, *American Presidency Project*, http://www.presidency.ucsb.edu/ws/?pid=43706; Patrick Owens, "Unionbuster at the N.L.R.B.," *Nation*, July 23, 1983, 71–74, 71–72 (includes "chicken coop" quote by Representative William Ford).

15 Parsons, "Black Conservatives." Reed Larson, "Blacks and Compulsory Unionism: 'The Classic Double Bind,'" *Right to Work News Service*, November 3, 1980, NRWC Papers, Box 1. See Chapter 8. John T. McQuiston, "Clarence M. Pendleton, 57, Dies," *New York Times*, June 6, 1988, D12. Ernest Holsendolph, "Skills, Not Bias, Seen as Key for Jobs," *New York Times*, July 3, 1982, 15.

16 Regents of the University of California v. Bakke, 438 U.S. 265, 319–20 (1978). A majority of justices found that promoting diversity in education was a sufficiently compelling interest to satisfy strict scrutiny. Ibid. at 314–19.

17 Legal Defense Foundation general counsel Whiteford Blakeney, a North Carolina segregationist, advocated a color-blind approach to equal protection in 1969. Whiteford S. Blakeney, "Segregation-Integration and the United States Constitution," *Charlotte Observer*, October 14, 1969, Wilkinson Papers, Box 166, Folder 2. Conservatives had since worked to distance this approach from its segregationist roots. See Nancy MacLean, *Freedom Is Not Enough: The Opening of the American Workplace* (Cambridge, Mass.: Harvard University Press, 2008), chap. 7. On the rise of color-blind conservatives see, generally, ibid.; Dennis Deslippe, *Protesting Affirmative Action: The Struggle over Equality after the Civil Rights Revolution* (Baltimore: Johns Hopkins University Press, 2012), chap. 6. Fullilove v. Klutznick, 448 U.S. 448 (1980); ibid. at 496 (Powell, J., concurring); ibid. at 523 (Stewart, J., dissenting). Justice Stevens was unclear in *Fullilove* about the standard he employed, but he stated that "racial classifications are simply too pernicious to permit any but the most exact connection between justification and classification." Ibid. at 537 (Stevens, J., dissenting). *Bakke*, 438 U.S. at 357–58 (Brennan, J., dissenting in part). Wygant v. Jackson, 476 U.S. 267 (1986). In *Wygant*, Stevens joined Brennan and the other benign remedialists while Chief Justice Burger and Justice Sandra Day O'Connor (Justice Stewart's replacement) joined the color-blind constitutionalists. Justice White remained hard to

place. He joined the benign remedialists in *Bakke*, 438 U.S. at 357–58 (Brennan, J., dissenting in part). In *Fullilove*, he and Burger refused to adopt either the color-blind constitutionalists' or the benign remedial-ists' approach (although they contended that the program passed muster under either). *Fullilove*, 448 U.S. at 472. They seemed to agree with the color-blind constitutionalists' fundamental premise, however, reasoning that a court should apply a single level of review to a "program that employs racial or ethnic criteria, even in a remedial context." Ibid. White concurred in *Wygant*, 476 U.S. at 294–95, that the minority layoff pro-gram was unconstitutional, but once again did not clearly adopt either the color-blind or the benign remedialist position.

18   United Steelworkers of America v. Weber, 443 U.S. 193, 200, 201–02 (1979). Ibid. at 222 (Rehnquist, J., dissenting). For different takes on *Weber*, see Cowie, *Stayin' Alive*, 242–44; Deslippe, *Protesting Affirmative Action*, 200–203; MacLean, *Freedom Is Not Enough*, 249–56; Deborah C. Malamud, "The Story of *United Steelworkers of America v. Weber*," in *Employment Discrimination Stories*, ed. Joel W. Friedman, 173–224 (New York: Foundation Press, 2006). For the argument that the program evaluated in *Weber* would have failed an equal protection analysis, see Sophia Z. Lee, "A Revolution at War with Itself? Preserving Employment Preferences from *Weber* to *Ricci*," *Yale Law Journal* 123 (2014): 2964–3000.

19   United Steelworkers of America v. Sadlowski, 457 U.S. 102, 122 n. 16 (1982). Brief of Appellants/Cross-Appellees [hereafter CWA Appellate Brief], May 16, 1984, Beck v. CWA, Nos. 83–1955 and 83–1956, U.S. Court of Appeals for the Fourth Circuit [hereafter Beck Appellate Case], CWA Papers, Box 218, Folder 21. Brief in Response to Appellants/ Cross-Appellees and in Support of Cross-Appeal, June 29, 1984 [here-after NRWLDF Appellate Brief], Beck Appellate Case, ibid., Folder 22, 24. Reply Brief on Appeal and Brief in Response on Cross-Appeal for Appellants/Cross-Appellees, August 1, 1984 [hereafter NRWLDF Appellate Reply Brief], Beck Appellate Case, ibid., Folder 21, 7.

20   These justices' narrow state action decisions continued a pattern they began earlier in the 1970s. See Chapter 10. Blum v. Yaretsky, 457 U.S. 991, 1004, 1009 (1982). Flagg Bros., Inc. v. Brooks, 436 U.S. 149, 162 n. 11, 164–65 (1978). Rendall-Baker v. Kohn, 457 U.S. 830, 841 (1982). See Chapter 10 for a discussion of the nexus doctrine's origins.

21   CWA Appellate Brief, 22–27 (quoting Kolinkse 712 F.2d at 478–80 and Lugar v. Edmondson Oil Co., Inc. 457 U.S. 922, 936 (1982)). This state-ment echoed both the current conservative justices and the midcentury labor pluralists discussed in previous chapters, especially Chapters 4–7.

22   *Lugar*, 457 U.S. 922 (1982). NRWLDF Appellate Brief, 26–29. Beck's attorneys noted, for instance, that the NLRA made these agreements a mandatory subject of bargaining and created unfair labor practice orders or court remedies if the employer refused to bargain for such an agreement

or failed to terminate an employee who did not pay the fees an agency shop agreement required. Ibid.

23 NRWLDF Appellate Brief, 18–21. Supplemental Br. of Appellees/Cross-Appellants on Rehearing En Banc, n.d. [1986], Beck Appellate Case, CWA Papers, Box 218, Folder 19, 12–13 (internal quotations omitted). "Russell, Winter, Chapman," notes on oral argument, November 1, 1984, CWA Papers, Box 217, Folder 16.

24 "Donald S. Russell Dies at 92," *New York Times*, February 25, 1998, B8. Federal Judicial Center, "Chapman, Robert Foster," in *Biographical Directory of Federal Judges*, available at http://www.fjc.gov/servlet/nGet Info?jid=411&cid=999&ctype=na&instate=na; Joseph Crespino, *Strom Thurmond's America* (New York: Hill and Wang, 2012), 175, 248.

25 NRWLDF Appellate Brief, 8–9, 30–34; "Russell, Winter, Chapman," November 1, 1984, CWA Papers. Beck v. CWA, 776 F.2d 1187, 1197–1209 (4th Cir. 1985).

26 Beck v. CWA, 800 F.2d 1280 (4th Cir. 1986) (rehearing en banc). "Federal Appeals Court Affirms Ruling That Compulsory Union Fees Were Misused," press release, September 17, 1986, Davenport Papers, Box 25, Folder 3. National Committee for Union Shop Abolition, "Its Background, Origin and Plan of Action," n.d. [1952–54], NRWC Papers, Box 1.

27 James B. Coppess to William [E.] Caldwell, February 3, 1981, CWA Papers, Box 217, Folder 2.

28 Robert E. Taylor, "Civil Rights Division Head Will Seek Supreme Court Ban on Affirmative Action," *Wall Street Journal*, December 8, 1981, sec. 1. Edwin Meese, "Constitution Day Speech," (speech, Dickinson College, Carlisle, Pa., September 16, 1985), Meese Papers, Box 15, "Dickinson College Constitution Day" Folder, 12, 14. In 1986, the Court struck down an affirmative action program under the Fourteenth Amendment, but the next year it upheld one under Title VII. Compare Wygant v. Jackson, 476 U.S. 267 (1986) with Johnson v. Santa Clara County Transportation Agency, 480 U.S. 616 (1987). On the Reagan Justice Department and affirmative action, see, generally, Charles Fried, *Order and Law: Arguing the Reagan Revolution* (New York: Simon & Schuster, 1991), 92–131; Douglas Kmiec, *The Attorney General's Lawyer: Inside the Meese Justice Department* (New York: Praeger, 1992), chap. 7; Reva B. Siegel, "Equality Divided," *Harvard Law Review* 127, no. 1 (2013): 1–94; Lee, "A Revolution at War with Itself?"

29 Steven M. Teles, "Transformative Bureaucracy: Reagan's Lawyers and the Dynamics of Political Investment," *Studies in American Political Development* 23, no. 1 (2009): 61–83; Dawn E. Johnsen, "Ronald Reagan and the Rehnquist Court on Congressional Power: Presidential Influences on Constitutional Change," *Indiana Law Journal* 78 (Winter/Spring 2003): 363–425. Compare the speech by Edwin Meese III before the D.C. Chapter of the Federalist Society Lawyers Division, Washington,

D.C., November 15, 1985, in DOJ Office of Legal Policy (OLP), *Original Meaning Jurisprudence: A Sourcebook*, December 11, 1986, Box 115, "Jurisprudence of Original Intent" Folder [hereafter *Originalism Sourcebook*], 8, with OLP, "Guidelines on Constitutional Litigation," February 19, 1988, 3. The term "strict construction" dated to the nation's founding, and Nixon campaigned against the Warren Court in 1968 by promising to appoint only justices who were "strict constructionists." See Jessica Low, *Sacred Texts, Sacred Interpretation: How America Became a Nation of the Word* (forthcoming); Chapter 10. In the 1970s and 1980s, conservative legal scholars shifted emphasis from treating the Constitution like a contract to divining the intent of the Framers or the understanding of the public that ratified it. While there are robust legal and political science literatures on originalism, there has been little historical work done of yet. An influential work outside history is Keith Whittington, "The New Originalism," *Georgetown Journal of Law and Public Policy* 2, no. 2 (Summer 2004): 599–613. Mary Ziegler, Ken Kersch, and Logan Sawyer are doing promising work in this area.

30 Meese's and Brennan's speeches are reproduced in Steven G. Calabresi, *Originalism: A Quarter Century of Debate* (Washington, D.C.: Regnery Publishing, 2007), chaps. 1–3. On the Federalist Society, see Steven M. Teles, *The Rise of the Conservative Legal Movement: The Battle for Control of the Law* (Princeton, N.J.: Princeton University Press, 2008), chap. 5. Terry Eastland to Edwin Meese, November 12, 1985, Meese Papers, Box 16, "Federalist Society/DC Lawyers Division" Folder. Stephen J. Markman to Edwin Meese III, December 11, 1986, Meese Papers, Box 115, "Jurisprudence of Original Intent" Folder. OLP, *Guidelines on Constitutional Litigation*, 10. See also *Originalism Sourcebook*; OLP, "The Constitution in the Year 2000: Choices Ahead in Constitutional Interpretation" October 11, 1988. Brief of Plaintiffs-Appellees, Buckley v. AFTRA, Case No. 73–1667, U.S. Court of Appeals for the Second Circuit, September 28, 1973, Davenport Papers, Box 25, Folder 4, 23.

31 Stuart Taylor Jr., "Court Voice of Reaganism: Charles Fried," *New York Times*, October 24, 1985, 9. Telephone interview with Charles Fried conducted by author, February 8, 2013 [hereafter Fried Interview].

32 Stuart Taylor Jr., "High Court Bars U.S. Role in 2 Cases," *New York Times*, September 19, 1985, A35. Charles Fried, "Individual and Collective Rights in Work Relations: Reflections on the Current State of Labor Law and Its Prospects," *University of Chicago Law Review* 51 (1984): 1012–40, 1037, 1039.

33 Stuart Taylor Jr., "Of Power and the Law," *New York Times*, December 28, 1985, 9. Fried, "Individual and Collective Rights."

34 NRWLDF, "Reagan Administration Urged to Squash Solicitor's Defense of Forced Unionism," May 13, 1987, Davenport Papers, Box 25, Folder 3, box 25. Fried, *Order and Law*, 176. Fried Interview. I think it accurate to characterize Fried as a strict constructionist as that term was used in the

1980s but respect that it is not a characterization he agrees with. The reader is also cautioned that the term's meaning has evolved since the 1980s.

35 Fried, *Order and Law*, 179. As discussed in Chapter 7, lawyers representing the sit-in protesters (Jack Greenberg among them) advanced broad sanctioning and sufficiency-of-contacts theories of state action to argue that the arrest and conviction of the protesters was unconstitutional. Brief of the United States as Amicus Curiae, April 30, 1987 [hereafter SG's Beck Brief], CWA v. Beck, No. 86-637, Supreme Court of the United States [hereafter Beck SC Records], 25–27, 29.

36 SG's Beck Brief, 18. Fried, *Order and Law*, 180. Fried sought to narrow *Weber* drastically, rather than overturn it, in part by importing strict scrutiny standards from the Court's constitutional affirmative action cases. Brief of the United States as Amicus Curiae, August 21, 1986, Johnson v. Transportation Agency, No. 85-1129, Supreme Court of the United States, esp. 9 n. 5. See, generally, Lee, "A Revolution at War with Itself?"

37 Fried, *Order and Law*, 180–81. Reed Larson to Howard Baker, April 27, 1987, Ronald Reagan Presidential Records [hereafter Reagan Papers], WHORM Subject File JL004–03, Casefile 478480, Ronald Reagan Presidential Library, Simi, Calif. Fried reports that the brief was leaked to the White House, (*Order and Law*, 180–81), but Larson wrote to the White House after seeing the draft and included information about the NLRB's internal reactions to the brief, suggesting that he got the brief from the board. Larson letters described in NRWLDF, "Reagan Administration Urged to Squash Solicitor's Defense of Forced Unionism," press release, May 13, 1987, Davenport Papers, Box 25, Folder 3; "Key Justice Official Sides with Union Bosses," *Human Events*, May 9, 1987, 1.

38 Fried, *Order and Law*, 178, 181. "Key Justice Official," *Human Events*, 1, 7. Ralph Z. Hallow, "Justice Official Sides with Labor on Partisan Use of Forced Dues," *Washington Times*, April 30, 1987, Davenport Papers, Box 25, Folder 3.

39 Stuart Taylor Jr., "Reagan Backs Unions in Court over Use of Fees," *New York Times*, May 1, 1987, A15. "Giving Workers Their Dues," *Wall Street Journal*, May 18, 1987, 26. Fried, *Order and Law*, 181. Reed Larson to Howard Baker, May 13, 1987, Davenport Papers, Box 25, Folder 3; also in Reagan Papers, Subject File JL002, Case File 491196. Brief of Amicus Curiae of Landmark Legal Foundation in Support of Respondents, September 30, 1987, Beck Supreme Court Records, pt. II.A; Brief of Amicus Curiae of Pacific Legal Foundation, S[creen]A[ctors]G[uild] Leaders for Labor Justice, et al., September 26, 1987, Beck Supreme Court Records, pt. I.A. On these conservative public interest legal organizations, see Teles, *The Rise of the Conservative Legal Movement*, chap. 3. Gerald Gidwitz to Ronald Reagan, December 17, 1987, Reagan Papers, WHORM Subject File ND018, Casefiles 164502 and 164503; Robert Luebke to Dianna Holland, May 5, 1988, ibid. Jesse Helms to Howard Baker, April 29, 1987, Reagan Papers, WHORM Subject File OA

19226, Benedict Cohen Files, "Helms/Beck v. CWA (1)(2)" Folder. Brief of Senator Jesse Helms as Amicus Curiae in Support of Respondents, draft, August 25, 1987, CWA v. Beck, No. 86–637, Supreme Court of the United States, ibid., 2. Jesse Helms to Ronald Reagan and George H. W. Bush, September 24, 1987, Reagan Papers, WHORM Subject File JL002, Casefiles 02683 and 067409. The other senators who signed Helms's filed brief were Strom Thurmond, Dan Quayle, and Steven Symms. Brief and Appendix by Senators Jesse Helms et al. as Amicus Curiae in Support of Respondents, September 30, 1987, Beck Supreme Court Records.

40 "Key Justice Official Sides with Union Bosses," 7. Howard H. Baker Jr. to Reed Larson, June 24, 1987, Reagan Papers, WHORM Subject File JL002, Casefiles 02683 and 067409. Howard H. Baker to Jesse Helms, June 11, 1987, Reagan Papers, WHORM Subject File OA 19226, Benedict Cohen Files, "Helms/Beck v. CWA (1)(2)" Folder.

41 Harry A. Blackmun, CWA v. Beck conference notes, January 11, 1988, Blackmun Papers, Box 492, Folder 3. I expanded Justice Blackmun's shorthand and added punctuation in this paragraph's quotes from his conference notes. William Rehnquist to William Brennan, May 17, 1988, Blackmun Papers, Box 482, Folder 1.

42 CWA v. Beck, 487 U.S. 735, 745, 761–62 (1988).

43 *Beck*, 487 U.S. at 780 (Blackmun, J., dissenting). Harry A. Blackmun, CWA v. Beck conference notes, Blackmun Papers.

44 Wilentz, *The Age of Reagan*; Teles, "Transformative Bureaucracy"; Johnsen, "Reagan and the Rehnquist Court." Assessments of Reagan's legislative achievements are more mixed. See W. Elliot Brownlee and Hugh Davis Graham ed., *The Reagan Presidency: Pragmatic Conservatism and Its Legacies* (Lawrence: University Press of Kansas, 2003).

Epilogue

1 After *Beck*, the Right to Work Foundation stopped trying to extend the state action doctrine to private sector workers. See, e.g., Nielsen v. International Ass'n of Machinists & Aerospace Workers, 94 F.3d 1107, 1113 (7th Cir. 1996). Twenty-first-century constitutional litigation that targets the workplace *without* contesting the state action doctrine includes the Coalition of Immoklalee Workers antislavery campaign on behalf of farmworkers, and the Institute for Justice's Economic Liberty project. NLRB, *An Outline of Law and Procedure in Representation Cases* (Washington, D.C.: Government Printing Office, August 2012), 59, 107–8. Kermit Roosevelt III, "Not as Bad as You Think: Why *Garcetti v. Ceballos* Makes Sense," *University of Pennsylvania Journal of Constitutional Law* 14 (February 2012): 631–60, 633. Harris v. Quinn, 573 U.S. __ (2014); Knox v. Service Employees International Union, 132 S.Ct. 2277, 2289–91 (2012). Charlotte Garden, "Citizens, United and Citizens United: The Future of Labor Speech Rights?" *William and Mary Law Review* 53,

no. 1 (2011): 1–53; Benjamin Sachs, "Unions, Corporations, and Political Opt-Out Rights after Citizens United," *Columbia Law Review* 112 (May 2012): 800–869. Extension of any right-to-work legal gains to private sector workers is unlikely, as it would require the Court to embrace the same early right-to-work decisions it would have to reject in order to recognize more robust rights for dissenting public sector employees. For more on the fate of the FCC's equal employment rules, including the FCC's persistent defense of those rules' constitutional underpinnings, see Sophia Z. Lee, "Race, Sex, and Rulemaking: Administrative Constitutionalism and the Workplace, 1960 to the Present," *Virginia Law Review* 96 (June 2010): 799–881, 870–80. Richard A. Primus, "The Future of Disparate Impact," *Michigan Law Review* 108 (June 2010): 1341–87. The scholars most actively engaged with the workplace Constitution today include James Gray Pope, "The First Amendment, The Thirteenth Amendment, and the Right to Organize in the Twenty-First Century," *Rutgers Law Review* 51 (1999): 941–70; Cynthia L. Estlund, "Free Speech and Due Process in the Workplace," *Indiana Law Journal* 71 (1995): 101–52; Rebecca E. Zietlow, "James Ashley's Thirteenth Amendment," *Columbia Law Review* 112 (November 2012): 1697–731; David E. Bernstein, *Only One Place of Redress: African Americans, Labor Regulations, and the Courts from Reconstruction to the New Deal* (Durham, N.C.: Duke University Press, 2001); David E. Bernstein, *Rehabilitating Lochner: Defending Individual Rights against Progressive Reform* (Chicago: University of Chicago Press, 2011). Some worker centers, a twenty-first-century alternative to unions, have embraced the Thirteenth Amendment. See, for instance, Coalition of Immokalee Workers, "150th Anniversary of Emancipation Proclamation Spurs Reflections on Campaign for Fair Food," September 24, 2012, available at http://ciw-online.org.

2 Michael Grabell, "The Expendables: How the Temps Who Power Corporate Giants Are Getting Crushed," *ProPublica*, June 27, 2013, www.propublica.org; Steven Greenhouse, "A Part-Time Life as Hours Shrink and Shift," *New York Times*, October 27, 2012; Katherine van Wezel Stone, *From Widgets to Digits: Employment Regulation for the Changing Workplace* (New York: Cambridge University Press, 2004).

3 My survey regarding workers' perception of their constitutional rights is described in the Introduction. Scholars have found similar results regarding employee understanding of legal protections for job security generally. Pauline T. Kim, "Bargaining with Imperfect Information: A Study of Worker Perceptions of Legal Protection in an At-Will World," *Cornell Law Review* 83 (1997): 105–60; Jesse Rudy, "What They Don't Know Won't Hurt Them: Defending Employment-at-Will in Light of Findings That Employees Believe They Possess Just Cause Protection," *Berkeley Journal of Employment and Labor Law* 23 (2002): 307–68.

4 Edward B. Rock and Michael L. Wachter, "Enforceability of Norms and the Employment Relationship," *University of Pennsylvania Law Review*

144 (1996): 1913–52; Rudy, "What They Don't Know Won't Hurt Them"; Michael L. Wachter, "The Striking Success of the National Labor Relations Act," in *Research Handbook on the Economics of Labor and Employment Law*, ed. Cynthia L. Estlund and Michael L. Wachter, 427–62 (Northampton, Mass.: Edward Elgar Publishing, 2012), 456–57.

5   Cecil B. deMille, dictation, April 30, 1945, DeMille Papers, Box 1143, Folder 2.

6   Christopher W. Schmidt, "The Sit-Ins and the State Action Doctrine," *William & Mary Bill of Rights Journal* 18, no. 3 (2010): 767–829, 779–81. See Chapter 7.

7   Clyde W. Summers, "The Privatization of Personal Freedoms and Enrichment of Democracy: Some Lessons from Labor Law," *University of Illinois Law Review* 1986 (1986): 696. Hendrik Hartog, "The Constitution of Aspiration and 'The Rights That Belong to Us All,'" *Journal of American History* 74, no. 3 (December 1987): 1013–34.

8   I have not been able to ascertain the union affiliations of the plaintiffs in *Abood* but the litigation was supported by the Detroit Education Association (DEA), the union that lost the election to represent Detroit's teachers, and the DEA filed its own suit. See Chapter 12; "Teachers Sue over Union Dues," Detroit Free Press, January 5, 1970, Smith Papers, Box 2, Folder 17.

Selected Bibliography of Primary Sources

Archival Collections

Archive of Labor and Urban Affairs (ALUA), Walter P. Reuther Library, Wayne State University, Detroit

- ~ CIO Secretary-Treasurer's Office Collection
- ~ Ernest C. Smith Papers
- ~ UAW Fair Practices Department Collection
- ~ UAW President's Office: Walter Reuther Papers
- ~ UAW Washington Office: Steve Schlossberg Collection

Arizona Historical Society, Phoenix

- ~ Personal and Political Papers of Senator Barry M. Goldwater

Gerald R. Ford Library and Archive, Ann Arbor, Mich.

- ~ WHCF Name Files, RG 689

Hagley Museum and Library, Manuscripts and Archive Department, Wilmington, Del.

- ~ Papers of the National Association of Manufacturers

Harvard Law School Library, Historical and Special Collections, Cambridge, Mass.

- ~ Papers of Archibald Cox

Hoover Institution Archives, Stanford, Calif.

~ John A. Davenport Papers
~ Edwin Meese Papers
~ National Right to Work Committee Papers
~ William H. Rehnquist Papers

John F. Kennedy Presidential Library and Museum (JFKPLM), Boston

~ Department of Justice Micro-copy No. NK-2
~ Papers of President Kennedy, Subjects, President's Office Files
~ Papers of Burke Marshall

Kheel Center for Labor-Management Documentation and Archives, Cornell University, Ithaca, N.Y.

~ Papers of James Gross
~ Papers of Frank McCulloch
~ U.S. National Labor Relations Board Oral History Project

Library of Congress Manuscript Division (LCMD), Washington, D.C.

~ Papers of Hugo Lafayette Black
~ Papers of Harry A. Blackmun
~ William J. Brennan Papers
~ Center for National Policy Review Records
~ William O. Douglas Papers
~ Leadership Conference on Civil Rights Records
~ Papers of Thurgood Marshall
~ National Association for the Advancement of Colored People Records
~ Joseph L. Rauh Papers

George Meany Memorial Archives (GMMA), Silver Spring, Md.

~ AFL-CIO Department of Civil Rights Discrimination Case Files, 1947–
  1984, RG 9–002, Series 1
~ AFL-CIO Office of the President, George Meany, 1952–1960, National
  and International Union Correspondence, RG 1–0027, Series 6
~ AFL-CIO Office of the President, George Meany Files, 1940–1980,
  Miscellaneous Correspondence and Subject Files, 1949–1979, RG
  1–0038, Series 3
~ Artificial Collections: George Meany Memorial Archives, Vertical Files,
  1881–1999, RG 98–002, Series 1

~ Department of Civil Rights Records, 1943–1967, RG 9–001, Series 1
~ Subject Files, 1955–1970, 1981, Organizing Department Records, 1955–1975, RG 28–002, Series 8

Moorland-Spingarn Research Center, Howard University, Washington, D.C.

~ Papers of Arthur Christopher, 1913–1967
~ Charles Hamilton Houston Papers

Seeley G. Mudd Manuscript Library, Princeton University, Princeton, N.J.

~ American Civil Liberties Union Records
~ Fund for the Republic Records

National Archives at College Park, Md. (NACP)

~ Records of the Department of Justice, RG 60
~ Records of the Department of Labor, RG 174
~ Records of the Federal Communications Commission, RG 173
~ Records of the Federal Power Commission, RG 138
~ Records of the National Labor Relations Board, RG 25
~ Records of Temporary Committees, Commissions, and Boards, Records of the President's Committee on Government Contracts, 1953–1961, RG 220

National Archives and Records Administration – Great Lakes Region (NARAGLR), Chicago

~ Records of the U.S. Courts of Appeals, Sixth Circuit, 1891–1964, RG 276.7
~ Records of the U.S. District Court for the Northern District of Ohio, 1803–1971, RG 21.37.1

National Archives at Atlanta (NAA)

~ U.S. District Court for the Middle District of North Carolina, RG 21.35.3

National Archives at Fort Worth, Tex. (NAFW)

~ Records of the U.S. District Court for the Southern District of Texas, 1846–1994, RG 21.46.5–6

National Archives at Philadelphia (NAP)

~ Records of the U.S. Courts of Appeals, Fourth Circuit, 1891–1986, RG 276.5

National Archives Building (NAB), Washington, D.C.

~ Records of the Supreme Court of the United States, 1790–1997, RG 267.3
~ Records of the U.S. Courts of Appeals, District of Columbia Circuit, 1893– 1967, RG 276.12

Penrose Library, University of Denver, Denver

~ Senator Peter H. Dominick Papers
~ Howard Jenkins Jr. Collection

L.Tom Perry Special Collections, Harold B. Lee Library, Brigham Young University, Provo, Utah

~ Cecil B. DeMille Papers, MSS 1400
~ Rosel Hyde Papers, MSS 142
~ Ernest L. Wilkinson Papers, UA 1000

Ronald Reagan Presidential Library, Simi, Calif.

~ Ronald Reagan Presidential Records

Wagner Archives, Tamiment Library, New York University, New York

~ Communications Workers of America Papers, WAG 124

University of Notre Dame Archives, Notre Dame, Ind.

~ Howard A. Glickstein Papers

Microfilm Collections

~ Boehm, Randolph, and August Meier, eds. *Papers of the NAACP, Part 1: Meetings of the Board of Directors, Records of Annual Conferences, Major Speeches, and Special Reports, 1909–1950.* Bethesda, Md.: University Publications of America [UPA], 1982.
~ Boehm, Randolph, August Meier, and John H. Bracey Jr., eds. *Papers of the NAACP, Supplement to Part 1, 1951–1955.* Bethesda, Md.: UPA, 1987.

~ Boehm, Randolph, August Meier, and John H. Bracey Jr. *Papers of the NAACP, Supplement to Part 1, 1956–1960.* Bethesda, Md.: UPA, 1991.

~ Bracey, John H. Jr., and August Meier, eds. *Papers of the NAACP: Supplement to Part 1, 1961–1965.* Bethesda, Md.: UPA, 1995.

~ Bracey, John H. Jr., and August Meier. *Papers of the NAACP, Part 13, Series A: Subject Files on Labor Conditions and Employment Discrimination.* Bethesda, Md.: UPA, 1991.

~ Bracey, John H. Jr., and August Meier. *Papers of the NAACP, Part 13, Series C: Legal Department Files on Labor.* Bethesda, Md.: UPA, 1991.

~ Bracey, John H. Jr., and August Meier. *Papers of the NAACP, Supplement to Part 13: The NAACP and Labor.* Bethesda, Md.: UPA, 1997.

~ Bracey, John H. Jr., and August Meier. *Papers of the NAACP, Part 23, Legal Department Case Files, 1956–1965, Series A: The South.* Bethesda, Md.: UPA, 1997.

Online Collections

~ *The American Presidency Project,* www.presidency.ucsb.edu/ws/.

~ *Congresslink*, Dirksen Congressional Center, www.congresslink.org/civil/cr1.html.

~ *The Making of Modern Law: U.S. Supreme Court Records and Briefs, 1832– 1978.* Farmington Hills, Mich.: Gale; http://gdc.gale.com.

~ "Members of Congress," *GovTrak,* www.govtrack.us/congress/members.

Monographs and Pamphlets

~ Berle, A. A. *Economic Power and the Free Society.* New York: Fund for the Republic, 1957.

~ Haake, Alfred P. *Faith and Fact: A Guide to Economics through Christian Understanding.* Pittsburgh, Pa.: Stackpole Co., 1952.

~ Harrison, William T. *The Truth about Right-to-Work Laws: The Union Arguments, the People's Case.* Washington, D.C.: National Right to Work Committee, 1959.

Opinions, Orders, Decisions, and Rulemakings

~ *Abood v. Detroit Board of Education,* 230 N.W.2d 322 (Mich. Ct. App. 1975) (per curiam), *aff'd,* 431 U.S. 209 (1977)

~ *American Communications Ass'n v. Douds,* 339 U.S. 382 (1950)

~ *Beck v. Communication Workers of America,* 468 F. Supp. 93 (D. Md. 1979), *aff'd,* 776 F.2d 1187 (4th Cir. 1985), 800 F.2d 1280 (1986) (en banc), *aff'd sub nom, Communication Workers of America v. Beck,* 487 U.S. 735 (1988)

~ Bekins Moving & Storage Co. of Florida, Inc., 211 N.L.R.B. 138 (1974)
~ Bell & Howell, 230 N.L.R.B. 420 (1977)
~ *Bell v. Maryland*, 378 U.S. 226 (1964)
~ Bethlehem-Alameda Shipyards, 53 N.L.R.B. 999 (1943)
~ *Betts v. Easley*, 161 Kan. 459 (1946)
~ *Bolling v. Sharpe*, 347 U.S. 497 (1954)
~ *Brotherhood of R.R. Trainmen v. Howard*, 343 U.S. 768 (1952)
~ *Brown v. Board of Education*, 347 U.S. 483 (1954)
~ *Burton v. Wilmington Parking Authority*, 365 U.S. 715 (1961)
~ *Business Executives' Move for Vietnam Peace v. FCC*, 450 F.2d 642 (D.C. Cir. 1971), *rev'd sub nom, Columbia Broadcasting System v. Democratic National Committee*, 412 U.S. 94 (1973)
~ *Carter v. Carter Coal Co.*, 298 U.S. 238 (1936)
~ *Civil Rights Cases*, 109 U.S. 3 (1883)
~ Communications Common Carriers: Nondiscrimination in Employment Practices, 34 Fed. Reg. 19200 (December 4, 1969)
~ *Conley v. Gibson*, 355 U.S. 41 (1957)
~ *Corrigan v. Buckley*, 299 F. 899, 901 (D.C. Ct. App. 1924), *aff'd*, 271 U.S. 323 (1926)
~ *DeMille v. American Federation of Radio Artists*, 175 P.2d 851 (Cal. Ct. App. 1946), *aff'd*, 31 Cal. 2d 139 (1947), *cert den'd*, 333 U.S. 876 (1948)
~ *Emporium Capwell v. Western Addition Community Organization*, 420 U.S. 50 (1975)
~ *Equal Employment Opportunity Commission v. Amer. Tel. & Telegraph*, 419 F. Supp. 1022 (E.D. Pa. 1976), *aff'd*, 556 F.2d 167 (3rd Cir. 1977), *cert den'd*, 438 U.S. 915 (1978)
~ Farmers' Cooperative Compress, 169 N.L.R.B. 290 (1968), *enforced and remanded sub nom, United Packinghouse, Food, & Allied Workers International*, 416 F.2d 1126 (D.C. Cir. 1969), *on remand sub nom*, Farmers' Cooperative Compress, 194 N.L.R.B. 85 (1971)
~ *Fullilove v. Klutznick*, 448 U.S. 448 (1980)
~ *Garner v. Louisiana*, 368 U.S. 157 (1961)
~ Handy Andy, Inc., 228 N.L.R.B. 447 (1977)
~ *Hanson v. Union Pacific Railroad*, 160 Neb. 669 (1955), *rev'd sub nom*, *Railway Employes' Department v. Hanson*, 352 U.S. 225 (1956)
~ Hughes Tool, 147 N.L.R.B. 1573 (1964)
~ *Hurd v. Hodge*, 334 U.S. 24 (1948)
~ *International Assoc. of Machinists v. Sandsberry*, 277 S.W.2d 776 (Tx. Ct. Civ. App. 1954), *rev'd sub nom, Sandsberry v. Intern'l Association of Machinists*, 295 S.W.2d 412 (Tex. S. Ct. 1956)
~ *International Assoc. of Machinists v. Street*, 215 Ga. 27 (1959), *rev'd*, 367 U.S. 740 (1961)
~ *Jackson v. Metropolitan Edison Co.*, 419 U.S. 345 (1974)

~ Larus & Brother Co., 62 N.L.R.B. 1075 (1945)
~ *Lombard v. Louisiana*, 373 U.S. 267 (1963)
~ *Lugar v. Edmondson Oil Co., Inc.*, 457 U.S. 922 (1982)
~ Mansion House Center Mgt Corp., 190 N.L.R.B. 437 (1971), *enforced and remanded sub nom, Mansion House Mgt. Corp. v. NLRB*, 473 F.2d 471 (8th Cir. 1973)
~ *Moose Lodge v. Irvis*, 407 U.S. 163 (1972)
~ Murcel Manufacturing Co., 231 N.L.R.B. 623 (1977)
~ *NAACP v. Fed. Power Comm'n*, 520 F.2d 432 (D.C. Cir. 1975), *aff'd*, 425 U.S. 662 (1976)
~ *National Federation of Railway Workers v. National Mediation Board*, 110 F.2d 529 (D.C. Cir. 1940)
~ Nondiscrimination in Employment Practices of Broadcast Licensees, 33 Fed. Reg. 9960 (July 11, 1968)
~ Nondiscrimination in Employment Practices of Broadcast Licensees, 35 Fed. Reg. 8825 (June 6, 1970)
~ Nondiscrimination in Employment Practices of Communication Common Carriers, 35 Fed. Reg. 12892 (August 14, 1970)
~ *Office of Communication for the United Church of Christ v. Federal Communications Commission*, 359 F.2d 994 (D.C. Cir., 1966)
~ *Oliphant v. Brotherhood of Locomotive Firemen and Enginemen*, 156 F. Supp. 89 (N.D. Ohio 1957), *cert. den'd*, 355 U.S. 893, *aff'd*, 262 F.2d 359 (6th Cir. 1958), *cert. den'd*, 359 U.S. 935 (1959), *rehearing den'd*, 359 U.S. 962
~ Pacific Gas & Elec. Co., 42 F.P.C. 243 (1969)
~ Pacific Gas & Elec. Co., 44 F.P.C. 1365 (1970)
~ Part 73 – Radio Broadcast Services: Equal Employment Opportunities, 36 Fed. Reg. 25012 (December 28, 1971)
~ Part 73 – Radio Broadcast Services: Nondiscrimination in Employment Practices, 34 Fed. Reg. 9284 (June 12, 1969)
~ *Peterson v. Greenville*, 373 U.S. 245 (1963)
~ Pioneer Bus Co. v. Transport Workers Union of America, 140 N.L.R.B. 54 (1962)
~ *Public Utilities Commission of District of Columbia v. Pollak*, 343 U.S. 451 (1952)
~ *Railway Employees' Department v. Hanson*, 351 U.S. 225 (1956)
~ *Regents of the University of California v. Bakke*, 438 U.S. 265 (1978)
~ *Reitman v. Mulkey*, 387 U.S. 369 (1967)
~ *Shelley v. Kraemer*, 334 U.S. 1 (1948)
~ *Smith v. Allwright*, 321 U.S. 649 (1944)
~ *Steele v. Louisville & Nashville Ry. Co.*, 323 U.S. 192 (1944)
~ *Teague v. Brotherhood of Locomotive Firemen and Enginemen*, 127 F.2d 53 (6th Cir. 1942)
~ Trumbull Asphalt Co., 240 N.L.R.B. 646 (1977)

~ *Tunstall v. Brotherhood of Locomotive Firemen and Enginemen*, 140 F.2d
    35, *rev'd*, 323 U.S. 210 (1944)
~ *United Steelworkers of America v. Sadlowski*, 457 U.S. 102 (1982)
~ *United Steelworkers of America v. Weber*, 443 U.S. 193 (1979)
~ *Washington v. Davis*, 426 U.S. 229 (1976)
~ *West Virginia Board of Education v. Barnette*, 319 U.S. 624 (1943)
~ *Wygant v. Jackson*, 476 U.S. 267 (1986)

Agency Reports and Executive Orders

~ *Eighteenth Annual Report of the National Mediation Board*. Washington,
    D.C.: Government Printing Office, 1953.
~ Executive Order 10479, 18 Fed. Reg. 4899 (August 13, 1953).
~ Executive Order 10925, 26 Fed. Reg. 44, 1977 (March 8, 1961).
~ *Tenth Annual Report of the National Labor Relations Board*. Washington,
    D.C.: Government Printing Office, 1946.
~ *Nineteenth Annual Report of the National Mediation Board*. Washington,
    D.C.: Government Printing Office, 1953.
~*Report of the National Advisory Commission on Civil Disorders.*
    Washington, D.C.: Government Printing Office, 1968.
~ *Seventeenth Annual Report of the National Mediation Board*. Washington,
    D.C.: Government Printing Office, 1952.
~United States Commission on Civil Rights, *Federal Civil Rights Enforcement
    Effort: A Report of the United States Commission on Civil Rights.*
    Washington, D.C.: Government Printing Office, 1970.

Statutes and Legislative Materials

~ Hearings before the Subcommittee of the Committee on Labor and
    Welfare on S.3296, 81st Cong., 2d Sess. (May 18, 1950)
~ Hearing on Federal Power Commission Oversight, before the Subcommittee
    on Energy, Natural Resources, and the Environment of the Senate
    Committee on Commerce, 91st Cong. 35–36 (January 30, 1970)
~ Hearing on Proposed Amendments to the National Labor Relations Act
    (NLRA), before the House Committee on Labor, 76th Cong. 1301
    (June 29, 30, and July 5, 1939)
~ Hearings on Responsibilities of the Federal Power Commission in the Area
    of Civil Rights, before the Subcommittee on Civil Rights Oversight of
    the House Committee on the Judiciary, 92d Cong. (March 2, 1972)
~ House Conference Report No. 510 on H.R. 3020, Labor-Management
    Relations Act, 80th Cong., 1st Sess. (June 3, 1947)
~ Labor-Management Reporting and Disclosure Act of 1959 (Landrum-
    Griffin Act), Pub. L. No. 86-257, 73 Stat. 519 (1959)
~ National Industrial Recovery Act, Pub. L. No. 73-90, 48 Stat. 195 (1933)

~ National Labor Relations Act, Pub. L. No. 74-198, 49 Stat. 449 (1935)

~ Railway Labor Act of 1934, Pub. L. No. 442, 48 Stat. 1185 (1934)

~ Statement of Donald R. Richberg before the Committee on Education and Labor, House of Representatives, on H. Res. 111, 80th Cong. (May 11–12, 1948)

~ Taft–Hartley Act, Pub. L. No. 80-101, 61 Stat. 136 (1947)

~Testimony of Joseph Waddy before the Senate Subcommittee of the Committee on Labor and Public Welfare, 81st Cong., 2d Sess., S. 3295 (May 18, 1950)

~ Testimony of Senator Howard Taft, 93 Cong. Rec. 4193 (April 29, 1947)

~Testimony of Theodore E. Brown before the House Committee on Interstate and Foreign Commerce, 81st Cong, 2d Sess. (June 7, 1950)

Index